F.V.

**St. Louis Community College**

Forest Park
Florissant Valley
Meramec

Instructional Resources
St. Louis, Missouri

# ALTERNATIVE VISIONS

# Philosophy and the Global Context

General Editor: Michael Krausz, Bryn Mawr College

This new series addresses a range of emerging global concerns. It situates philosophical efforts in their global and cultural contexts, and it offers works from thinkers whose cultures are challenged by globalizing movements. Comparative and intercultural studies address such social and political issues as the environment, poverty, consumerism, civil society, tolerance, colonialism, global ethics, and community in cyberspace. They also address related methodological issues of translation and cross-cultural understanding.

**Titles in the Series**

# ALTERNATIVE VISIONS:

## Paths in the Global Village

Fred Dallmayr

ROWMAN & LITTLEFIELD PUBLISHERS, INC.
*Lanham • Boulder • New York • Oxford*

ROWMAN & LITTLEFIELD PUBLISHERS, INC.

Published in the United States of America
by Rowman & Littlefield Publishers, Inc.
4720 Boston Way, Lanham, Maryland 20706

12 Hid's Copse Road
Cummor Hill, Oxford OX2 9JJ, England

British Library Cataloguing in Publication Information Available

**Library of Congress Cataloging-in-Publication Data**
Dallmayr, Fred R. (Fred Reinhard), 1928–
    Alternative visions : paths in the global village / Fred Dallmayr.
        p.    cm.—(Philosophy and the global context)
    Includes bibliographical references and index.
    ISBN 0-8476-8767-8 (cloth : alk. paper).—ISBN 0-8476-8768-6
(pbk. : alk. paper)
    1. Multiculturalism.    2. Intercultural communication.
3. Philosophy, Comparative.    4. East and West.    5. Civilization,
Modern—20th century.    I. Title.    II. Series.
BD175.5.M84D33    1998
303.48'2'01—dc21                                                        97-29035
                                                                                CIP

ISBN 0-8476-8767-8 (cloth : alk. paper)
ISBN 0-8476-8768-6 (pbk. : alk. paper)

Printed in the United States of America

♾ ™ The paper used in this publication meets the minimum requirements of
American National Standard for Information Sciences—Permanence of Paper for
Printed Library Materials, ANSI Z39.48–1984.

*For Rajni Kothari, Chandra Muzaffer,*
*and Sulak Sivaraksa*
*in fond admiration*

Ah, so pleasantly we live
without enmity among those with enmity.
*Dhammapada*

Can you continue befriending
with no prejudice, no ban?
Can your learned head take leaven
from the wisdom of the heart?
*Tao Te Ching*

You have read in the Qur'an "they love Him"
placed in a single verse with "He loves them."
*Jalal ad-Din Rumi*

Let thy aim be the good of all or world maintenance
and thus carry on thy task in life.
*Bhagavad Gita*

# Contents

# Preface

This book continues a journey whose previous way station was my *Beyond Orientalism: Essays on Cross-Cultural Encounter*. As indicated then, the journey was motivated in large measure by a certain malaise pervading much of contemporary Western intellectual life: a sense of inner weariness and unease, coupled with the urge for self-transgression and transformation. Curiously, this unease has been spreading under the veneer of a very opposite mood: robust self-assuredness and self-congratulation celebrating modern Western culture as the zenith of human evolution. As it so often is, noisy self-confidence may also be deceptive here, functioning more as a symptom of an unavowed grief. In my own case, nonassuredness and self-decentering have been the springboard for a transgressive journey leading in the direction not of an abstract or speculative "otherness," but of those concrete others—themselves inhabited by transcendence—situated in the welter of historically sedimented cultures around the globe. To this extent, my journey has been aided and abetted, but also complicated, by the ongoing process of globalization, the emergence of the "global village"—a process that is tarnished by the intrusion of instrumental-managerial designs and by the standardizing effects of hegemonic power.

Since publication of the previous study, my travels have taken me still farther afield: beyond South Asia to Africa, the Near East, and the Far East (with a few additional visits to South America). The main purpose of these travels was always to learn—and to teach or lecture only when specifically asked. Through learning about other cultures I have discovered more about my own background and perhaps have become more discerning or discriminating in this respect. As I should add, hermeneutical learning and appreciation for me do not constitute barriers to critical judgment, prudently exercised—although I tend to subscribe to Charles Taylor's notion of a "presumption of worth" (that can be challenged or rebutted). In all these matters I have greatly benefited from the example of the three individuals to whom this book is dedicated: Rajni Kothari, Chandra Muzaffer, and Sulak Sivaraksa. Located in very different cultural settings—respectively in postindependence India, Malaysia, and Thailand—all three have for several decades served as voices of conscience, and often as intellectual gadflies, in their communities, bent on articulating "alternative visions" for the future of their societies and the world. While strenuously resisting the hegemonic designs of colonialism and neocolonialism, they have never been reluctant to critique oppressive or aggressive tendencies present in their own cultural milieu. As founder and longtime director of the Centre for the Study of Developing Societies in Delhi, Kothari has persistently denounced elitist and exploitative structures both at home and abroad, seeking to reorient India along more Gandhian lines. As director of the Just World Trust (NGO) in Malaysia, Chandra Muzaffer focuses his publications on abusive or violent Western behavior toward Islamic countries, without flattering Islamic militancy and fundamentalism. A leading figure in the far-flung International Network of Engaged Buddhists (INEP), Sivaraksa seeks to reform and revitalize Buddhism as an agency of change, while simultaneously deploring Buddhist co-optation by ruling elites. Authors of numerous books and articles, these three individuals have admirably combined academic discourse with (nondomineering) social praxis.

In singling out these three, I certainly do not wish to diminish the impact of many other people on my intellectual journey. In the South Asian context I also need to mention Thomas Pantham, Ashis Nandy, R. Sundara Rajan, and Rajeev Bhargava. In the East Asian context I want to acknowledge my indebtedness to Masao Abe, James Heisig, and Shiro Matsumoto. Closer to home, I have been for many years the beneficiary of the insights of such friends and academic colleagues as Bhikhu Parekh, Anthony Parel, Tu Wei-Ming, Charles Taylor, Graham Parkes, Eliot Deutsch, Marietta Stepaniants, and Hwa Yol Jung. At my own university I have enjoyed intellectual stimulation and continued encouragement from David Burrell, Robert Johansen, Joseph Buttigieg, and many others. My gratitude is extended to Cheryl Reed, who diligently typed and retyped the manuscript. As always, my deepest thanks go to my family, especially to my wife Ilse who has lent patient and cheerful support to my sometimes extensive peregrinations. May our children—and the young generation everywhere—be blessed with a more peaceful and humanly sustaining environment than our now waning century has been able to provide.

# Introduction

Ever since the demise of the Cold War, the world finds itself in a situation that is unprecedented in human history, in which the entire globe is under the sway of one hegemonic framework: that of Western civilization, with its economic, technological, and intellectual corollaries. None of the previous empires in history—neither the Roman, Spanish, and British empires nor the Chinese Middle Kingdom—had been able to extend their "civilizing mission" to the entire globe or humankind as a whole. Today, all the countries and peoples in the world stand under a universal mandate or directive: to "develop" or "modernize" and hence catch up with the civilizational standards established and exemplified by the West (and some of its non-Western proxies). "Globalization" involves to a large extent the spreading or dissemination of modern Western forms of life around the globe.

To be sure, some aspects of these life-forms have a benign character, at least at first glance: where development coincides—or promises to coincide—with liberation from want, poverty, and oppression, few sensible people would wish to demur on principle. Most importantly, where modernization equals democratization, that is, the replacement of feudal autocracies by democratic regimes wedded to freedom and equal rights, the change might garner near universal assent. Yet, at a closer look, things are more complex. Modernity is a "package deal," including individual rights along with huge state bureaucracies and giant corporations, backed up by the immense military and technological arsenal of a quasi-imperial, hegemonic power.[1] In light of the radical asymmetry of status and influence between North and South, "developed" and "undeveloped" countries, development sometimes operates as a massive steamroller granting rights to some while crushing the rights of others (for instance, indigenous peoples). In this context, democratization becomes contestable—and legitimately contestable—on democratic grounds.

Both politically and intellectually, this kind of contestation is hazard-

1

ous in numerous respects. On the one side, friends of democracy loyal to local contexts face the danger of being co-opted by traditionalist, perhaps even fundamentalist, movements bent on adamantly resisting any type of social transformation and cultural learning. Often allied with feudal patriarchal structures of domination, such reactionary movements typically evince little sympathy for democracy or democratization. On the other hand, locally or regionally engaged democrats may encounter the wrath of international experts, of the new "managerial elite" of development planners, for whom local contexts and cultural traditions are nothing but obstacles in the global modernization process. Although mostly pragmatic, development managers can invoke the aid of Western (or Westernized) intellectuals and theorists to whom context and local tradition likewise appear as mere defects or curable diseases. In the eyes of these intellectuals prominent in the academy and the media modernity is equivalent to the project of the Enlightenment, which symbolizes the triumph of knowledge over ignorance, reason over superstition, and freedom over bondage. Given the eloquence and vaunted progressivism of these intellectuals, it is important to remember Michel Foucault's comments on the "blackmail of the Enlightenment" which glibly equates critical reservations about modernity with a virulent antimodernism and antirationalism. In the words of Foucault (himself hardly suspect of reactionary leanings), our contemporary situation demands that we "free ourselves from the intellectual blackmail of 'being for or against the Enlightenment.' " We must "refuse everything that might present itself in the form of a simplistic and authoritarian alternative: you either accept the Enlightenment and remain within the tradition of its rationalism" or "you criticize the Enlightenment and try to escape from its principles of rationality."[2]

As is well known, Foucault on other occasions has defended the virtues of local or decentralized politics, of democracy operating at the "grassroots," against centralized panaceas, including those of (perhaps well-meaning) global planners. In doing so, he has lent his support to dispersed local struggles and movements, to the travails of people engaged in a "vernacular" politics in concrete contexts—which is not the same as a retreat into narrow parochialism at the expense of broader visions. In one of his lectures (in 1976), Foucault spoke eloquently of the need for an "insurrection of subjugated knowledges," where "subjugated knowledges" referred to "historical contents that have been buried and disguised" in privileged modes of expertise. More specifically, the term denoted what he called "people's knowledge" (*le savoir des gens*), or those "naive knowledges" that are "located down on the hierarchy, beneath the required level of cognition or scientificity." Far from depressing or squashing the possibility of social transformation, subjugated knowledges and their concomitant life-forms were the only possible harbingers of genuine democratic renewal for Foucault; it is on the level of people's knowledge, he noted, that criticism today "performs its work." With this formulation, he boldly rescued change from the grasp of universal intellectuals and global experts who, since Kant, had monopolized "critique." Foucault explicitly notes this shift in an interview (given roughly at the same time as the aforementioned lecture) in which he championed the role of "specific intellectuals" against the pretensions of intellectual universalism:

> For a long period, the "left" intellectual spoke and was acknowledged the right of speaking in the capacity of master of truth and justice. He was heard, or purported to make himself heard, as the spokesman of the universal. To be an intellectual meant something like being the consciousness/ conscience of us all. I think we have here an idea transposed from Marxism, from a faded Marxism indeed. . . . The intellectual was there taken as the clear, individual figure of a universality whose obscure, collective form was embodied in the proletariat. . . . [But now] intellectuals have to get used to working, not in the modality of the "universal," the "exemplary," the "just-and-true-for-all," but within specific sectors, at the precise points where their own conditions of life or work situate them.[3]

The idea of a vernacular democracy, of a grassroots approach to social life and change, is not unique to Foucault, but has been ably seconded by other French writers sometimes loosely grouped together under the label "postmodernists." On repeated occasions, Gilles Deleuze has vindicated locally contextualized politics as a corrective or counterresponse to the centralizing ambitions of managerial elites often linked with globally hegemonic power structures.[4] In a particularly instructive fashion, some of Jacques Derrida's writings have challenged the continuous demand to be "for or against the Enlightenment" by articulating democratic politics that avoid the pitfalls of both universalism and regressive localism. His *The Other Heading: Reflections on Today's Europe* formulates a "double injunction" that may be a double bind but has liberating potential. Derrida writes of the necessity "to make sure that a centralizing hegemony not be reconstituted" and of the parallel need "not to multiply borders," that is, "not to cultivate for their own sake minority differences, untranslatable idiolects, national antagonisms, or the chauvinisms of idiom." Political and social responsibility today, he adds, consists "in renouncing neither of these conflicting imperatives." Like Foucault, Derrida denounces universalizing intellectual schemes which under the pretext of promoting "transparency," the "univocity of democratic discussion," or "communication in public space," impose a model of communication that represses "anything that bends, overdetermines, or even questions" them. Derrida advocates the double injunction of acknowledging the "universality of formal law" while at the same time fully respecting "differences, idioms, minorities, singularities." With specific reference to the Enlightenment and the possible blackmail of rationality, *The Other Heading* states:

> The *same* duty dictates cultivating the virtue of *critique*, of the critical idea, the critical tradition, but also submitting it, beyond critique and questioning, to a deconstructive genealogy that exceeds it without yet compromising it. . . . The *same* duty demands tolerating and respecting all that is not placed under the authority of reason. It may have to do with faith, with different forms of faith. It may also have to do with certain thoughts . . . that, while attempting to think reason and the history of reason, necessarily exceed its order, without becoming, simply because of this, irrational, and much less irrationalist. For these thoughts may in fact also try to remain faithful to the ideal of the Enlightenment, the *Aufklärung*, the *Illuminismo*, while yet acknowledging its limits, in order to work on the Enlightenment of this time: the time that is ours, today.[5]

In these bold and "timely" lines, Derrida has issued a challenge to our age that so far has been mostly unheeded: the challenge to pursue reason into its margins and recesses. If classical Enlightenment has meant (in Kant's famous phrase) an "awakening from immaturity," Derrida's lines beckon us into a new and more complex phase of maturity, where without abandoning reason we are also willing to reflect on reason's underside, its costs as well as its preconditions. The passage extends the old motto "*sapere aude*" (dare to think) by daring us to ponder the hidden side of thought, including the historical and ontological conditionality of Enlightenment itself. In Derrida's (and Foucault's) vocabulary, this kind of inquiry might be called "genealogy." What the contemporary *sapere aude*, in any case, brings into view are new and largely unexplored areas of thought or dimensions of experience. To the extent that Enlightenment rationality, anchored in the Cartesian *cogito*, was predicated on a traditional spirit-matter or mind-body bifurcation, the contemporary phase of maturity urges us to ponder more carefully spirit's inherence in "nature," that is, the "ecological" matrix of rational understanding. To the extent that the same rationality had in many ways a masculine-patriarchal cast, the rethinking of reason implies a reconsideration of the "feminine," without any endorsement of fixed gender roles. Most importantly for present purposes, the *sapere aude* of "the time that is ours, today" forces us to reflect on the imperialist or colonial legacy of Western modernity and the status and relevance of non-Western cultures and societies. In Merleau-Ponty's words, the "crisis" or ongoing self-critique of Western modernity compels us to reassess our relation to that part of the world we have subjugated or excluded (under the label "Orient"). "From this angle," he writes,

civilizations lacking our philosophical or economic equipment take on an instructive value. It is not a matter of going in search of truth or salvation in what falls short of science or philosophical awareness, or of dragging chunks of mythology as such into our philosophy, but of acquiring—in the presence of these variants of humanity that we are so far from—a sense of the theoretical and practical problems *our* institutions are faced with, and of rediscovering the existential field that they were born in and that their long success has led us to forget. The Orient's "childishness" has something to teach us, if it were nothing more than the narrowness of our adult ideas.[6]

For Merleau-Ponty (as for Derrida), the issue is not the abandonment of rational thought, but rather the imperious self-enclosure and hence possible ossification of Western modernity. His uppermost hope, evident in all his writings, was for a renewed learning experience, achieved through an opening of the West to its excluded "other." "Western philosophy can learn from them [non-Western thinkers] to rediscover the relationship to being and initial option which gave it birth, and to estimate the possibilities we have shut ourselves off from in becoming 'Westerners' and perhaps reopen them."[7] On this point, Merleau-Ponty's writings have fallen mostly on deaf ears, at least among Western intellectuals and philosophers. Apart from some anthropologists and area specialists, Western intellectuals on the whole have been disinclined to learn from "underdeveloped" cultures—although they have not been averse to retaining their teaching role (in keeping with the West's "civilizing mission"). Uncomfortable with overt modes of neo-colonialism, prominent Western philosophers, rationalists and pragmatists alike, have professed a supposedly benign form of ethnocentrism, predicated either on philosophical principle or, more frequently, on a casual brand of *laissez-faire* ("leave us alone") attitude. What is more surprising is that this dismissive stance is shared by many postmodernists otherwise attentive to the writings of Derrida and Foucault. In this case, an exaggerated notion of "difference" according to which everything radically differs from itself has engendered a brave "ultrapostmodernism," where every difference or distinct identity is ultimately submerged in indifference. When identities are seen as totally fluid and originating from arbitrary whim, encounters with them result (and cannot help but result) in "hybridity" or indiscriminate fusionism; but in the absence of distinct elements, this fusion remains vacuous, a fusion of nothing. In our global situation, hybridity basically advises non-Western peoples to divest themselves of their vernacular moorings—a counsel of Westernization (perhaps Americanization).[8]

This outcome is surprising in light of Derrida's and Foucault's circumspect formulations, their insistence on "double injunctions" and multiple duties or tasks. It is also puzzling in view of postmodernism's emphatic celebration of the "other" or "otherness" that sometimes borders on panegyrical self-effacement. No theme in postmodern literature is more frequently invoked than that of otherness, though often in terms leaving it shapeless and devoid of content. This applies even to the foremost spokesman of radical otherness in contemporary Western thought, Emmanuel Levinas. No doubt, Levinas's shift to "alterity" constitutes a salutary antidote to virulent modes of egocentrism and "logocentrism" prevalent in Western modernity; this salutary effect also extends to his recuperation of the ethical dimension of self-other relations. Yet, meritorious features of this kind are offset by deficiencies that cannot be overlooked but are frequently ignored by his commentators. Prominent is the predilection for antinomial, "black-and-white" types of argument that completely foil the notion of double injunctions. When Western philosophy is portrayed (as repeatedly happens in Levinas's *Totality and Infinity*) as uniformly self-centered and imperialistic, the only road open seems to be the exit from philosophy as such—a strategy that sidesteps the laborious process of the "overcoming of metaphysics" demanded in our time. Likewise, the depiction of otherness as radical "exteriority" (and the derivation of ethics from it) affronts not only ethical autonomy but more importantly the interlacing of "inside/outside" or "immanence/transcendence" that has been a major concern of postmodern (or post-Husserlian) thought. For present purposes, the main drawback is a lingering ethnocentrism beneath the rhetoric of alterity. Both in his early and his later phases, Levinas's thought remained explicitly wedded to a Western biblical and monotheistic tradition, in a manner that seems to preclude any transit to South Asian or Far Eastern forms of reflection.[9]

By and large, postmodernism's turn to "otherness" has remained speculative and ineffectual with regard to cross-cultural encounters in our time; to some extent, its rhetoric has even reinforced deep-seated "Orientalist" leanings among Western intellectuals disdainful of vernacular contexts or traditions. The reasons for this outcome are not hard to detect: both in the case of indiscriminate fusionism—the merger of indistinct elements—and in that of an absolute privileging of the "other," the chances of a concrete learning experience are undercut or at least severely curtailed. A learning experience can only occur through mutual interrogation and interpellation, through a mode of interaction stopping short of both instant hybridization and pliant surrender. Such interaction, in turn, presupposes the encounter of situated, but not absolutized, differences where a distinct life-form—a concrete mode of "being-in-the-world"—opens itself up to the challenge of otherness in a manner yielding a deeper, transformative understanding of self and other. This, in a nutshell, is the lesson of contemporary hermeneutics or of a hermeneutically construed existentialism attentive to the place of human existence or *Dasein* in the world. As formulated by a string of thinkers from Heidegger to Gadamer and beyond, existential hermeneutics is predicated on a dialogical interplay where the other's revelatory power is released only through a questioning that necessarily proceeds from the vantage of situated modes of self-understanding (what Gadamer calls "prejudgments"). Viewed under hermeneutical auspices, self-other relations resist both the lure of a domineering appropriation of difference—the posture of an aggressive "logocentrism"—and that of indifference through self-effacement. The former temptation has been more virulent in Western thought than the latter, although each is really the reverse of the other. To counter domineering impulses, hermeneutical interrogation has to be animated by both sympathy and reticence, a willingness to balance understanding and self-transgression; relinquishing the goal of full transparency, a differential hermeneutics (or a "hermeneutics of difference") must leave distances intact, thereby practicing the liberating gesture of what Heidegger calls "letting-be."[10]

Hermeneutical considerations of this kind apply with particular force to the contemporary global arena and the ongoing process of globalization. As indicated before, this process of globalization is well underway, promoted and engineered in large part by global managers and experts bent on "developing" or "modernizing" everything in the world from the top down. In opposition to global panaceas, hermeneutics insists on the need for a vernacular or grassroots approach starting from concretely situated human life-forms, what Foucault called "subjugated knowledges" or "people's knowledge" (*le savoir des gens*). By starting from this vantage, a hermeneutical approach guards against the peril of a hegemonic globalization under Western auspices—a latter-day form of Orientalism and imperialism—and also against a naive hybridization that postulates the quick submergence of cultural differences in a global melting pot, oblivious to persisting asymmetries of power. At the same time, wedded to interrogation and self-transformation, hermeneutics refuses the trap of parochialism and instead encourages ongoing self-critique carried on by Foucault's "specialized" or situated intellectuals (attentive to *le savoir des gens*). Most importantly, hermeneutical engagement supports and enables the kind of learning experience that alone holds the promise of genuine global cooperation and cobeing (*Mitsein*). Cut loose from vernacular moorings and beliefs, cosmopolitanism remains a mere flight of fancy, unable to engage the hearts and minds as well as the existential agonies of human beings; if at all, hearts and minds are transformed only in the crucible of sustained engagement and situated encounter. This point was well expressed by Václav Havel in a recent address at Harvard. As Havel observed, the current state of affairs

> contains a clear challenge not only to the Euro-American world but to our present-day civilization as a whole. It is a challenge to this civilization to start understanding itself as a multicultural and a multipolar civilization, whose meaning lies not in undermining the individuality of different spheres of culture and civilization but in allowing them to be more completely themselves. . . . [Such understanding] must be an expression of the authentic will of everyone, growing out of the genuine spiritual roots hidden beneath the skin of our common, global civilization. If it is merely disseminated through the capillaries of this skin, the way Coca-Cola ads are—as a commodity offered by some to others—such a code can hardly be expected to take hold in any profound or lasting way.[11]

The present volume has been written and composed in the spirit of Havel's address. Faithful to the tenor of a vernacular or differential hermeneutics, the successive chapters explore the margin or border zone between self and other, localism and globalism, and situated traditions or practices and future prospects. They chart diverse "paths in the global village"—neither prefabricated highways nor pointless cul-de-sacs. In every instance, they explore hitherto sidestepped or underprivileged "alternative visions," especially alternatives to hegemonic domination and parochial myopia. In uncovering such visions, successive chapters enlist the aid of a host of past and present thinkers and engaged intellectuals, from Confucius and Nagarjuna to Adorno, Gandhi, Cabral, and Nancy. In particular, this volume pays tribute to the legacy of Gottfried Herder, a thinker often sidelined as a mere spokesman of Romantic nationalism.

A contemporary of Kant and Holbach, Herder was confronted directly and intensively with the "blackmail of the Enlightenment": the demand to opt unequivocally either for enlightened universalism or a backward-looking, reactionary parochialism. In a bold and innovative move, Herder refused both options as equally pointless and desultory—a refusal that retains exemplary significance in our own age. In opposition to the global ambitions of universal intellectuals, especially the "philosophers of Paris" addicted to Europe's "civilizing mission," Herder preferred to take his bearings from historically sedimented contexts, that is, from the grassroots level of popular wisdom or "people's knowledge." In contrast with enlightened "absolutism" and centralized planning, his writings celebrated the merits of democracy (or a vernacular republicanism) animated by underprivileged or "subjugated" modes of thought and experience. To Herder, loyalty to people's knowledge also meant attentiveness to people's religious beliefs; such attention characterized his

lifework as a philosopher and preacher. Yet none of his grassroots preferences ever induced him to succumb to antirationalism or anti-Enlighten-
ment. Local or national contexts were for him precisely preconditions for
transformative encounters; in turn, such encounters were gateways to a
learning experience, which by engaging "head and heart" would lift peoples steadily to the level of *Humanität*.[12]

The discussion of Herder's lifework that opens this volume seeks to
place the distinctiveness of his thought against the backdrop of some
prominent contemporary interpretations, especially those offered by
Charles Taylor and Isaiah Berlin. The following chapter is devoted to an
issue that might present a challenge to a hermeneutical approach inspired
by Herder's legacy. Recent Western thought has in some quarters been
leaning toward a brave "ultrapostmodernism," where the celebration of
difference shades over into a cult of indifference or nondistinctiveness. A
legitimate critique of "foundational" or "essentialized" identity and an
equally legitimate emphasis on self-transgression become the harbingers
of an erasure of identity as such and hence an endorsement of uniform
sameness (sometimes styled "hybridization"). Chapter 2 investigates this
issue by taking its bearings from Theodor Adorno, whose later writings
in large part centerstaged the notion of "nonidentity" (in opposition to
modernist forms of egocentrism). Adorno was careful, however, to differentiate between "nonidentity" as a decentered form of selfhood and "no-
identity" viewed as hybrid sameness, a differentiation in large measure
reflecting the continued influence of Hegelian teachings recuperated in
Adorno's "negative dialectics." To illustrate the importance of Adorno's
differentiation, the chapter turns its attention to Edward Said, whose
writings frequently oscillate precariously between the postures of "nonidentity" respectful of difference and "no-identity" sliding into indifference, or between postmodernism and ultrapostmodernism. Although
valuable as a weapon against Orientalist constructions, diffusion of identity into "no-identity," or nomadic hybridity, jeopardizes Said's commendable support for the "subjugated knowledges" of marginalized or
oppressed peoples in the Near East.

The importance of vernacular contexts and people's knowledge are
starting points for the critique of fixed identities and "essentialized"
forms of domination. Many critical or insurgent movements in our time
take their departure not from a universalized sameness or hybridity but
precisely from situated cultural traditions, including religious faith.
Chapter 3 provides an overview of prominent "liberation perspectives,"
often blending philosophy and theology both in the West and the East
with a focus on Christianity, Buddhism, and Islam. Often emerging in
conjunction with Marxist or secular-socialist movements, liberation theologies also faced, and learned to deal with, the Enlightenment black-

mail. In an instructive fashion, the tension between and eventual change from cosmopolitan indifference to a more concrete and historically situated outlook is manifest in the writings of Gustavo Gutierrez, especially in the differences between his early book *A Theology of Liberation* and his later work *Las Casas*, subtitled *In Search of the Poor of Jesus Christ*. With particular eloquence and forcefulness, the Enlightenment challenge has also been taken up by Iranian philosopher-sociologist Ali Shari'ati, the lifelong opponent and eventual victim of the Shah's oppressive regime. Shari'ati's basic opposition occurs not between an enlightened universalism and a backward-looking clerical parochialism, but between two kinds of religious outlook: a religion of domination and a religion of liberation, the former reflecting the legacy of Cain and the second the legacy of Abel. As he noted, in a passage which ably captures the gist of liberation theologies throughout the world:

> The weapon of Cain has been religion, and the weapon of Abel has also been religion. It is for this reason that the war of religion against religion has also been a constant of human history. . . . There has existed throughout human history, and there will continue to exist until the last day, a struggle between the religion of deceit, stupefaction, and justification of the status quo and the religion of awareness, activism, and revolution. The end of time will come when Cain dies and the "system of Abel" is established anew . . . [then] equality will be realized throughout the world, and human unity and brotherhood will be established, through equity and justice.[13]

In relying on the "weapon of Abel," religious liberation struggle cannot possibly be an exercise in violence and rampant terrorism, given that Abel symbolizes gentleness and peace. The latter point has been powerfully underscored by the most inspiring and exemplary liberation leader in our century: the Mahatma Gandhi, who is the focus of chapter 4. Gandhi's preferred formula for liberation struggle was *satyagraha*, a term usually translated as "truth force" or as the doing or enactment of truth. As the chapter tries to show—partly by way of a commentary on Erik Erikson's renowned *Gandhi's Truth*—"truth" was not simply an epistemic category for Gandhi, but the name for an existential-ontological engagement on the side of rightness, equity and brotherhood/sisterhood—Abel's legacy. However, truth enactment or "truth force" mandated a peculiarly "unforced" or nonaggressive type of action or praxis, a mode of conduct thoroughly governed by nonviolence (*ahimsa*) and by the willingness to suffer rather than inflict violence and injustice on others. It is this aspect of self-suffering and endurance that leads Erikson to describe Gandhi as a *homo religiosus*, or a "religious actualist," following the lead of great religious teachers. Although Western-educated and by no means disdainful of reason and knowledge, Gandhi was a severe critic of modernity's vaunted accomplishments, especially when erected into a universal panacea. In his own liberation struggle, Gandhi stayed close to the vernacular insights of people's knowledge and people's religion in his native India—just as he preferred decentralization in economics and politics to technocratic planning. Yet reliance on vernacular beliefs never equaled self-enclosure, serving instead as a springboard for continued self-transformation inspired by the prophetic promises contained in religious literature and sacred texts.

Religious commitment—in Gandhi's case and that of other liberation thinkers—does not amount to antihumanism, as secularist intellectuals often claim (in a variation of the Enlightenment blackmail). For Shari'ati, Islam is a species of humanism, although divinely guided and supported.[14] Chapter 5 explores the "humanism versus antihumanism" issue, with a central focus on Confucian teachings. Confucianism is often accused of harboring a repressive traditionalism that stifles human initiative, especially the exercise of individual human rights. Concentrating on the role of "humaneness" (*jen*) in the *Analects*, some leading experts in the West have sought to defend Confucianism against this charge by offering a more "modern" or enlightened reading; in their *Thinking Through Confucius*, Roger Ames and David Hall approximate *jen* to a radical quasi-existentialist mode of self-constitution and "self-making"—an interpretation that perhaps assimilates the alien too quickly within the familiar, thus shortchanging the hermeneutics of difference. More cautious readings advanced by Herbert Fingarette and Tu Wei-Ming, without in any way relinquishing "humaneness," embed *jen* into the complex network of Confucian ideas. In particular, Tu Wei-Ming's writings steer a sensitive course between Western-style humanism and antihumanism, between anthropocentric self-assertion and pliant surrender; in doing so, they also strike a balance between the demand for human rights and the Confucian emphasis on "rites" (*li*), the concrete obligations and responsibilities to others involved in contextual relationships. One benefit of this approach is that it renders Confucianism a supplement and corrective, rather than a mere duplicate, of Western preferences. In addition, Tu's construal of *jen* as self-cultivation and transformation establishes a linkage with Herder's teaching—by pinpointing the path of "humanization" lifting people up to the level of *Humanität*.

This path of humanization offers the potential for renewal that is never cut loose from historically sedimented moorings and situated vernacular beliefs. To avoid rupture, what is needed along this path is memory-work, attention to the still untapped resources of the past; in our time of

rapid globalization with a bent toward global amnesia such memory-
work emerges as a crucial requisite for the preservation of critical humaneness. Memory-work does not mean memorizing past events or a
rummaging or wallowing in historical grievances and resentments. Instead, what such work aims at is the recovery or excavation of the redemptive qualities and liberating promises latently present in traditional
practices and cultural or religious beliefs. To a large extent, recovery of
this kind implies attentiveness to human suffering, to the agonies and
tribulations undergone by the victims of history, but again, not as an
exercise in self-pity or resentment, but as a roadmarker in the direction
of self-transformation and social transformation. In our century, suffering and its redemptive recollection have been stirringly thematized by
members of the early Frankfurt School, particularly by Walter Benjamin
as well as Adorno and Marcuse. Chapter 6 offers a discussion of their
main arguments regarding memory-work and its ethical and political implications; it also draws a parallel between these arguments and Heidegger's formulation of a "recollective" or "commemorative" mode of
thinking (*Andenken*) mindful of the always already present call of
"being" existing prior to calculative reasoning. Such thinking is not
merely retrospective, but forward-looking, bent on retrieving liberating
possibilities buried in the past. Derrida similarly formulates an "idea of
democracy," describing it as

> something that remains to be thought and *to come* (*à venir*): not something
> that is certain to happen tomorrow, not the democracy (national or interna-
> tional, state or trans-state) of the *future*, but a democracy that must have
> the structure of a promise—*and thus the memory of that which carries the
> future, the to-come, here and now.*[15]

Derrida's comments on national and transnational perspectives provide a bridge to the second part of this volume. While part I deals primarily with philosophical (and theological) concerns affecting the global
village, part II examines the more concrete issues of nationalism, transna-
tionalism, and global development. In light of the fascist and genocidal
excesses of our century, the idea of nationalism has unsurprisingly gained
a bad reputation; its role is particularly castigated and disdained by liberal Western intellectuals wedded to universal progress but neglectful of
the double injunction demanded in our time. This disdain obscures or
sidesteps the long-standing complicity of Western liberalism with colonialism, imperialism, and contemporary neocolonial offshoots—a legacy
that has been, and continues to be, the target of national liberation movements around the globe.

Chapter 7 examines the liberation movement in Africa, with a focus on the work of Amilcar Cabral. For Cabral, national liberation was a struggle involving both political and cultural resistance, equally removed from submissive modernization (or Westernization) and a nostalgic "nativism." To counter the lure of Western-style assimilation, Cabral coined the motto "return to the source." The phrase by no means counsels an atavistic revivalism or an antiquarian worship of the past; instead—as does memory-work—it returns to the source, signaling a retrieval of alternative resources buried in cultural traditions, for the sake of furthering the aim of national or people's liberation and resistance. The chapter also explores the work of some leading contemporary African thinkers who, often directly in the footsteps of Cabral, seek to delineate the character of African distinctiveness and of a practical, political, but nonessentialist African "identity" in our time. Returning to the source again means steering a path between sameness and absolute difference, avoiding the dual pitfalls of a nostalgic "ethnophilosophy" and an abstract "pure philosophy" and accentuating a historically situated mode of reflection geared toward vernacular or people's emancipation.

Cabral's posture implicitly challenges a major thesis advanced by theorists of nationalism: that nationalism has had liberating or progressive effects only in the context of Western history, while inevitably denoting xenophobic regression outside the Western orbit. Chapter 8 turns to the example of the national liberation struggle in South Asia, particularly the Indian subcontinent. Despite the undeniable presence of stridently extremist voices, the chapter demonstrates the predominately moderate and "progressive" tenor of the Indian nationalist or independence movement, opposed in equal measure to colonialism and to regressive chauvinism or parochialism. Apart from the Mahatma Gandhi, the leading figures in this story are Vivekananda, Sri Aurobindo, and Rabindranath Tagore, as well as Muhammad Iqbal (during his early phase) and Abul Kalam Azad. Their target was foreign domination—without any pampering of ethnic or religious forms of "fundamentalism" averse to cross-cultural learning. The chapter carries the discussion of nationalism into the postindependence period in India in an effort to distill and juxtapose some major strands in the contemporary debate: particularly strands accentuating the modern nation-state as opposed to views privileging cultural traditions and lifeworld practices.

The state versus culture (or government versus civil society) nexus is pursued further in chapter 9, which deals with two leading intellectuals in contemporary India: Rajini Kothari and Ashis Nandy, both associated with the Centre for the Study of Developing Societies in Delhi. Kothari has established himself as an eloquent and thoughtful defender of democracy in India—more precisely of a vernacular or grassroots type of democracy organized partly along Gandhian lines with only limited con-

cessions to the centralized apparatus of the nation-state. These concessions are even further restricted, if not entirely canceled, by Nandy, who
invokes cultural practices as a crucial source of resistance to homogenizing tendencies operative both on the state and global levels. Several of
Nandy's writings explicitly attack the subordination of vernacular beliefs
to hegemonic structures and, above all, the instrumental (ab)use of culture in the service of political agendas on the Left and Right. To this
extent, Nandy's work illustrates important issues troubling contemporary social-political thought: the relation between state and society, politics and culture, policy goals and historically grown lifeworld.

The role of culture in democratic development, especially on a global
level, is discussed in greater detail in chapter 10. Culture in this context
means vernacular or people's culture (in line with Foucault's "people's
knowledge"), a historically sedimented mode of life amenable to diverse
forms of retrieval and reconstruction. While not a substitute for economic and political analysis, culture functions as a necessary presupposition of social inquiry by providing a frame of reference; taken in this
sense, the term denotes a matrix of symbolic meanings and taken-for-
granted assumptions. However, there are deeper and more dynamic connotations. By being available for recollective retrieval, historically sedimented meanings can surface as a reservoir of "counterculture," a vital
source of resistance marshalling vernacular understandings against the
standardizing tendencies present on the state and global levels. Particularly in the context of hegemonic globalization, counterculture serves as
a practical-political arsenal for safeguarding the aspirations of vernacular
democracy. Yet this arsenal can be, and has repeatedly been, exploited for
repressive nostalgic aims, especially the aims of nativism or a xenophobic
parochialism. To counter this danger, the chapter invokes a further dimension or connotation of the term, where "culture" means a process of
educational formation and transformation (in the sense of the German
*Bildung*). At this point, the discussion takes the themes of "humaneness"
and progressive "humanization," whose roots point back prominently to
Herder, to a new level. With specific reference to global development,
formation (*Bildung*) postulates an open-ended encounter between societies and cultures, a reciprocal learning process animating a "global village" continuously in the throes of formation.

The concluding chapters take up important theoretical and practical
dimensions of life in the global village. Chapter 11 tackles the problem
of the ethical standards (or standards of *Sittlichkeit*) that will hopefully
inform social and transcultural relations on the level of global democracy. To make some headway in this largely unexplored terrain, the
chapter re-invokes the Derridean notion of a double injunction: simultaneously to transgress and to "sublate" or preserve Enlightenment princi-

ples. With respect to the issue of global "justice," adherence to the Derridean notion requires a complex move of contestation and negotiation: namely, the attempt to juxtapose and contaminate Western-style proceduralism, wedded to a uniform rule of law, with more open-ended forms of equity attentive to individual and cultural diversity and singularity. In the pursuit of this aim, the proverbial "blindness" of justice to difference needs to be counterbalanced with a "seeing eye" type of justice respectful of otherness. Borrowing from the Confucian tradition, justice here involves a contest or negotiation between universally equal "rights" and "rites" (seen as contingently situated contexts), a negotiation requiring a prudential and culturally informed type of political judgment.

Questions of justice and equity are closely related to the emergent structure or structural design of the global village—the topic of the final chapter. Taking its departure from Samuel Huntington's thesis of a looming "clash of civilizations," chapter twelve explores possible alternatives (or alternative visions) to this new version of international *Realpolitik*. After consulting a number of expert views on international politics, including Immanuel Wallerstein's "systemic" perspective, the chapter finally sides with the vision of an "inoperative" (that is, nonmanagerial and nonhomogeneous) community, as this vision is articulated by Jean-Luc Nancy. The concept intimates an open-ended, cross-cultural relationship equally at odds with standardized uniformity and local fragmentation, which is the only proper path for the global village. To conclude with Nancy's eloquent words, which accentuate the always expectant or "promised" quality of global democracy:

> It is thus not an absence but a movement; it is "inoperative" in its very activity. It is the propagation, even the contagion, or again the communication of community itself that propagates itself or communicates its contagion by its very interruption [or inoperation].[16]

Resorting to a more Heideggerian idiom, one might say that the world as global village is ours only in a very elusive sense: a kind of trust rather than a securely manageable abode or possession.

## Notes

1. Compare Edward W. Said, *Culture and Imperialism* (New York: Knopf, 1993); also John Tomlinson, *Cultural Imperialism: A Critical Introduction* (Baltimore, Md.: Johns Hopkins University Press, 1991).

2. Michel Foucault, "What Is Enlightenment?" in *The Foucault Reader*, ed. Paul Rabinow (New York: Pantheon Books, 1984), pp. 43, 45.

3. Foucault, "Two Lectures" and "Truth and Power," in *Power/Knowledge:*

*Selected Interviews and Other Writings (1972–1977) by Michel Foucault*, ed. Colin Gordon (New York: Pantheon Books, 1980), pp. 81–82, 126. In "Two Lectures" Foucault also speaks of the "inhibiting effect of global, totalizing theories" (p. 80). In a subsequent interview, "Power and Strategies," he observed that "the role for theory today seems to be just this: not to formulate the global systematic theory which holds everything in place, but to analyze the specificity of mechanisms of power, to locate the connections and extensions, to build little by little a strategic knowledge (*savoir*)" (p. 145).

4. As he observed at one point: "Against this global policy of power, we initiate localized counter-responses, skirmishes, active and occasionally preventive defenses. We have no need to totalize that which is invariably totalized on the side of power; if we were to move in this direction, it would mean restoring the representative forms of centralism and a hierarchical structure. We must set up lateral affiliations and an entire system of networks and popular bases; and this is especially difficult." See "Intellectuals and Power: A Conversation between Michel Foucault and Gilles Deleuze," in Foucault, *Language, Counter-Memory, Practice: Selected Essays and Interviews*, ed. Donald F. Bouchard, trans. Bouchard and Sherry Simon (Oxford: Blackwell, 1977), p. 212.

5. Jacques Derrida, *The Other Heading: Reflections on Today's Europe*, trans. Pascale-Anne Brault and Michael B. Naas (Bloomington: Indiana University Press, 1992), pp. 44, 54–55, 78–79. See also the essay "Call It a Day for Democracy," pp. 84–109.

6. Maurice Merleau-Ponty, "Everywhere and Nowhere," in *Signs*, trans. Richard C. McCleary (Evanston, Ill.: Northwestern University Press, 1964), p. 139. As he adds: "The relationship between Orient and Occident, like that between child and adult, is not that of ignorance to knowledge or non-philosophy to philosophy; it is much more subtle, making room on the part of the Orient for all anticipations and 'prematurations.' "

7. Merleau-Ponty, "Everywhere and Nowhere," p. 139. Merleau-Ponty was by no means ready simply to abandon Western philosophy: "Husserl had understood: our philosophical problem is to open up the concept without destroying it. There is something irreplaceable in Western thought. The attempt to conceive and the rigor of the concept remain exemplary, even if they never exhaust what exists" (p. 138).

8. On this point, I find Deleuze's unqualified endorsement of hybridity and his occasional championing of a "nomadic" vagrancy which comes and goes nowhere somewhat misleading. Such vagrancy is too uncomfortably close to a bland cosmopolitanism or the jet-setting nomadism of multinational managers at home everywhere and nowhere. Compare, e.g., Deleuze, "Nomadic Thought," in *The New Nietzsche: Contemporary Styles of Interpretation*, ed. David B. Allison (New York: Dell Publishing Co., 1977), pp. 148–149.

9. See Emmanuel Levinas, *Totality and Infinity: An Essay on Exteriority*, trans. Alphonso Lingis (Pittsburgh, Pa.: Duquesne University Press, n.d.), especially pp. 42–48: "the idea of Socratic truth thus rests on the essential self-sufficiency of the same, its identification in ipseity, its egotism" (p. 44) and, about the later Heidegger: "ontology becomes ontology of nature, impersonal fecundity,

faceless generous mother, matrix of particular beings, inexhaustible matter for things" (p. 46). His chiding comments on Heidegger's "four-fold" (p. 46)—a metaphor for the immanence/transcendence nexus—seem to apply with equal scorn to Hindu and Taoist conceptions of the world. Most specifically, the derivation of ethics from outside or exteriority would appear to be unintelligible in a Buddhist context (remembering that the Buddha's "awakening" happened after seven weeks of solitary meditation). In this respect, I disagree with Gillian Rose when she describes Levinas's perspective as a "Buddhist Judaism." On the other hand, I am strongly in sympathy with her notion of an "activity beyond activity." See Gillian Rose, *Mourning Becomes the Law: Philosophy and Representation* (Cambridge: Cambridge University Press, 1996), pp. 37–38; also *The Broken Middle: Out of Our Ancient Society* (Oxford: Blackwell, 1992).

10. Relying largely on some of Gadamer's later writings, and in part on Derridean teachings, I have elaborated upon the notion of a "hermeneutics of difference" in my *Beyond Orientalism: Essays on Cross-Cultural Encounter* (Albany, N.Y.: SUNY Press, 1996), pp. 39–62 (chapter 2, "Gadamer, Derrida, and the Hermeneutics of Difference"). Compare also Paul Ricoeur, *Oneself as Another*, trans. Kathleen Blamey (Chicago: University of Chicago Press, 1992). The idea of an aggressive Orientialism was powerfully delineated in Edward W. Said's *Orientalism* (New York: Vintage Books, 1979).

11. Václav Havel, "A Challenge to Nourish Spiritual Roots Buried Under Our Thin Global Skin" (Convocation Address presented at Harvard University in June 1996), in *Just Commentary*, 28 (July 1966): 2.

12. Herder's legacy is strongly contested today on liberal (and partly on postmodern) premises. From a liberal or libertarian perspective, Herder's main shortcoming is his presumed neglect or de-emphasis of modern individualism in favor of collective beliefs. In response, however, one can argue that Herder's concern was neither with individualism nor with collectivism, but with the cultural and linguistic parameters of both. Seen in this light, the modern Western accent on individual preferences is the result of a long process of cultural-historical sedimentation. Liberal individualism thus constitutes a distinct cultural framework that can only be critiqued or decentered from alternative frameworks. As an opponent of colonialism, Herder in any case was keenly aware of the disempowering effects of liberal (capitalist) individualism on indigenous populations around the world.

13. Ali Shari'ati, "The Philosophy of History: Cain and Abel," in *On the Sociology of Islam: Lectures by Ali Shari'ati*, trans. Hamid Algar (Berkeley, Calif.: Mizan Press, 1979), pp. 108–109.

14. See Shari'ati, "On Humanism" and "Humanity Between Marxism and Religion," in *Marxism and Other Western Fallacies: An Islamique Critique*, trans. R. Campbell (Berkeley, Calif.: Mizan Press, 1980), pp. 15–31, 49–96.

15. Derrida, *The Other Heading*, p. 78 (italics in original). Compare also his somewhat later comments: "Even beyond the regulating idea in its classical form, the idea (if that is still what it is) of democracy to come, its 'idea' as an event of a pledged injunction that orders one to summon the very thing that will never present itself in the form of full presence, is the opening of this gap between an

infinite promise . . . and the determined, necessary but also necessarily inadequate forms of what has to be measured against this promise." See *Specters of Marx: The State of the Debt, the Work of Mourning, and the New International*, trans. Peggy Kamuf (New York: Routledge, 1994), p. 65.

16. Jean-Luc Nancy, *The Inoperative Community*, ed. Peter Connor, trans. Peter Connor et al. (Minneapolis: University of Minnesota Press, 1991), p. 60. (I have altered the translation slightly for purposes of readability.)

*Part 1*

# Modernity and Its Discontents

# 1

# Truth and Difference: Some Lessons from Herder

> If one could connect the most diverse scenes without confusing them
> . . . what a feat!
>
> J. G. Herder

Ours—we are told—is an age of multiple ruptures, of profound sea changes in many domains. The celebrated "death of god" has been followed by the equally vaunted "death of man," accompanied by the death of reason and truth. In lieu of the foundational moorings of modernity or modern metaphysics—subjectivity, consciousness, the *cogito*—we have plunged into a bottomless abyss where seemingly "anything goes." Instead of serving as an antidote to prejudice, truth (at least epistemic truth) has itself been unmasked as a prejudice, a fabrication governed by the will to power. Thus, in place of older notions of adequation or correspondence (*adaequatio mentis ad rem*), knowledge is now widely assumed to depend on cognitive frameworks and constructed or invented designs that apparently reflect the sole whim of their designers. The cognitive-metaphysical rupture is paralleled by a comparable political transformation, or at least by a widening rift besetting the heart of modern political thought. The facile, rose-colored optimism of Western liberalism has been thrown into disarray in our century by two world wars and the grim spectacles of genocide and holocaust. More recently, the global vision nurtured by modern liberalism as well as Marxist internationalism has been upset by the powerful upsurge of political particularisms, by the sometimes militant resurgence of local, ethnic, or national claims to self-determination. Just when cosmopolitanism seems to triumph under the aegis of Western science, technology, and industry, the world is plunged into fragmentation and ethnic rivalries rising from the passion for difference or diversity.

Individual observers or analysts are prone to assign different weights to these discontinuities and assess them in differing lights. Moreover, the two ruptures are not unavoidably synchronized or joined in indissoluble union; spokesmen of the "end of metaphysics" do not necessarily support political fragmentation, and vice versa. Still, there is a bent toward convergence. In attacking metaphysical "foundationalism" and the reign of epistemic truth, Richard Rorty also champions a mild form of Western ethnocentrism. In non-Western countries, the espousal of "postmodernism" (seen here as the reversal of modern metaphysics) is often linked with a fervent return to native or indigenous resources. My aim here is not to explore instances of convergence or divergence. Instead I want to raise some general questions. Are we really forced into a "no exit" situation, constrained to choose between polar opposites that may be equally unpalatable? Does the rejection of foundations or metaphysical banisters really entail a surrender to happenstance and arbitrary whim? Does the deconstruction of "truth" (especially epistemic truth) inevitably consign us to the abyss of no-truth or untruth or to a stance of cynical indifference between the former and the latter? Is there a truth of life or of experience that we may not wish to surrender even in our age of post-metaphysics? Does the collapse of "logocentrism," anchored in the *cogito*, really compel us to abandon every type of "humanism" or commitment to humanity even when it transgresses human self-indulgence? In the political domain: does the rejection or critique of liberal universalism inevitably force us to embrace the alternative of parochialism and hateful xenophobia? Is it not possible—indeed, are there not good practical and philosophical reasons—to cherish cultural and ethnic diversity while at the same time opposing the blandishments of both cosmopolitanism and local narcissism?

Posed in this manner, all these questions are probably too abstract—or too "universal"—to permit tangible and fruitful exploration. To render them more accessible, this chapter focuses on the legacy of a man whose lifework has revolved around these questions and elucidated them profoundly: Johann Gottfried Herder (1744–1803). Herder's work has a deep relevance in our time—a fact that is rarely perceived or acknowledged. Outside the circle of intellectual historians specializing in the eighteenth century, his writings do not figure prominently in contemporary (philosophical and political) discussions. During his own lifetime, he was eclipsed by the ascent of the Weimar Olympians (especially Goethe and Schiller), which he witnessed with some anguish and unease. During the nineteenth century, parts of his work were appropriated by the successive waves of Romanticism, historicism, and nationalism. Curiously, it was precisely this appropriation that promoted Herder's own oblivion by suggesting the mistaken notion of a progressive sublation or *Aufhebung* of his seminal ideas. But his legacy is not reducible to Romanticism, historicism, and/or nationalism (especially of a chauvinistic kind). A contemporary of both Kant and Johann Georg Hamann, he was exposed simultaneously to the former's defense of Enlightenment rationalism and the latter's radical, antifoundationalist plumbing of the abysses of reason.[1] Keenly aware of the "dialectic of Enlightenment," Herder throughout his life sought to steer a course between reason and nonreason, truth and nontruth, and the Scylla of political globalism or cosmopolitanism and the Charybdis of ethnic fragmentation or exclusivism. The chapter proceeds in three steps. First is the portrayal of Herder's work by some influential Anglo-American philosophers in recent times. This serves as background for an assessment of Herder's complex navigation between universal "progress" and historical discontinuity, between humanity and "people" (*Volk*). The concluding section outlines some of the areas where Herder's legacy seems today particularly salient and fruitful.

# I

Herder has not been in the forefront of philosophical concerns in our century, shaped successively by logical positivism, analytical philosophy, and (post)structuralism. Still, neglect has not been complete and there are notable exceptions to the reigning temper of the times. Among Anglo-American philosophers and political thinkers, the most prominent of these are Charles Taylor and Isaiah Berlin. Taylor has missed no opportunity to retrieve Herder from obscurity. His magisterial study of "absolute idealism" presented Hegel's philosophy as the confluence of two powerful sources or tributaries: the streams of Enlightenment rationalism, epitomized by Kant, and of *Sturm und Drang*, literary imagination, typified by Herder. In Taylor's work, Kant's critical perspective nourished the analytical rigor and rational-systematic structure of Hegel's work, while Herder provided Hegel with historical depth, cultural and ethical substance (*Sittlichkeit*), and a taste for self-expression or "expressivism." Taylor's subsequent publications strengthened and amplified his Herderian sympathies. In his *Sources of the Self*, Herder emerged as a crucial builder in the formation of the modern (Western) conception of individuality or individual distinctiveness, a watershed figure who transformed older Christian and Renaissance notions of spiritual and moral autonomy into the characteristically modern idiom of personal uniqueness and irreplaceability. More recently, Taylor has underscored the crucial significance of Herder for the status and meaning of modernity itself.

Countering one-sided identifications of modernity (or the "discourse of modernity") with Enlightenment principles, Taylor—both in *The Ethics of Authenticity* and his work on multiculturalism—has again emphasized the dual tributaries of our age: Enlightenment rationality and Herderian Romanticism. Politically and ethically, while the former buttresses the commitment to universal human rights, the second vindicates cultural autonomy and self-determination.[2]

Although highly commendable in the contemporary context, Taylor's "rehabilitation" of Herder (in my view) portrays him too narrowly as merely a tributary to Hegel's work and the character of modernity as such: a tributary largely identified with Romanticism, historicism, and nationalism (or national self-determination). One may wonder how such disparate elements—Kantian rationalism and Herderian sentiment—could ever merge or fuse in synthesis, especially the "absolute" synthesis envisaged by Hegel. Are we not faced here with an antinomic union that would at best yield a discordant patchwork? More importantly, Taylor tends to truncate the character and significance of Herder's work. Far from serving merely as tributary or underlaborer to a later synthesis, one can legitimately argue that Herder himself forged the kind of balanced outlook celebrated by Taylor, though one far removed from Hegel's absolute idealism. To speak metaphorically: far from being a one-eyed cyclops limited to a segmental view, Herder was a profoundly bifocal thinker capable of reconciling in his own (non-Hegelian) way the pulls of reason and sentiment, truth and diversity, as well as cosmopolitanism and localism. Generally speaking, Taylor associates Herder too closely with the later Romantic and historicist movements, thereby neglecting Herder's mediating role between the Baroque age and the (post) Napoleonic era, between Spinoza and Leibniz, on the one hand, and Fichte and Hegel, on the other. One label that Taylor frequently pins on Herder is particularly dubious or misleading: "expressivism." By suggesting the disclosure of a human "inside" to an outside world, the label is too deeply imbued with late-Romantic subjectivism to suit Herder's perspective in which larger, cosmic forces (*Kräfte*) express themselves in and through the individual without shrinking into it.

Taylor seemingly borrowed the label from Sir Isaiah Berlin, who had used "expressionism" as one of several catch-all formulas to pinpoint Herder's thought. Berlin's *Vico and Herder*, written during the heyday of linguistic analysis, is an admirable display of nonconformism. It contains a plethora of valuable insights that no student of Herder can afford to ignore. According to Berlin, Herder was continuously fascinated by cultural and personal diversities and their reciprocal interplay, to the point that the "tension of the One and the Many" could be singled out as his "obsessive *idée maîtresse.*" Compared with other Enlightenment figures,

Herder was endowed with an uncanny talent for empathy or "sympathetic imagination," which allowed him to understand or reconstruct the most diverse forms of life, and "the odder, the more extraordinary a culture or an individual, the better pleased he was." To quote Berlin on this point:

> He can hardly condemn anything that displays color or uniqueness; Indians, Americans and Persians, Greece and Palestine, Arminius and Machiavelli, Shakespeare and Savonarola, seem to him equally fascinating. . . . He conscientiously looks for uniformities, but what fascinates him is the exception. He condemns the erection of walls between one genus and another; but he seeks for the greatest possible number of distinctions of species within a genus, and of individuals within the species.

What particularly annoyed and repelled him was the trend of standardization and systematization, the powerful predilection nurtured by the Encyclopedists "for uniformity, for the assimilation . . . of one culture or way of life to another." In this respect, he was clearly influenced by Hamann, that archenemy of systems, who always insisted on the need to "preserve sensitiveness to specific historical and cultural phenomena" and to "avoid becoming deadened . . . by networks of tidy concepts." Together with Hamann, Herder (in Berlin's account) always managed to retain an almost naive "impressionability," the capacity to "react spontaneously to the jagged, irregular, not always describable data provided by the senses, by imagination, by religious revelation, by history, by art."[3]

The three catchphrases or "cardinal ideas" that Berlin uses to characterize Herder's outlook are populism, expressionism, and pluralism. Among these, the notion of populism—described as the "belief in the value of belonging to a group or culture"—deserves primary attention. Berlin immediately, and correctly, challenges a widespread view according to which Herder started as an almost "routine defender" of enlightened cosmopolitanism and later retreated into an uncritical, reactionary type of nationalism. (The reverse view is also sometimes found in the literature: an early nationalistic sentiment gave way later to a rationalist universalism.) Berlin debunks this periodization as entirely "untenable"; "whatever may have been the evolution of Fichte or Friedrich Schlegel, Herder's form of nationalism remained unaltered throughout his life." Berlin also takes issue with the notion that the nationalism or national populism embraced by Herder, whether in his early or later period, was ever tainted by chauvinist militancy. One of the main theses of Berlin's book is that Herder's national populism was purely cultural and not "political"; it promoted cultural distinctiveness without demeaning other ethnic or national cultures as inferior or possible targets of conquest. To buttress this point, Berlin cites eloquent statements from Herder's early and late writings, such as: "To brag of one's country is the stupidest form of boastfulness." "An innocent attachment to family, language, one's own city, one's own country, its traditions, are not to be condemned"; but "aggressive nationalism" is detestable in all its forms because it leads to war, and "all large wars are essentially civil wars since men are brothers." What Herder particularly opposed was the streamlining of ethnic or national culture into a political movement, especially into an organized "state" that only serves as an instrument of centralization and domination. Berlin notes, "For him, as for Nietzsche, the state is the coldest of all cold monsters." Nothing in history is more hateful to Herder than "churches and priests [and intellectuals] who are instruments of political power"; as for the state, "it robs men of themselves."[4]

In Berlin's view, several consequences follow from this benign type of national populism. First, all cultures have some intrinsic qualities and merits, though they may also have blemishes or defects. Basically, there is no chosen or privileged culture or nation, and certainly no room for racial superiority; in Herder's phrase, there is no *"Favoritvolk."* Second, a nation or culture is not a compact entity but a historically grown fabric with an internal variety of strands and self-interpretations. To this extent, Herder was not a metaphysical essentialist; a nation or culture was not simply a "natural kind" or a "real essence" or foundational category. Generally speaking, Herder's view of the world was not mechanistic in the Newtonian sense, nor was it wedded to a biological organicism or collectivism. Despite all the talk about "organic growth," human life for Herder was separated from animal organisms by virtue of its thoughtful understanding or *"Besonnenheit."* In Berlin's account, Herder's cultural approach managed to sidestep "three great eighteenth-century myths" that later nourished the stream of nineteenth-century nationalism and evolutionism. One such myth is the idea of the progressive amalgamation of cultures, accomplished chiefly under the guidance of the most advanced Western nations. Herder was most adamant in his defense of cultural and historical diversity against this doctrine. As he noted in *Yet Another Philosophy of History*, "Every nation has its own inner center (*Mittelpunkt*) of happiness, as every sphere its own center of gravity." To understand the significance of a culture, an experience, or an event one must grasp it in its distinctiveness, not subsume it under a general category. A second myth was the preferential status of some historical epochs over others, such as that of Renaissance humanism over the supposed "darkness" of the Middle Ages, which sometimes encouraged a nostalgic longing for past periods (ancient Greece or the Germanic forests) over the present. Closely linked with these doctrines was the central myth of the Enlightenment: the universal, linear "progress" of humankind. As

Berlin shows, Herder did not replace progress with the reverse idea of stationary repetition or chaotic discontinuity. Opposed to both uniformity and chaotic indifference, Herder subscribed to a kind of human advancement (*Fortgang*) that involved the unfolding of individual or cultural capacities to their highest possible level. *Fortgang*, Berlin notes, means that "each society, each culture develops in its own way."[5]

The second catchphrase employed by Berlin is "expressionism," and doubts begin to surface with its use. Berlin quite correctly stresses the role of language and tradition in Herder's thought and thus embeds "expression" in a broader historical, and even cosmic, context. Human groupings, large and small, he writes, obtain their distinctiveness from "common traditions and common memories, of which the principal link and vehicle—indeed, more than vehicle, the very incarnation—is language." Without entirely sharing Hamann's language mysticism (or mystical nominalism), Herder completely endorsed the former's belief that language is the "central organ of understanding" and that the ability of humans "to speak to others (to men or God or themselves)" is basic to this understanding. Language was neither a miraculous exogenous gift of God nor a technical invention of human reason, but rather part of human being itself, of human thoughtfulness (*Besonnenheit*) displayed in internal or communicative deliberation. Given the fact that the attempt to invent words already presupposes language, Herder consistently opposed every kind of arbitrary constructivism; as he noted, thinking in words is always a "swim in an inherited stream of images and words; we must accept these media on trust: we cannot create them." Together with Vico, Herder saw creativity in language not as willful fabrication but as poetic or "mythopoetic" world-disclosure that ultimately remains "magical in character." Despite this insightful account, Berlin subsequently proceeds to infuse Herder with a heavy dose of late-Romantic subjectivism that is alien to his thought. Although acknowledging that Herder was "uncompromisingly hostile to . . . egomania," Berlin also characterizes him as one of the originators of the "doctrine of artistic commitment" and artistic self-expression. For Herder, he asserts, art is "the expression of men in society in their fullness." Hence Herder was "bitterly opposed" to the view that the artist's purpose is "to create an object whose merits are independent of the creator's personal qualities or his intentions, conscious or unconscious." To Berlin, Herder was the "true father" of the maxim "it is the artist's mission, above others, to testify in his works to the truth of his own inner experience."[6]

Berlin's third, and most dubious, catchphrase, which also serves as the capstone of his entire presentation, is "pluralism." Here a curious reversal takes place. Despite the earlier emphatic differentiation of Herder's populism from myopic types of chauvinism, and despite eloquent pas-

sages attesting to Herder's "Christian humanism" and his devotion to
"*Humanität*," seen as a mediating standard between universalism and
particularism, pluralism is now harshly portrayed as the "rejection of
absolute values." According to Berlin, this rejection runs counter to a
premise of Western culture crucial since the time of Plato: the assumption
that it is in principle possible "to draw some outline of the perfect society
or the perfect man, if only to define how far a given society or a given
individual fell short of the ideal." Termed the "keystone of the classical
arch," this assumption allegedly "began to crumble" with and after
Herder. Although recognizing the prominence of *Humanität* in *Ideas for
a Philosophy of History* and elsewhere, Berlin now insists that Herder's
entire skill and imagination went into "the evocation of the individual
cultures and not of the alleged links between them." Despite Herder's
vast historical panorama ranging over many cultures and containing
many positive and negative judgments, emphasis is now placed entirely
on incomparability, incommensurability, and untranslatability: "We are
forbidden to make judgments of comparative value, for that is measuring
the incommensurable." Herder's early *Yet Another Philosophy of History* is styled a "classical statement of historical relativism," while all his
works—including *Critical Forests* and *Letters for the Advancement of
Humanity*—are claimed to "celebrate the uniqueness, the individuality,
and above all, the incommensurability with one another of each of the
civilizations which he so lovingly describes and defends." Given this celebration of the "equal validity" of incommensurable cultures, the traditional concepts of an "ideal state" or of an "ideal man" obviously
become incoherent; in fact, they are not merely "difficult to formulate,
or impossible to realize in practice," but are "patently absurd" and "unintelligible." Berlin reaches this somber conclusion:

> The consequences of Herder's doctrines did not make themselves felt imme-
> diately. . . . The full effect was felt only when the Romantic Movement, at
> its most violent, attempted to overthrow the authority both of reason and
> of dogma on which the old order rested. The extent of its explosive potenti-
> alities was not fully realized until the rise of modern anti-rationalist move-
> ments—nationalism, fascism, existentialism, emotivism, and the wars and
> revolutions made in the name of two among them; that is to say, not until
> our own time, and perhaps not altogether even today.[7]

## II

Berlin's conclusion—surprising in light of his earlier remarks and his historical sensibilities—seems off the mark and fraught with incoherence.
By pressing Herder into the straitjacket of late Romanticism and histori-

cism, he appears to lack precisely the kind of empathy or "sympathetic imagination" that he praises in Herder's work and which he himself often displays as an eminent historian of ideas. The incoherence derives from the one-sided emphasis on incomparability and incommensurability, on cultural exclusivism. Taking this premise seriously, what would cross-cultural empathy be if not an exercise in utter futility? What meaning would Herder's far-flung historical investigations—from the Babylonians to the Incas and the Chinese—have if cultural boundaries were truly impermeable and if cultures could not somehow learn from each other without thereby reaching a synthesis or fusion of horizons? Moreover, how could one assert the "equal validity" of cultures in the absence of some criteria, however inchoate, buttressing judgments of equality and normative validity? How could one even assert the distinctiveness of a certain culture or group without some comparative differentiation of this distinctiveness both from the nondistinctive and the characteristic features of other cultures? And how could one render such a differential judgment without invoking a broader frame of reference in terms of which distinct features appear significant or insignificant? It is to Charles Taylor's credit to have stressed the role of frames of significance in differential judgments: "To come together on a mutual recognition of difference—that is, the equal value of different identities—requires that we share more than a belief in this principle. . . . Recognizing difference, like self-choosing, requires a horizon of significance."[8] Although recently formulated, Taylor's insight is not novel. One cannot plausibly assume that Herder—an eminent philosopher—was ignorant of such elementary considerations.

Berlin's concluding verdict is all the more puzzling in light of some acknowledged scholarly influences. In his preface to *Vico and Herder*, Berlin voices his indebtedness, among others, to Herder scholar F. M. Barnard, noting that his reliance upon the latter's "excellent anthology," *Herder on Social and Political Culture*, is "particularly great." However, Barnard does not at all concur with Berlin's judgment of a relativistic and exclusivist pluralism. In his introduction to *Herder on Social and Political Culture*, Barnard carefully separates Herder from later Romanticism and from the "explosive potentialities" manifest (according to Berlin) in the rise of "modern anti-rationalist movements." Later Romantics, especially in their political leanings, have "often been acclaimed as followers of Herder," and it cannot be denied that "a number of their ideas" derived from Herderian sources. These shared ideas have led many commentators mistakenly to identify the outlook of later Romanticism with that of Herder and even to "hold him responsible for the different forms of perversion which Romanticism has undergone." Such identification in Barnard's view, however, "blurs crucial differences" and contrasts, especially the fact that Herder's notion of pluralism was entirely "transmuted." In place of Herder's conception of a "co-operative pluralism" with a popular-democratic thrust, the Romantics returned to the old regime notion of functional stratification. In contrast to Herder's advocacy of "*multiple* affiliations," where individuals can "move between, and belong to, a diversity of groups," the Romantics revived the medieval legacy of "social immobility" and of the "total and exclusive submission of a member to a single social group" (and ultimately to the authority of the state). In lieu of the hermetic organicism of the Romantics, Herder used the notion of "organism" in a metaphorical sense, just as his view of populism always strove to uphold the notions of "both *Volk* [people] and *Humanität*" as "equally relevant value considerations." In light of these differences, Barnard's conclusion departs sharply from Berlin's verdict. Instead of the dire "consequences" ominously intimated by Berlin, Barnard holds that Herder's central legacy found "no immediate heirs."[9]

Rather than pursuing these divergences further, we turn now to some of Herder's own writings (using mainly Barnard's excellent English translations). Herder's prizewinning "Essay on the Origin of Language" (1770) contains many instructive comments on "the One and the Many," universalism and particularism. It takes issue with the doctrines of an external, divine, as well as a purely instrumental origin of language, placing the accent instead on the distinctiveness of human being as such and thus sidestepping the conundrum of an origin of origins. The difference between humans and animals is not only a matter of degree, or one revolving around an added faculty like reason; rather, it involves a holistic mutation, a *Gestalt* change affecting the "entire economy" of dispositions. Bereft of a circumscribed instinctual habitat, human knowing and acting has to rely on interpretive understanding for which language and speech are constitutive. Herder polemicizes here against a separation of mind and language, the argument that thought can proceed without distinguishing symbols. This separation, he counters, is "not only improbable but actually impossible." "[T]he difference between two things can be determined only by means of a third," and "it is this third which constitutes the significant characteristic and which fashions the identifying symbol we apply to it within our mind." The polemic also extends to the fiction of "man in the state of nature," including Rousseau's "phantom" of an itinerant nomad or *bon sauvage*. Before experiencing and understanding his natural condition, Herder notes, this nomad must "*already* have possessed the art of thinking and, with it, the art of speaking, since the former entails the latter in its operation." Given the linkage of thinking and speaking, language attests to the "natural" sociability of humans, their character as a "gregarious creature, born to live in society." From families to larger societies, language is the fabric linking generations and kinship groups together, by virtue of which everyone is "knit into the texture of the whole." Herder celebrates the poetic or mythopoetic qualities of language in forging the lives of peoples:

> What a treasure language is when kinship groups grow into tribes and nations! Even the smallest of nations in any part of the globe, no matter how undeveloped it may be, cherishes in and through its language the history, the poetry and songs about the great deeds of its forefathers. The language is its collective treasure, the source of its social wisdom and communal self-respect. Instruction, games and dances are associated with it.[10]

Although stressing the holistic quality of language, its character as a social bond, Herder is far from presenting it as a stable essence or indissoluble synthesis. On the contrary, human diversity, manifest in differences between individuals, groups, and peoples, quite naturally accounts for the prevailing diversity of languages and idioms, even among the "most closely neighboring nations." Human sociability does not rule out divergence, competition, and even struggle and conflict. "Man," Herder asserts, is not a "Hobbesian wolf" nor a "lone creature of the forest" as Rousseau would have it; he has a "communal language in which to communicate." Yet, neither is he a "helpless lamb, inseparably bound up with one herd," a creature "incapable of adjusting to novel surroundings or of developing new dispositions, habits or languages." Hence, the existing diversity of languages does not have to be attributed to exogenous forces (like climate or geographical distance) but can quite sensibly be traced to endogenous factors such as divergent dispositions and attitudes; "Conflict and mutual aversion, in particular, have greatly favored the emergence of language differentiation." It is in this manner that Herder also interprets the biblical story of the tower of Babel. Without entering into theological disputes, he states, readers cannot fail to perceive the "principal idea" in this allegorical tale: "Distinct nations were formed, each with its own language, not only as a result of migrations, but also because of discord in the course of great common concerns." Thus, national differences are the "debris of the confusion of peoples." However, recognition of divergence and discord is not Herder's last word. Differences between individuals, groups, and peoples also prevent self-isolation and stimulate competition and a mutual learning process that is beneficial to humanity at large; "Let the nations freely learn from one another, let one continue where the other has left off." For Herder, this learning process has been, and continues to be, especially salutary for Germans:

> Have we Germans not learned most of what we know as a "civilized nation" from other people? Indeed we have. In this and in many other such cases nature has forged a new chain of transmission, from nation to nation. Arts, sciences, languages, the totality of social cultures, have been developed

and refined in a powerful progression in this very manner. This international transmission of social cultures is indeed the *highest form of cultural
development which nature has elected*.[11]

The same interlacing of divergence and commonality is also a central
theme in Herder's *Yet Another Philosophy of History* (1774)—a work
styled by Berlin as the epitome of historical relativism. Attacking the abstract generalizations dear to Enlightenment rationalism, Herder immediately launches into the praise of differentiation and diversity. "Have you
noticed," he asks, "how inexpressible is the individuality of one man,"
in fact, how difficult it is to "know distinctly what distinguishes him,
how he feels and lives, how differently his eyes see, his soul measures, his
heart experiences, everything?" What is true of individuals also applies
to peoples and nations. Who, indeed, could plumb the depth in the character of a single nation that even after sustained inquiry manages to
"evade the word that would capture it"? The diversity of talents and
perspectives extends further to the concept of happiness, which is sometimes treated as the universal yardstick of humanity at large. "Who can
compare," he queries, "the different forms of satisfaction perceived by
different senses in different worlds? Who can compare the shepherd and
the Oriental patriarch, the ploughman and the artist, the sailor, the run-
ner, the conqueror of the world?" Different perceptions of happiness and
of the sense of life ultimately derive from different horizons or frames of
reference, which in turn are due to different traditions and sedimented
judgments. "But prejudice is good," Herder affirms (anticipating Gadamer by two hundred years), "in its time and place, for happiness may
spring from it. It urges nations to converge upon their center, attaches
them more firmly to their roots, causes them to flourish after their kind."
All of these notions, to be sure, are diametrically opposed to the reigning
Enlightenment philosophy with its longing for uniformity and standardization guided by the model of the most "advanced" European nations:

> The general, philosophical, philanthropical tone of our century wishes to
> extend "our own ideal" of virtue and happiness to each distant nation, to
> even the remotest age in history. But can one such single ideal act as an
> arbiter praising or condemning other nations or periods, their customs and
> laws; can it remake them after its own image? Is good not dispersed over
> the earth?[12]

Lingering on the process of standardization, Herder astutely probes
some of its implications, which, in his own time, were still somewhat
recessed or embryonic. Behind or beneath the vaunted triumph of reason,
he detects tendencies at work in the Enlightenment age that were often
repressed by its devotees, especially progressive mechanization guided by

instrumental rationality and the expansion of capitalism. Once the rhetoric of the age is critically sifted, Herder notes, one perceives that "a large part of this so-called new civilization is actually a piece of mechanism." Closer inquiry reveals that mechanism and mechanization are the "essential characteristic of the new spirit." Under the impact of this ongoing mechanization, older virtues or practices pertaining to civil life and government have atrophied or become obsolete, making room for the cult of efficiency entrusted to experts; "The machine can be controlled by one single person, with one single thought, with one single sign." Thus, the presumed emancipatory thrust of the Enlightenment gives way again to status hierarchy; enlightened absolutism replicates the despised despotism of the feudal age. "It is always a matter of master and servant, of despot and vassal. This system of relationships finds its most sublime political expression in the new-fangled philosophical concept of *sovereignty*." An important corollary of mechanization was the new "political economy" with its effort to give a scientific account of mercantilism and the budding spirit of capitalism, a spirit not averse to monopolistic control:

> We no longer require religion, (that childish sanction!) honor, spiritual freedom and human happiness as mainsprings for the existence of states, for these have effectively been replaced by fear and money. How well we know how to seize upon Mammon as our sole god, and to transform him into a second Proteus, so that by enlisting his aid we can acquire and enforce whatever we happen to want![13]

As opposed to the standardizing bent of the age and its belief in linear progress, *Yet Another Philosophy of History* counsels a much more subdued and modest approach without simply replacing unity with rupture, teleology with chaos. The idea of progress remains a target of Herder's unrelenting critique. In support of this idea, he notes, its devotees have "embellished or invented facts, minimized or suppressed contrary facts"; above all, they have "taken words for works, enlightenment for happiness, greater sophistication for virtue" and in this manner invented the "fiction of the 'general, progressive amelioration of the world'," which remains unpersuasive to the "true student of history and the human heart." Although he assailed the *idola fori* of his time, Herder was not content with a simple reversal or a cynical slide into disbelief. Some, he writes, who perceived the "harmfulness of this dream" of progress determined despairingly that there were only "vices and virtues alternating like climates" and "perfections sprouting and dying like spring leaves." Thus, instead of plan or progress, they centerstaged endless cyclical repetition, "weaving and unraveling like Penelope." Repelled by the doctrine of amelioration, these observers fell into a whirlpool of doubt "about all virtue, about all happiness and the destiny of man." Unwilling to surrender himself to this whirlpool, Herder is still intensely aware of the hazards of any affirmative move. The complex pattern of history would be "a miserable, little thing," he exclaims, "if I, insect that I am, could survey it all!" Still, even as a mere finite creature, as just "one letter" in the book of history, Herder detected a process of "becoming" to which, without the privilege of an overview, his own life inevitably belonged: the process of the experiential learning of humanity. Thus, there was "becoming on a grand scale," perhaps even something like a "passage of God over the nations"; this becoming could be seen as a "long, leavening" or seasoning movement that Herder described as the "fermentation of the culture (*Bildung*) of man." Anticipating Walter Benjamin, *Yet Another Philosophy* depicts history as a grand Baroque drama whose overall design was perceptible only in its gaps and fragments:

> History may not manifestly be revealed as the theater of a directing purpose on earth—of which our shallow histories boast so much—for we may not be able to espy its final end. But it may conceivably offer us glimpses of a divine theater through the openings and ruins of individual scenes.[14]

The balance of unity and diversity is still preserved in Herder's *Ideas for a Philosophy of the History of Mankind* (1784–1791), although with a slightly more affirmative tone. Herder again emphasizes human diversity, operative in a single life as well as in the lives of peoples and nations. "A man's life," he notes, "is one continuous series of change and its phases read like sagas of transformation." Likewise, "the species as a whole goes through a ceaseless metamorphosis. Flowers drop and wither: others sprout and bud." The affairs of humanity are an inexhaustible welter of differences, sometimes to the point of confrontation and conflict. Human history in particular is a patchwork of multiple plots and subplots whose connections the human mind can scarcely fathom. History is ultimately "a theater of transformations which only He, who animates these events and lives and feels Himself in all of them, can review." Yet, cultural and historical diversity does not entirely cancel a certain commonality, a link fashioned by universal human "sympathy" that together with self-preservation constitutes a mainspring of human behavior. What Herder envisions is not an abstract species concept nor a lowest common denominator, but a bond of feeling nurtured by historical experience and a long-standing reciprocal learning process. Thus years before the French "Declaration of the Rights of Man and the Citizen," Herder proclaimed and eloquently defended the notion of a general human brotherhood or fraternity that is still far removed from bland standard-

ization: "But thou, O man, honor thyself: neither the pongo nor the gib-
bon is thy brother, but the American [Indian] and the Negro *are*. These,
therefore, thou shouldst not oppress, or murder, or rob; for they are men
like thee."[15]

# III

The preceding discussion provides a glimpse of the wealth of Herder's
insights and of the complex, tensional character of his thought, which
completely resists streamlining into a simple formula or program. Drawing on some of his major writings, it also counteracts some dubious or
lopsided interpretations of his work by various contemporary thinkers.
As it seems to me, Herder holds definite relevance for intellectual and
political constellations of our time, particularly for the ruptures, dilemmas, or sweeping changes affecting our contemporary self-understanding: above all the dilemmas of truth and nontruth, humanism and
antihumanism, and universalism and particularism. In all these domains,
Herder's work offers a powerful stimulus for renewed reflection and a
reconsideration of prevailing views. F. M. Barnard is quite correct when
he says that, although devoid of "immediate heirs," Herder may yet find
followers today. It does not seem "fanciful" to suggest, he states, that
Herder's "ingenious attempt" to resolve dichotomies commonly thought
to be "irrevocably opposed to each other" has lost none of its relevance
to current discussions in politics, history, and philosophy. Barnard
stresses these troubling tensions or dichotomies: "individualism *versus*
collectivism; reason *versus* feeling; nature *versus* culture; state *versus*
non-state political cultures; uniqueness *versus* generalization; conserva-
tion and tradition *versus* change and the progressive emergence of new
goals; nationalism *versus* internationalism."[16]

Herder's work is particularly instructive or strongly suggestive when
examined in terms of the metaphysics-postmetaphysics debate in philosophy. A critic of Cartesianism and its Enlightenment offshoots, Herder
challenged the "foundational" status of the *cogito*, the centrality of subjectivity, and the subject-object relation, as linchpins of epistemological
truth. A corollary of this critique was the resolute turn to language and
speech, sometimes celebrated as a very recent achievement, and the dis-
carding of anthropocentism in favor of the contextualizing of human
being in family, society, and world. Among philosophers of our age affinities can be detected in the existential ontology of Martin Heidegger,
particularly in his portrayal of human *Dasein* as "being-in-the-world."
As for Herder being-in-the-world constitutes a countermove to the Cartesian *cogito* and the radical decontextualization of human existence. Par-

allels between the two thinkers extend to numerous other features of their respective works. When Herder locates a distinctive quality of human being—as differentiated from animal species—in human "thoughtfulness" (*Besonnenheit*), his argument is clearly evocative of Heidegger's notion of "recollective," as opposed to calculative, thinking (*Andenken*) and also of the central trait ascribed to *Dasein* in *Being and Time*: the capacity for "care" for and about being. Closely linked with this reflectiveness is the emphasis of both thinkers on interpretation or understanding: human beings, though "in-the-world," are not simply instinctually enmeshed and hence have to make sense of their lives through interpretive efforts. Understanding for Herder and Heidegger implies language—the latter seen not as a handy tool but as constitutive of human being as such. Mutual resonances can also be found in the domain of humanism-antihumanism. Heidegger's *Letter on Humanism* strongly denounces the human narcissism endemic to modern Western thought, while simultaneously seeking to salvage "humanity" on a more recessed, custodial level, an outlook not too distant from Herder's *Humanität*.[17]

Herder's legacy for social-political theory deserves attention on several counts. One concerns political culture, or the role of culture in politics, as opposed to a purely utilitarian and organizational focus centered on individual benefits or governmental efficiency. Although not craving the feudal arrangements of medieval times, despite an appreciation of some of their merits, Herder was a strong opponent of modern absolutism, especially of the absolute "state" seen as a "machine" of standardization (or, in Weberian terms, as the wielder of the monopoly of force). His denunciation of the modern state—recurrent throughout his writings—is passionate and relentless, in a manner that strikes a responsive chord in contemporary critics of state sovereignty: "Those who expect or even demand enlightenment from the state as such . . . cherish ideas that are wholly unintelligible to me. The state as an entity is an abstraction incapable of seeing or hearing." Herder's denunciation of the state is based on its wholly artificial character, centralization of power (hence its anti-populism), and tendency toward militarism. In addition to being a standardizing machine, the state like all "despotic" forms of government was also an engine of war and military conquest: "What has given Germany, what has given civilized Europe, its governments? The answer is *war*." Herder's indictment of militarism and the history of military conquest is again eloquent and stirring and shows no trace of relativism:

Our old planet has been a prey to violence and its history presents a melancholy picture of manhunts and conquests. Almost every little variation of a boundary, every new epoch, is inscribed in the book of Time with the blood of human victims and the tears of the oppressed. The most celebrated names are those of the murderers of mankind, crowned or crown-seeking execu-tioners, and, even more distressingly, the worthiest of men have often been compelled by necessity to help in forging the chains of their brethren.[18]

Although a universal phenomenon in human history, military conquest in modern times has not been equally distributed among nations and peoples. As Herder is keenly aware, Western or European nations have been particularly proficient in modernity in imposing their military, eco-nomic, and cultural yoke on non-European societies. Herder is probably the most passionate eighteenth-century opponent of European colonial-ism, which was premised in equal measure on greed and the theory of progress (styled as the "white man's burden"). His comments on the topic make sobering reading in our postcolonial era. Addressing the en-lightened elite of his time, *Yet Another Philosophy* castigates the arro-gance of the presumed Western superiority. In the name of progress, "soon there will be European colonies everywhere. Savages all over the world will become ripe for conversion as they grow fonder of our brandy and our luxuries; they will soon approach our culture and become, so help me God, good, strong and happy men, just like us!" Europe's civiliz-ing mission was always buttressed by the profit motive, that cornerstone of the vaunted "system of (free) trade" espoused by political economy, opening native societies to Western commerce, including the slave trade. In Europe itself, Herder grants, slavery has been abolished, but only because it has been "actuarially established" that slaves are more costly and less productive than free labor. Yet this did not prevent "our raiding three other continents for slaves, trading in them, banishing them to silvermines and sugar plantations." But "they are not European, not Christian! What is more, we get silver, precious stones, spices, sugar and—secret diseases, in return." These, in sum, have been the benefits of the system of trade and free commerce. And "who does not have a hand in this grand European sponging enterprise? Who does not compete as a trader, even of his own children?" Twenty years later, in *Letters for the Advancement of Humanity*, Herder still decries colonialism in the most acerbic language:

> Can you name a land where Europeans have entered without defiling them-selves forever before defenseless, trusting mankind, by the unjust word, greedy deceit, crushing oppression, diseases, fatal gifts they have brought? Our part of the world should be called not the wisest, but the most arrogant, aggressive, money-minded: what it has given these peoples is not civilization but the destruction of the rudiments of their own cultures wherever they could achieve this.[19]

Herder does not limit himself to general condemnation, but repeatedly delves into concrete instances of colonial conquest and exploitation. His

*Ideas* refers to the wretched lot of native American Indians in North and South America following European invasion. "The ferocious way," he writes, "the American natives are fighting for their country and for their brethren and children that have been deprived of it and crucially degraded and oppressed, is another example worth citing." Even when they are "reasonably well treated," natives are bound to "feel cheated" and only to wait for the day when their repressed longing for freedom will "burst out into open flames." Two decades later, in his periodical *Adrastea*, Herder depicted an imaginary conversation between an Asian Indian and a European, where the Indian says, "Tell me, have you still not lost the habit of trying to convert to your faith peoples whose property you steal, whom you rob, enslave, murder, deprive of their land and state, to whom your customs seem revolting?" As a result of the farflung extension of colonial empires, Europe was emerging as the acme and metropolis of the world, with the rest of the globe serving as dependent supplier of resources. "From what height we look down upon the world!" *Yet Another Philosophy* exclaims. "In a sense, all peoples and continents stand in our shadow, and if a storm in Europe shakes two tiny branches, how the whole world trembles and bleeds!" Concentration of power, capital, and machines was reaching a point where "by pressing one finger" entire nations could be "thrown into turmoil." Faced with the enormity of these developments, *Yet Another Philosophy* struck a somber note for Westerners:

> The more we Europeans invent methods and tools with which to subjugate the other continents, the more we defraud and plunder them, the greater will be their final triumph over us. We forge the chains with which they will bind us: the upturned pyramids of our constitutions will stand erect on their soil; they, along with us—but enough, everything tends visibly towards a great end! We encircle the globe, with whatever it may be, and what follows can probably never more diminish its foundation. We are approaching a new stage in our development, even if it is only one of decay![20]

Herder views European Enlightenment not from the vantage of counterenlightenment, but from a position akin to Adorno's and Horkheimer's "dialectic of enlightenment"—the complex interlacing of advancement and regression, of triumph and defeat. Herder despised the pretense and arrogance of his century, its self-proclaimed superiority over all competing life-forms in the past or in other parts of the globe; but his thought is free of sentimental nostalgia, given that historical temporality cannot be reversed, although aspects of the past can be retrieved through recollection. What he termed his century's "pet philosophy" was the belief that "human destiny is forever marching forward in giant steps" and that the present spreading of light was preceded only by darkness and shadows. According to this belief, previous centuries and experiences were only stepping-stones to the advancements of the present age, becoming obsolete and disposable once the higher stage was reached: "so many corners had first to be forcibly rubbed off before the round, smooth, pretty thing that we are could appear." In opposition to this vision of steady ameliorization and progressive perfection, *Yet Another History* establishes a ledger carefully recording both gains and losses: the simultaneous advances in rationality and shallowness, the concurrent growth of human mastery and human servility—"Let anyone cast the balance." "[L]ight is infinitely heightened and diffused whilst inclinations and vital instincts are infinitely weakened"; "principles of liberty, honor and virtue" are commonplace and loudly acknowledged by everyone, while people lie in chains of "cowardice, shame, luxury, servility, and miserable desultoriness." Techniques and technical improvements are widespread, but in the end they are appropriated by experts, by "one person, or a few, who do all the thinking." The vaunted humanitarianism of the age is largely a sham unsupported by real commitment to human fellowship: "Ideas of universal love for humanity, for all nations, and even enemies, are exalted, whilst warm feelings of family and friendship are allowed to decay."[21]

Herder's critique of universal humanitarianism or cosmopolitanism deserves careful attention, especially in view of his own endorsement of *Humanität*. The two kinds of humanism can and should be differentiated and not simply be ascribed to theoretical ambivalence (as some commentators have done). What Herder challenged and deplored was the claim of some intellectuals to speak on behalf of the human species or humanity at large without any concern for the agonies and aspirations of actual human beings. *Yet Another Philosophy* castigates the illusion of "the philosophers of Paris" who pretend to "civilize 'toute l'Europe' and 'tout l'univers' "—a pretense that, for Herder, is unlikely to touch or liberate "men's hands and hearts." Under the aegis of this pretense, ethnic and national attachments and loyalties are forever banished: "We love each and every one, or rather, we can dispense with love; for we simply *get on* with one another, being all equally polite, well-mannered and even-tempered." As a result, the notion of a homeland or of kinship vanishes or recedes into the background; instead, "we are all philanthropic citizens of the world." French is promulgated as the universal medium (substitute English today), and thus the "golden age" is dawning again, when "all the world will speak one tongue, one universal language." Herder's countermove to this cosmopolitanism was not antihumanism but *Humanität* seen as devotion to concrete human beings in their time and place. This concept—a close corollary of his populism or trust in popular self-rule—was brought out forcefully in *Letters for the Advancement of Humanity* and here in his *Ideas*:

> The savage who loves himself, his wife and his child . . . and works for the good of his tribe as for his own . . . is in my view more genuine than that human ghost, the . . . citizen of the world, who, burning with love for all his fellow ghosts, loves a chimera. The savage in his hut has room for any stranger, . . . the saturated heart of the idle cosmopolitan is a home for no one.[22]

To be sure, it is precisely this kind of grassroots humanism, this accent on local and temporal concreteness, that has earned Herder the charge of ethical or cultural relativism. In the same way, his rejection of a linear teleology and his insistence on the inherent worth of historical periods have pushed him into the proximity of historicism or historical relativism. But these charges are unfounded. Although opposed to grand "foundationalist" schemes, Herder was by no means a simple defender of nontruth or the will to power. He emphasizes the nonexclusiveness of local contexts and the importance of cross-cultural learning, as in the preceding statement that "the savage in his hut has room for any stranger." More importantly, there is a way of bolstering his stress on cultural-temporal specificity in nearly Kantian terms: namely, by invoking the maxim that human beings everywhere should be treated as "ends" and never merely or solely as means. This maxim is clearly violated by a teleology that regards previous centuries as mere means or stepping-stones to our age and alien cultures as way stations to our own. No theme in Herder's opus is more pervasive or recurrent than this belief in the distinctive quality and "valuableness" of different times and places that gives them perhaps not an "equal validity" but a strong claim to empathetic attention: "I cannot persuade myself that anything in the kingdom of God is *only* a means—everything is both a means and an end simultaneously, now no less than in the centuries of the past." What differentiates Herder's multicultural and multitemporal attentiveness from Kantian ethics is his insistence on rescuing the "ends" principle from its noumenal abstraction and inserting it into the thick of ongoing historical experience, in which he is not so much a "transcendental spectator" as an engaged participant.[23]

Contrary to the assumption of relativism and parochialism, it is precisely Herder's contextualism—his concern with local and temporal human finitude—that opens his heart and mind to a broader engagement, *Humanität*. Precisely because he is not a mere onlooker or spectator of human affairs, he cannot be content with a purely contemplative teleology nor with a cynical indifference that indiscriminately fuses truth and nontruth, good and evil; exactly because he does not "know" or control the grand scheme of things, he has to make an effort in his own time and place to tilt the balance, however slightly, in favor of goodness, human kindness or *Humanität*. Herder's work is thus not a purely "philosophical" exercise but an intensely practical endeavor, as Berlin obliquely recognizes when presenting him as an "*engagé*" writer." The linkage of thinking and doing—or, to use later vocabulary, the nexus of theory and praxis—is a *leitmotif* in all of Herder's writings, highlighted by the recurrent celebration of *Bildung* (meaning both individual and collective education or cultivation). Herder's denunciation of a purely theoretical approach to *Bildung*—the belief that theory alone could yield *Bildung*—was outspoken and unwavering. "How inundated we are with fine principles, elaborations, systems, interpretations," he exclaims in *Yet Another Philosophy* "—inundated to the extent that almost nobody can see the bottom of the floodwaters, or keep his feet, and for that very reason merely floats on the surface." As he continues bitingly: "It could be that all these tired generalities are nothing but a foam which dissolves in the air of all times and peoples." Against this universalizing foam Herder pits the sustaining power of contextual commitments, of concrete enterprises where head and heart are joined: "How different all this is from nourishing the veins and sinews of one's own people, from strengthening their hearts and refreshing them to their marrow. What an abyss there is between the finest general truth and the least of its applications to a given sphere, to a particular purpose and in any one specific manner!" To conclude his comments on this theme, Herder adds some personal remarks and also some caveats that contemporary Western philosophers might suitably wish to heed:

> If, therefore, my voice had power and scope enough, I would appeal to those who contribute to the *Bildung* of mankind: let us have no more generalizations about improvement, no more paper-culture, but wherever possible, implementation and action! . . . The noblest legislator [of mankind] in appearance may in reality be the most ardent destroyer of his age. With no thought for inner improvement, *Humanität* and happiness, he swims with the tide of his century, deludes his century into acclaiming him its savior, and claims the brief recompense for it all, the fading laurel of vanity which tomorrow becomes dust and ashes. But the really great and, indeed, divine work of civilizing mankind is quiet yet strong, hidden yet enduring, and has little in common with paltry vanity.[24]

# Notes

1. For some good biographical accounts of Herder's life and intellectual development see Robert T. Clark, Jr., *Herder: His Life and Thought* (Berkeley:

University of California Press, 1955); Francis McEachran, *The Life and Philosophy of Johann Gottfried Herder* (Oxford: Clarendon Press, 1939); Friedrich W. Kantzenbach, *Johann Gottfried Herder* (Hamburg: Rowohlt, 1970), and Alexander Gillies, *Herder, Der Mensch und sein Werk* (Hamburg: von Schröder, 1949). For insightful treatments of Johann Georg Hamann (1730–1788) see Larry Vaughan, *J. G. Hamann: Metaphysics of Language and Vision of History* (New York: P. Lang, 1989) and James C. O'Flaherty, *Unity and Language: A Study in the Philosophy of J. G. Hamann* (Chapel Hill: University of North Carolina, 1952).

2. See Charles Taylor, *Hegel and Modern Society* (Cambridge: Cambridge University Press, 1979), pp. 1–3; *Sources of the Self* (Cambridge, Mass.: Harvard University Press, 1989), pp. 368–378; *The Ethics of Authenticity* (Cambridge, Mass.: Harvard University Press, 1992), pp. 28–29, 61–62; "The Politics of Recognition," in Amy Gutman, ed., *Multiculturalism and "The Politics of Recognition"* (Princeton, N.J.: Princeton University Press, 1992), pp. 31–32. Compare also "The Importance of Herder," in Taylor, *Philosophical Arguments* (Cambridge, Mass.: Harvard University Press, 1995), pp. 79–99.

3. Isaiah Berlin, *Vico and Herder: Two Studies in the History of Ideas* (New York: Viking Press, 1976), pp. 154–155.

4. *Vico and Herder*, pp. 153, 156–158, 162. Compare also Berlin's emphatic assertion: "Even though he seems to have coined the word *Nationalismus*, his conception of a good society is closer to the anarchism of Thoreau or Proudhon or Kropotkin, and to the conception of a culture (*Bildung*) of which such liberals as Goethe and Humboldt were proponents, than to the ideals of Fichte or Hegel or political socialists. For him *die Nation* is not a political entity" (p. 181). Berlin quotes J. G. Herder, *Sämtliche Werke*, ed. Bernhard Suphan (Berlin: Weidmannsche Buchhandlung, 1877–1913), vol. 12, pp. 211, 319.

5. Berlin, *Vico and Herder*, pp. 163, 169–170, 186, 190–191. The quote is from Herder, *Sämtliche Werke*, vol. 5, p. 509.

6. Berlin, *Vico and Herder*, pp. 165–168, 171, 200–201, 204. The citation is from Herder, *Sämtliche Werke*, vol. 17, p. 59.

7. Berlin, *Vico and Herder*, pp. 206–209, 212–213. Compare also Berlin's assertion: "Herder had deep affinities with the *Aufklärung* [Enlightenment]. . . . But what lies at the heart of the whole of his thought, what influenced later thinkers, particularly the German Romantics and, through them, the entire history of populism, nationalism and individualism, is the theme to which he constantly returns: that one must not judge one culture by the criteria of another; that differing civilizations are different growths, pursue different goals, embody different ways of living, are dominated by different attitudes to life" (p. 210). In rendering his concluding verdict of relativism, Berlin basically follows the lead of Friedrich Meinecke in *Die Entstehung des Historismus* (Berlin: Oldenbourg, 1936), trans. by J. E. Anderson as *Historism* (New York: Herder and Herder, 1972).

8. Taylor, *The Ethics of Authenticity*, p. 52. A similar argument, though couched in different vocabulary, is advanced by Ernesto Laclau and Chantal Mouffe when they assert the interpenetration of the "logic of difference" (incom-

mensurability) and the "logic of equivalence" (commensurability); see their *Hegemony and Socialist Strategy* (London: Verso, 1985), pp. 182–184. Regarding the charge of historical relativism, compare also the judicious comment of Hans-Georg Gadamer: "However dramatic his critique of the Enlightenment doctrine of progress may have been, his keen insight into the diversity of times, peoples, and cultures did not entail a surrender to relativistic historicism. One fails to do justice to his work when reading it from the angle of a full-fledged historicism." See his *Nachwort* (postscript) to J. G. Herder, *Auch eine Philosophie der Geschichte zur Bildung der Menschheit* (Frankfurt-Main: Suhrkamp, 1967), p. 150.

9. F. M. Barnard, Introduction to *J. G. Herder on Social and Political Culture* (Cambridge: Cambridge University Press, 1969), pp. 53–59. Among those identifying Herder with later Romantic "perversions" Barnard cites R. G. Collingwood, *The Idea of History* (Oxford: Clarendon Press, 1946), pp. 86–92; K. R. Popper, *The Open Society and Its Enemies*, 3rd ed. (London: Routledge, 1952), vol. 2, p. 52; and H. S. Reiss, *The Political Thought of the German Romantics* (New York: Macmillan, 1955), pp. 2–8.

10. Herder, "Essay on the Origin of Language," in *Herder on Social and Political Culture*, F. M. Barnard, pp. 131–132, 137–139, 161–165.

11. "Essay on the Origin of Language," in *Herder on Social and Political Culture*, F. M. Barnard, pp. 167–169, 173–174 (italics in the original). Herder adds, "We Germans would, like the Indians of North America, still be living contentedly in our forests, waging cruel wars as heroes, if the chain of foreign cultures had not pressed in upon us and, with the impact of centuries, had not forced us to join in" (p. 174).

12. Herder, "Yet Another Philosophy of History for the *Bildung* of Mankind," in *Herder on Social and Political Culture*, F. M. Barnard, pp. 181, 186–187. Barnard translates *Bildung* (education, culture) in the title as "enlightenment," which seems to me somewhat misleading.

13. "Yet Another Philosophy of History," pp. 196–197, 207.

14. "Yet Another Philosophy of History," pp. 187–188, 217, 223. Compare also his statement: "He has not considered—this omniscient [Enlightenment] philosopher—that there can be a great, divine plan for the whole human race which a single creature cannot survey, since it is not he, philosopher or monarch of the eighteenth century though he may be, who matters in the last resort. Whilst each actor has only one role in each scene, one sphere in which to strive for happiness, each scene forms part of a whole, a whole unknown and invisible to the individual, self-centered actor" (p. 215).

15. Herder, "Ideas for a Philosophy of the History of Mankind," in *Herder on Social and Political Culture*, F. M. Barnard, pp. 268, 282–284. In stipulating self-preservation *and* sympathy as the two mainsprings of human behavior Herder is following the lead of the Scottish moralists and of Rousseau.

16. Barnard, *Herder on Social and Political Culture*, p. 59. As one may note, a main effort of postmetaphysics or postmodernism in our time has been precisely to overcome or "deconstruct" some of these antinomies (though overcoming here often takes the form of a retreat into abstract conditions of possibility and impossibility).

17. See Martin Heidegger, "Letter on Humanism," in *Heidegger: Basic Writings*, ed. David F. Krell (New York: Harper & Row, 1977), pp. 193–242. Further affinities can be seen between Herder's attack on modern mechanization and standardization and Heidegger's conception of *Gestell*. For a reading of Heidegger's own work along nonnationalistic (even antifascist) lines see my *The Other Heidegger* (Ithaca, N.Y.: Cornell University Press, 1993). Herder's portrayal of human being also shows some similarities with recent "philosophical anthropology" (an offshoot of existential phenomenology); particularly his notion of the premature birth and instinctual deficiency of humans—a deficiency compensated by language—parallels arguments advanced by Helmuth Plessner in *Conditio Humana* (Pfullingen, Germany: Neske, 1964).

18. Herder, "Ideas for a Philosophy of the History of Mankind," in *Herder on Social and Political Culture*, F. M. Barnard, pp. 319, 321, 324 note 18. See also Herder, *Sämtliche Werke*, vol. 13, p. 453. Herder's cultural approach to politics also implies attention to (popular) religion as an important spring of human motivations and aspirations that is at odds both with enlightened indifference and militant fundamentalism. His observations on the role of religion have lost none of their relevance in our time. Compare these comments: "If you say, O man, that revelation is too archaic for you, in the wisdom of your gray hairs, just look around you. You will see that the bulk of the nations of the earth are still in their childhood. . . . Wherever you travel among, and listen to, so-called savages, you hear sounds that illustrate Holy Writ and catch a breath of living commentary upon Revelation." Or: "It is equally conceivable, as some great man may indeed have prophesied, that the next century may be one of superstition, in reaction against the perverse skepticism of ours. Whatever the course of things (and *it would be sad if only superstition could succeed unbelief, and this wretched vicious circle never be broken*) religion, reason and virtue are in time bound to defeat the maddest attacks of their adversaries." See "Yet Another Philosophy of History," pp. 218, 221 (emphasis mine). While applauding Herder's emphasis on political culture, I cannot deny that his thoughts on political structure are somewhat elusive or underdeveloped; in particular, his attack on the modern "state" is not supplemented by an elaboration of alternative arrangements beyond a general recommendation of decentralization and popular self-rule on the local level. Still, his work provides a forceful incentive for reflecting on possible alternatives to the bureaucratic state.

19. Herder, "Yet Another Philosophy of History," pp. 206, 209; also Herder, "Briefe zur Beförderung der Humanität," in *Sämtliche Werke*, vol. 17, p. 63.

20. Herder, "Yet Another Philosophy of History," in *Herder on Social and Political Culture*, F. M. Barnard, pp. 206, 221; "Ideas for a Philosophy of the History of Mankind," p. 286. For the citation from *Adrastea* (another name for Nemesis) see Berlin, *Vico and Herder*, p. 161. Herder's comments can fruitfully be compared with Gandhi's indictment of modern Western civilization in his early work on Indian self-rule. See M.K. Gandhi, *Hind Swaraj, and Other Writings*, ed. Anthony J. Parel (Cambridge: Cambridge University Press, 1997), esp. pp. 30–38.

21. Herder, "Yet Another Philosophy of History," pp. 194, 200.

22. Herder, "Yet Another Philosophy of History," pp. 202, 209; also Herder, *Sämtliche Werke,* vol. 13, p. 339.

23. Herder, "Yet Another Philosophy of History," p. 194. Empathetic attention to other cultures and periods, to be sure, does not eliminate the possibility of critique and suggestions for improvement. As Herder repeatedly argues, all cultures and times are mixtures of virtues and vices, achievements and defects that the empathetic student needs to sort out. In the helpful vocabulary used by Charles Taylor, there is a "presumption" in favor of the inherent quality of other cultures and their ability to teach us something—a presumption which can be defeated. See Taylor "The Politics of Recognition," pp. 72–73.

24. Herder, "Yet Another Philosophy of History," pp. 202–205; Berlin, *Vico and Herder,* p. 204. Herder's critique of pure philosophy is sometimes entertainingly harsh. Compare these comments: "If there is one thing in the world you want to see badly done, entrust it to a philosopher. On paper, everything is neat, smooth, beautiful and great; in performance it is a disaster." Or: "It is presumably part of our excellence that we should be able to boast of a philosophy second to none in its insipidity, myopia, arrogance, complacency and, above all, its futility. The Orientals, Greeks and Romans could not boast of such achievements." See "Yet Another Philosophy of History," pp. 198, 213.

# 2

# The Politics of Nonidentity: Adorno, Postmodernism, and Edward Said

> . . . the liberation of the subject from itself.
>
> Theodor Adorno

Despite proclamations of happy endings (especially the ending of history) ours is not a restful era. Properly understood, antifoundationalism and postmodernism are shorthand for rupture, exodus, and the urge of emigration, in Nietzschean terms, the "longing for the other shore." In lieu of the modern infatuation with certainty and self-identity, postmodernism is intent upon opening windows onto alterity, difference, and non-identity—a profound destabilization of cognitive boundaries and frameworks. Although maligned by traditionalists including defenders of liberal modernity, this yearning may well be the most ennobling and redeeming quality in contemporary Western thought—by cleansing that thought of its tendencies toward egocentrism, acquisitiveness, and intellectual cannibalism. In philosophical terms, postmodern transgression invites the transformation of philosophy from a sequence of school doctrines into an again open field of inquiry. Politically, the trangressive mood responds to our changed international constellation: the replacement of a Eurocentric or Western-centered world by a properly global and multicultural environment.

In departing from established markers postmodernism seems to venture into a dark abyss where in Hegel's memorable phrase "all cows are black" and nothing and everything can equally be asserted at will. Like all first impressions, this may be deceptive. Transgression of "foundations" cannot mean a simple departure from the past, and certainly not a departure from thinking, but only an invitation to a more patient and sustained kind of thoughtfulness. As soon as established markers of the

47

past like the *cogito* are destabilized, all kinds of difficult questions surge forward and cannot be shunted aside in the name of postmodern "originality." Among these questions are: What does destabilizing the *cogito* effectively mean? Does it mean the simple demise or "end of the subject" in favor of some kind of objectivism or reifying heteronomy? Does destabilization mean the erasure of boundaries between self and other, giving way to a general non-distinction or indifference and thus to a universal kind of "sameness" taking the place of the identity of the ego? Equally and more importantly: What does the move to otherness, difference, and nonidentity imply? Does it signal a leap beyond the *cogito* into a quasi-Kantian "thing-in-itself," a kind of objective *counter*identity beyond the pale of cognition and interpretation? Or does it again herald an exodus into a no-man's-land bereft of all distinctions, into a realm of radical negativity, of a *non*identity that negates every identity? But then how could anyone persist in this realm (or pretend to *"be* nothing")? Moreover, how could one honor the other's nonidentity in the absence of a recognition of the distinctness and differential relation of self and other?

These questions are not postmodern inventions, although they require special attention in our time. In diverse guises, they are found in the work of the last great systematic thinker of the modern era: Hegel. Building upon and sharpening the accents of earlier formulations, Hegel's thought revolved relentlessly around the complex relationship between self and other, sameness and difference, universalism and particularism. Postmodern thinkers are thus ill advised to neglect or brush aside the richly nuanced legacy of Hegel's dialectics—notwithstanding the need to move beyond idealist-metaphysical boundaries. This chapter explores some of the issues associated with the turn to difference or nonidentity. The first section reviews in detail the arguments of one of the precursors of postmodernism—Theodor Adorno—whose writings centerstage with particular urgency the issue of nonidentity. While shunning "foundationalism," including Hegel's absolute idealism, Adorno in many ways remained faithful to key Hegelian insights, thereby preserving "negative dialectics" from vacuity or a slide into the no-man's-land of indistinction or non-differentiation. In this respect, Adorno's approach has not always been followed by some of the leaders of recent postmodernism (the topic of the second section) whose writings often combine a fervent embrace of nonidentity with the wholesale rejection of Hegel's legacy. Largely due to this rejection, nonidentity in their writings often gives way to an externalized *counter*identity or else to an indifferent *no-*identity. The concluding section explores implications of these diverse approaches for contemporary politics on a global scale, where the slide of nonidentity into non-distinction (or no-identity) can take the form of intellectual nomadism or an indifferent cosmopolitanism. The work of

Edward Said, whose intellectual mentors prominently include Adorno but whose outlook tends to hover instructively on the border between vagrancy and a differentially committed politics, illustrates these implications.

# I

Among writers of the early and middle part of our century, no one has been more intensely preoccupied with both the philosophical and the political saliency of nonidentity than Adorno. Although adumbrated and cautiously prepared in some of his earlier writings, the topic found its most trenchant formulation in the *magnum opus* of Adorno's later years: his *Negative Dialectics* (1966).[1] Written in a dense, compact style, the work has the reputation of being opaque. Yet its dense texture precisely testifies to Adorno's postmetaphysics: his profound urge to transgress the linear transparency of the *cogito* and Enlightenment rationalism. Adorno's nonidentity basically means a surplus of being over knowing, especially an excess of social and historical reality over the appropriating grasp of conceptualization epitomized in Hegel's notion of *Begriff*. The introduction to *Negative Dialectics* announces the work's central theme: the attempt to formulate a post-Hegelian (but not simply an anti-Hegelian) mode of dialectics in which the relation of self and other, of thought and reality, would not culminate in a final synthesis or conceptual unity. The rudimentary notion of dialectics, he notes, is that things do not "dissolve into their concept without a rest" and that hence they exceed the traditional "rule of correspondence" (*adaequatio*). Much of traditional metaphysics—including Hegel's idealism—sought to cancel this excess by insisting on the identity of being and concept. According to this tradition, "to think means to identify," with the "conceptual order" absorbing and monopolizing the content of thought. This totalizing tendency can only be reversed or corrected by another kind of dialectics that preserves and cultivates a "keen sense of non-identity." That sense, in turn, is fostered by reason's own "inevitable insufficiency," by reason's "culpability" toward the target of its thought.[2]

As Adorno recognizes, traditional preoccupation with *logos* and conceptualization was not simply a mistake that could be remedied through a leap into irrational intuitionism. Philosophical concepts also testify to the labor of thought, to reason's endeavor to gain knowledge about reality and ultimately to give an account both of the world and itself. Coupled with this is a process of human emancipation, the emergence of human awareness from the constraints of a naturalistic or environmental determinism. What is problematical in Adorno's view is not the labor of thought itself, but the proclivity of modern reason to self-enclosure or self-sufficiency, which surrenders reality to the sway of cognitive categories while simultaneously elevating human subjects to a position of mastery or domination over the world. The corrective is not the abandonment of thought but a kind of double gesture or double movement of thought: a reflection on self-reflection through which reason recalls its embeddedness in being or reality and which allows the self to move from self-enclosure in the direction of a freer recognition of otherness or nonidentity. Philosophy, in the traditional sense, seeks to "grasp the nonconceptual realm through concepts," which, though a necessary first step, is also a mode of compulsion; by becoming conscious of this fact philosophical reflection is able to "cancel the autarchy of the concept" and thus "strip the blindfold from our eyes." This kind of "demystification of the concept" (*Entzauberung des Begriffs*) is the "antidote" offered by contemporary, postmetaphysical philosophy. Postmetaphysics inaugurates a new form of dialectics, styled by Adorno as "negative dialectics" that does not lead to indifferent negativism but reflective openness indefinitely postponing the moment of positive-affirmative closure:

> To change the direction of conceptuality by turning it toward nonidentity is the decisive pivot of negative dialectics. Insight into the constitutive character of the nonconceptual in the concept would end the compulsiveness of identification which is a corollary of the concept in the absence of such reflection. The apparent self-sufficiency of the concept as the locus of rational unity is transgressed through reflection on its intrinsic meaning.[3]

In Adorno's account, negative dialectics entails an exit from Hegel's philosophical system, but in a way that does not simply cancel Hegel's dialectical insights, especially the notion of dialectical mediation. The crucial distinction hinges on Hegel's insistence on a final affirmative synthesis encompassing identity and nonidentity alike. Negation as nonaffirmation is Adorno's basic departure from Hegel's system, which postulated the "coincidence of identity and positivity" and ultimately the inclusion of nonidentity in the "higher subjectivity of absolute spirit." With this postulate Hegel violated the inner momentum of his own thought, evident in his own obsessive preoccupation with logical contradiction; but contradiction is only the other side of the identitarian coin and a result of the neglect of nonidentity (beyond the thesis-antithesis syndrome). Under "negative" (nonaffirmative) auspices, the character of dialectics is qualitatively transformed: the claims of linear teleology and systematic unity are soberly cast aside; chastised and doubly reflective, human reason no longer dominates but assists in the emancipation of the phenomena of the world from conceptual constraints. Phenomena at this point are no longer, as with Hegel, mere "exemplifications of their concept," but heralds of meaning disclosure in their own right. Hegel's vaunted labor of reason is not abandoned, but intensified, because conceptual thought is required to struggle with and against itself, in an effort to "immerse itself almost unconsciously in phenomena." No longer victimized by human rationality, phenomena would be able to "gain their own voice" under the "lingering glance of thought":

> Turning against [Kantian] epistemology, Hegel had argued that one becomes a smith only in the activity of smithing, by the actual cognition of things that resist cognition . . . There we have to take him at his word. This view alone would return to philosophy its "freedom to the object" in Hegel's sense, something it had lost under the spell of conceptual "freedom" or the constitutive autonomy of subjectivity.[4]

While deviating from Hegel's idealism, Adorno is nevertheless careful to avoid the shortcuts, or *cul-de-sacs*, which Hegel's philosophy had clearly pinpointed and sought to overcome. In doing so, Adorno's negative dialectics involves no bland denial of Hegel's teachings. One such *cul-de-sac* is the portrayal of nonidentity as a realm of radical otherness or externality, as a Kantian "thing in itself" completely beyond the purview of thought or reflection. Nonidentity here congeals into a mode of heteronomy (or external positivity) to which consciousness is expected blindly to surrender. Adorno notes, "Weary of identity, thought readily capitulates before the utterly intangible and then transforms this intangibility of things into a taboo for human reflection, requiring it to resign itself irrationally or scientistically and not to tackle what is different." Apart from its stultifying effects, the same portrayal also leads dialectics quickly back into the most traditional metaphysical dualisms or antinomies: those between form and content, subject and object, universalism and particularism. Hegel's lasting and most incontrovertible achievement was the exposure of the artificiality of these dichotomies and the reciprocal mediation of the opposing categories. In centerstaging nonidentity, Adorno is far from eliding this achievement. Above all, his nonidentity is not simply a paean to particularity, to an immediately given singularity or counteridentity: "According to one of the most lasting results of Hegel's logic, particularity does not exist utterly by itself but is in itself 'other' and linked with otherness. What is, is more than what it is."[5]

Most importantly, in Adorno's formulation nonidentity is not equivalent to a mere erasure of identity, a leap into a radical negativity or no-identity. This leap is probably the most serious and persistent temptation of postmetaphysical thought, fostered and nourished by the constraints of the identitarian paradigm. Yet, though understandable in its motives, the leap cannot stand up to closer scrutiny. First, the status of negativity demands reflection. Conceived as a vacuum or absolute emptiness, how could nonidentity "be" anything at all; above all, how could it serve as a habitat or a place of refuge for those exiled from identity? To treat it is as such implies a paradoxical reification of negativity or nonbeing. Adorno is adamant in rejecting this construal. Nonidentity, he writes, "cannot directly be found as something in turn positively real, not even through a negation of negation" (in Hegel's sense); "the equation of the negation of negation with positive reality is the very essence of identification, the identity principle in its purest form." Nonidentity is not a separate realm juxtaposed with identity, but the difference and self-transgression slumbering in every identity, the absence in every presence. Adorno's turn toward nonidentity thus heralds not a retreat into indifferent vacuity, but the encounter and contestation of distinct or differentiated identities, marked by a reciprocal transgression of self-enclosure. In a pregnant and daring formulation, Adorno conceptualizes nonidentity as the "genuine identity of phenomena in opposition to their identification." A proper thinking of being or reality requires neither an abstract conceptualism nor a gross reification of phenomena, but an attempt to think "nonidentity in and through identity itself."[6]

Adorno's denial of synthesis does not endorse a crude atomism or social anarchism devoid of guideposts, nor is it equivalent to moral indifference or "nihilism" (in the popular sense). Given their self-transgressive, nonessentialist character, the encounter of identities implies a mutual learning process, a "struggle for recognition" where contestants come to acknowledge each other both as different and as partners. Adorno's negative dialectics thus preserves the deepest intention of Hegelian philosophy: its commitment to "ethical life" or *Sittlichkeit*, and its hope for a "reconciliation" of opposites beyond consensual uniformity. This hope is repeatedly and eloquently expressed in *Negative Dialectics*, with language completely free of "defeatism" or "pessimism," labels sometimes thoughtlessly applied to Adorno's work. In the book's introduction reconciliation, though at this point only a distant hope given prevailing forms of exploitation, denotes the emancipation of nonidentity, its release from the constraints of systematizing rationality, and hence the "surging forth of the multiplicity of differences." Reconciliation results from the "anamnesis of a no longer maligned and now pacified multiplicity, stigmatized by subjective rationality"; negative dialectics serves this anamnetic goal. Among the many hopeful and ethically moving passages in *Negative Dialectics* one of the most stirring is the following, which seeks to chart a course beyond "alienation":

> Phenomena congeal as fragments of a system dominated by conceptualism; their recovery restores a love to things. Beyond the pale of Romanticism—

construed as *Weltschmerz* and as a suffering from alienation—we hear Eichendorff's word of the "beautiful strangeness" (*schöne Fremde*). The reconciled condition would no longer annex the alien in an exercise of philosophical imperialism, but would be happily content to accept it as distant and different even in proximate surroundings—beyond the limits of heterogeneity and sameness.[7]

# II

The theme of nonidentity and multiplicity broached soberly and circumspectly in *Negative Dialectics* has developed into a predominant passion in postmodern thought, sometimes ceding place to facile slogans. In large measure, the changed mood is due not only to a certain intellectual trendiness, which Adorno would have abhorred, but also and mainly to the cancellation of any sensibility or sympathy for Hegel's legacy and the deeper aspirations of his dialectics. This cancellation is clearly evident in the programmatic manifesto of postmodern thought: Jean-François Lyotard's *The Postmodern Condition*.

Lyotard's postmodernism signals an exodus from traditional metaphysics, more specifically, a stark reversal or denial of the affirmative content of that metaphysics. Without acknowledgment of possible Hegelian resources, reversal here operates in the mode of logical negation or antithesis. For Lyotard traditional metaphysics—including its modern variant rooted in the *cogito*—involved a celebration of *logos*, rational consensus, and universal teleology, accents that in their combined force had a "totalizing" effect ominously prefiguring recent forms of totalitarianism. According to *The Postmodern Condition*, metaphysical preferences of the past found expression in a series of "grand metanarratives"—from Adam Smith's capitalist *Wealth of Nations* to Marx's vision of proletarian world revolution—all of which are characterized by the effort to unify all knowledge and experience in a comprehensive synthesis. Rebelling against these synthesizing stories, postmodernism heralds a radical switch of priorities: from *logos* to "paralogy," from unity to fragmentation, from homogeneity to heterogeneity, and from unified identity to the negation or dispersal of identities. In a curious blending of Kantian and Nietzschean motifs, this shift to nonidentity focuses on local particularity, or rather on the agonistic struggle among particularities, devoid of possible mediation or mutual recognition. In Lyotard's words, what postmodernism centerstages is not so much a "theory of communication" aimed at consensual understanding but rather a "theory of games which accepts agonistics as a founding principle."[8]

In *The Postmodern Condition*, the focus on agonistics and dispersed identities is linked explicitly with the rejection of the metanarrative of Hegelian idealism. In order to recount his teleology, Lyotard asserts, Hegel had to ascend beyond the local particularities of lifeworlds and discourses to the level of a transhuman "metasubject," of the universal world spirit—a move that is both illegitimate and dangerous in its consequences. Propelled by a "transcendental illusion," Hegel flung himself into a totalizing overview; but as Kant, Nietzsche, and the experiences of our century have taught us, "the price to pay for such an illusion is terror." Lyotard intensified his attack on Hegel in *The Differend*— "differend" meaning an "agonal contest" or struggle marked by the heterogeneity of contestants and the absence of a common or commensurable bond. In an "excursus" specifically devoted to Hegelian philosophy, the book critiques the notion of dialectical mediation and historical teleology as purely "speculative," again the result of a "transcendental illusion." Hegelianism is said to privilege consensus over dissensus, continuity over discontinuity, and cumulative meaning over its dispersal—a favoritism ultimately rooted in the primacy of spirit over reality, or otherness, and of identity over nonidentity. Based on the premise of agonistics or the incommensurability of lifeworlds and discourses, Lyotard dismisses this primacy as logically untenable and politically obnoxious. Seen from the vantage of Nietzsche and the theory of language games, he insists, resort to a metadiscourse or metaphysics is no longer feasible; in any event, the claim of "an absolute triumph of one discourse over others is senseless."[9]

A similar outlook privileging agonistic difference can be found in some of the writings of Foucault, though his formulations tend to be more nuanced and multivocal. In opposing the reign of traditional metaphysics, Foucault's argument frequently proceeds through a strategy of reversal designed to overturn the metaphysical predominance of unity, homogeneity, and universal teleology or dialectics. Thus, in articulating or adumbrating a philosophy of "transgression"—transgressing especially the metaphysics of the *cogito*—his writings tend to favor multiplicity over unity, contestation over consensus, rupture over teleology, and nonidentity (or the dispersal of identity) over any stable self-conception. This shift unsettles intellectual moorings that reach the beginnings of Western philosophy. In his words, the experience of transgression forms "the exact reversal of the movement which has sustained the wisdom of the West at least since the time of Socrates": the wisdom anchoring philosophy in "the serene unity of a subjectivity which would triumph in it, having been fully constituted by it and through it." The breakdown of this constitutive unity or identity and its "dispersal in a language that dispossesses it while multiplying it within a space created by its absence" can be seen as "probably one of the fundamental structures of contemporary thought." Buttressed by the legacy of Nietzsche, Foucault depicts a restless struggle for power permitting no respite among contending forces:

> Humanity does not gradually progress from combat to combat until it arrives at universal reciprocity where the rule of law finally replaces warfare; humanity instills each of its violences in a system of rules and thus proceeds from domination to domination. The nature of these rules allows violence to be inflicted on violence and the resurgence of new forces that are sufficiently strong to dominate those in power.[10]

Like Lyotard and other postmodern thinkers, Foucault is explicit in his effort to transgress Hegel, not working through him in some novel way, but leaving him behind. As he noted in an essay devoted to his friend Gilles Deleuze, the postmetaphysical "freeing of difference" requires a "thought without contradiction, without dialectics, without negation," one that "accepts divergence" or otherness; it requires a "thought of the multiple—of the nomadic and dispersed multiplicity that is not limited or confined by the constraints of similarity" or by the "blurred image of an Idea that eternally retains our answers in some upper region." The dismissal of Hegelianism is closely linked with the valorization of Nietzschean agonistics and contestation. After portraying history as the scene of discontinuous struggle, Foucault's essay on Nietzsche's genealogy postulates a break with the dominant themes of idealist thought. In light of Nietzsche's teachings, he notes, it is time to put aside or surmount the "two great problems of nineteenth-century philosophy, passed on by Fichte and Hegel (the reciprocal basis of truth and liberty and the possibility of absolute knowledge)," in favor of Nietzschean life-affirmation.[11]

Although powerfully suggestive (and deserving of much closer scrutiny than these pages permit), the quoted writings of Lyotard and Foucault also exhibit profound tensions and antonomies, especially with respect to the issue of nonidentity. In large measure, their postmodern exit from metaphysics places heterogeneity over sameness, local particularism over unity or holistic meaning; nonidentity thus tends to coincide with the contingent stubbornness of particularity, with something concretely "real" beyond the grasp of totalizing conceptual categories. Yet this coincidence is not complete and, almost by necessity, contends with competing connotations. Given the demise or dismissal of identity, local particularity likewise cannot aspire to achieve closure or a stable content but remains vulnerable to the pull of fragmentation and dispersal. Once this pull is given free reign, nonidentity moves into a vacant space marked

by the absence of all distinctive differences and inhabited only by a nomadic thought equally aloof from others and itself. Paradoxically, nonidentity can thus be the emblem of both factual-particular distinctness
(counteridentity) and indifference (no-identity).

Nowhere is this tension more clearly evident than in the work of Gilles
Deleuze, to whom Foucault felt in many ways indebted. In many of his
writings, Deleuze celebrated concrete experience as the locus of sensual
particularities, the latter construed along quasi-Nietzschean lines as unequal, antagonistic forces locked in relentless combat. His study of Nietzsche presented the German thinker as the great iconoclast of the Western
metaphysical tradition intent on deconstructing or "decodifying" the
universal categories of traditional thought. In opposition to these totalizing categories, Nietzsche was said to espouse the radical disjuncture or
agonistics of particular elements, the contest between "active" (or life-
affirming) and "reactive" (or life-denying) forces that perennially yields
the hierarchy of dominance and submission:

> There are nothing but quantities of force in mutual "relations of tension."
> Every force is related to others and it either obeys or commands. . . . In a
> body the superior or dominant forces are known as *active* and the inferior
> or dominated forces are known as *reactive*. . . . This difference between
> forces qualified according to their quantity as active or reactive will be called
> *hierarchy*.[12]

While emphasizing the role of concrete particularities as quantifiable
forces, Deleuze on another level undermined or deconstructed concrete
identifiable particularities, making room for a "nomad thought" completely outside the realm of stable identity. Nomad thought figured, at
least tendentially, as a kind of nonidentity diametrically opposed to the
constraints and totalizing "codifications" of settled societies and thought
systems (a curious restoration of metaphysical inside-outside schemes):
"The nomad and his war machine oppose the despot with his administrative machine: an extrinsic nomadic unit as opposed to an intrinsic despotic unit." Traditional philosophy and metaphysics, in Deleuze's view,
have been essentially codifying and hence related to laws and institutions
that together have shaped "the history of sedentary peoples from the
earliest despotic states to modern democracies." In contrast, Nietzsche
was the first to conceive of "another kind of discourse as counter-philos-
ophy": a discourse that is "above all nomadic" and whose statements
function as "the products of a mobile war machine," not the utterances
of a rational administrative system "whose philosophers would be bureaucrats of pure reason." The last phrase was aimed primarily at German idealism and above all at the work of Hegel, whose thought,

although generally on the side of codification, is denounced as giving aid and comfort to merely "reactive" (or life-sapping) forces due to its embroilment in mediation and dialectical negation. In Deleuze's version of postmodernism

> There is no possible compromise between Hegel and Nietzsche. Nietzsche's philosophy has a great polemical range; it forms an absolute anti-dialectics and sets out to expose all the mystifications that find a final refuge in the dialectic. . . . The Hegelian dialectic is indeed a reflection on difference, but it inverts its image. For the affirmation of difference as such it substitutes the negation of that which differs; for the affirmation of the self it substitutes the negation of the other, and for the affirmation of affirmation it substitutes the famous negation of the negation. . . . The dialectic expresses every combination of reactive forces and nihilism, the history or evolution of their relations.[13]

## III

The issues touched upon in the preceding discussion are not merely esoteric concerns reserved for academics. Directly or indirectly, the issues resonate with, or have a bearing on, crucial "real-life" agonies and dilemmas in our contemporary world. With the retreat or demise of Eurocentrism and Western colonialism, nonidentity acquires a profound political saliency, giving rise to a number of urgent questions. Does the shift to nonidentity imply the axiom of an alien and incommensurable realm completely outside the range of Western-style understanding and negotiation? Does the same shift involve the valorization of concrete ethnic or national particularities beyond the pale of dialectical mediation, approximating global politics to a Hobbesian *bellum omnium* or to a quasi-Nietzschean struggle for power among relentlessly competing active and reactive forces? Alternatively, does the bracketing of unifying conceptual categories signal a leap into a vacuous sphere of nondistinction, a place inhabited by free-floating nomadic intellectuals or jet-setting cosmopolitans equally at home everywhere and nowhere? Or is nonidentity perhaps an absence or negation slumbering in the heart of every identity, a motive for open-ended encounter beyond the conundrum of heterogeneity and sameness?

Among contemporary Western intellectuals attentive to global politics, few have wrestled with these issues in a more sustained fashion than Edward Said, whose sprawling and seminal work vividly illustrates some of the mentioned agonies and dilemmas. Said is chiefly renowned as the author of "Orientalism," a theoretical construct pitting Occident and Orient against each other as agonistic forces and vigorously exposing the complicity of Western scholars (styled "Orientalists") in European colonial expansion. In recounting the story of Orientalism, Said has not remained on the sidelines as a mere onlooker or *raconteur*, but has assumed the role of an eloquent, sometimes impassioned, spokesman of victims against victimizers, of the colonized against colonizers, of the Orient against the Occident. He has stirringly raised his voice on behalf of the Palestinians, who display the pernicious and long-range effects of colonial intervention and domination he describes. Yet, while thus situating himself in an agonistic and perhaps incommensurable conflict, Said is also a learned Western intellectual ill at ease with all kinds of local or parochial attachments and sensitive to the lure of a free-floating nonidentity congruent with the practice of literary deconstruction. Thus, though warmly taking up the cause of Palestinians, Said does not seem particularly concerned with the distinctiveness of Palestinian traditions nor inclined to share or participate in their life-forms or religious beliefs. This kind of critically distanced partisanship raises the question of theoretical articulation and coherence. Said is not reticent about citing his theoretical mentors—prominent among them are Adorno, Foucault, and Deleuze, as well as Gramsci and Raymond Williams—but the counsel of these mentors is tensional and by no means readily compatible.

Theoretical tensions are clearly apparent in Said's early, groundbreaking study *Orientalism*. Through far-ranging historical and literary investigations, Said uncovers a basic antagonism pervading much of Western history and culture—struggle between Occident and Orient, European or Western self-conception and its constructed antipode—that has the shape of a contest between active and reactive forces, with the West actively constructing its identity and the Orient being the mere recipient of a weak and demeaning counteridentity. In this respect, Said's Orientalism is a type of identity politics: "a Western style for dominating, restructuring, and having authority over the Orient"; by reason of its image construction, Western or European culture "gained in strength and identity by setting itself off against the Orient as a sort of surrogate and even underground self." Orientalism is deeply pervaded by traditional metaphysical (or categorial) distinctions, especially the dualisms of inside and outside, familiar and unfamiliar; it encoded and promoted "the difference between the familiar (Europe, the West, 'us') and the strange (the Orient, the East, 'them')." In this dualist structure, weights were hierarchically distributed: Europe being rational, mature, and "normal" and the Oriental irrational, childlike, and depraved. Basically Europe was the rational "knower," the Orient the "known," or the recipient of knowledge; intellectually and politically, the former was the master, the latter the servant. Given the systematic character of Orientalism and its merger of knowledge and force, Said approvingly invokes Foucault's notion of discourse or discursive formation:

> Without examining Orientalism as a discourse one cannot possibly understand the enormously systematic discipline by which European culture was able to manage—and even produce—the Orient politically, sociologically, militarily, ideologically, scientifically, and imaginatively during the post-Enlightenment period. . . . Orientalism can thus be regarded as a manner of regularized (or Orientalist) writing, vision, and study, dominated by imperatives, perspectives, and ideological biases ostensibly suited to the Orient.

Sharpening this analysis with Nietzschean views on truth and will, Said depicts Orientalism as "fundamentally a political doctrine willed over the Orient because the Orient was weaker than the West, which elided the Orient's difference with its weakness."[14]

While thus rehearsing the conflict between Occident and Orient Said occasionally refers to a realm of otherness completely outside the Orientalist model, a "real" or actual Orient untouched by Western categories. His account of identity politics thus makes room for a radical non- or counteridentity, conceived of as a concrete, transconceptual particularity. Although cautiously formulated, the references are too frequent to be overlooked. Immediately after introducing the Orientalist model, Said concedes that it would be "wrong" to conclude "that the Orient was *essentially* an idea, or a reaction with no corresponding reality": for clearly "there were—and are—cultures and nations whose location is in the East" and whose "lives, histories, and customs have a brute reality obviously greater than anything that could be said about them in the West." About this reality *Orientalism* admittedly has "very little to contribute, except to acknowledge it tacitly." Somewhat later, in discussing various European novelists and poets imaginatively writing about the East, Said notes that "the 'real' Orient" at best provoked their vision and "rarely guided it." The contrast between identity and counteridentity as it relates to the Orientalist paradigm is emphatically asserted in a passage summarizing an overview of literary examples. "Underlying all the different units of Orientalist discourse . . . [is] a set of representative figures or tropes." These figures are to the "actual Orient" as "stylized costumes are to characters in a play"; hence, "we need not look for correspondence between the language used to depict the Orient and the Orient itself, not so much because the language is inaccurate but because it is not even trying to be accurate."[15]

Juxtaposed with this invocation of a real or actual Orient is another account that completely undermines the implied dualist metaphysics of fiction versus reality, of cognition versus thing-in-itself. Countermanding the notion of a willful injury inflicted by Orientalist discourse, *Oriental-ism* repeatedly takes recourse to a radical constructivism according to which all views of the world are equally fictive and imaginary and hence equally "deconstructible"; relinquishing its role as a concrete (particular-ist) counterforce, nonidentity here enters a hazy netherworld of denial, a place of indifference or non-distinction against which all distinct identi-ties are furtive inventions. Countering Rudyard Kipling's famous polar-ization, Said voices the "main intellectual issue raised by Orientalism": "Can one divide human reality, as indeed human reality seems to be genuinely divided, into clearly different cultures, histories, traditions, so-cieties, even races, and survive the consequences humanly?" Shortly af-terwards, Said takes up the issue of constructivism and finds its argument persuasive, at least more than a naive realism. "There is always a mea-sure of the purely arbitrary in the way distinctions between things are seen," he writes. "And with these distinctions go values whose his-tory"—if completely unearthed—would "show the same measure of arbitrariness." A general skepsis regarding historical and cultural differ-ences arises; once it is agreed that "all things in history, like history itself, are made by men," one will also appreciate how readily times and places can be "assigned roles and given meaning that acquire objective validity only *after* the assignments are made." The conclusion of the study com-pletely abandons the distinction between the Orientalist model and the real Orient and thereby, unwittingly, the moral edge directed against the former (for how could the West have acted otherwise?):

> It is not the thesis of this book to suggest that there is such a thing as a real or true Orient (Islam, Arab, or whatever); nor is it to make an assertion about the necessary privilege of an "insider" perspective over an "outsider" one, to use Robert K. Merton's useful distinction. On the contrary, I have been arguing that "the Orient" is itself a constituted entity, and that the notion that there are geographical spaces with indigenous, radically "differ-ent" inhabitants who can be defined on the basis of some religion, culture, or racial essence proper to that geographical space is equally a highly debat-able idea.

In lieu of a plea for diversity and agonistics, *Orientalism* ultimately coun-sels sameness and indifference: "If it eliminates the 'Orient' and 'Occi-dent' altogether, then we shall have advanced a little on the road suggested by Raymond Williams."[16]

Since *Orientalism*, Said has been prodigiously productive, both as a literary critic and a social commentator. His outlook has not been sta-tionary, but has undergone subtle changes in emphasis and formula-tion.[17] Despite such changes, however, there is a strong continuity of themes and theoretical accents. This continuity is clearly evident in his recent and widely acclaimed *Culture and Imperialism*. The new study is a sequel to *Orientalism* in that it carries the issue of East-West relations forward to the present global situation: rather than focus on European colonialism and its scholarly offshoots, *Culture and Imperialism* draws attention to the looming North-South conflict and the chasm between development and underdevelopment—a contest waged under the aegis of the "American ascendancy" to global hegemony. As Said observes, imperialism did not become a thing of the past with the dismantling of the "classical [European] empires"; on the contrary, the emergence of the United States as the last superpower suggests "that a new set of force lines will structure the world." Traditional empires have always been characterized by a "twinning of power and legitimacy," the juncture of domination in the political and cultural spheres. This juncture has not changed; what is different in the "American century" is only the "quantum leap in the reach of cultural authority," due in large measure to "the unprecedented growth in the apparatus for the diffusion and control of information." Citing approvingly the findings of Anthony Smith (in *The Geopolitics of Information*) and Herbert Schiller (in *Culture, Inc.*), Said observes that "rarely before in human history has there been so massive an intervention of force and ideas from one culture to another as there is today from America to the rest of the world." The methods of intervention have become more subtle and sophisticated in comparison with old-style colonialism, but subtlety enhances rather than diminishes efficiency of control:

> It is not a question of a directly imposed regime of conformity in the correspondence between contemporary United States cultural discourse and United States policy in the subordinate, non-Western world. Rather, it is a system of pressures and constraints by which the whole cultural corpus retains its essentially imperial identity and its direction.[18]

What emerges from this portrayal is the vision of a new imperial structure and discourse, a global sort of agonistics building upon and expanding the earlier conflict between Occident and Orient (as seen in the Orientalist model). As in earlier times, this conflict rages between masters and servants, rich and poor, "developed" knowers and "backward" recipients of knowledge; indications are that the gulf is widening. Said echoes the Brandt report of 1980: "The powerful are likely to get more powerful and richer, the weak less powerful and poorer; the gap between the two overrides the former distinctions between socialist and capitalist regimes." Faced with this hegemonic-imperial setting, weaker countries in the South or East have to pursue strategies of resistance to ward off the homogenizing tentacles of global power; they must nurture counter-identities in opposition to the pervasive imperial identity (counteridentity means nonidentity in the sense of concrete particularity). This is indeed Said's counsel; throughout his new study, he champions the cause of victims and of liberation movements in all parts of the world—from the Palestinian intifada to black insurgency against Apartheid to the demands of Native Americans in the United States. As he writes, Western imperial policy toward the non-Western world has been "consistent" during recent decades, as is evident in its "support for dictatorial and unpopular regimes," its endorsement of massive retaliation "out of all proportion to the violence of native insurgency against American allies," and its "steady hostility to the legitimacy of native nationalism." Although not condoning any kind of xenophobic chauvinism, Said remains attentive to the strategic imperatives deriving from the global asymmetry of power: "If you are part of a Philippine, or Palestinian, or Brazilian oppositional movement, you must deal with the tactical and logistical requirements of the daily struggle."[19]

As in *Orientalism*, however, Said's endorsement of counteridentity and of national or local particularism is circumscribed and traversed by a completely different focus: an exodus or escape from identity as such. In fact, *Culture and Imperialism* centerstages this kind of exodus in eloquent and nearly rhapsodic language to the point of nearly blotting out the topic of political insurgency. What motivates this accent, at least in part, is the dismal performance of many newly independent countries and the rise of a chauvinistic type of cultural and religious fundamentalism in many parts of the Orient and elsewhere. Said is vehement in denouncing these problematic occurrences. Almost everywhere in the non-Western world, he writes, "the effort to homogenize and isolate populations in the name of nationalism (*not* liberation) has led to colossal sacrifices and failures." The rise of nationalism and fundamentalism has led to the upsurge of a narrow and xenophobic identity politics. In the Near East, more energy is spent "bolstering the idea that to be Syrian, Iraqi, Egyptian, or Saudi is a sufficient end, rather than in thinking critically, even audaciously, about the national program itself." Hence: "Identity, always identity, over and above knowing about others." In the global setting, the insistence on local identity or counteridentity is the reverse side of the imperial identity; both are "expressions of essentialization": "Muslims or Africans or Indians or Japanese, in their idioms and from within their own threatened localities, attack the West, or Americanization, or imperialism, with little more attention to detail, critical differentiation, discrimination, and distinction than has been lavished on them by the West." This is an "ultimately senseless dynamic." Surveying the present postcolonial scene, Said finds that the process of decolonization and national liberation has widely given way to petty parochialism:

> All those nationalist appeals to pure or authentic Islam, or to Afrocentrism, *négritude*, or Arabism had a strong response, without sufficient consciousness that those ethnicities and spiritual essences would come back to exact a very high price from their successful adherents. Fanon was one of the few to remark on the dangers posed to a great socio-political movement like decolonization by an untutored national consciousness. Much the same could be said about the dangers of an untutored religious consciousness. . . . National security and a separatist identity are the watchwords.[20]

In *Culture and Imperialism*, critique of political derailments is strongly buttressed—even overshadowed—by general theoretical considerations. As in his earlier study, constructivism surfaces as an attractive model for viewing the world. In the contemporary world the job facing the "cultural intellectual" is "not to accept the politics of identity as given, but to show how all representations are constructed, for what purpose, by whom, and with what components." Constructivism implies (again) that all identities or distinct differences are basically arbitrary, furtive, substitutable, and hence deconstructible; they certainly do not have any kind of "ontologically given and eternally determined stability, or uniqueness, or irreducible character." As in much of postmodern literature, this (de)constructive view is closely linked with a dismissal of Hegel. As Said observes (invoking the testimony of Homi Bhabha), the fact that all culture is "hybrid and encumbered, or entangled and overlapping with what used to be regarded as extraneous elements—this strikes me as *the* essential idea for the revolutionary realities today . . . we can no longer afford conceptions of history that stress linear development or Hegelian transcendence." The theme of an exodus or exile from identity is struck, together with the corollary of a diasporic existence beneath or beyond spatial and temporal constraints: "Far from being the fate of nearly forgotten unfortunates who were dispossessed and expatriated," exile today becomes "something closer to a norm, an experience of crossing boundaries and charting new territories in defiance of the classic canonic enclosures." In shouldering this experience, the cultural critic assumes the role of a cosmopolitan wanderer freely moving across times and places. *Culture and Imperialism*'s concluding section on "Movements and Migrations" approvingly invokes Paul Virilio's notion of "counter-habitation" and even more ardently Deleuze's conception of nomadism and nomadic thought. Referring to Deleuze and Guattari's *Mille Plateaux*, Said finds in nomadism the highly suggestive idea of the "eccentric" operation of an "itinerant war machine," a metaphor illustrative of "intellectual mobility in an age of institutionalization." Seen from this angle, he adds, liberation as an intellectual mission

> has now shifted from the settled, established, and domesticated dynamics of culture to its unhoused, decentered, and exilic energies, energies whose incarnation today is the migrant, and whose consciousness is that of the intellectual and artist in exile, the political figure between domains, between forms, between homes, and between languages.[21]

With this turn to nomadism, we are back in the netherworld of vacant signifiers, of a no(n)-identity denying distinct features. An initial philosophical question is prompted: How can denial provide a place of habitation (even counter-habitation)? How can negation *"be"* something with describable contours? More important and pressing are social and political considerations. How would nomadic intellectuals—by definition *dis*engaged from concrete contexts and loyalties—be able and willing to engage themselves again with real-life problems or events? Having sundered all concrete attachments, how would they manage to commit themselves to anything except the principle of nomadism? As Gadamer has taught us, local prejudices are not only limitations but also productive premises of mutual interrogation; by contrast, a vagrant spectatorial stance is liable to lack the "traction" required for genuine encounter. On a still more concrete level, one wonders about the political implications of Said's endorsement of nomadism. What concrete consequences are entailed, for example, in the present Near East situation? Are Palestinians now asked to abandon their quest for a homeland and to remain content with refugee camps or with a dispersal into diasporic existence? Would similar advice be offered to the Kurds or American Indians? As Said would probably agree, it is always an awkwardly embarrassing matter to preach poverty to the poor or homelessness to the homeless. The message is particularly embarrassing in the present global situation dominated (as Said insists) by an imperial identity intent on homogenizing and standardizing the world. Cutting loose from local moorings, in this setting, aids and abets this process of homogenization, the production of a global nondistinction or sameness. But if all people are the same and substitutable, then what difference does it make if the world is governed from a hegemonic center, say America, especially if that center is, in Richard Barnet's words, the "bearer" of universal law?[22]

This conclusion is clearly at odds with the basic thrust of Said's study, which aims at a critical insurgency against cultural imperialism. Testifying to Said's integrity as a scholar and *engagé* writer, his endorsement of nomadism is at least occasionally muted, especially when it comes to the problem of real-life homelessness. As he invokes Deleuze, he also compassionately deplores the plight of homeless people all over the world. "For surely," he states, "it is one of the unhappiest characteristics of the age to have produced more refugees, migrants, displaced persons, and exiles than ever before in history, most of them as an accompaniment to and, ironically enough, as afterthoughts of great postcolonial and imperial conflicts." Said resolutely takes the side of the *raison du coeur* against a complacently vagrant intellectualism. "It would be the rankest Panglossian dishonesty to say that the bravura performances of the intellectual exile and the miseries of the displaced person or refugee are the same" or of the same order. Clearly there is a vast difference between "the optimistic mobility, the intellectual liveliness, and the logic of daring" marking the "various theoreticians on whose work I have drawn" and "the massive dislocations, waste, misery, and horrors endured in our century's migrations and mutilated lives." Curiously, but perhaps not surprisingly, it is in the context of these observations that Said refers to the work of Adorno, especially to the latter's *Minima Moralia*, subtitled *Reflections from a Damaged Life*. In that text, Adorno ponders the loss of any traditional grounding as a result of world wars and holocaust. What Said leaves somewhat opaque—but what would need to be recovered—is the complex dialectical (in fact, negatively dialectical) character of Adorno's notion of the homelessness of home or his plea to find one's home in homelessness. This aspect does seem to be present in Ali Shari'ati, the Iranian Islamic writer whom Said invokes as a distant soulmate of Adorno—particularly in Shari'ati's description of human being as a "dialectical phenomenon."[23]

Said is much more faithful to the central point of his study—and to the point of Adorno's negative dialectics—when he maintains the perspective of an engaged struggle with imperial domination, an engagement which is equally far from yielding a bland synthesis and from sliding into the blind alleys of parochial exclusivism and global vagrancy. How could one demur from Said's pleas for a new "paradigm for humanistic research," where scholars would be concerned not with the survival of "disciplinary fiefdoms" or "manipulative identities," but with "the improvement and noncoercive enhancement of life in a community struggling to exist among other communities"? And how could one object or fail to be strongly drawn to his notion of "opposing and alleviating coercive domination," of "transforming the present by trying rationally and analytically to lift some of its burdens," and of situating various literatures "with reference to one another and to their historical modes of being"?

In these passages Said is able to capture the subtle dialectic of both embracing and transgressing identity, of a seriously engaged encounter where difference provides traction and attraction. As he observes in the final pages of *Culture and Imperialism*, there is nothing amiss with teaching students about their own "identity, history, tradition, uniqueness" because this may incite them to "name their basic requirements for democracy and for the right to an assured, decently human existence." However, one needs to situate this background "in a geography of other identities, peoples, cultures" and study "how, despite their differences, they have always overlapped one another, through unhierarchical influence, crossing, incorporation, recollection, deliberate forgetfulness, and, of course, conflict." At the very end of his study, Said cites a passage by Hugo of St. Victor, a twelfth-century monk following the monastic ideal, that equates human perfection with the ability to extinguish one's "love to all places." However, Said points out:

> Hugo twice makes it clear that the "strong" or "perfect" person achieves independence and detachment by *working through* attachments, not by rejecting them. Exile is predicated on the existence of, love for, and a real bond with one's native place; the universal truth of exile is not that one has lost that love or home, but that inherent in each is an unexpected, unwelcome loss.[24]

## Notes

1. Theodor W. Adorno, *Negative Dialektik* (Frankurt-Main: Suhrkamp, 1966), trans. by E. B. Ashton as *Negative Dialectics* (New York: Seabury Press, 1973). I refer subsequently to the English translation, but since the latter is often very unsatisfactory, I correct the translation in light of my understanding of the German original. Adorno was not the first to articulate a postmetaphysical view of identity and nonidentity. Such a view had already been formulated in rigorous philosophical terms by Martin Heidegger in *Identität und Differenz* (Pfullingen, Germany: Neske, 1957). In this study, Heidegger delineated both a differentiated notion of "identity" and a novel, post-Hegelian version of "difference." Adorno's book makes no reference to Heidegger's initiative.

2. Adorno, *Negative Dialectics*, pp. 4–5.

3. *Negative Dialectics*, pp. 11–13.

4. *Negative Dialectics*, pp. 5–6, 27–28, 141–142. In a footnote on p. 142, Adorno elaborates on the various meanings of "identity" in the history of Western philosophy. Regarding the difference between negative dialectics and Hegelian dialectics compare also the sections "On the Dialectics of Identity," pp. 146–148; "Synthesis," pp. 156–158; "Critique of Positive Negation," pp. 158–161; "Relapse into Platonism," pp. 329–331; "Dialectics Cut Short by Hegel," pp. 334–338; and "Self-Reflection of Dialectics," pp. 405–409.

5. *Negative Dialectics*, pp. 136, 139, 161. Compare also the sections "Particularity and the Particular," pp. 173–174; "Subject-Object Dialectics," pp. 174–176; and "Dynamics of Universal and Particular," pp. 313–314. As

transconceptual, nonidentity cannot be approached or thematized directly, nor simply *via negativa*, but only through "constellations" or interwoven strands of vantage points, for which ordinary language (in its nonsystematized texture) offers an analogue. See esp. pp. 162–166.

6. *Negative Dialectics*, pp. 158, 161, 189.

7. *Negative Dialectics*, pp. 6, 191 (the reference to Eichendorff is omitted in the translation). Regarding hope and reconciliation, see also the passage on pp. 206–207 (which speaks of "bodily resurrection" and reconciliation with matter) and pp. 391–392 (which speaks of recovery through transformative renunciation). Regarding the implications of Adorno's work for a postmetaphysical ethics compare Drucilla Cornell, "The Ethical Message of Negative Dialectics," *Social Concept* 4 (1987): 2–25; also my *Between Freiburg and Frankfurt: Toward a Critical Ontology* (Amherst, Mass.: University of Massachusetts Press, 1991), pp. 121–128.

8. Jean-François Lyotard, *The Postmodern Condition: A Report on Knowledge*, trans. Geoff Bennington and Brian Massumi (Minneapolis: University of Minnesota Press, 1984), pp. 15–17. Lyotard is quite explicit regarding the social and political implications of such agonistics: "The society of the future falls less within the province of a Newtonian anthropology [with its unifying assumptions] than a pragmatics of language particles. There are many different language games—a heterogeneity of elements; they only give rise to institutions in patches—local determinism." Postmodernism is said to strengthen "our sensitivity to differences" and "our ability to tolerate the incommensurable" (pp. xxiv–xxv).

9. *The Postmodern Condition*, pp. 33–35, 53–56, 59–61. See also Lyotard, *The Differend: Phrases in Dispute*, trans. Georges Van den Abbeele (Minneapolis: University of Minnesota Press, 1988), pp. 92, 138. For a more detailed review and critique of Lyotard's position see my *Margins of Political Discourse* (Albany, N.Y.: SUNY Press, 1989), pp. 10–15, 149–152; also my "Modernity in the Crossfire: Comments on the Postmodern Turn," in *Postmodern Contentions: Epochs, Politics, Space*, ed. John Paul Jones III, Wolfgang Natter, and Theodore R. Schatzki (New York: Guilford Press, 1993) pp. 17–38. Lyotard has further elaborated and slightly modified his position; see his *The Postmodern Explained: Correspondence 1982–1985*, trans. Don Barry et al. (Minneapolis: University of Minnesota Press, 1992).

10. Michel Foucault, *Language, Counter-Memory, Practice: Selected Essays and Interviews*, trans. Donald F. Bouchard and Sherry Simon (Oxford: Blackwell, 1977), pp. 42–44 ("A Preface to Transgression") and 151 ("Nietzsche, Genealogy, History"). The strategy of reversal is also manifest in his more systematic "archaeological" investigations, where difference prevails over sameness, discontinuity over teleology, and dispersal of meaning over stable identity. See Foucault, *The Archaeology of Knowledge*, trans. A. M. Sheridan Smith (New York: Pantheon Books, 1972), especially pp. 3–17.

11. *Language, Counter-Memory, Practice*, pp. 163 ("Nietzsche, Genealogy, History") and 185 ("Theatrum Philosophicum"). In more circuitous langue but no less emphatically, the need to depart from Hegel was asserted in Foucault's

inaugural lecture at the Collège de France, "The Discourse on Language," curiously in the context of a tribute paid to the Hegel scholar Jean Hyppolite. One of the deep aspirations of our age was said to be the desire to "flee Hegel." See "The Discourse on Language," in *The Archaeology of Knowledge*, p. 235.

12. Gilles Deleuze, *Nietzsche and Philosophy*, trans. Hugh Tomlinson (New York: Columbia University Press, 1983), p. 40. Compare also Deleuze, "Active and Reactive," in *The New Nietzsche: Contemporary Styles of Interpretation*, ed. David B. Allison (New York: Dell Publishing Co., 1977), pp. 80–81.

13. Deleuze, *Nietzsche and Philosophy*, pp. 195–196; also his "Nomad Thought" in *The New Nietzsche*, pp. 148–149. For an instructive critique of Deleuze's construal (or misconstrual) of both Hegel and Nietzsche see Stephen Houlgate, *Hegel, Nietzsche and the Criticism of Metaphysics* (Cambridge: Cambridge University Press, 1986). Compare also the section on "Poststructuralism and Deconstruction" in my *G. W. F. Hegel: Modernity and Politics* (Newbury Park, Calif.: Sage Publications, 1993), pp. 233–238. In the above citations one may wonder how a nomadic thought can also congeal into a "nomadic unit" and a "mobile war machine" without ceasing to be extrinsic to identifiable codes.

14. Edward W. Said, *Orientalism* (New York: Vintage Books, 1979), pp. 3, 20, 40, 43, 202, 204. Foucault and Nietzsche, to be sure, are not Said's only mentors here but share the spotlight with Gramsci's theory of "hegemony" and Williams's notion of cultural change: "My whole point is to say that we can better understand the persistence and the durability of saturating hegemonic systems like culture when we realize that their internal constraints upon writers and thinkers were *productive*, not unilaterally inhibiting. It is this idea that Gramsci, certainly, and Foucault and Raymond Williams in their different ways have been trying to illustrate" (p. 14).

15. *Orientalism*, pp. 5, 22, 71. Even in the context of an explicit invocation of Nietzsche (and his notion of the "will to truth"), an effort is made to distinguish neatly between truth and fiction, between reality and its discursive construction. "The Orient," we are told, "was a word which later accrued to it a wide field of meanings, associations and connotations"; however, the latter "did not necessarily refer to the real Orient but to the field surrounding the word" (p. 203).

16. *Orientalism*, pp. 28, 45, 54, 322. As one should add, of course, Said's assertions are always cautiously formulated; thus, his endorsement of constructivism is somewhat qualified. As he notes, for example: "This universal practice of designating in one's mind a familiar space which is 'ours' and an unfamiliar space beyond 'ours' which is 'theirs' is a way of making geographical distinctions that *can be* entirely arbitrary" (p. 54). (Italics in the original.)

17. While *Orientalism* still treats hermeneutics as a mere accomplice to the domineering aims of Orientalist discourse, subsequent writings make room for a more positive assessment of hermeneutical understanding. See *Orientalism*, p. 222, and Said, *Covering Islam: How the Media and the Experts Determine How We See the Rest of the World* (New York: Pantheon Books, 1981), pp. 154–164. Initiatives of this kind are pursued and further explored in my *Beyond Orientalism: Essays on Cross-Cultural Encounter* (Albany, N.Y.: SUNY Press, 1996).

18. Said, *Culture and Imperialism* (New York: Knopf, 1993), pp. 282, 291, 319, 323. Compare also Anthony Smith, *The Geopolitics of Information: How Western Culture Dominates the World* (New York: Oxford University Press, 1980), and Herbert Schiller, *Culture, Inc.: The Corporate Takeover of Public Expression* (New York: Oxford University Press, 1989).

19. Said, *Culture and Imperialism*, pp. 284, 311, 322.

20. *Culture and Imperialism*, pp. 299, 307, 311. Given his support of the Palestinian movement, Said's critique of Near Eastern politics is particularly forthright: "Democracy in any real sense of the word is nowhere to be found in the still 'nationalistic' Middle East: there are either privileged oligarchies or privileged ethnic groups" (p. 300).

21. *Culture and Imperialism*, pp. 314–315, 317–318, 331–331. Compare also Gilles Deleuze and Felix Guattari, *Mille Plateaux* (Paris: Minuit, 1980). More recently, Said has elaborated the role of critical cultural intellectuals; see his *Representations of the Intellectual: The 1993 Reith Lectures* (New York: Pantheon Books, 1994).

22. Richard J. Barnet, *The Roots of War* (New York: Atheneum, 1972), p. 21. The phrase is quoted by Said in *Culture and Imperialism*, p. 286. One might also fruitfully ponder the connection between nomadic intellectuals and the rise in our time of jet-setting cosmopolitans and multinational corporate executives—a phenomenon Said critiques eloquently in his book, especially in the context of "American media imperialism" (p. 292).

23. *Culture and Imperialism*, pp. 332–334. Compare also Said, "Reflections on Exile," in *Out There: Marginalization and Contemporary Culture*, ed. Russell Ferguson et al. (Cambridge, Mass.: MIT Press, 1990), pp. 357–366; Theodor W. Adorno, *Minima Moralia: Reflections from a Damaged Life*, trans. E. F. N. Jephcott (London: New Left, 1974); and Ali Shari'ati, *On the Sociology of Islam: Lectures by Ali Shari'ati*, trans. Hamid Aegar (Berkeley, Calif.: Mizan Press, 1979). Shari'ati was a defender of an open-ended, nonaggressive Islam. In his *Representations of the Intellectual*, Said comments at greater length on Adorno, especially on *Minima Moralia*; see pp. 54–60.

24. Said, *Culture and Imperialism*, pp. 312, 319, 330–331, 335–336.

# 3

# Liberation Perspectives East and West

To free a neck
(from the burden of debt or slavery) . . .

Qur'an

The year is 1550; the place is Valladolid in Spain. People are gathered to hear a debate concerning a matter crucial for Spain and Spanish imperial ambitions. Juan Ginés de Sepúlveda, a doctor of philosophy and theology, is holding forth on the legitimacy of empire, buttressing it with reason and faith alike. Based on classical teachings and scriptures, Sepúlveda affirms that truth (in the absolute sense) is accessible to humans through reason and revelation and that, once perceived, it must never be compromised; in comparison with truth, error has no standing, and its defense is both irrational and impious and even heretical. Given these premises, the Spanish conquest of the Americas is the victory of truth over untruth, of goodness over evil, and hence justified on the highest grounds. Counterpoised to Sepúlveda is a Dominican friar (now bishop of Chiapa), Bartolomé de Las Casas, who comes armed with firsthand experience of the New World. For Las Casas, the distinction between truth and untruth is not nearly as clear-cut as for the learned doctor; truth is to be searched for constantly, and faith is a gift, not a secure possession. In contrast to Sepúlveda's depiction of the conquistadors as Christ's batallions on earth, Las Casas perceives the face of Jesus in the persecuted, tortured, and mutilated bodies of the American Indians:

> I leave, in the Indies, Jesus Christ our God scourged and afflicted and buffeted and crucified, not once but millions of times, on the part of the Spaniards who ruin and destroy these people and deprive them of the space they require for their conversion and repentence, depriving them of life before their time. . . . The Spaniards who traverse the land with their violence and wicked example . . . make the name of Christ into a blasphemy.[1]

71

The significance of the meeting in Valladolid extends beyond the confines of the Spanish conquest. The dispute highlights a crossroads in Christianity, in fact, a parting of the ways in religion and culture of every kind. On the one side are those who consider philosophical knowledge and religious faith a badge of privilege, a property whose possession entitles its owners to public preeminence and political domination. On the other are those who view philosophy and religion simply as emblems of a special seasoning, a distinctive mark calling its bearers into service, self-transformation, and a willingness to suffer rather than inflict violence and injustice. The watershed between these two positions is deep and cannot be bridged or readily mediated; it also marks a difference between historical epochs.

In ancient or premodern times, philosophy and religion were often closely linked with public power or political dominance; in the West, following its establishment as a state religion under Constantine, Christianity was cast in an imperial mold. Against this background, what is loosely called "modernity" or "modernization" can be seen as the progressive dissociation of philosophy and religion from public dominance—a process sometimes mistakenly, or at least one-sidedly described as "secularization" or the spreading of an antireligious secularism. Actually, the dissociation inaugurated by modernity can also be perceived as the advent of a new "liberation," not just for secularist politics, but also for philosophy and religion, which are now released from extraneous entanglements with public power. This beneficial effect of modernity upon religion was clearly noted by Paul Ricoeur when he wrote that today the secular city or the "non-parish" may "save the parish" or religious faith by reminding the latter of its calling as the "salt of the earth" rather than the imperial administrator of the world.[2]

Ricoeur's comments throw light on the ambivalent status of modern secularism and the meaning of liberation. Western civilization or culture today stands again at a crossroads—which is in many ways reminiscent of, yet different from, the Spanish conquest and the meeting at Valladolid. While then Spanish imperial might and culture were appropriating the "Indies" (Americas), Western civilization today is in the process of extending itself to the entire globe, specifically to non-Western societies and cultures. Whereas the *conquista* pitted an imperial and missionary religion against non-believers and their freedom to disbelieve, modern Western civilization has ostensibly shed this legacy and made itself the standard-bearer of human liberty in all its forms—including the secularist freedom from religion. Ever since the Enlightenment, Western societies have been wedded to the motto of liberation or emancipation, terms designating the freeing of human agency (individual or collective) from spiritual and other controls.

In the aftermath of the Cold War, Western liberalism and liberalization have emerged as the triumphant ideological panacea, spreading its effects around the globe. Yet precisely at this point, a curious dilemma has arisen: the embroilment of liberty and liberalism itself with domination. This entanglement is by no means fortuitous or merely the result of hegemonic designs. Just as under market auspices liberal individualism easily shades over into egocentrism, the rise of modern science and technology has transformed the Cartesian *cogito* into a surveyor and master of the natural universe, a transformation often captured by such labels as "logocentrism" or "anthropocentrism." The question that surfaces—in the footsteps of Las Casas—is whether human liberty can be severed from domination and mastery or, in Nietzschean terms, whether human freedom can be cultivated without animosity or resentment against nature, the world, and the variety of human cultures.[3]

The same question has clear implications for the familiar Western motto of liberation or emancipation and its conventional understanding; it also profoundly complicates the meaning of such terms as "liberation theology" and "liberation philosophy." In light of the modern complicity of freedom and mastery, liberation theology cannot designate a straightforward exodus from nature and history in favor of the cultivation of an anthropocentric or self-contained human agency. In the spirit of Las Casas again, the watershed of our time urges us to turn from the official doctrine of liberalism and its global defenders (the *beati possidentes*) to the netherworld of the dispossessed; differently phrased: we need to ask whether in these dispossessed we discover again the face of the "other" or the "divine" (what Emmanuel Levinas calls the "absolute Other" or *l'Autrui*), the face of infinite forbearance and gentleness.

The present chapter explores various contemporary forms of liberation theology and liberation philosophy under the combined rubric of "liberation perspectives" (in recognition of the frequently blurred boundary between philosophy and religion).[4] The first section reviews the difficult meaning of liberation or emancipation in Western liberation perspectives, especially those influenced in some fashion by postmodernism (or postmetaphysics). The same difficulty is next illustrated by reference to Christian liberation theology, as formulated chiefly by Gustavo Gutierrez. A third section turns to non-Western perspectives, more specifically, orientations originating outside the confines of the so-called "Judeo-Christian" tradition. The journey will lead first to Buddhism, where the main focus will be placed on recent developments in Japanese and South Asian Buddhist thought. The final leg examines liberation perspectives in the Islamic world and also some developments occurring at the crossroads of Islamic and Hindu traditions.

# I

In modern Western thought, liberation has often, and perhaps predominantly, been construed in a binary fashion, with liberty being seen as a deliberate exodus from, and hence the negation or opposite of, servitude and oppression. Liberty in this connection occupies a position similar to that of reason and subjectivity in major strands of Enlightenment philosophy: rationalization was viewed as an exit from prejudice and tradition, with reason denoting the negation of unreason.[5] As it happens, binary conceptions of this kind have been challenged or called into question by recent philosophical trends in the West, especially those showing the imprint of the so-called "linguistic turn" as well as the turn to "worldhood" (the lifeworld context of reason).

Significant strides beyond traditional binary metaphysics were made by Martin Heidegger, in a manner that remained closely attentive to the crucial issue of liberty. For Heidegger, reflection means openness to the liberating call of "being"; to this extent, genuine philosophy is necessarily liberative or liberationist, but not in the sense of a purely negative liberty. As presented in his work, freedom, or liberty, is basically "relational," but "relation" must not be confused with a restrictive conformism nor with a contractual exchange. In a preeminent sense, human existence is portrayed as a relational "being-in-the-world," with the hyphens indicating both closeness and distinction. Heidegger's so-called "ontic-ontological difference" has sometimes been construed as a radical separation—an untenable view. Far from denoting an abstract category, "being" in a strong sense can only mean the "being of beings," a phrase that points beyond both coincidence and negation (even dialectical negation) to a relational difference or differential "entwinement." It is in this sense that one should read Heidegger's famous comments on freedom in "On the Essence of Truth," where freedom is said to be truth as such, the latter seen as openness to the being of beings: "In letting beings be, freedom is the open, that is, not-self-encapsulating relationship (*Verhältnis*). All comportment is grounded in this relation which directs it toward beings and their disclosure."[6]

The issues of freedom and liberation have also received prominent attention in recent social and political thought, often in a manner resonating with Heidegger's (and post-Heideggerian) views. In a broad overview essay on the status of liberty and emancipation today, the Dutch theorist Jan Pieterse has emphasized the need to distinguish, without radically segregating, "modern" from "postmodern" treatments of the topic. In Pieterse's presentation, the terms have been bequeathed to us by the Enlightenment and its liberal offshoots, a tradition that understood "emancipation" as a linear process or movement, that is, as an exodus from oppression to the "reign of freedom." In modified form, this tradition was also accepted by classical Marxism, which translated human liberation into a collective project underwritten by the proletariat, seen as the "privileged revolutionary subject." In its liberal and its Marxist molds, liberation tended to be viewed as an exit or *via negativa*, an attempt by individuals or collectives to negate and thus gain "freedom from" existing contexts. This approach, Pieterse notes, is contested and intensely problematized in recent postmodern and poststructuralist literature. While the "grand theme" of modernity, he writes, revolved around "human beings taking responsibility for their own destiny" and thus around the "conscious programming and production of society," postmodernism offers a critical postscript to this trajectory (without denying freedom as such). Recent theoretical initiatives suggest an "emancipation *from* emancipation" (that is, from its modernist or Enlightenment version); in any event, the nexus of context and liberation can no longer be viewed as a binary or "simple adversarial relationship":

> If modernity is about the promise of human power, postmodernism is about the problem of power. As such it represents heightened sensibilities. Unlike Marxism, it is not an "in-house" critique of the Enlightenment project but it brackets the premises of modernity and the Enlightenment itself. It interrupts the familiar duets of liberals and radicals. Since it is concerned with paradigm transgression, it generates irritability among paradigm partisans.[7]

In a more poignant and probing fashion, the issue of liberation/emancipation has been explored by Ernesto Laclau, with an accent on the quandaries besetting the modernist version. In Laclau's portrayal, the modern paradigm has been wedded to a number of dubious premises, including a binary metaphysics and the utopia of ultimate social transparency. Emancipation in this version presupposed "the elimination of power, the abolition of the subject/object distinction, and the management—without any opaqueness or mediation—of community affairs by social agents identified with the viewpoint of social totality." Replicating the dualisms of essence/appearance and of a priori/a posteriori domains, individual or collective carriers of emancipation were assumed to "preexist" the actual process of liberation, relegating that process to the mere stripping away of a façade. For Laclau, the paradigm suffered not only from quandaries but from logically incompatible claims: on the one hand, emancipation holds the promise of a plenitude of freedom untarnished by power or opacity; on the other hand, this promise can only be kept through an exclusionary act: the imperialist purging of freedom of all residues of power, irrationality, and prejudice. The task is to reconceive liberation along "postmodern" lines, not to discard it. In the latter

approach, conflicting claims are not eliminated but reassessed as nonex-
clusionary antagonisms. Once the metaphysics of plenitude is put aside,
liberation becomes a mode of agonistic interaction, a process in which
individuals and groups meet in a setting devoid of a privileged foundation and marked both by mutual implication and contestation. Laclau
formulates:

> We are today coming to terms with our own finitude and with the political
> possibilities that it opens. This is the point from which the potentially liber-
> ating discourses of the postmodern age have to start. We can perhaps say
> that today we are at the end of emancipation and at the beginning of
> freedom.[8]

Unsurprisingly, the quandaries besetting the modernist paradigm of
liberation have been critiqued acutely by intellectuals in non-Western,
especially so-called "developing," societies. Having been the targets first
of Western colonialism and later of Western-style "modernization" projects, these countries were bound to experience with particular intensity
the subtle linkage between Western modernity, including its emancipation model, and the political agenda of control and domination. In their
effort to extricate themselves from colonial (and postcolonial) tutelage,
non-Western societies had to engage in a complex "double gesture" of
liberation: a course of action which, while aiming at social and political
freedom and autonomy, would simultaneously recast liberation in a nondomineering and nonmodernist mold. This two-fold process has been
articulated by Ashis Nandy, a leading intellectual in postcolonial India,
in his essay "Liberation of Those Who Do Not Speak the Language of
Liberation." Nandy argues that modern Western colonialism was not
simply an external garment spread lightly over colonized lands, but a
massive incursion into the inner mind and ordinary lifeworld of peoples.
To this extent, colonizers were transformed from external oppressors to
an "intimate enemy" or internalized double. Even those wishing to extricate themselves from colonial control can do so initially only within the
framework and the terminology offered by the Western model; they must
learn to "speak the language of liberation" and thus to internalize "the
oppressor's language and worldview" before being able to qualify as
"proper dissenters." Genuine liberation, for Nandy, requires a more subtle and difficult mode of divergence, a paradigm shift from the modernist
to a (loosely) "postmodern" model; in Jan Pieterse's terms, this shift involves an emancipation from Western modernity or an "emancipation
from (modernist) emancipation" that does not abandon the idea of freedom and liberation as such. Departing from modern Enlightenment
metaphysics, the shift signals a liberation in and through such contexts,

prominently including the culture and religion sedimented in popular beliefs. As Nandy has noted in another essay, "Cultural Frames for Social Transformation: A Credo," the aggressive predominance of Western-style modernity around the globe calls for a movement of cultural resistance against such fashionable catchwords as "development, growth, history, science and technology"—a resistance that refuses to be simply captive to an indigenous past.[9]

# II

In its appeal to nonelitist historical and cultural memories, Nandy's argument bears a close resemblance to a critical perspective prominent in many "developing" societies both inside and outside the Western orbit: "liberation theology." The term was first coined and elaborated in Latin America as a counterpoint to prevailing social-economic inequities and established ecclesiastical hierarchies. As inaugurated and propounded by Christian theologians, liberation theology was clearly meant as a complex double gesture: the attempt to preserve the liberating legacy of Christ's teachings by purging it of its entanglement with powerful elites in society and church. Proceeding in this manner, liberation theologians sought to undercut or disprove the alleged incompatibility between faith and human freedom that had been asserted in diverse ways by the "modernist" model of emancipation and unwittingly sanctioned by reactionaries in the church. Despite their nuanced aims, however, early formulations of liberation theology were often sidetracked or reappropriated by the modernist paradigm they sought to correct. Faced with overwhelming social-economic disparities engendered by capitalism, liberation theologians often aligned themselves with Marxist intellectuals and radical popular movements bent on overturning existing class structures. Although politically invigorating, this alliance exacted a price: Marxist theologians were forced to subscribe to the notion of a "privileged revolutionary subject" and hence to the modernist concept of a self-constituting subjectivity or agency. As a corollary, they were led to embrace the trajectory toward not only a society without classes but a society without faith—a condition where "man" (in Marx's memorable phrase) "has lost his illusions" and hence can "revolve about himself as his own true sun."[10]

The problem of a modernist appropriation can be detected not only in popular religious tracts but also in the text that sounded the clarion call of Christian emancipation: Gustavo Gutierrez's *A Theology of Liberation.* Following the lead of some European "political" theologians, Gutierrez in that text delineated a relatively unproblematical linkage between Marxism and Christianity based on a shared transformative project. Citing Sartre's famous statement that Marxism as a philosophical framework "cannot be superseded" in our time, he explained how Christian theology in fact finds itself "in direct and fruitful confrontation with Marxism," adding that "it is to a large extent due to Marxism's influence that theological thought, searching for its own sources, has begun to reflect on the meaning of the transformation of this world and the action of man in history." The somewhat derivative status of "theological thought" was clearly reflected in the discussion of the book's central concept, liberation. In Gutierrez's presentation, the term comprised three dimensions or "interpenetrating levels of meaning": political liberation, social-historical emancipation, and religious salvation, with the first two tending to overshadow if not marginalize the third dimension. Gutierrez's encapsulated formulation of these levels clearly reveals its modernist overtones:

> In the first place, *liberation* expresses the aspirations of oppressed peoples and social classes, emphasizing the conflictual aspect of the economic, social, and political process which puts them at odds with wealthy nations and oppressive classes. . . . At a deeper level, *liberation* can be applied to an understanding of history. Man is seen as assuming conscious responsibility for his own destiny. . . . In this perspective the unfolding of all of man's dimensions is demanded—a man who makes himself throughout his life and throughout history. . . . Finally, . . . the word *liberation* allows for another approach leading to the Biblical sources which inspire the presence and action of man in history. In the Bible, Christ is presented as the one who brings us liberation [from sin].[11]

Given these accents, Jan Pieterse seems justified in noting that, in this text, "the scripts of Enlightenment, Marxism, national liberation, and Christianity" are fused in a curious and somewhat uneven amalgam. In the meantime, however, Gutierrez's thinking—and much of Christian liberation theology—has undergone a kind of paradigm shift from a linear-modernist model to a perspective more attuned to historical sedimentations and the distinctiveness of the Christian message. This change is clearly evident in Gutierrez's more recent, magisterial study on the friar from Seville, titled *Las Casas: In Search of the Poor of Jesus Christ.* In that study, Las Casas is portrayed as the ardent and caring defender of the American Indians, that multitude of "scourged Christs of the Indies," but not as the pioneer of a sovereign and self-constituting subjectivity or agency in the modernist vein. Gutierrez is even unwilling to apply the terminology of his own previous text to the friar's lifework. As he comments, Las Casas has often been described as someone ahead of his time, due to his ability to employ apparently "modern language" when speaking of the rights and liberties of the Indians. Although perhaps well intentioned, the description reveals a contemporary bias. This treatment, Gutierrez writes sharply, is an outgrowth of "the arrogance of the modern spirit" that regards itself as "the final arbiter of history" and "distorts past reality" accordingly. The same reservations extend to the use of the label "liberation theology." While alluding to a certain "liberative dimension of Christian faith," the label seems to Gutierrez unhelpful as a vehicle for expressing our contemporary appreciation of the friar's work. That work and witness "transpired in a context very different from today's," at both the social and theological levels; "their depth accrues to them from their gospel roots and from the way in which Las Casas managed to live his fidelity to the Lord." Hence, we cannot and should not ask him "to speak after the fashion of a person of the twentieth century."[12]

In accentuating historical and religious distinctiveness, Gutierrez's book resists the lure of a bland cosmopolitanism tied to a modernist trajectory. To do justice to Las Casas, to "this witness to God's love in the Indies," he insists, requires us to respect him "in his world, in his era, in his sources" without resort to a narrow historicism. Far from alienating or distancing us from the friar's work, such an approach will actually "move us closer" to him—without any modern-imperialist pretense of being able to identify his position with "the way in which we today defend causes." To be sure, our sensibilities toward social injustice and oppression have been sharpened by the experiences of our own age, but they are not simply the product of modern liberalism and Marxism. Gutierrez emphasizes Las Casas's religious calling, the fact that the friar was one of those who "on the basis of their faith" denounced "the poverty and plundering of which the oppressed of history were the victims." It would "not be forcing things" to say that Las Casas's task consisted above all "in letting it be known in the Indies that there is a God, and that God is the God of Abraham, Isaac, Jacob, and Jesus" and the enemy of injustice and oppression. For Gutierrez, it is precisely this distinctive proclamation of faith that provides the basis for the continued appeal of Las Casas across the centuries and across continents. The friar's prophetically inspired voice speaks to colonizers and colonized alike, to the "natives" of both the new and old world:

> This is one of the reasons why the figure of Las Casas is of such striking universality: here we have someone who, still today, issues a challenge to persons at various corners of the planet. . . . This is why his proclamation of the Christian message is invested with characteristics of prophetic denunciation that maintain all their validity today. The situation in the Indies in the sixteenth and seventeenth centuries was the occasion of some person's rediscovery of the very fonts of faith.[13]

## III

Theoretically and practically, the travails of liberation or emancipation are not restricted to Western and Latin American contexts. As an outgrowth of anticolonial struggles and a result of modernization and the worldwide diffusion of ideas and discourses, liberation is today a prominent issue in virtually all non-Western societies and cultures. This prominence is particularly striking in two cultural arenas often perceived as indifferent to social freedom: Buddhism and Islamic civilization. Before examining them, one should again note differing linguistic conventions. By comparison with Western terminology, non-Western cultures are much less preoccupied with the neat differentiation and labeling of intellectual pursuits. Thus, in contrast with the "separation of value spheres" often hailed as the trademark of Western modernity,[14] discourse in these societies is often marked by an easy symbiosis or interpenetration of the domains of reason and faith, rational argument and tacit knowledge. The distinction made between theology and philosophy is similarly less absolute than in some traditional Western settings.

In traditional Buddhism, the central point of the four "noble truths" is liberation from suffering (*dukkha*) induced primarily by self-centeredness or selfish desire (*tanha*) as well as blind ignorance and delusion (*avidya*). In the teachings of the Buddha Sakhyamuni, the overcoming of suffering was articulated in detail as an "eightfold path" of enlightenment and emancipation pointing ultimately to a realm of freedom beyond desire (*nirvana*, *nibbana*). As elaborated by versions of the Mahayana school, pursuit of this path requisitely involved the exit from self-delusion, particularly the deluded assumption of a fixed selfhood or essential self-nature (*atman*, *svabhava*); once this assumption was bracketed, the road was cleared for the experience of "emptiness" (*sunya*, *sunyata*), which, in turn, is a concomitant of soteriological freedom. This self-deflation has proved a significant stimulus to Buddhist-Christian dialogue in recent decades. As the Japanese Buddhist Masao Abe has pointed out with great astuteness and eloquence, a crucial link between Buddhist and Christian teachings can be found in the Pauline notion of *kenosis* or "self-emptying," the doctrine that Christ "emptied himself" of his divine essence or self-nature in order to share and redeem the lives of mortal sinners:

> I realize that the *kenosis* of God is a crucial issue for our dialogue. Is it not that the *kenosis* of Christ—that is, the self-emptying of the Son of God—has its origin in God "the Father," that is, the *kenosis* of God? Without the self-emptying of God "the Father," the self-emptying of the Son of God is inconceivable. In the case of Christ, *kenosis* is realized in the fact that one

who was in the form of God emptied himself and assumed the form of a servant. . . . In the case of God, *kenosis* is implied in the original "nature" of God which is love.[15]

Given its traditional emphasis on freedom and emancipation, Buddhism seems to be well equipped to provide inspiration for a liberation perspective, even liberation movements, in our time. Moreover, in light of the accent on self-emptying or self-deflation, this impulse seems to be relatively free of the modernist conundrums of anthropocentrism or a self-constituted revolutionary agency (or subjectivity). However, things are more complicated; the very denial of self-nature (*svabhava*) appears to obstruct rather than further any viable conception of concrete human liberation. For, one may ask: in the absence of self or self-nature, who or what would be the subject or agent of liberation? Who or what is going to be liberated in a process of enlightenment seen as an exit from delusion? Questions like these, to be sure, are not new and have accompanied and prodded Buddhist reflections for centuries. In the eyes of many Western observers, the focus on emptiness and self-deflation has earned Buddhism the reputation of a doctrine of world-denial and pessimistic retreat. Schopenhauer interpreted the deflation of selfhood and subjective will—even to the point of pessimistic withdrawal—as a praiseworthy feature of Eastern thought, enabling it to counter Western Promethean ambitions. Nietzsche, by contrast, held that the same deflation signaled a lapse into debilitating nihilism, that must be overcome by a new world-affirmation and the celebration of human will to power.

The questions surrounding a "selfless" liberation have not escaped the attention of Buddhist thinkers and religious leaders. In fact, Buddhist reflections on the topic provide some of the most innovative and stimulating contributions to contemporary liberation debates.[16] Nevertheless, practical considerations or concerns frequently override the task of theoretical elaboration. Under the impact of (post)colonial struggles and/or the pressure of modernizing agendas, many non-Western societies in recent times have witnessed the emergence of Buddhist-inspired and Buddhist-led movements dedicated to the goal of social change and the removal of oppressive inequities. In their study on *Engaged Buddhism*, subtitled *Buddhist Liberation Movements in Asia*, Christopher Queen and Sallie King have assembled impressive evidence testifying to a widespread stirring of social and political consciousness in Asian societies that flatly contradicts Buddhism's reputation of social escapism or world-denial. A crucial ingredient of this upsurge is a redefinition of the traditional Buddhist notion of suffering (*dukkha*) and its overcoming that shifts attention to social and political causes of human suffering and the possibility of their correction or removal. Queen finds that it is precisely a "new awareness of the social and institutional dimensions of suffering and the liberation from suffering" that has provided fuel for the rise of contemporary Buddhist liberation movements. In light of the focus on socially or politically induced misery, liberation movements also have to shoulder the task of social organization and mobilization, transgressing the confines of individual enlightenment.[17]

Yet caution is indicated at this point. As Queen fully recognizes, the phenomenon of "Buddhist liberation movements" investigated in his text does not merely affect Buddhist teachings in a marginal or tangential way. The idea of such movements, he acknowledges, involves a "profound change in Buddhist soteriology" from "a highly personal and otherworldly notion of liberation to a social, economic, this-worldly liberation." This change implicates other traditional features of Buddhism, including the concept of "karma and rebirth," the veneration of the "*bhikkhu sangha*" (monastic community), and the focus on "ignorance and psychological attachment to account for suffering in the world." Under the auspices of the new movements, these traditional features have taken "second place" to a concentration on "the institutional and political manifestations of greed, hatred, and delusion" and "new organizational strategies for addressing war and injustice, poverty and intolerance."[18] The question that arises here concerns the "Buddhist" character of these movements. If liberation movements become completely embroiled in "this-worldly" struggles and activities, what happens to the liberating transcendence of such embroilment? If Buddhist "engagement" denotes the wholehearted pursuit of worldly ends by any means, what happens to such traditional virtues as nonattachment, nonviolence, and compassion? More sharply phrased: If Buddhist movements completely adopt the strategies and modus operandi of other ("secular") organizations, the distinctive "Buddhist" label becomes redundant and can readily be dropped.

As historical experience teaches, the hazards of politicization are multiple and cannot be ignored; problems emerge for both politics and religion. In politics, there is the danger of a religious "dogmatization" of public life, the polarization of society into "good" and "evil" (here *dhammic* and *adhammic*) portions. Religion's main issue is the integrity of religious-philosophical teachings. In the context of developing societies today, Buddhism, like other religions, faces the lure of social cooptation, which, in its milder forms, may involve adaptation of beliefs to the yardsticks of modern consumerism and capitalist free enterprise, leading to a "marketing" of religion. In its more virulent manifestations, cooptation involves surrender to the ideological blueprints of a chauvinistic nationalism that completely negates any lingering trace of nonattachment and nonviolence. In his study *Buddhism Betrayed?* Stanley Tambiah has vividly portrayed the dismal effects of nationalist intoxication on Sinhalese Buddhism in Sri Lanka. As Tambiah shows, Sri Lankan Buddhism was initially mobilized politically to counter Western colonialism and the panoply of internal and external threats in the region. In its early phase, this mobilization mainly had an educational character, manifest in the creation of Buddhist universities and the elevation of Sinhala to official language. Subsequently, however, political rhetoric increasingly seeped into Buddhist discourse, finally submerging the latter in nationalistic frenzy. The "primary slogans" for monks as well as laity, Tambiah comments, became the "unity and sovereignty of the motherland"; what was left was a "militant, populist, fetishized" Buddhism that, stripped of traditional meanings, served merely as a "marker of crowd and mob identity" and an "instigator of spurts of violence."[19]

Political mobilization does not necessarily have this outcome, however. Pursued with sobriety and integrity, religious liberation initiatives can have a salutary effect both religiously and sociopolitically by reawakening society to the demands of social equity or justice, which may be stifled by prevailing class divisions as well as by religious dogmatism and clerical elitism. In order to promote this salutary outcome, however, attention must be given to both the theoretical and the practical dimensions of liberation; most importantly, care must be taken to differentiate or distance religion (and philosophy) from totalizing political ideologies or blueprints. In the case of Buddhism, this involves a careful reassessment of the concept of nonattachment or nonattached action, an agency that is wedded to social service yet remains unattached to selfish gain or the lure of power and dominion. With specific regard to liberation, this reassessment brings back into view the idea of a "double gesture" of affirmation and transcendence of constitutive agency: in traditional Mahayana terminology, the project of a "self-emptying" of emptiness itself (*sunyata sunyata*). Two prominent intellectual initiatives, one taken from Japanese Zen Buddhism, the other from the Theravada school in Thailand, illustrate the meaning of this kind of liberation.

Apart from being a major voice in Buddhist-Christian conversation during recent decades, Masao Abe has also made important contributions both to the praxis and the theoretical clarification of "liberation" in the Buddhist context. On the level of praxis or practical engagement, Abe has been actively involved in a loosely structured lay movement called the "F.A.S. Society" (dedicated to the "awakening of the formless self" everywhere), which had been initiated by one of his teachers, Hisamatsu Shin'ichi. This lay movement was meant to transgress the traditional Zen focus on monastic practices and private individual illumination in favor of a concern for social transformation on both the domestic and global levels; in order to promote this transformation, the liberation of people from oppression and injustice, lay Buddhists had to be ready to serve as emancipatory agents, without, however, embracing the modernist premises of anthropocentrism or sovereign self-constitution. Faithful to central Buddhist teachings, Hisamatsu thus championed liberation in a loosely "postmodern" sense by embracing the double gesture of affirmation and transcendence manifest in the liberating role of an unattached or "formless self" liberating people from both oppression and self-delusion. As a participant in and occasional spokesman of this lay society, Masao Abe has pursued his teacher's path, as is evident in some of his own practical-political statements. As he observes in an essay postulating a new "cosmology" or global awakening, humankind today must assert its supremacy over traditional power politics; however, this supremacy must itself be based on "self-negation" and take "wisdom and compassion as its principles" rather than the usual *libido dominandi*. Only in this way will it be possible to fashion an "ethics of mankind" beyond anthropocentrism that renders humans fully responsible to each other and to the nonhuman (ecological) universe.[20]

On a more theoretical or philosophical plane, Abe has made significant strides toward the formulation of a liberating, yet not substantializing or essentializing, agency. In his exchange with Christian and Jewish theologians, Abe developed the intriguing notion of an affirmative and dynamic *sunyata*, an emptiness that transcends or transmutes itself in the direction of a compassionate social engagement. As he noted at the time, *sunyata* cannot be conceived as a mere vacuum or pure negativity hovering outside plenary being, an antithesis standing "somewhere outside of or beyond one's self-existence." Construed in this manner, emptiness quickly turns into a distinct, though negative, entity or substance juxtaposed with the array of positive (ontic) substances. In the tradition of Mahayana Buddhism, efforts have always been made to guard against this substantializing danger. Abe perceives here a parallel between Mahayana Buddhism and strands in recent Western philosophy. "Following Martin Heidegger," he writes, who put "a cross mark X" on the term "being" (*Sein*), Buddhists are well advised to put a cross mark on *sunyata*, thereby highlighting its intrinsic ambivalence without erasing it. Once this is done, *sunyata* can be located neither inside nor outside of being or "self-existence," for it occupies a terrain that is "neither external nor internal, neither transcendent nor immanent." This insight, in turn, allows *sunyata* to be seen as a dynamic process of transformation, a continual transgression of self-being toward nonexternal otherness. Such a process, however, implies existential engagement:

> We are *sunyata* at each and every moment of our lives. For true *sunyata* is not *sunyata* thought by us, but lived by us. In this living realization of true

*sunyata*, self and *sunyata* are dynamically identical [or entwined]. . . . And this dynamic identity [entwinement] of self and *sunyata* is equally true of everyone and everything throughout the universe. Consequently, although the term *sunyata* may sound negative, it has positive, soteriological meanings.[21]

As a mode of existential engagement, *sunyata* has clear implications for human agency and its role in social liberation. Given the close entwinement of inside and outside, Abe's liberation cannot be confined to solitary enlightenment and must include struggle against avoidable social ills. At this point, self-awakening and enlightenment reveal their intimate connection with social service and the still broader arena of compassion (*karuna*) with all living beings. *Sunyata* properly understood harbors within itself a deep compassion through which existing forms of oppression or domination can be "freely turned over," or at least alleviated. Invoking the classical doctrine of "dependent co-arising" (*pratityasamutpada*), Abe interprets emptiness as a pathway not to solitary self-withdrawal but to an understanding of existential mutuality, the realization of "the sympathetic universality and the cosmic solidarity of *karma*." Regarding agency as a corollary of *karma*, he boldly proposes a "kenotic" rendering of human willing and acting—a reformulation that both preserves and transcends human initiative by embedding the latter in the framework of emptiness. Free will as a source of agency is clearly "one's own free will"; and yet, it also empties itself into the "free will of *sunyata*." Conversely, happenings in the world are thoroughly *sunyata*'s doing, but they are also the result of human agency and design. According to Abe, the connection of willing and not willing (or un-willing) forms the basis of the Buddhist "vow" or engagement in the world (*pranidhana*). At its core, this is the pledge "to save others, however innumerable they may be, as well as one's self," a pledge in which "the mind to seek enlightenment and the desire to save all sentient beings are dynamically one."[22]

In may ways, Abe's initiatives find a parallel in Thai Buddhism, particularly in the lifework and teachings of Ajarn Buddhadasa, also known as Buddhadasa Bhikkhu. Like Abe, Buddhadasa has always insisted on the need to (re)connect theoretical insights with the domain of lived praxis. Reflecting this conviction, one of his central efforts has been rendering Buddhism meaningful to ordinary people, an aim which put him at odds with both clerical monastic hierarchies and ruling power structures and prevailing state ideologies. To further the goal of radical renewal, in 1932 Buddhadasa established a center (a forest retreat) for the study and concrete practice of Buddhism that came to be known as Suan Mokkh or "Garden of Liberation." Initially inhabited by only a small group of followers, the center attracted a steadily growing number of visitors from all echelons of the monastic and lay communities in Thailand, thus emerging as a seedbed of spiritual and social reform. It was at Suan Mokkh that Buddhadasa first articulated some of his more overtly sociopolitical ideas that were subsequently promulgated on lecture tours throughout the country. Foremost among them is the concept of a Buddhist or "Dhammic Socialism" meant to contrast with both Western capitalism, with its celebration of private profit, and Soviet communism, with its glorification of totalitarian state power. For Buddhadasa, "Dhammic Socialism" is a form of democracy—but a democracy respectful of the spiritual authority of *dhamma* (or *dharma*) and mindful of the continuous need for human self-transformation.[23]

In his religious-philosophical teachings, Buddhadasa recognizes the centrality in Buddhism of the four "noble truths" with their focus on suffering (*dukkha*) and its removal. As previously indicated, suffering is commonly traced to wanton desire and self-delusion. Deviating from traditional construals, Buddhadasa views desire as including both individual wantonness and the craving for social-political status, power or dominion, which Buddhism is meant to cure. The Buddhist striving for enlightenment and liberation from suffering thus extends from private life to the arena of social or "worldly" arrangements.[24] Although trained in the Theravada tradition, Buddhadasa's thoughts on liberation are quite flexible and freely embrace a number of Mahayana and Zen concepts, including no-self-nature (*anatman* or *anatta*) and emptiness (*sunyata* or *sunnata*). As for Abe, emptiness is not a static entity but a dynamic transformer: precisely by virtue of no-self-nature, individuals as well as societies can detach themselves from stifling habits or ingrained power structures and embark on the process of moral experimentation and liberating renewal. Buddhadasa, as does Abe, recognizes the role of agency in this process while giving it a Buddhist or *"dhammic"* cast. Although taken by itself agency is not properly liberating (but only *karma*-producing in a confining way), nonattached or self-transcending action can pave the road to genuine freedom (or *nibbana*). In this context, Buddhadasa also reformulates the concept of "dependent co-arising" (*paticca-samuppada* in its Pali version) by extricating it from a doctrinaire *karma*-wheel. Inserted into concrete social life, "co-arising" means that removal of oppression cannot occur through private self-withdrawal but only through the cooperative struggle and reform that is the heart of "Dhammic Socialism."[25]

## IV

Among the great world religions today, at first glance none seems less hospitable to liberation than Islamic civilization. In the eyes of many observers, Islam is almost completely identified with a fanatical and "il-liberal" fundamentalism, a "totalizing" political agenda fueled by unexamined religious dogmas or beliefs. Despite undeniable tendencies in this direction, this identification is nevertheless mistaken, at least when placed in a historical context. Although urging human "surrender" to God or the divine, Islam in its long history has never counseled blind surrender to the "powers that be," whether they are clerical or political elites. On the contrary, precisely by differentiating between divine and merely "worldly" rule, Islamic thought has nurtured a suspicion of human power and its proclivity to unjust oppression, which can be a motive for liberation. Both the suspicion and the motive are amply evident in the Qur'an, especially in Suras 1 and 90. While the former exhorts people to pursue the path of justice or righteousness (*zirat al-mustaqim*), the second spells out the direction of this path, now called the path of the "steep ascent." What is this steep ascent? the Sura asks, and responds:

> To free a neck
> (from the burden of debt or slavery),
> Or to feed in times of famine
> The orphan near in relationship,
> or the poor in distress;
> And to be of these who believe,
> and call upon one another to persevere,
> and urge upon each other to be kind.[26]

The seed of liberation is thus planted in the Qur'an, not as a mere corollary or sideline of faith, but as its very point and meaning. The close connection of faith and freedom is corroborated by many other passages in the Qur'an and also by many of the sayings of the Prophet (*hadith*) recorded by his companions. One of the guiding maxims of the Qur'an is the principle "no compulsion in matters of faith" (*la ikhra fid-din*), a maxim that could serve as an appropriate guidepost for all religions. Several recorded sayings attest to the Prophet's intense love of freedom and his abhorrence of arbitrary political domination or oppression. "One who walks with a tyrant," one passage states, "in the full knowledge that he is a tyrant, and in order to strengthen him, . . . has already left the fold of Islam [*dar al-Islam*]." "On the day of judgment, the tyrant's own tyranny will descend upon him in the form of darkness." With regard to religious fanaticism and the indiscriminate blending of faith and power, the Prophet commented to his companions, "He who preaches bigotry is not one of us. . . . And he who dies for such a cause is not one of us either."[27]

Love of freedom and denunciation of oppression are not limited to the

founding period of Islam; in diverse ways, the same attitude has reverber-
ated throughout the historical unfolding of Islamic civilization. A prominent and often memorialized example of this attitude is the great Muslim
mystic Husain ibn Mansur, better known as al-Hallaj. Of modest Persian
origins, al-Hallaj came to live and work in Baghdad, which then was the
seat of a sprawling Muslim empire under the rule of the Abbasid caliphs.
Moving in the inner circles of public life, he experienced with growing
dismay the effects of political corruption and the growing ossification of
religious faith in the hands of orthodox clerical elites. Adopting the
stance of a prophetic critic, al-Hallaj challenged with increasing vehe-
mence both governmental oppression and clerical dogmatism, for which
he was executed, or martyred (922 A.D.), on charges of heresy. Heresy
was his insistence on cutting through legalistic formulas in search of a
more direct and intimate union with the divine. In searching for this
union, al-Hallaj curiously adopted a "kenotic" image of selfhood (without any apparent borrowing from Asian sources), stating, "When God
takes a heart, He empties it of all that is not Himself." Herbert Mason
ably pinpoints the saint's outlook: "Clearly the Hallajan way implies a
certain surrender of self, an expatriation of mind, an absorption with the
life and spirit of another than oneself." This surrender is at the same time
a source of affirmation and enabling empowerment: "Friendship and fidelity are its keynotes and infectuously become those of others who come
to know him."[28]

Today this legacy of prophetic liberty is under siege in many parts of
the Islamic world. Due partly to global pressures and internal political
restrictions, the spirit of liberating and enabling inquiry seems to be less
prevalent than in the past. Annemarie Schimmel, a sympathetic student
of Islam, finds a disturbing tendency toward intellectual closure: "In a
civilization whose traditional greeting is *salam* (peace)," she states, "we
observe at the moment a great narrowing and stiffening of dogmatic and
legalistic positions." In lieu of the search for spiritual enrichment and a
closer union with the divine, "we are confronted in large areas with sheer
power politics, with ideologies which utilize Islam more or less as a catch-
word, and have very little in common with its religious foundations."[29]
Nevertheless, despite this troubling tendency, the potential of liberating
Islamic faith is by no means vanquished or extinguished today, although
it is often sidelined or put on the defensive; there are important voices in
contemporary Islam testifying to the continuing legacy of both religious
and philosophical renewal. In the following, two such voices will be highlighted, one taken from a Sunni context, the other from the context of
Shiism.

An Algerian expatriate teaching at the Sorbonne in Paris, Mohammed
Arkoun is the author of numerous books and essays on the contemporary

significance of Islam. By all accounts, he is one of the most subtle and sophisticated interpreters both of Islam and of the present-day intellectual scene in the West. In his writings and lectures, Arkoun has placed himself in sharp opposition to clerical dogmatism and elitism, exhorting Muslim intellectuals to become active participants in debates concerning the present condition and future prospects of the evolving global village. While adopting a "liberal" stance of openmindedness, his writings have also been critical of certain routinely, or dogmatically, held liberal predilections, especially those for an agnostic secularism and market-centered politics. According to Robert Lee, one of his English translators, Arkoun's lifework has always addressed a question crucial to both Muslims and non-Muslims in the contemporary world: the proper relation between self and other, or how can people "be thoroughly themselves without isolating themselves, by virtue of this identity, from their neighbors and the rest of humanity"? In wrestling with this question, Arkoun is situated at the crossroads of (Western) modernity and postmodernity, tradition and renewal, and (philosophical or scientific) reason and faith. While challenging the presumed self-sufficiency of modern reason, he also refuses himself the comfort of a self-enclosed religious particularism. In pursuing this course, Lee comments, Arkoun attempts to navigate through "dangerous shoals" between "a Western universalism that tends to marginalize the entire Islamic tradition" and "an Islamic resurgence that puts itself at odds not only with Western tradition but also with the Islamic tradition as most Muslims have understood it for the past fourteen centuries." Rekindled as a partner in the conversation of humankind, Islam reemerges as a "liberal" or liberating faith—provided that (Western) liberalism itself sheds its imperial or triumphalist aura.[30]

Arkoun's views are most readily accessible to English-speakers in the stimulating volume *Rethinking Islam: Common Questions, Uncommon Answers*. In his introduction, Arkoun lucidly profiles his general intellectual stance. His basic aim has been, and continues to be, to "liberate" discourse on Islam from dogmatic limitations and contradictions, especially from an approach that tends to "enclose and marginalize Islam in 'specificity,' particularism, and singularities." Although largely ignored in the West, such a liberating impulse is by no means lacking in Islam. In fact, alongside the fundamentalist tendencies "so obligingly observed, reported, and echoed in the Western media," there exists a "liberal, critical Islam open to change, an Islam still little known and rarely taken into consideration." Venturing into this hidden Islam requires an effort to stir up frozen or congealed thought patterns; as Arkoun explains (with phrasing vaguely reminiscent of Heidegger), it requires a retrieval of the "unthought" in traditional Islamic thought. Such retrieval, in turn, is predicated on an emancipatory premise: breaking new ground not only

in Islam but in the three monotheistic religions depends on "the liberation of thought from all theories, dogmas, and imageries bestowed by the
self-founding and self-proclaiming theologies of each community against
its rivals." To some extent, this liberation or emancipation is patterned
after the Western Enlightenment model—but with a twist that problema-
tizes this model by insisting on the mutual embroilment of universal/
particular, or global/local, polarities. Reflecting on recent intellectual
trends in the West, Arkoun sees the need and the opportunity to shift the
understanding of Islam from the purely epistemic level, what Foucault
called the "historico-transcendental theme," to "the level of postmodern
reason which has become critical of Enlightenment reasoning itself." He
remarks pointedly, "I believe Islam will not escape the upheavals of postmodernism."[31]

The implications of this emancipatory perspective are detailed in subsequent chapters of *Rethinking Islam*. Liberating faith, especially a socially and politically engaged faith, needs to be carefully distinguished
from the vogue of "fundamentalism" marked by the indiscriminate fusion of religion and politics and the ultimate surrender of faith to power
objectives. Arkoun's book differentiates between a properly religious or
"mythical" discourse and a purely "ideological" discourse intent on in-
strumentalizing religion. Contemporary fundamentalist movements, he
notes, owe their partial success to the availability of impoverished and
frustrated masses of people "still sensitive to Messianic promises and eschatological expectations." In enlisting these sentiments, fundamentalist
strategies tend to have corrosive and even "devastating effects" on religious faith by promoting "ideological" platforms that slyly substitute
"unrealizable political programs" for the "millenary, transhistorical
hopes" of the past. This substitution was particularly evident in Kho-
meini's so-called "Islamic revolution" in Iran; here the confusion between "mythical religious discourse" and a "mobilizing, desanctifying
ideological discourse" reached the greatest height of "mobilizational efficacy," while also spreading its destructive impact on the "semantic ordering of the community." As opposed to ideological-fundamentalist
mobilization, liberation must tap deeper religious resources located beyond, and even repressed by, sheer power politics. The idea of reflective
retrieval becomes crucial. In Arkoun's words: "The *unthought* and the
*unthinkable* in Islamic thought have been accumulating ever since ideologies of struggle for political liberation took over the *whole* of the social
arena." What is needed to regain access to these repressed domains is a
critical awareness capable of critiquing itself (a kind of double gesture):
We need to enter a new phase where critical thought—"anchored in modernity but criticizing modernity itself and contributing to its enrichment
through recourse to the Islamic example"—would "accompany, or even

for once precede, political action, economic decisions, and great social movements."[32]

As these comments indicate, Arkoun's liberation is at odds both with religious fundamentalism and an agnostic power politics that is often wedded to a dogmatically affirmed "secularism." Focusing on the latter issue, *Rethinking Islam* calls attention to the emergence of modern Turkey under the leadership of Atatürk. In charting Turkey's course, Atatürk sought a radical rupture with the past: by replacing the sultanate with the nation-state, the Arabic with the Latin alphabet, the turban and fez with the hat, and the Shari'a with the Swiss legal code. In Arkoun's view, however, Atatürk's understanding of both Islam and Western modernity was highly defective and in fact reflected the "naïve state of consciousness" prevalent among Muslim intellectuals during the heyday of colonialism. These "generations believed naïvely that it was enough to take the 'prescriptions' for the success of Western civilization and apply them to Muslim countries." Among other panaceas, secularism was perceived as one of the "effective prescriptions" designed to cure backward societies of their religious traditions. Later emulated by many nation-builders in the Third World, Atatürk's "revolution" installed an ideological elitism disdainful of sedimented symbols; for Arkoun, it signaled "the triumph of positivist, historicist reason, radically cut off from the mythic consciousness in which the great mass of believers, ulema and illiterate alike, continued to move." In its long-range repercussions, it opened a breach between revolutionary leaders and the masses they claimed to emancipate that severely "impaired the symbolic capital cultivated by the living tradition."

In this context Arkoun carefully distinguishes between "open-minded secular thought" and dogmatic "secularism" and agnosticism. While the former can be valuable in preserving the integrity of religion and politics, the latter is liable to yield indifference and even illiteracy regarding important well-springs of popular culture and belief: It is "secularist thought," which, "on the pretext of neutrality," has eliminated from public schools all instruction in "the history of religions understood as a permanent and universal dimension of human societies." As a result, the general public has become "illiterate in all that touches religious life and expression" and thus incapable of thinking about "myth, symbols, symbolic capital."[33]

In our time, the liberating potential of Islam has been articulated not only by expatriate scholars like Arkoun, but also by Muslim intellectuals active in their homelands, where their work has often exposed them to political ostracism or persecution. A prominent case in point is the Iranian intellectual and sociologist Ali Shari'ati who lived and struggled, often from a prison cell, during the Shah's reign and died in 1977 shortly before the Iranian revolution, presumably at the hands of the Shah's agents. Educated in Iran and in Paris, Shari'ati was an astute observer and critic of modern Western and of traditional Muslim society and culture. Although appreciating the freedom of inquiry and individual initiative promoted by Western modernity, he was appalled by, and fiercely attacked, the Western propensity toward materialism, consumerism, and secularist anthropocentrism; at the same time, he had no sympathy for clerical traditionalism, and certainly not for any kind of "fundamentalism" that exploited religious beliefs for purely mundane objectives of political power. Against these diverse tendencies or temptations, Shari'ati invoked the liberating energies of a critically self-reflective Islamic faith, which, in his view, were alone capable of moving people and effecting genuine human and social transformation. In the words of one of his biographers, Shari'ati fought "on two fronts simultaneously": "He opposed the extreme traditionalists who had spun a web around themselves, separated Islam from society, retreated into a corner of the mosque and the madrasa, and often reacted negatively to any kind of intellectual movement within society." But he also challenged the "rootless and imitative intellectuals" who had made "the new scholasticism," that combined positivism, secularism, and materialism, their stronghold. Both groups, the biographer adds, had "severed their relations with society and the masses of the people" and ultimately "bowed their heads before the manifestations of corruption and decadence" of the age.[34]

For Shari'ati, genuine liberation can proceed only from spiritual or religious impulses—provided they are not corrupted for worldly aims. Among world religions, he finds the great virtue of monotheism precisely in its liberating or emancipatory élan. Whereas the founders of other religions almost immediately turned to secular power in the hope of propagating their message by means of that power, monotheism operates differently: "All the prophets of the Abrahamic line," he asserts, "from Abraham down to the Prophet of Islam, proclaim their missions in the form of rebellion against the secular power." As Shari'ati realizes, even in monotheistic religions this liberating spirit was subsequently subdued through policies of compromise and accommodation. In Judaism, the original message of Moses came under the spell of "rabbis and Pharisees" aligned with worldly elites, just as Christianity, after an initial period of persecution, succeeded to "the throne of the Roman Empire," thereby "perpetuating the imperial order." Even Islam, after a time of struggle, was later reshaped by imperialistic caliphates, turning into a "rationale for the acts of the most savage conquerors" and a cloak for the "feudal order of the Saljuqs and Mongols." In Shari'ati's account, the basic reason for this decay or contamination is the transformation of religion from a path into a fixed doctrine or destination: Religion is nothing but a path "laid down from clay to God," of "an infinite migration" and inner transformation. Historically, all the ills afflicting religious societies arise from the fact that "religion has changed its spirit and direction" by becoming a destination rather than a road. Shari'ati strongly indicts the clerical establishment of his country:

> You have made the path a place of recreation, you have turned the highway into some sort of sacred park or clubhouse. Look at the Shi'a. In their belief, the Imam is a person who leads and guides them. But he has become for them, in effect, a sacred and invisible essence, a suprahuman entity to be praised and worshipped and extolled, but nothing else![35]

Shari'ati's strongest affirmation of Islam as a liberating message, or a theology of liberation, occurs in his essay "The Philosophy of History: Cain and Abel." The story of Cain and Abel provides the key to a profound "philosophy of history" propelled by the conflict of two opposing elements in the form of an evolving "dialectic." The drama begins with the killing of Abel by Cain, where Abel represents "the age of a pasture-based economy" and of "the primitive socialism that preceded ownership," and Cain represents "the system of agriculture and individual or monopoly ownership." Following this opening event, history evolved as a struggle involving economics, and political power, as well as religion. As Shari'ati notes, Abel the pastoralist was killed by Cain the landowner; with this murder, the period of "common ownership of the sources of production," the age of pastoralism, hunting and fishing and also that of "brotherhood and true faith," came to an end and was replaced by the establishment of the system of private ownership "together with religious trickery and transgression against the rights of others." During the pastoral age, nature was the source of all production and placed her bounty at the disposal of all. Morally or religiously, social life was pervaded by "paternal respect," "steadfastness in fulfilling obligations," "sincerity of religious conscience," and a "pacific spirit of love and forbearance." All this changed with the introduction of agriculture and private ownership of land. Shari'ati comments, in a quasi-Rousseauan vein, that human and social life were "exposed to a profound revolution which, in my view, constitutes the greatest revolution in history." It "produced a new man, a powerful and evil man, as well as the age of civilization and discrimination."[36]

Over time, the revolution brought a radical and far-reaching change in moral and religious attitudes. With the advent of property, the earlier ties of kinship were replaced by "bonds of servitude," while equality was sacrificed to discrimination and brotherhood to fratricide; likewise, the earlier spirit of "humanity, conciliatoriness, and compassion" gave way

to the passions of "hatred, rivalry, oppression, and self-worship." Shari'-
ati also perceives this change as the upsurge of two different human personality types: Abel "the man of faith, peaceable and self-sacrificing"
opposing Cain "the worshipper of passions, the transgressor, the fratricide." The conflict of personalities is not a difference of "human nature,"
but rather a difference of social and moral contexts. Abel was a man of
"sound disposition" because an inhuman social and economic system
had not yet "alienated, disfigured, perverted or polluted him"; though
born of the same parents, Cain responded to evil propensities unleashed
by "an anti-human social system, a class society, a regime of private ownership that cultivates slavery and mastery and turns men into wolves,
foxes or sheep." *Pace* Freud, the difference is not that Cain's libidinal
instincts were inherently stronger than those of others, but that the cultivation of human virtues was stifled in his situation. During ensuing centuries, history testifies to the struggle between the descendants of Abel,
those oppressed people who throughout history have been "slaughtered
and enslaved" by power, and the "system of Cain" that has always been
upheld by the ruling classes. Contrary to Marx's theory, this conflict involves not only a class struggle but also a struggle of morals and religions.
For Shari'ati, the crucial historical battle is not between religion and irre-
ligion, or knowledge and superstition but "the war of religion against
religion":

> There has existed throughout human history, and there will continue to
> exist until the last day, a struggle between the religion of deceit, stupefaction
> and justification of the status quo and the religion of awareness, activism
> and revolution. The end of time will come when Cain dies and the "system
> of Abel" is established anew. That inevitable revolution will mean the end
> of the history of Cain; equality will be realized throughout the world, and
> human unity and brotherhood will be established through equity and jus-
> tice.[37]

Given its aspiration toward human brother- and sisterhood, commitment to the liberating faith of Abel also implies a liberation from the
shackles of religious sectarianism, and hence an openness to interreli-
gious goodwill and understanding. This openness is clearly illustrated by
the traditions of Sufism and *bhakti* religiosity on the Indian subcontinent
for which Shari'ati shows considerable empathy.[38] Over long stretches of
time, this legacy of popular religiosity in India, while contrary to the
dictates of clerical elites, has encouraged Muslims and Hindus to live in
peace. Among contemporary Muslim leaders, this outlook is well exemplified by the Maulana Wahiduddin Khan, director of the Centre for Islamic Studies in Delhi. For many years, the Maulana has acted as the

spokesman of an open-minded, conciliatory, and freedom-loving Islam, a religious posture carefully guarding itself against political co-optation and manipulation. In his readiness to insert Islam into the broader conversation of humankind, the Maulana has aligned himself with the path taken earlier by such "progressive" Indian or South Asian Muslims as Syyed Ahmad Khan and Muhammad Iqbal. Iqbal, half a century ago, had pleaded for a "reconstruction of religious thought in Islam" as an antidote to clerical elitism and legalistic orthodoxy. Under the combined influence of the mystical Sufi tradition and partly of Western "life philosophy," Iqbal charted a course that cautiously sought to revitalize Islamic faith while screening it against both fundamentalist abuse and modernist, or "secularist," indifference. Whereas Iqbal ultimately cast his lot with the new "Islamic" state of Pakistan, Wahiduddin Khan carries on his lifework on the more difficult terrain of modern India often marked these days by the violent clash of competing fundamentalisms.

In the midst of these conflicts, the Maulana's Centre has been spreading the message of a gentle, nonmilitant religious piety which—like that of Arkoun—is willing to respect a secular politics animated by "open-minded, secular thought," while resisting a "secularist" myopia. In an essay titled "Religion and Politics," the Maulana has pondered the condition of both India and Pakistan since the partitioning of the subcontinent. Both countries have in recent decades been in the grip of a contest between secular and religious agendas, the latter aiming to seize political or governmental power—if necessary, by force. In Pakistan the religious agenda is termed "Nizam-e-Mustafa," and in India it is named "Ramrajya" (and more recently "Hindutva"). In Khan's view, these forms of religious mobilization are misguided in the worldwide context of progressive democratization; in fact, they are counterproductive by undermining the integrity of religious faith. "What has come into being," he writes, "and what is going to be achieved in the effort to consolidate the position of religion is in no way a religious system, but is rather a course of destruction" adding to the "general ruination" of social and political life. Precisely from the angle of religious faith, ideological mobilization presents a grave danger; hence neither the "Hinduization" of India nor the "Islamization" of Pakistan can be a desirable goal.

In another essay, the Maulana distinguishes between two methods for bringing about change: one by revolutionary violence, the other by persuasion or exhortation (*da'wa*). Aligning himself with the path of exhortation, the Maulana sternly rebukes militant or fundamentalist Muslims "who are everywhere to be found in armed encounters with their supposed rivals." The basic difference of methods is that between a willful striving for power and a "self-emptying" liberation from injustice: "Where revolution calls for precipitateness, *da'wa* advises patience, caution. Where revolutionary acts earn one popularity, *da'wa* leads one into self-obliteration and the readiness to be the target of others' stones."[39] In taking this position, Wahiduddin Khan stands in the tradition of several generations of nonmilitant Muslim intellectuals in India that can actually be traced back much further in Indian history, to the time of popular Puranas and the great "poet saints." The weaver Kabir is one of these saints; his work stands at the crossroads of faith, between Islamic Sufism and Hindu *bhakti*. Although presumably of Muslim background, Kabir alienated himself from the reigning clerical establishment; while living among Hindus in Benares, his lifestyle did not endear him to Brahmanic elites. This alienation is clearly reflected in one of his poems:

> Hindus, Muslims—where did they come from?
>     Who got them started down this road?
> Search inside, search your heart and look:
>     Who made heaven come to be?
> Fool, now
>     Throw away that book, and sing of Ram [God] alone.

The intended impact of Kabir's poetry is liberating or emancipatory—but not in a modernist or secularist sense; liberation here works through and for faith:

> If caste was what the Creator had in mind,
>     Why wasn't anyone born
>     with Shiva's three-lined sign?
> If you're a Brahman,
>     from a Brahman woman born,
>     why didn't you come out some special way?
> And if you're a Muslim,
>     from a Muslim woman born,
>     why weren't you circumcised inside?
> Says Kabir: No one is lowly born.
>     The only lowly ones are those
>     who never talk of Ram.[40]

# Notes

1. Bartolomé de Las Casas, *Historia de las Indias*, in *Obras escogidas*, vol. 2, ed. J. Pérez de Tudela (Madrid: Biblioteca de Autores Españoles, 1957), p. 511. The English translation is taken from Gustavo Gutiérrez, *Las Casas: In Search of the Poor of Jesus Christ*, trans. Robert R. Barr (Maryknoll, N.Y.: Orbis

Books, 1993), p. 62. Regarding Sepúlveda's position compare this statement: "To correct human beings caught in a most dangerous error, who are headed straight for damnation whether knowingly or out of ignorance, and to bring them to salvation is an obligation of natural and divine law and a duty that all persons of good will would wish to perform even toward those who might not wish them to. He is no Christian, then, who doubts that they will die an everlasting death who wander about at a distance from the Christian religion. It is right, then, to force the barbarians, for their salvation, into the way of justice." See Juan Ginés de Sepúlveda, *Apologia* (Madrid: Editoria Nacional, 1975), p. 65; English translation taken from Gutierrez, *Las Casas*, p. 250.

2. Paul Ricoeur, *Political and Social Essays*, ed. David Stewart and Joseph Bien (Athens, Ohio: Ohio University Press, 1974), pp. 121, 197. He adds soberly, "Even today, however, all the churches still have far more political influence than is warranted by their religious faith. . . . The illusion that we are still living in a Christian era is a formidable hypocrisy which poisons the political life of the West: the so-called 'Christian' parties, 'Christian' trade unions, and the influence of clericalism form a heritage which it is not easy to get rid of. . . . When it emerges from this illusion, the church will be able to give light once more to all men—no longer as a power, but as a prophetic message" (p. 123).

3. As I see it, this question is the motivating impulse behind Max Horkheimer's and Theodor W. Adorno's *Dialectic of Enlightenment*, trans. John Cumming (first German ed. 1947; New York: Herder & Herder, 1972). The same motivation animated Martin Heidegger's critique of modern technology under the rubric of "enframing" or *Gestell*; see his *The Question Concerning Technology and Other Essays*, trans. William Lovitt (New York: Harper & Row, 1977).

4. Regarding this blurred boundary compare J. L. Mehta, "Beyond Believing and Knowing," in *India and the West: The Problem of Understanding* (Chico, Calif.: Scholars Press, 1985), pp. 202–220. See also Emmanuel Levinas, *Totality and Infinity*, trans. Alphonso Lingis (Pittsburgh, Pa.: Duquesne University Press, n.d.), p. 39.

5. To a considerable extent, this binary conception is still operative in Jürgen Habermas's work; see especially his *Toward a Rational Society*, trans. Jeremy J. Shapiro (Boston: Beacon Press, 1970) and *Knowledge and Human Interests*, trans. Jeremy J. Shapiro (Boston: Beacon Press, 1971). The primacy of negative liberty has been particularly vindicated or championed by Isaiah Berlin in his "Two Concepts of Liberty," in *Four Essays on Liberty* (New York: Oxford University Press, 1969), pp. 118–172.

6. Martin Heidegger, "Vom Wesen der Wahrheit," in *Wegmarken* (Frankfurt-Main: Klostermann, 1967), pp. 81, 90. For an English translation (by John Sallis) see David F. Krell, ed., *Martin Heidegger: Basic Writings* (New York: Harper & Row, 1977), pp. 125, 133–134. Freedom in the essay is by no means rooted in a subject-centered or anthropocentric agency, nor in the simple negation of agency. As Heidegger insists: "Freedom is not merely what common sense is content to let pass under this name: the caprice manifest occasionally in our choosing or inclining in this or that direction. Freedom is not mere absence of constraint with respect to what we can or cannot do. Nor is it on the other hand

mere readiness for what is required and necessary. . . . Prior to all this ('negative' and 'positive' freedom), freedom is the engagement in the disclosure of beings as such." See *Wegmarken*, p. 84; Krell, *Martin Heidegger: Basic Writings*, p. 128. Compare also my "Ontology of Freedom: Heidegger and Political Philosophy," in *Polis and Praxis* (Cambridge, Mass.: MIT Press, 1984), pp. 104–132. Regarding "entwinement" (or "intertwining") see Maurice Merleau-Ponty, *The Visible and the Invisible*, ed. Claude Lefort, trans. Alphonso Lingis (Evanston, Ill.: Northwestern University Press, 1968), pp. 130–155.

7. Jan Nederveen Pieterse, "Emancipations, Modern and Postmodern," *Development and Change* 23 (1992): 6–7, 13, 19, 23–24. He adds: "The main difference between the modern and the postmodern emancipations appears to be that the former situate themselves within the Enlightenment tradition and secondly that they take an instrumental attitude to power, whereas the latter problematize power to a much greater degree" (p. 31).

8. Ernesto Laclau, "Beyond Emancipation," *Development and Change* 23 (1992): 121–123, 125, 131–132, 136–137. The essay is reprinted in Laclau, *Emancipation(s)* (London: Verso, 1996), pp. 1–19. The critique of the notion of a "fully revolutionary foundation"—especially of the status of the proletariat as "universal class" (as it was conceived by Marx and his heirs)—had already been elaborated by Laclau and Chantal Mouffe in their *Hegemony and Socialist Strategy: Towards a Radical Democratic Politics*, trans. Winston Moore and Paul Cammack (London: Verso, 1985).

9. See Ashis Nandy, "Liberation of Those Who Do Not Speak the Language of Liberation," in *Theory and Practice of Liberation at the End of the Twentieth Century*, ed. Lelio Basso International Foundation (Brussels: Bruylant, 1988), pp. 165–173; "Cultural Frames for Social Transformation: A Credo," *Alternatives* 12 (1987): 113–117. Compare also Nandy, *The Intimate Enemy: Loss and Recovery of Self Under Colonialism* (New Delhi: Oxford University Press, 1983). Regarding the notion of "double gesture" see Jacques Derrida, *Positions*, trans. Alan Bass (Chicago: University of Chicago Press, 1981), pp. 41–42.

10. Karl Marx, "Contribution to the Critique of Hegel's *Philosophy of Right*: Introduction," in *The Marx-Engels Reader*, ed. Robert C. Tucker (New York: Norton & Co., 1972), p. 12. As Marx added: "Religion is only the illusory sun about which man revolves so long as he does not revolve about himself."

11. Gustavo Gutierrez, *A Theology of Liberation*, trans. and ed. Sr. Caridad Inda and John Eagleson (Maryknoll, N.Y.: Orbis Books, 1973), pp. 9, 36–37, 176.

12. Gutierrez, *Las Casas: In Search of the Poor of Jesus Christ*, p. 8. See also Jan Pieterse, "Emancipations, Modern and Postmodern," p. 10.

13. Gutierrez, *Las Casas*, pp. 9–11. In a more oblique fashion, a similar shift of paradigms can be found in another Latin American perspective: the so-called "philosophy of liberation" articulated by Enrique Dussell. While initially adhering to a quasi-Marxist doctrine of "dependency" (*dependencia*), Dussell has recently embraced a more prophetic, quasi-religious stance inspired in part by a Levinasian attention to "radical otherness" (as the source of ethical-political demands). See Enrique Dussell, *Philosophy of Liberation*, trans. Aquilina Martinez

and Christine Morkovsky (Maryknoll, N.Y.: Orbis Books, 1985) and *The Invention of the Americas: Eclipse of "the Other" and the Myth of Modernity*, trans. Michel D. Barber (New York: Continuum, 1995). For a critique of some absolutist tendencies in Dussell's work see Ofelia Schutte, *Cultural Identity and Social Liberation in Latin American Thought* (Albany, N.Y.: SUNY Press, 1993), pp. 188–189.

14. See Habermas, *The Philosophical Discourse of Modernity: Twelve Lectures*, trans. Frederick Lawrence (Cambridge, Mass.: MIT Press, 1987), pp. 16–18, 40–43.

15. Masao Abe, "Kenotic God and Dynamic Sunyata," in *The Emptying God: A Buddhist-Jewish-Christian Conversation*, ed. John B. Cobb, Jr. and Christopher Ives (Maryknoll, N.Y.: Orbis Books, 1990), p. 14. Radicalizing his point further, Abe adds, "God is God, not because God had the Son of God take a human form and be sacrificed while God remained God, but because God is a suffering God, a self-sacrificial God through total *kenosis*. The kenotic God who totally empties Godself and totally sacrifices Godself is, in my view, the true God." For the Pauline notion of *kenosis* see Philippians 2:5–8. For other treatments of the Buddhist-Christian dialogue compare Abe, *Buddhism and Interfaith Dialogue*, ed. Steven Heine (Honolulu: University of Hawaii Press, 1995); Ninian Smart, *Buddhism and Christianity: Rivals and Allies* (Honolulu: University of Hawaii Press, 1993); and Paul O. Ingram and Frederick J. Streng, eds., *Buddhist-Christian Dialogue: Mutual Renewal and Transformation* (Honolulu: University of Hawaii Press, 1986).

16. Compare in this context David Loy, "Freedom: A Buddhist Critique," *Journal of the Faculty of International Studies* (Bunkyo University) 6 (1966): 25–34.

17. Christopher S. Queen, introduction to *Engaged Buddhism: Buddhist Liberation Movements in Asia*, ed. Queen and Sallie B. King (Albany, N.Y.: SUNY Press, 1996), p. 10. Several contributors to the volume reflect on the relation between "engaged Buddhism" and Christian liberation theology; see especially pp. 309–312, 350–352.

18. Queen, *Engaged Buddhism* introduction, p. 10.

19. Stanley J. Tambiah, *Buddhism Betrayed? Religion, Politics, and Violence in Sri Lanka* (Chicago: University of Chicago Press, 1992), pp. 91–92.

20. Masao Abe, "Sovereignty Rests with Mankind," in his *Zen and Western Thought*, ed. William R. LaFleur (Honolulu: University of Hawaii Press, 1985), pp. 252–256. On this point, Abe's argument coincides with recent initiatives for the formulation of a global ethics; compare, e.g., Hans Küng, *Global Responsibility: In Search of a New World Ethic* (New York: Crossroad, 1991); and Küng and K.-J. Kuschel, eds., *A Global Ethic: The Declaration of the Parliament of the World's Religions* (New York: Continuum, 1995). See also Abe, "Hisamatsu's Philosophy of Awakening" and "Hisamatsu Shin'ichi, 1889–1980," *The Eastern Buddhist* (n.s.), 14 (1981): 26–42 and 142–147. Regarding Hisamatsu's writings compare, e.g., *Zen and the Fine Arts* (Tokyo: Kodansha International, 1971); *Nothingness* (Kyoto: Association of Self-Awakening, 1957); "Postmodernist Manifesto," *FAS Society Newsletter* 1 (1976); and "For the Postmodernist," *FAS*

*Society Newsletter* 2 (1977). For a general discussion of Hisamatsu and his relation to Abe see Christopher Ives, *Zen Awakening and Society* (Honolulu: University of Hawaii Press, 1992), pp. 69–90, and his introduction to *The Emptying
God*, pp. xiv–xviii.

21. Abe, "Kenotic God and Dynamic Sunyata," in *The Emptying God*, pp.
27–28.

22. *The Emptying God*, pp. 32, 50, 57–58.

23. For some of this background see Santikaro Bhikkhu, "Buddhadasa Bhikkhu: Life and Society through the Natural Eyes of Voidness," in *Engaged Buddhism*, ed. Queen and King, pp. 147–179. Regarding "Dhammic Socialism"
Santikaro writes perceptively, "Ajarn Buddhadasa seemed to try to accomplish
two things here. First, he legitimated socialism as an issue and an approach appropriate to Buddhism, Thai culture, and the current situation. Socialism is not
something to be shunned as Western or foreign, for it can be found in Thailand's
cultural and religious heritage. In fact, it is more appropriate for Thailand than
the Western forms (capitalism, consumerism, technocracy, etc.) currently being
mimicked. Socialism as he understood it, would allow Thai society, as well as
Asian culture as a whole, to preserve and further develop those elements of their
heritage that are superior to what is being imported from the West. Finally, he
argued for a more religious understanding of socialism, one based in Dhamma
principles" (p. 170).

24. To quote Santikaro Bhikkhu again: "The Buddhist goal of quenching or
ending *dukkha* is not to be falsely spiritualized into an other-worldly end, for the
genuinely spiritual does not designate or reject the body. *Nibbana* can only be
found right here in the middle of *samsara*, the whirlpool of birth and death. So
when we talk about ending *dukkha*, we mean both personal and social problems." See *Engaged Buddhism*, p. 163.

25. See Buddhadasa Bhikkhu, *What Is Paticcasamuppada?* (Bangkok: Group
for the Propagation of Excellent Way of Living, 1974). Buddhadasa has also been
active in the Buddhist-Christian dialogue for several decades. Paralleling Abe's
"kenotic" reading, he interprets the Christian sign of the cross as the simultaneous affirmation and crossing out of the "I." See his *Buddhadasa's View on Buddhism and Christianity* (Bangkok: Tianwaan Press, 1984). On the above points
compare also Suwanna Satha-Anand, "Religious Movements in Contemporary
Thailand: Buddhist Struggles for Modern Relevance," *Asian Survey* 30 (1990):
395–408. Buddhadasa's teachings are continued today by the Spirit in Education
Movement (SEM) in Thailand, especially by Sulak Sivaraksa, one of SEM's chief
promoters and a key figure in the "International Network of Engaged Buddhists"
(INEB). Among Sivaraksa's publications see *A Socially Engaged Buddhism*
(Bangkok: Thai Inter-Religious Commission for Development, 1988); *Religion
and Development*, 3rd ed. (Bangkok: Thai Inter-Religious Commission, 1987);
*A Buddhist Vision for Renewing Society* (Bangkok: Thai Inter-Religious Commission, 1994); Sivaraksa, ed., *The Quest for a Just Society: The Legacy and
Challenge of Buddhadasa Bhikkhu* (Bangkok: Thai Inter-Religious Commission,
1994). Compare also Donald K. Swearer, "Sulak Sivaraksa's Vision for Renewing Society," in *Engaged Buddhism*, ed. Queen and King, pp. 195–235.

26. *Al-Qur'an: A Contemporary Translation*, by Ahmed Ali (Princeton, N.J.: Princeton Univesity Press, 1984).

27. See *Words of the Prophet Muhammad: Selections from the Hadith*, compiled by Maulana Wahiduddin Khan (New Delhi: Al-Risala Books, 1996), pp. 78, 80, 95. Compare also Maulana Wahiduddin Khan, *Muhammad: The Ideal Character* (New Delhi: Al-Risala, n.d.), a study that emphasizes the gentle and nondomineering character of the Prophet.

28. Herbert Mason, *The Death of al-Hallaj: A Dramatic Narrative* (Notre Dame, Ind.: University of Notre Dame Press, 1979), pp. xiv, xix.

29. Annemarie Schimmel, "A Good Word is like a Good Tree" (speech delivered in October 1995 on the occasion of the bestowal of the German Book Trade's annual Peace Prize); reprinted in English translation in *JUST Commentary* 21 (March 1996): 4. She adds, "The fundamentalists try to recruit followers from among the unemployed, rootless youth whom they supply with a few simple formulas to manipulate them easily. But such a politically misused Islam is something completely different from lived Islam; it is, as Tahe Ben Jalloun writes, a caricature of true Islam" (pp. 4–5).

30. Robert D. Lee, foreword to Mohammed Arkoun, *Rethinking Islam: Common Questions, Uncommon Answers*, trans. and ed. R. D. Lee (Boulder, Colo.: Westview Press, 1994), pp. viii–xi. "Arkoun follows contemporary analysts in suggesting that liberalism depends upon a religious tradition and not, as Mustafa Kemal (Atatürk) seems to have thought, upon a radical separation of politics and religion; he embraces liberalism on the condition that liberalism itself be reinterpreted." Lee also points to the difficult intellectual climate in the contemporary Islamic context: "Arkoun has repeatedly said that no genuinely independent, creative work on the Islamic tradition can currently be done in the Arab world. The close ties between nationalist, authoritarian governments bent on using Islam for their own purposes or preoccupied with fending off militant, Islamist movements for equally clear reasons makes genuine scholarship impossible" (p. xi).

31. Arkoun, *Rethinking Islam*, pp. 1–3. Arkoun is well aware that his "postmodern" reading of Islam will be resisted not only by traditional Islamicists but also by Western modernists wedded to Western supremacy: "The West has not accepted the challenge—or even the objection—that arises from within its own culture; even in the midst of a generalized crisis such as that opened by the end of Marxist eschatology, Western reason has maintained its pressure on the rest of the world and its refusal to entertain forms of thought coming from the outside. . . . In this fashion the history of the hegemonic world rolls on, perpetuating a sovereignty over human beings that was once attributed to God, while secondary actors exhaust themselves in imitating, adapting, reproducing and confirming the productivity and insuperability of that world" (p. 4).

32. Arkoun, *Rethinking Islam*, pp. 12–13. In Arkoun's presentation, the merger of faith and public power is not the invention of contemporary fundamentalism, but can be in part traced back to the classical age of Islamic civilization. "The linking of political action to symbolic creativity ended definitively with the rise of the imperial Umayyad state. Instead, there triumphed an inverse

process whereby the symbolic capital carried by the Qur'an was utilized for the construction and imposition of an official, orthodox Islam: *official* because it resulted from political choices of the state, which physically eliminated opponents who stood for any other interpretations and uses of the symbolic capital (the Shi'ite and Kharijite protests, most notably); *orthodox* because the experts accredited by the political authorities gave credence to the idea that it is possible to read the Word of God correctly, to know the prophetic tradition exhaustively" (p. 22).

33. Arkoun, *Rethinking Islam*, pp. 20, 24–26.

34. See Gholam A. Tavassoli, "Introduction: Biobibliographical Sketch," in *On the Sociology of Islam*, Ali Shari'ati, trans. Hamid Algar (Berkeley, Calif.: Mizan Press, 1979), pp. 20–21. Although committed to human liberation, Shari'ati questioned the modern Western paradigm of liberation in both its liberal-capitalist and its orthodox Marxist forms. Modern humanism "which all post-Renaissance humanitarian intellectuals hoped would take over the task of human liberation from religion," has in fact become a scholastic doctrine, a "sacred article of faith for all the atheistic schools of recent centuries." See Shari'ati, "Humanity Between Marxism and Religion," in *Marxism and Other Western Fallacies: An Islamic Critique*, trans. R. Campbell (Berkeley, Calif.: Mizan Press, 1980), p. 91.

35. See Shari'ati, *On the Sociology of Islam*, pp. 66–67 ("Approaches to the Understanding of Islam"), pp. 93–94 ("Anthropology: The Creation of Man"); also *Marxism and Other Western Fallacies*, pp. 37–38 ("Modern Calamities"). At another point, Shari'ati offers an intriguing interpretation of "*hijra*," migration. Far from being a singular event during the emergence of Islam, he writes, *hijra* involves a "profound philosophical and social principle," one which has been "the primary factor in the rise of civilization throughout history. All the twenty-seven civilizations we know of in history have been born of a migration that preceded them. . . . The converse is also true: that there is no case on record in which a primitive tribe has become civilized and created an advanced culture without first moving from its homeland and migrating." See *On the Sociology of Islam*, pp. 43–44. The statement obviously militates against any kind of ethno-centric fundamentalism.

36. Shari'ati, "The Philosophy of History: Cain and Abel," in *On the Sociology of Islam*, pp. 98–99. While emphasizing the role of the ownership of the means of production, Shari'ati disagrees with Marx on the precise sequence of events. In effect, "the exact opposite of Marx's theory applies: it is not ownership that is a factor in the acquisition of power, but the converse. Power and coercion were the factors that first bestowed ownership on the individual" (p. 100).

37. *On the Sociology of Islam*, pp. 102, 106–109.

38. Compare his essay on "Mysticism, Equality, and Freedom," in *Marxism and Other Western Fallacies*, pp. 97–122, where we read (p. 99) that "mysticism is a manifestation of the primordial nature of man and it exists as a means of journeying to the unseen." In Iran today, Shari'ati's legacy is ably continued and deepened by Abdolkarim Soroush, a philosopher trained both in Iran and England. An opponent of the Shah's regime before the revolution, Soroush has

emerged in recent years as a highly articulate defender of a "liberal," open-minded Islam and a trenchant critic of the Iranian clerical establishment, a stance that has made him the target of repeated abuse and persecution.

39. Maulana Wahiduddin Khan, "Religion and Politics" and "Two Methods," in *Al-Risala* 122–123 (March-April 1995): 5–7, 21–22. He adds, "The revolutionary path is that of reaction, and just explaining it in Islamic terms does not transform it into an Islamic method. *Da'wa*, on the other hand, calls for patience and avoidance of confrontations. This method, as opposed to that of reaction, is doubtless the more difficult of the two, but, in the long run, is the best calculated to bear fruit" (p. 22). Compare also his *Islam As It Is* (New Delhi: Al-Risala Books, 1992).

40. John Stratton Hawley and Mark Juergensmeyer, eds., *Songs of the Saints of India* (New York: Oxford University Press, 1988), pp. 52, 54. Compare also *Songs of Kabir from the Adi Granth*, trans. Nirmal Dass (Albany, N.Y.: SUNY Press, 1991); Muhammad Hedayetullah, *Kabir: The Apostle of Hindu-Muslim Unity* (Delhi: Motilal Banarsidass, 1989).

# 4

# Satyagraha: Gandhi's Truth Revisited

> To perceive the spirit of truth one must be able to love the meanest
> of creation as oneself.
>
> M. Gandhi

The problem of "truth," and more specifically the meaning of Gandhi's
"truth," is a difficult topic resisting easy resolution. A story that comes
from a so-called "Western" religion (Christianity), and thus is likely to
be familiar or readily accessible to Western readers, may serve to introduce the topic. During the Easter week Christians celebrate or commemorate what is called the "passion" (suffering) of Jesus. Following the
betrayal by one of his disciples, Jesus has been apprehended. He is first
taken to the high priests in Jerusalem and then to the house of Pontius
Pilate, who was then Roman governor of Judaea. A man versed in legal
proceedings, Pilate asks Jesus many questions to find out who he is and
what he has done. Jesus does not answer all these questions, but he does
say this, as recorded in John's gospel: "I was born and I have come into
the world to bear witness to the truth. Everyone who is of [or in] the truth
hears my voice" (John 18:37). Pilate, who was a skeptic and perhaps an
aspiring pragmatist-deconstructionist, responds, shrugging his shoulders,
"What is truth?"

We are today not so far away from Pilate. In dominant strands of modern Western thought the relation between truth and action or truth and
human life has become apocryphal. Under the impact of modern scientific epistemology, truth tends to be associated entirely with empirical
observations or with propositional statements capturing empirically as-
certainable states of affairs. Action, by contrast, is seen as guided by indi-
vidually chosen goals or collective ideologies, motivations or intentions
that are purely subjective and cut loose from the moorings of truth.
Against this background, Gandhi's politics and political self-understand-

ing appear enigmatic. As is well known, Gandhi titled his autobiography *The Story of My Experiments with Truth,* a title which refers neither to scientific experiments nor to playful subjective experimentations with lifestyles. This aspect is further underscored by another term which is crucial to Gandhi's self-understanding: *satyagraha,* which is commonly translated as "truth force" (or soul force) or as the enactment or perform- ance of truth, where performance does not mean just the enactment of prior theoretical principles, but the infusion of truth into the perform- ance itself. What sense can one make of such terms or phrases and of the self-understanding connected with them?

In seeking to clarify these issues, some guidance can be found in a book that approaches the topic from a deeply experiential angle: the study of the noted psychoanalyst and social psychologist Erik Erikson, *Gandhi's Truth* (first published in 1970). Erikson died in May 1994; thus, the pres- ent pages are dedicated both to his memory and, more centrally, that of Gandhi, whose one-hundred-twenty-fifth anniversary was celebrated recently. The chapter proceeds in three main stages. The first section recapitulates some of the central arguments of Erikson's study, while simultaneously trying to embed these arguments in Erikson's broader psychological framework. Next, in addition to critical comments on Erikson's study, some competing or alternative interpretations of Gan- dhi's "truth" are delineated. The conclusion reflects briefly on Gandhi's sources of inspiration and also on the continuing importance of his poli- tics and lifework in our time, drawing attention to some prominent con- temporary *satyagrahis*—most notably the Czech "truth-doer" Vaclav Havel.

I

In his study *Gandhi's Truth,* Erikson constructs a psychological portrait of Gandhi around a concrete episode that, though mentioned only pass- ingly in Gandhi's autobiography, constitutes for Erikson a crucial forma- tive event in the course of Gandhi's self-discovery and his emergence as a political leader. This event was a strike that Gandhi organized and led in Ahmedabad in 1918 against the mill owners of that city, prominently employing fasting and nonviolent resistance. Thus, from the beginning, Erikson places the accent not on a private intention or a whimsically chosen goal but on a public happening that decisively shaped Gandhi's life and the character of his leadership. Erikson's focus on the strike has to do only in part with its "objective" significance; it is more directly concerned with the issue of public leadership and its exercise. As Erikson observes, the historical context of the strike was monumental and likely to dwarf the Ahmedabad episode:

> For mark the year: it was on the Ides of March of 1918, the year of massive mechanized slaughter on the front in France, the year when empires collapsed and new world alliances were formed, the year of Wilson and above all of Lenin. And here in Ahmedabad one of the great charismatic figures of the postwar world was concentrating on a strictly local labor dispute, putting his very life on the line by fasting—an event scarcely noticed even in India at the time.

The discrepancy between global context and local action is not an obstacle for Erikson but rather an inducement to further inquiry. Precisely in light of this discrepancy he became "fascinated with these months in Gandhi's middle years" and decided to reconstruct "the Event" as a catalyst for "extensive reflections on the origins, in Gandhi's early life and work, of the method he came to call 'truth force'."[1]

This fascination deserves further elaboration and assessment, because its motives are far from self-evident. Erikson, though faithful in many ways to Freud's legacy, departed from the teachings of his mentor chiefly by shifting the accent from a "psychosexual" to a "psychosocial" level of analysis, a shift involving a broadening of the Freudian concentration on early infancy to the entire spectrum of human psychological development from infancy to early and late adulthood. One of the most distinctive features of Erikson's approach is the theory of an "epigenetic" life cycle, according to which human maturation involves recurrent tensional encounters between psychic dispositions and social environment that demand ever renewed efforts of renegotiation and management. Early in *Gandhi's Truth*, Erikson refers to the classical Hindu doctrine of "stages of life" (*ashramas*), which he finds broadly suggestive and not incompatible with his own epigenetic account. Erikson divides the human life cycle into three major periods: early infancy and childhood (further subdivided into four phases), adolescence, and adulthood (in turn broken down into three phases). While earliest infancy is overshadowed by the conflict between trust (or hope) and mistrust and early childhood witnesses the clash between autonomy and shame, the subsequent phases of the "play age" and the "school age" are permeated respectively by the struggle of initiative against guilt and industry (achievement) against inferiority. The main developmental problem of adolescence resides in the tension between identity maintenance and identity diffusion, or between career objective and role ambivalence. During the mature period, young adulthood wrestles with the antagonism of intimacy and isolation, whereas the middle and late phases of adulthood struggle successively with the conflicting pulls of "generativity" and self-absorption and of personal integrity and despair.[2]

For present purposes, what needs to be retrieved from this scheme is the formulation of middle adulthood, which centers on the challenge or task of "generativity." According to Erikson, middle adulthood is centrally preoccupied with intergenerational conflict and management, the problem of establishing viable relations with the next generation based on adult leadership and example. The term "generativity" designates "the interest in establishing and guiding the next generation or whatever in a given case may become the absorbing object of a parental kind of responsibility." What is involved here is the ability to "lose oneself in the meeting of bodies and minds," leading to "a general expansion of ego interests and of libidinal cathexis over that which has been thus generated and accepted as a responsibility." The same notion of generativity is invoked in *Gandhi's Truth*, with specific reference to the middle period of Gandhi's adult life. As Erikson states, his growing interest in the Ahmedabad strike led him into "an 'in-between' period of Gandhi's life" when the "South African Gandhi" had already become historical while the history of "Gandhi, the Mahatma of all India" had not yet begun. It was at this point that Gandhi—in a genuine display of "generativity"— emerged as the generative leader of a new India about to break from the colonial yoke:

> At the time of the Ahmedabad strike, Gandhi was forty-eight years old: middle-aged Mahatma, indeed. That the very next year he emerged as the father of his country only lends greater importance to the fact that the middle span of life is under the dominance of the universal human need and strength which I have come to subsume under the term *generativity*. I have said that in this stage a man and a woman must have defined for themselves what and whom they have come to care for, what they care to do well, and how they plan to take care of what they have started and created.[3]

What enabled Gandhi to become the caring parental leader of the younger generation of Indians, and how, in particular, did he choose to exercise his caring guidance and leadership? For Erikson, the answer is clear (and his formulation of it is the major insight and contribution of his study): Gandhi's firm devotion to "truth" (*satya*) and his consistent reliance on "truth force" (*satyagraha*). Erikson repeatedly insists on this aspect in passages that are both instructive and revealing. Reporting on the background of Gandhi's involvement in the South African struggle, Erikson comments perceptively on problems of terminology and their adequate handling in the English language. As he notes, *satyagraha* was the "Sanskritic combination" that Gandhi chose as a name for his way of life and action, meaning "truth and force, in literal translation." In other studies, the term is often rendered as "passive resistance" or "nonviolent resistance"—falling far short of the original. Even the phrase "militant nonviolence," preferred by Martin Luther King, Jr., fails to convey "the spiritual origin of nonviolent courage in Gandhi's 'truth'." Erikson favors the expression "truth force," adding, "I will speak of the 'leverage of truth' when, in addition to truth and force, I want to suggest the skillful use of a sensitive instrument." To be sure, care must be taken not to mistake the character of this "force." For, paradoxically stated, it simultaneously signifies a "non-force," the radical renunciation of the lust for force or power coupled with a complete self-abnegation or self-surrender to the force of truth. Also rendering *satyagraha* as "actualism"—a term that requires further explanation—Erikson captures this point in a remarkable passage:

> Gandhi's actualism, then, first of all consisted in his knowledge of, and his ability to gain strength from, the fact that nothing is more powerful in the world than conscious nothingness if it is paired with the gift of giving and accepting actuality. It is not for me to say what this power *is*; yet obviously it demands the keenest of minds and a most experienced heart, for otherwise it would be crushed between megalomania and self-destruction.[4]

This passage occurs in a section of Erikson's book devoted to the discussion of Gandhi's "leverage of truth," more specifically, in the chapter "Homo Religiosus." In employing this somewhat unusual vocabulary, Erikson is careful to differentiate between "actualism," or "actuality," and mere "factual reality" which can be empirically ascertained and demonstrated. Gandhi is described as a "religious actualist," one whose whole life revolved around the faithful performance or enactment of truth predicated on self-renunciation and devoted service. By virtue of these qualities, Erikson holds, Gandhi can be compared to other religious leaders, especially to Martin Luther (to whom Erikson devoted another book), who pinpointed the nature of actualism or *satyagraha* in such phrases as "*via Dei est qua nos ambulare facit*" (God's way is what makes us move) or "*quotidianus Christi adventus*" (Christ comes everyday). From this religious perspective, actualism indicates a midpoint between activity and passivity, between being and nonbeing, and hence also between force and non-force. As Erikson writes, in an almost Buddhist turn of phrase: "Out of the acceptance of nothingness emerges what can be the most central and productive, timeless and actual, continuous and active position in the human universe." Dedication to the performance or enactment of truth in this context means neither a mindless activism nor a simple retreat into passivity or nonbeing; instead, performative actuality properly construed is "complementary to nothingness" and "deeply and unavoidably endowed with the instinctual energy and the elemental concern of generativity," with self-surrender and an exemplary mode of self-giving. Hovering between action and passion, actualism also confounds the boundary between masculinity and femininity. In effect, Gandhian *satyagraha* has an affinity to "the experience of women who, in their hereness and practical religiosity, weave together in the chores of daily life what really 'maintains the world' " (*lokasamgraha*) and "who—while heroes court death—can experience death as an intrinsic part of a boundless and boundlessly recreative life."[5]

Committed to the maintenance of society across generations, Gandhian *satyagraha* carries a profoundly ethical significance, with ethics distinguished (for some purposes) from private morality or moralism. As interpreted by Erikson, Gandhian "truth force" involves the willingness to respect the intrinsic integrity or truth of fellow humans, and in fact of all living beings; in Heideggerian vocabulary, it implies the readiness to "let being be" without mandating acceptance of the status quo or an empirical state of affairs. This readiness of "letting-be," in turn, presupposes the abandonment of the will to mastery, that is, an acceptance of suffering in lieu of the desire to inflict suffering on others and hence an attitude of self-surrender of the ego to the persuasive truth disclosed in all beings. For Gandhi, Erikson notes, truthful action was governed by "the readiness to get hurt and yet not to hurt," ultimately by the "principle of *ahimsa*" (or nonviolence). Following Joan Bondurant, he describes the "only dogma" in Gandhian thought as the maxim "the only test of truth is action based on the refusal to do harm." Yet, by itself *ahimsa* is only a means and not fully intelligible without recourse to its deeper ethical and religious moorings. "With all due respect for the traditional translation of *ahimsa*," Erikson adds, "I think Gandhi implied in it, besides a refusal not to do physical harm, a determination not to violate another person's essence." Only a wholehearted respect for the other's truth, a careful responsiveness to the other's being without managerial or manipulative intent, can foster the emergence of genuine ethical bonds both in family life and society at large. This insight lends support to Erikson's own psychological theory, which in addition to the categories of competence and integrity lists "mutuality" as a crucial ingredient in human maturation or development.[6]

Returning to the "Event" in Ahmedabad, it is clear that the strike involved a confrontation with the mill owners—a confrontation predicated not on a contest of sheer power or force, but on the exercise of "truth force" and thus on a deep-seated sense of ethical responsibility. By embracing nonviolence and the readiness to suffer (rather than to inflict suffering), *satyagraha* softens hardened battle lines and fosters the restoration of mutuality or reciprocal goodwill. Pursued with integrity and unspoiled by resentment, Erikson comments, Gandhi's approach teaches that "only the voluntary acceptance of self-suffering can reveal the truth latent in a conflict—and in the opponent." Although the mill owners, and the British colonizers on other occasions, did not fully rise to the occasion, they could not entirely escape the ethical appeal addressed to them by the performers of *satyagraha*. This explains the fact that both the strike and many later confrontations were largely conducted in a spirit of celebration rather than of bitter hostility. "The mood of the Event," Erikson writes, "was above all pervaded by a spirit of *giving the opponent the courage to change* even as the challenger remained ready to change with the events." "At such periods of his life," he adds, "Gandhi possessed a Franciscan gaiety and a capacity to reduce situations to their bare essentials, thus helping others both to discard costly defenses and denials and to realize hidden potentials of good will and energetic deed." In the end, Gandhi's acceptance of suffering and self-surrender entailed the surrender or sacrifice of his life at the hands of a fanatic. In light of this somber conclusion, which casts its shadow backward over the Ahmedabad strike, Erikson feels justified in interpreting, and interpreting "with humility," the "truth force" of the religious actualist in these terms: "to be ready to die for what is true now means to grasp the only chance to have lived fully."[7]

## II

The preceding recapitulation of Erikson's work was meant to demonstrate the experiential depth and innovative richness of his interpretation. Yet "revisiting" an earlier acclaimed work also implies reinterpretation and reassessment in a critical vein. Despite Erikson's subtle insights, several reservations or caveats having to do with some (explicit or implicit) tendencies of his study arise. A main query concerns the issue of "psychologism," the occasional tendency on Erikson's part to "psychologize" Gandhi's life and hence to internalize or privatize both the Ahmedabad "Event" and the character of the "truth force" manifested in that episode. This tendency is entirely natural and perhaps inevitable for a psychologist and practicing psychoanalyst; yet, readers today are bound to ask questions pointing beyond a Gandhian psychology or "psychohistory," such as: Was Gandhi's truth or truth force simply the outgrowth of a particular psychological disposition or idiosyncratic preference, or does it convey a broader and more enduring lesson? On this point, Erikson's study appears somewhat undecided or ambivalent.

Erikson closely links psychohistory and psychoanalysis with Gandhian *satyagraha.* Detailed study of Gandhi's life, he affirms, has buttressed his conviction that psychoanalysis—stripped of its "physicalistic terminology"—"amounts to a *truth method,* with all the implications which the word truth has in *satyagraha.*"[8] What accounts for the affinity, and even convergence, of psychoanalysis and *satyagraha* is their shared attachment to psychotherapy or rather to a generalized therapeutic model in terms of which internal as well as interpersonal conflicts are resolved or overcome through a process of psychic adjustment. Psychohistory as illustrated in the Ahmedabad strike thus concurs with psychoanalytic practice, where the therapeutic encounter of analyst and patient seeks a cure seen as the "joint experience of a truth which relieves and restores as it enlightens." On the basis of this concurrence, Erikson is led to postulate the idea of a "universal therapeutic" committed to the principle that "one can test truth (or the healing power inherent in a sick situation) only by action which avoids harm" or at least by action that "minimizes the violence caused by unilateral coercion or threat." This idea, in turn, encourages him to formulate a concept of historical (or psychohistorical) development that points to a therapeutically achieved universal peace.[9]

Arguments of this kind, though well intentioned, cannot hide from view several suspect premises. For one thing, the elevation of psychoanalytic therapy to a universal model harbors the danger of manipulative designs when society is cast in the role of a patient subject to psychic management.[10] More importantly, Erikson's vision of psychohistory seems strongly beholden to the (Western) theory of "progress" guided by human self-emancipation and control, which is hardly congenial to the Indian (and Gandhian) view of temporality and time.[11] Lurking behind these features is the continuing though recessed influence of modern metaphysics and its twin pillars of subjectivism (or subjectivity) and anthropocentrism. The subjectivist strand is manifest in the repeated reliance on internal feelings or private emotions. Thus, in presenting Gandhi as a "religious actualist," Erikson distinguishes between "factual reality" that is merely empirically "correct" and genuine "actuality" that "feels effectively true in action." Even the notions of "truth" and "truth force" are occasionally drawn into the circle of intuitive feelings: for example, in the statement that "truth" will "reveal itself only in intuitive fusion with the innermost self or (or *and*) the will of the masses."[12]

To correct subjectivist or emotive accents of this kind, care must be taken to strengthen the socially interactive components of Erikson's approach. This may be accomplished through recourse to interactive discourse or a kind of "communicative pragmatics" in the Habermasian sense. In his study *Gandhi's Political Philosophy: A Critical Examination,* Bhikhu Parekh comes close to recommending the latter option. In Parekh's account, Gandhian "truth force" or *satyagraha* is basically a cooperative search for truth in which rational discussion and persuasion play crucial roles: truth emerges from discursive argumentation. Since no one can initially claim to be already in possession of truth in this cooperative search, each agent or participant must first acknowledge his or her ignorance or fallibility, while placing trust entirely in the outcome of the common search. If a given party or agent refuses to participate in the search for truth, political pressure—in the form of nonviolent resistance—can be applied with the goal of establishing or restoring the conditions of rational discourse. Referring to terminological issues, Parekh observes that *satya* denotes "truth," while *agraha* (in its ordinary Gujarati sense) means "insisting on something without becoming obstinate or uncompromising." The joining of the two terms in *satyagraha* thus suggests a combination of rational truth and political pressure or else of theory and practice:

> A moral agent insists *on* truth as he sees it, but acknowledges that he might be wrong or only partially right and invites his opponent to join him in a cooperative search *for* truth. When the invitation is declined, he *insists* on it in a truthful manner and continues to do so until his opponent is ready to talk. Insofar as it is concerned to *discover* truth, Gandhi's theory of *satyagraha* is an integral part of his theory of truth; insofar as it is an attempt to insist on and *realize* truth, it is an inseparable part of this theory of nonviolence. Gandhi's theory of *satyagraha* is at once both epistemological and political.[13]

Strictly construed, the correlation of epistemology and politics yields something akin to the model of rational action or interaction, or, again, to the theory of communicative pragmatics. Parekh on the whole endorses this outcome, though with important qualifications designed to mitigate the rationalist structure of discourse in favor of a "non-rationalist theory of rationality." As he notes, for Gandhi, rational discussion and persuasion were the preferred ways of dealing with interactive situations, especially situations of conflict. Given the diversity of individual perspectives, discussion required an act of reciprocal empathy, a willingness to "step into each other's shoes" and thus ultimately to arrive at a rational consensus based on insights "acceptable to both" (or all participants). The possibility of such consensus was predicated on a number of assumptions—in Parekh's view chiefly on three. First, since searching for truth implies initial ignorance, each participant was expected to enter the discussion "in a spirit of humility and with an open mind." Next, given the initial distance between competing or possibly contrasting perspectives, each party must be animated by a sense of truthfulness or sincere empathy, especially the sincere readiness to "enter into the other's world of thought." Sincerity of this kind, finally, presupposes a bracketing or overcoming of selfishness and ill will, attitudes that block rational discourse and hence frustrate the goal of consensual impartiality. At this point, Parekh oversteps the narrow confines of rationalism, making room for emotive or "non-rationalist" elements. For Gandhi, he writes, impartiality or objectivity demanded "an open mind, and an open mind presupposed an 'open heart.' " Rational understanding is foiled when the other's world is approached without personal empathy or sympathy, when that world is not allowed to "form part of one's emotional and moral universe." Hence, in the Gandhian view, "sympathy, love or goodwill was a necessary precondition of rationality, and only universal love guarantees total objectivity."[14]

Although perceptively and eloquently stated, Parekh's communicative (*cum* emotive) approach still leaves something out of account or falls short of the complexity of "Gandhi's truth." The quandaries of subjectivism are not fully overcome by a coupling of friendly feelings and a discursively anchored truth theory or epistemology. What is missing or still underemphasized is the "otherness" or demand quality of truth: the aspect that a search for truth, while proceeding in ignorance, is yet impelled by something that exceeds the range of human management or disposition, including the prevailing frame of rational discourse. In this respect, Erikson's account actually has the advantage of insisting (at least occasionally) on the need for a human "surrender" to truth, a need that clearly transgresses psychologism. Such surrender involves a form of radical self-transcendence and transformation not only of a psychological or epistemological but an ontological kind. This aspect deserves further attention.

Interactive discourse or conversation—including rational argumentation—is never self-enclosed or complete; as participants in such discourse we are never fully "amongst ourselves" or *chez nous*. As we know (at least since Wittgenstein), discussion always occurs in a given context of understanding or "language game," and language games always presuppose certain shared assumptions or premises that help to stabilize available meaning contents. Meaningful or intelligible participation in discourse thus requires, in large measure, adaptation to or conformity with prevailing semantic agreements. Yet, there is something more: a kind of linguistic excess or non-closure. Every language game, one might say, is also inhabited by an "other" voice—or a voice of otherness—which traverses it from within or from its margins. In religious vocabulary, this voice may be called a transgressive or "prophetic" voice, which uncannily unsettles and stirs up presently shared meanings in the direction of unfamiliar and possibly transformative modes of human and social life. The theologian Nicholas Wolterstorff speaks of "divine discourse," meaning not an unintelligible mumbling or "speaking in tongues," but rather a discourse penetrating our ordinary understandings in the form of a challenge or demand.[15]

Without discounting other dimensions, this transgressive aspect is also involved in Gandhi's notions of truth and truth force or *satyagraha*. It is captured in Erikson's emphasis on the need for a human "surrender" to (rather than domestication of) truth, and it is the same quality that surfaces in his portrayal of Gandhi as *homo religiosus* or a "religious actualist." Gandhi himself was by no means reticent to acknowledge this tranformative dimension of *satyagraha*. As he wrote in a letter to C. F. Andrews, "I have taken up things as they have come to me and always in trembling and fear. . . . I fancy that I followed His will and no other and He will lead me 'amid the encircling gloom.' "[16]

To be sure, in making room for divine discourse or a prophetic voice, we must guard against being led astray and abandoning the domain of ordinary discourse. The danger that looms in any transgression of ordinary speech is willful caprice, arrogant dogmatism, and possibly violent fundamentalism. In our own age, we are only too familiar with this danger and its often destructive manifestations (ranging from the incident at Waco, Texas, to suicide bombers in West and South Asia). However, we can and must differentiate between a prophetic voice or transgression that is genuinely transformative or "religious" and a sham transgression that is merely a form of human conceit and self-aggrandizement. The distinguishing criterion is this: genuine transgression leads to human flourishing, to the enhancement of life or what is called the "good life," whereas sham transgression leads to violence (against others), destruction, and death. The former involves self-giving or self-surrender, while the latter aims at power and domination. The first accepts self-suffering, even suffering unjustly, while the second seeks to inflict suffering and injustice on others.

In light of this distinction, there can be no doubt about the character of Gandhi's truth and *satyagraha*. Throughout this life, he accepted suffering—in the form of fasting, imprisonment, abuse, and ultimately death—while always being careful not to inflict suffering on others and to respect them in their "essence" or being. In this way, *satyagraha* and *ahimsa* are not just accidentally but necessarily linked. As indicated before, Gandhian *satyagraha* was never a form of dogmatic self-assertion and intolerance. Gandhi's search for truth implied an openness to the opinions and arguments of others—but not to the point of abandoning the commitment to justice and truth in favor of a shallow compromise or empty consensualism. If discussion and attempts at persuasion bog down, Gandhian *satyagraha*, instead of endorsing a "liberal" compromise or a bland status quo, moves to a higher or deeper level of intensity:

noncooperation and civil disobedience, to the point of self-suffering. In the practice of *satyagraha*, self-suffering makes an appeal to opponents that neither rationality nor violence or threats of violence can match:

> Suffering is the law of human beings; war is the law of the jungle. But suffering is infinitely more powerful than the law of the jungle for converting the opponent and opening his ears, which are otherwise shut, to the voice of reason. . . . [So] if you want something really important to be done, you must not merely satisfy the reason, you must move the heart too. The appeal of reason is more to the head, but the penetration of the heart comes from suffering. It opens up the inner understanding of men. Suffering is the badge of the human race, not the sword.[17]

Somewhat circuitously, this leads back to the Easter story with which these pages began, which was also probably one of Gandhi's sources of inspiration. In the Easter passion, after Pilate had finished his questioning, he handed Jesus over to the soldiers who brutally attacked him, spat on him, and put a crown of thorns on him. After this, Pilate took Jesus out to show him to the people. And there something unexpected happened: the same Pilate who just a while ago had said "What is truth?" on seeing this bloodstained figure became unwittingly the conveyor of a profound truth; when pointing at Jesus he said "*Ecce homo*," "Look, a human" or "Look, there is humanity."

## III

This reference to the Easter story is not meant to cast Gandhian *satyagraha* in a narrowly denominational or theological mold, which would be quite alien to Gandhi's legacy and his commitment to the reconciliation among cultures and religions. In a telling fashion, one can also illustrate the meaning of *satyagraha* by turning to a classical text of Hinduism that was always close to Gandhi's heart and a constant companion in his struggles: the Bhagavad Gita. As is well known, Gandhi considered himself a *karmayogin*, a practitioner of the path of *karma yoga* or *karma marga* as spelled out in the classical text. Although allowing for different approaches to truth or the divine, the Bhagavad Gita attributes a particularly elevated status to *karma yoga* seen as a nonpossessive or nonmanagerial form of action, as a mode of self-giving service that remains unattached to the fruits or benefits of action. The role of the *karmayogin* is that of an active "doer of truth"—a performer of *satyagraha*—who yet refuses the blandishments of external success, especially of power, domination, and self-aggrandizement. As we read in a central passage of the Bhagavad Gita, "Great is the human who, free from attachment and with the soul in serene harmony, works on the path of *karma yoga,* the path of consecrated action. . . . Let thy actions then be pure, free from the bonds of clinging desire." Elsewhere, Krishna, as divine mentor, instructs his disciple in these words: "Let thy aim be the good of all or world maintenance [*lokasamgraha*] and thus carry on thy task in life."[18]

By way of conclusion, it may be appropriate to highlight briefly some of the broader implications and lasting contributions of Gandhian truth and truth force, that is, of a worldly activity guided by the search for, and the demands of, (nonepistemological) truth.[19] A primary implication and contribution is the rejection of narrowly "ideological" politics, particularly a politics wedded to teleological doctrines, grand metanarratives, or worldviews (*Weltanschauungen*). Gandhi at no point articulated a political doctrine or set of general marching orders—a fact that is sometimes denounced as a sign of incoherence. At every juncture, Gandhian politics involved a nonviolent engagement and struggle with the concrete challenges of the day, and above all an engaged surrender to the claims of the most vulnerable, oppressed, or underprivileged segments of society—in a manner that "let" these segments "be" without manipulative ideological designs. In our time, marked by the breakdown of grand ideological blueprints, Gandhian truth force or *satyagraha* may yet acquire an unexpected and perhaps heightened significance. That breakdown is glaringly manifest in the collapse of communism in the former Soviet Union (and East European countries), traceable to the stifling effects of totalitarian management and the blatant contamination of utopia with violence. The only grand ideology still surviving in our time, apart from sporadic outbursts of chauvinism, is free enterprise liberalism; but apart from various internal fissures and contestations, that ideology is increasingly troubled and besieged by its complicity with anthropocentrism and, more generally, with root premises of modern Western metaphysics.[20]

As Gandhi's life amply testifies, abandonment of ideological blueprints does not in any way signal a retreat into apathy or sheer passivity, just as his "experimenting with truth" was not a recipe for cynicism or willful relativism. In a genuinely Socratic manner, confession of ignorance is an emblem of truthfulness—which, in turn, remains beholden to the search for, and demands of, truth. In like fashion, relinquishing the pretense of ideological marching orders and a political mastery of the world is an index not of indifference but of a genuine concern for the well-being of the world, and thus a commitment to the task of "world maintenance" (*lokasamgraha*). Shunning the vanity of managerial power and control thus implies an active and concrete engagement in the affairs of the world that releases the "power of the powerless" beyond the pale of resentment, vengefulness or malice. The practice of *karma yoga* or *satyagraha* in this sense is not the exclusive province of Gandhian politics, if the latter is identified with a particular struggle for independence on the Indian sub-continent. Although he pursued that path with supreme dedication, Gandhi's example radiates far beyond the confines of his native Indian context. To that extent, Gandhian truth force may yet add a gentle redeeming glow to a century otherwise wallowing in warfare, genocide, and massive destruction.

In our time, other political leaders have emulated Gandhi's example without any narrow discipleship and in a completely independent and innovative fashion. One such figure, mentioned by Erikson, was Martin Luther King, Jr., whose motto of "militant nonviolence" steered the Civil Rights movement in America in a direction broadly akin to Gandhian *satyagraha*. Another example, still closer to recent memory, is that of Vaclav Havel whose ideas, in conjunction with those of his friends, guided the so-called "velvet revolution" in Czechoslovakia along the path of a radical, but nonviolent, transformation of political life. In an essay on "The Power of the Powerless," Havel described the life of "dissidents" or "dissenters"—those transgressing the bounds of domination—as an attempt of "living within the truth." As a mode of resistance to control, such an attempt demands the cultivation of a sense of responsibility and responsiveness, which is "clearly a moral act, not only because one must pay so dearly for it, but principally because it is not self-serving." Shunning systematic violence as well as counterviolence, the attempt of "living (with) the truth" also implies for Havel a rejection of grand ideological blueprints:

> A genuine, profound and lasting change for the better . . . can no longer result from the victory (were such a victory possible) of any particular traditional political conception, which can ultimately be only external, that is, a structural or systemic conception. More than ever before, such a change will have to derive from human existence, from the fundamental reconstitution of the position of people in the world, their relationships to themselves and to each other, and to the universe. . . . This is not something that can be designed and introduced like a new car. If it is to be more than just a new variation on the old degeneration, it must above all be an expression of life in the process of self-transformation.[21]

## Notes

1. Erik H. Erikson, *Gandhi's Truth: On the Origins of Militant Nonviolence* (New York: Norton & Co., 1993), p. 10. "The fact," he continues, "is that without a knowledge of its place in Gandhi's life and in India's history, the Event could indeed be considered a rather minor affair, hardly contributive to the fact that Gandhi was to emerge exactly a year later as the leader of the first nation-

wide act of civil disobedience" (p. 12). For Gandhi's own account of the episode see M. K. Gandhi, *An Autobiography or The Story of My Experiments with Truth* (Ahmedabad: Navajivan, 1992), pp. 355–362.

2. See the chapter "Eight Stages of Man" in Erikson, *Childhood and Society* (New York: Norton & Co., 1950), pp. 219–234; also the chapters "Growth and Crises of the Healthy Personality" and "The Problem of Ego Identity" in *Identity and the Life Cycle: Selected Papers by Erik H. Erikson* (New York: International Universities Press, 1959), pp. 50–164. Compare further the chapter "The Life Cycle" in Paul Roazen, *Erik H. Erikson: The Power and Limits of a Vision* (New York: Free Press, 1976), pp. 107–120.

3. Erikson, *Gandhi's Truth*, p. 395; see also *Childhood and Society*, p. 231.

4. *Gandhi's Truth*, pp. 198, 397.

5. *Gandhi's Truth*, pp. 390, 398–400. Regarding the feminine or loosely "bisexual" character of Gandhian *satyagraha* compare also Ashis Nandy, "Towards a Third World Utopia" and "From Outside the Imperium: Gandhi's Cultural Critique of the West" in his *Traditions, Tyranny and Utopias: Essays in the Politics of Awareness* (Delhi: Oxford University Press, 1987), esp. pp. 38–40, 141–144.

6. Erikson, *Gandhi's Truth*, pp. 412–413. See also Joan Bondurant, *Conquest of Violence: The Gandhian Philosophy of Conflict*, rev. ed. (Berkeley, Calif.: University of California Press, 1965), p. 25. In stressing mutuality, Erikson's position clearly conflicts with the insistence on radical non-reciprocity in Levinasian ethics; compare, e.g., Emmanuel Levinas, *Totality and Infinity: An Essay on Exteriority*, trans. Alphonso Lingis (Pittsburgh, Pa.: Duquesne University Press, n.d.), pp. 35–52, 212–216.

7. Erikson, *Gandhi's Truth*, pp. 399, 413, 444.

8. *Gandhi's Truth*, pp. 244–245. It may be recalled here that "psychologism" was a central critical target for both Husserl and Heidegger. For recent critiques of the subjectivism or "subjectifying" metaphysics of psychology and psychoanalysis, compare Michel Foucault, *Madness and Civilization*, trans. Richard Howard (New York: Pantheon, 1965); also his *The History of Sexuality*, vol. I, trans. Robert Hurley (New York: Pantheon 1978).

9. Erikson, *Gandhi's Truth*, pp. 247, 439.

10. This concern was voiced some time ago by Hans-Georg Gadamer in his debate with Jügen Habermas; see especially Gadamer, "On the Scope and Function of Hermeneutical Reflection" (1967), in *Philosophical Hermeneutics*, trans. and ed. David E. Linge (Berkeley: University of California Press, 1976), pp. 18–43.

11. Compare in this context, e.g., Anindita N. Balslev, *A Study of Time in Indian Philosophy* (Wiesbaden: Harrassowitz, 1983).

12. Erikson, *Gandhi's Truth*, pp. 41, 242, 396. Erikson at one point (p. 101) uses the phrase "experimental existentialism" to characterize Gandhi's general outlook.

13. Bhikhu Parekh, *Gandhi's Political Philosophy: A Critical Examination* (Notre Dame, Ind.: University of Notre Dame Press, 1989), pp. 142–143. There are several statements by Gandhi that support this communicative-pragmatic

reading. As he affirmed at one point, "We must try patiently to convert our opponents. If we wish to evolve the spirit of democracy out of slavery, we must be scrupulously exact in our dealings with opponents. . . . We must concede to our opponents the freedom we claim for ourselves." Elsewhere he states, "If intolerance becomes a habit, we run the risk of missing the truth. Whilst . . . we must act fearlessly according to the light vouchsafed to us, we must always keep an open mind and ever be ready to find that what we believed to be truth was, after all, untruth." See Roland Duncan, ed., *Selected Writings of Mahatma Gandhi* (Boston: Beacon Press, 1951), p. 79; Mohandas K. Gandhi, *Democracy: Real and Deceptive*, ed. R. K. Prabhu (Ahmedabad: Navajivan, 1961), pp. 34–35; also Ronald J. Terchek, "Gandhi and Democratic Theory," in *Political Thought in Modern India*, ed. Thomas Pantham and Kenneth L. Deutsch (New Delhi: Sage Publications, 1986), pp. 311–312.

14. *Gandhi's Political Philosophy*, pp. 143–144. A similar distinction between Gandhi's outlook and Habermasian communicative pragmatics is made by Thomas Pantham: "The main difference between Habermas and Gandhi is that while the former's practico-political discourse centers around communicative rationality and the force of better arguments, the latter's *satyagraha* is based not only on reason but also on love and self-suffering. Moreover, Habermas's practical discourse is largely a thought experiment, while Gandhi's *satyagraha* is a mode of direct action that ruptures the theory-practice dichotomy." See Pantham, "Habermas' Practical Discourse and Gandhi's *Satyagraha*," in *Political Discourse: Explorations in Indian and Western Political Thought*, ed. Bhikhu Parekh and Thomas Pantham (New Delhi: Sage Publications, 1987), p. 292.

15. See Nicholas Wolterstorff, *Divine Discourse: Philosophical Reflections on the Claim that God Speaks* (New York: Cambridge University Press, 1995). Compare also David Loy, "Dead Words, Living Words, and Healing Words: The Disseminations of Dogen and Eckhart," in *Healing Deconstruction: Postmodern Thought in Buddhism and Christianity*, ed. David Loy (Atlanta, Ga.: Scholars Press, 1966), pp. 33–51.

16. See Erikson, *Gandhi's Truth*, p. 411; compare also Margaret Chatterjee, *Gandhi's Religious Thought* (Notre Dame, Ind.: University of Notre Dame Press, 1983). It was precisely this outlook that prompted some critics of Gandhi to attack him as "other-worldly" or "antihumanist." As George Orwell argued, we "must choose between God and Man"; from this angle, "Gandhi's teachings cannot be squared with the belief that man is the measure of all things and that our job is to make life worth living on earth." See Orwell, "Reflections on Gandhi," *Partisan Review* 16 (January 1949); quoted in Thomas Pantham, "Beyond Liberal Democracy: Thinking with Mahatma Gandhi," in *Political Thought in Modern India*, ed. Pantham and Deutsch, p. 342.

17. Mohandas K. Gandhi, *India's Case for Swaraj* (Ahmedabad: Yeshanand, 1932), p. 369. Elsewhere Gandhi stated, "Hitler and Mussolini on the one hand and Stalin on the other are able to show the immediate effectiveness of violence. But it will be as transitory as that of Chengis' slaughter. But the effects of Buddha's non-violent action persist and are likely to grow with age." See Gandhi, *Nonviolence in Peace and War*, vol. 1 (Ahmedabad: Navajivan, 1942) pp. 128–129; quoted in Pantham, "Beyond Liberal Democracy," pp. 341, 343.

18. The Bhagavad Gita, trans. Juan Mascaró (New York: Penguin Books, 1962), pp. 56–58 (chapter 3, verses 7, 9, 20). On the relation between Christianity and Hinduism compare Harold Coward, ed., *Hindu-Christian Dialogue: Perspectives and Encounters* (Maryknoll, N.Y.: Orbis, 1990); Swami Satprakashananda, *Hinduism and Christianity* (St. Louis, Mo.: Vedanta Society of St. Louis, 1975).

19. As one might mention, recent and contemporary philosophy has seen various efforts to rethink the notion of "truth" in a manner that meshes in many ways with Gandhi's understanding of *satya*. Pioneering in this respect has been Martin Heidegger, with his "ontological" formulation of truth, pointing beyond both pragmatic and emotive construals (truth is what "works" for me) and cognitive-epistemological frameworks (truth means "correspondence" with facts). Heidegger's lead has been followed by Gadamer and others. See especially Heidegger, "On the Essence of Truth," in *Martin Heidegger: Basic Writings*, ed. David F. Krell (New York: Harper & Row, 1977), pp. 17–141; Hans-Georg Gadamer, *Truth and Method*, 2nd rev. ed., trans. Joel Weinsheimer and Donald G. Marshall (New York: Crossroad, 1989), and Gadamer's "Was ist Wahrheit?" in *Kleine Schriften I: Philosophie, Hermeneutik* (Tübingen: Mohr, 1967), pp. 46–58.

20. This does not mean that liberalism cannot perhaps be freed of its metaphysical baggage and thus remain relevant to future politics. Likewise, the collapse of Soviet-style communism does not in any way signal the demise of crucial Marxist insights. On the latter point see, e.g., Jacques Derrida, *Specters of Marx*, trans. Peggy Kamuf (New York and London: Routledge, 1994).

21. "The Power of the Powerless: To the Memory of Jan Patocka," in *Vaclav Havel or Living in Truth*, ed. Jan Vladislav (London and Boston: Faber & Faber, 1987), pp. 62, 70–71. As Havel is careful to point out, the so-called "Declaration of Charter 77"—the chief dissident document—did not offer a political program or ideological platform. The essay repeatedly points to the teachings of both Patocka and Heidegger.

# 5

# Humanity and Humanization: Comments on Confucianism

> He whose heart is in the smallest degree set upon *jen* will dislike no one.
>
> Confucius

At a recent East-West meeting held in Hawaii, a prominent American philosopher raised this question during a discussion period: "What good has Confucianism ever done for China?" Addressed to a panel of distinguished experts on Asian philosophy, the question was provocative and even offensive—and was clearly perceived as such by the panelists and most members of the audience. Apart from its brusqueness, the query displayed an ethnocentrism unbecoming at any time, but especially in the context of that particular meeting. It also seemed to apply a narrowly pragmatic yardstick to Asian thought that appeared to measure worth or goodness in terms of use-value or pay-off. Stripped of its pragmatic and ethnocentric overtones, however, the question may well contain a kernel of truth deserving to be rescued. For after all, is it not desirable to ponder the continued relevance of traditional thought in our changed circumstances? In this case, is it not legitimate to inquire into the benefit of the Confucian legacy not just for China, but also—and more importantly—for those living in the West today? It is in this latter sense, in any event, that the American philosopher's question will be salvaged for the present chapter.

To be sure, "Confucianism" cannot be assessed here in all its multiple facets and dimensions; such an undertaking would vastly exceed both the author's capacities and limitations of space. Instead, the focus will be upon an aspect that is a central (perhaps *the* central) feature of the Confucian legacy: its understanding of humanity or of what it means to be properly "human." A crucial category in both the *Analects* and later Confucian literature is the notion of *jen*, a term commonly rendered as fellow feeling, humaneness, or humanity (in the sense of the German *Humanität*). Focus upon this concept is prompted not by idle curiosity but by developments in recent Western, especially Continental, philosophy, having to do with the decentering of "subjectivity" or of the Cartesian *cogito* formerly seen as the pivot of both epistemic knowledge and moral action. In challenging traditional parameters of knowing and acting, these developments have also unsettled and called into question the status of "humanism" in Western thought. When promoted by such labels as "death of the subject" or "death of man," this unsettling process has sometimes been associated with the upsurge of a blatant antihumanism—an upsurge which in turn has led to the re-vindication of humanism under the rubric of "anti-antihumanism" (to use Richard Bernstein's phrase).[1] Viewed in broader terms, these arguments are part of the pervasive debate in Western philosophy regarding the demise of foundationalism and the so-called "overcoming of metaphysics."

Confucian thought holds several possible lessons for the ongoing humanism-antihumanism debate. This kind of exploration is warranted on hermeneutical grounds: only by proceeding from one's own concerns and "prejudgments" is it possible to gain access to alien texts or discourses—provided these prejudgments are not willfully foisted on alien life-forms in a manner that would deprive them of their distinctive voice. This chapter's investigation relies on available translations and prominent or well-reputed interpretations of Confucian thought and proceeds in three steps. In order to gain bearings in this field, the first section turns to the well-known *Thinking through Confucius* by Roger Ames and David Hall, a study that ranges probingly over the whole corpus of Confucian thought, while repeatedly giving special attention to the role of humanity or *jen*. Although erudite and perceptive, the book carries too many of the authors' prejudgments into the Confucian world, thereby (at least incipiently) assimilating Confucian *jen* into current, Western-style modes of humanism. In order to correct this tendency, the second section examines other equally visible or prestigious interpretations of Confucian ideas, particularly those advanced by Herbert Fingarette and Tu Wei-Ming; a promising interpretive strategy which, if pursued, is prone to overcome the vexing humanism-antihumanism conundrum, is especially notable in the writings of Tu Wei-Ming. By way of conclusion, the third section returns to the context of modern Western philosophy in order to discover possible "elective affinities" or "family resemblances" with Confucian *jen*. The entire discussion is animated by the query: What lessons might be derived from Asian thought for a cross-cultural learning experience today?

# I

*Thinking through Confucius* is impressive not only for its scope and careful scholarship, but also for its cross-disciplinary character. Written jointly by an Asian specialist and a philosopher reared in the Western tradition, the book brings together a set of diverse competencies that rarely mesh today in the compartmentalized structure of academia. This joining of knowledge encourages and supports a decidedly cross-cultural or "transcultural" approach. As the authors note in a preface to the book, titled "Apologia," their approach diverges both from a bland universalism neglectful of differences and from a radical relativism insisting on the incommensurability of cultures. In pursuing a broadly hermeneutical route of inquiry, their study in effect seeks to promote "that sort of dialogue which eventually may result in a mutual recognition of both commonalties and differences" between Western and Asian philosophy. In challenging cultural separateness, the authors clearly reject a purely antiquarian treatment of texts where the *Analects* would appear as "a mere repository of culture-bound ethical norms relevant [only] to the origin and development of classical Chinese culture." Rather than embarking on such a backward-looking reconstruction, Hall and Ames are willing to shoulder even the accusation of "cross-cultural anachronism," the charge that their interrogation proceeds from issues and concerns originating in contemporary Western thought, which in this form were unfamiliar to Confucius himself. Countering this charge, the authors boldly affirm that one always and inevitably "begins to think *where one is*" and that only in this way will it be possible to rescue Confucian thought "as a potential participant in present philosophic conversations."[2]

These initial arguments—valuable if not pushed to the extreme of "relevantism"—are augmented (and qualified) in the book's opening chapter by a number of additional stipulations that are said to guide the subsequent inquiry. The basic intent of these stipulations is to alert readers to the fact of cultural distance, despite commonalities, and thus to caution against a facile appropriation of Asian thought. One such guidepost is the notion of "radical immanence," a term referring to the absence of a transcendent creator-God, as well as strictly transcendent principles, in Asian thought, including Confucianism. As the authors assert, recognition of this premise is crucial for a proper understanding of the *Analects*, although they acknowledge a certain terminological quandary arising from the fact that the immanence/transcendence distinction is entirely of a Western origin and that "immanence" itself seems to presuppose "transcendence" as its corollary. Coupled with the presumed premise of immanentism is the rejection of the radical dualisms or antinomies characterizing Western thought, such as those between God and world, subject and object, reality and appearance. In lieu of these contrasts, Hall and Ames propose as a further guidepost the notion of "conceptual polarity"—better termed "counterpoint" or "complementarity"—where polarity is a relationship between elements or events in which "each requires the other as a necessary condition for being what it is." The final guidepost or presupposition animating the study is the priority of "tradition" over "history" in Asian, especially Confucian, thought. While history is said to centerstage the "concept of agency," tradition proves resistant to the idea of "originators and creators"; while history "thrives on the actions of rebels," tradition accentuates continuities with the past. In their combination, these premises lead the authors to some general comments relevant to the issue of humanism:

> The distinction between Western forms of individualism and the Confucian concept of the person lies in the fact that difference is prized in Western societies as a mark of creativity and originality, while in China the goal of personality development involves the achievement of interdependence through the actualization of integrative emotions held in common among individuals.[3]

The emphasis on cultural distance is an important reminder, particularly in a study that deliberately takes its departure from contemporary Western concerns. Properly pursued, the reminder would seem to entail a kind of hermeneutical reticence, marked by a constant readiness to test and revise initial presuppositions or prejudgments in the light of what Gadamer has called the "primacy of the *interpretandum*." As it happens, this reticence is not consistently maintained in the bulk of the study, especially in its discussion of Confucian *jen*. As a result, the initial guideposts or "uncommon assumptions" placed at the very threshold of inquiry are allowed to give way, at least tendentially, to much more "common" conceptions and perspectives (common, that is, from a Western viewpoint). In some respects, this tendency nearly approximates a reversal. Thus, the accent placed on "tradition" quickly cedes centerstage to the "concept of agency" (initially associated with "history"), while the notion of polarity or complementarity steadily takes a more one-sided focus on origination and creativity styled "making." Among the initial guideposts, the only one steadfastly preserved throughout the study is the concentration on immanentism or cosmic immanence; however, immanence is progressively interpreted in the sense of "this-worldliness," which permits it to take on connotations of secularism and agnostic humanism congruent with the Western model of secularization. This transformation of outlook is surprising in light of the book's opening caveats, and particularly so in view of the authors' repeated emphasis on interpretive vigilance. As they observe at one point, "vigilance is essential," for "the temptation to construe an alien culture in the more comfortable terms of one's own interpretive constructs is altogether too powerful to ignore."[4]

In large measure, the shift is traceable to the philosophical parameters or frames of reference chosen for comparative purposes, parameters which are basically derived from American pragmatism and French existentialism. In the case of pragmatism, the chosen mentors are Dewey, Mead, and, to a lesser extent, Whitehead, while French existentialism is basically reduced to the Sartrean variety. What links pragmatism and existentialism, in the authors' view, is the turning away from epistemic knowledge toward practice understood as a form of production or making, and hence also toward a humanism construed as "self-formation, self-articulation, self-creation." Rather than being passive products of nature, humans are perceived as creative agents or "makers of meaning," as the makers of society, culture or civilization, which, as human products, reveal the transformative quality of their makers. As Hall and Ames state, "The human being, as a cultural object, is primarily a maker of cultural objects and is, thereby, a maker of himself." More sharply phrased: "The human being as a maker of meaning has as his initial product his self, his person." This aspect was clearly elaborated by Sartre in his notion of free action, designed to "bring into being what is not" and to reveal human consciousness as a creative "consciousness for itself—*pour soi*." According to Hall and Ames, missing in Sartre's approach is attention to the social context of human action, to the necessary correlation between freedom and societal or cultural lifeworlds. Whatever the correctness of this charge, the authors find a remedy in American pragmatism with its emphasis on social interaction and adaptation. Given that society and culture are themselves human products, social adaptation here can only mean a form of self-adaptation or a kind of "closed circuit" movement between producer and product. This type of circuit is plainly evident in the work of George Herbert Mead—singled out as the most helpful pragmatist—with its articulation of social interaction as a relation between "I" and "me" (where "me" designates social context). What attracts the authors to Mead is chiefly his view of humanism. Unlike Dewey, whose endorsement of "naturalism" remained highly ambivalent, Mead was more straightforward: whereas the character of Dewey's naturalism oscillated between "scientific" on the one hand, and "nonsupernatural," "worldly," and "secular" on the other, Mead's version was meant "primarily in the latter, humanistic sense."[5]

These comments, of course, are meant not merely as a profession of philosophical faith, but as yardsticks for comparative inquiry. This aspect is repeatedly underscored in the study. Rooted in the notion of *jen*,

Confucian humanism is said to involve a process of "person making" and "culture making." The Confucian understanding of "person making" in particular, we read, has "its closest analogues" in the Western tradition "among the existentialists and the American pragmatists." The same point is reiterated somewhat later in the statement that "with appropriate caution" the accounts of "Sartre, and particularly of Dewey and Mead" can be helpful in the attempt to "understand Confucius' thought." Among pragmatists, it is again Mead who is given pride of place. Hall and Ames's study takes recourse to "this relatively unheralded pragmatist" for his ability of providing "perhaps the best introduction to the Confucian notion of person making"; in particular, Mead's version of naturalism is said to approximate closely "the kind of humanism that may be attributed to Confucius." The upshot of this invocation of existentialism-*cum*-pragmatism (or pragmatically revised existentialism) is a reading of Confucian *jen* as the origin of progressive self-creation and culture-creation, accentuating the "primary role of the particular human being as the ultimate source and maker of meaningful action." Seen as the source of social action, the properly humane or humanized person (*jen*) can also be described as the "author" of personhood and culture, and further as the "authoritative" warrant of cultural meaning—which is the reason why Hall and Ames also translate *jen* as "authoritative person." In his capacity as originator and "significator" of meaning, the human or "consummating" person engages himself in "authoring his cultural tradition." It is the interchange between "his embodiment of the *authority* of consensus" and "his *authorship* of the emerging culture" that makes such a person "*authoritative*."[6]

In more closely probing the meaning of Confucian humanism, Hall and Ames pay attention to a number of concepts in addition to and including *jen*—particularly "*li*" and "*yi*." Although the assumption of such a constellation of factors is common among Confucian scholars, its treatment in *Thinking through Confucius* is revealing of the authors' approach. *Li* is difficult and complex and has variously been rendered as "ritual action," "rite," "propriety," and "ceremony"; it could also be rendered as authentic tradition. The term *yi*, on the other hand, denotes something like "meaning," "significance," or (intuitive) "judgment." Among Confucian scholars, it has been customary to assume a close linkage between *jen* and *li*—a view that seems to concur with Confucius's statement in the *Analects* (16/13) that "If you do not learn the rites [*li*], you will not be able to take your stand" (as a human being). *Thinking through Confucius* sharply departs from this customary view by deemphasizing the role of *li*. As Hall and Ames recognize, the concept has its origin in ancient religious ceremonies having to do "with the sacred and sacrificial." Although the notion was later extended to cover social conventions more broadly, *li* "never lost the sense of sacredness and sacrifice"; in fact, "the original religious function of integrating the specifically human sphere with the whole remained the same." Notwithstanding this admission, the authors proceed to divest *li* of its religious connotations in large measure and thus to integrate the concept into the process of person making and culture making animated by a secularized humanism:

> Ritual actions are certainly not perceived as divinely established norms. If they have normative force, it is because they have been generated out of the human situation, and hence render informed access to it. They are patterns of behavior initiated and transmitted in order to refine and enhance life in a community.[7]

While thus reducing or downplaying the importance of *li, Thinking through Confucius* assigns a major role to the concept of *yi*, or significance—certainly a greater role than that in customary interpretations of the *Analects*. Commenting on a dictionary definition that simply renders the term as "dignity of demeanor," the authors assert the basic equivalence of *yi* with "a notion of self-construing identity." From a Confucian angle, the human self should be seen as "the source, the locus, the impetus and, at least initially, that which is determined by its own disclosure of *yi*." Congruent with the focus on person making, *yi* understood as "personal disclosure of significance" thus emerges as "coextensive with the process of self-realization." More boldly and emphatically stated, *yi* as the "unique personal contribution" to self-realization is the capacity through which the self "originates unique activity and construes itself on its own terms in a novel and creative way." The authors are not completely neglectful of the contextualism of Confucian thought, that is, the correlation of action and social context. However, as a corollary of person making, this correlation is portrayed simply as a process of meaning bestowal and appropriation, in which the self constantly expands or enlarges itself through creative assimilation (along the lines of the Meadian "I" and "me"). According to Hall and Ames, disclosure of *yi* reveals the human self as a "self-realizing person-in-context." The term "person-in-context" designates a processual conception of selfhood where the self functions as "a dynamic and changing focus of existence characteristically expanding and contracting over some aspect of the process of becoming." Without abandoning its centrality, the self is said to achieve meaning through "the interplay between bestowing its own accumulated significance and appropriating meaning from its context."[8]

The stress on self-creation or self-construction seems to run counter to a number of passages in the *Analects*, particularly to Confucius's saying

(12/1) that, in order to become properly human, one needs "to discipline oneself [*ko-chi*] and practice ritual action [*li*]." Although acknowledging the importance of the saying, the authors treat it as an "often misinterpreted phrase." Properly read, the phrase merely buttresses human self-realization that can alternatively be described "as the objectification of self in that it recognizes the correlative and coextensive relationship between person making and community making, and ultimately, world making." In the presentation of the authors, the centerstaging of *yi* (vis-à-vis *li*) has not only philosophical but also political motives. The argument of their study is not only that "a full appreciation of the meaning of *yi* is fundamental to an understanding of the dynamics of person making" but that the neglect or misconstrual of *yi* has "made possible rigidly narrow and conservative interpretations of Confucianism." In their account, this neglect or misconstrual is not of recent origin. The failure to appreciate fully the role of *yi* in person making, they note, is "not only characteristic of current conservative readings of Confucius but dates back as least as far as the early Taoists." Among recent and contemporary interpreters of Confucius, the study singles out Herbert Fingarette, who, in a number of writings, has insisted on the close linkage of *jen* and *li*, and thus of humanity and ritual or sacred tradition. Although conceding that Fingarette may have "best appreciated the central character of custom and tradition in Confucian thought," Hall and Ames fault him for underestimating the role of *yi* and hence for failing to give "an adequate account of that personal creativity necessary to overcome the inertia of the past." It is "far better" to claim that ritual and tradition have their "origins in *yi* acts, which make us persons in the truest sense"; for only such a reading allows us to see Confucius "as something other than a rigid conservative."[9]

Hall and Ames specifically treat the concept of *jen* as the central pillar in Confucian humanism and in person making seen as a self-expanding and integrating process. Person making, from this angle, involves some kind of self-transformation, but nothing like self-abandonment or self-denial. Rather, self-realization as a synonym for person making proceeds in a series of steps through which the self expands or enlarges itself in order to appropriate or integrate the rest of society. As the authors note, self-realization for Confucius meant "the extension of one's range of concern and the appropriate application of one's own intentionality to this broader context." Differently phrased, Confucian person making or humanization denotes "the taking in of other selves to build a self" as well as "the application of one's own personal judgment (*yi*)." This approach is again said to be congruent with that of Mead, whose notion of a "field of selves" results from "taking in other selves and making them part of our communal self." Seen in this light, the self/

other boundary is blurred through self-development; as a result, there emerges "an indivisible continuum between 'self' and 'other,' between 'I' and 'we,' between 'subject' and 'object,' between 'now' and 'then'." In accord with this general framework, the level of one's humanity or humanization, as well as the authorial quality of the "authoritative person," depends upon "the degree of one's extension and integration," the extent of a person's capacity of " 'taking in' the selves of others." Even the Confucian concept of love—more specifically his association of *jen* with "loving others" (*ai jen*)—is interpreted as a form of self-extension and appropriation, not of surrender or devotion:

> This concept of love in the classical Chinese tradition, consistent with the "taking in" aspect of person making, conveys a sense of appropriation. *Ai* is to take someone into one's sphere of concern, and in so doing, make him an integral aspect of one's own person.[10]

The focus on person making as self-extension is preserved in a later chapter devoted to Confucian "cosmology," particularly to a discussion of the key terms *tien, te,* and *tao.* In conformity with their general model, the authors present *tien* as an "authorial concept," *te* as an "authoring" concept, and *tao* as an authored or "authoritative notion." While recognizing that *tien* is commonly rendered as "heaven" or "sky," they immediately dissociate the term from any "transcendent" connotations. In their view, *tien* as used in the *Analects* is "unquestionably anthropomorphic" and "unqualifiedly immanent" (where immanent clearly stands for "this-worldly," and anthropomorphic can also be read as anthropocentric). *Tien* is a "general designation for the phenomenal world as it emerges of its own accord," or a corollary of person making. The related notion of "*tien ming*" (mandate of heaven) is likewise divested of "mandatory" or normative dimensions and interpreted as part of human culture making and world making, where culture and society—as human products—can always be remade: "Since the human being is the ultimate source of meaning and value, cultural consensus is always open to reformulation and reinterpretation." The concept of *te*—commonly rendered as "virtue" or "moral force"—is also embedded in the process of self-realization. For Hall and Ames, the Confucian *te* is basically synonymous with the capacity for self-expansion. As one's person is extended, "his range of possibilities and the influence or power of his person are proportionately extended" so that he becomes a "large person"; this concurs with Confucius's belief "that the human being is a world maker, and the greater his proportions, the greater his efficacy as world maker." Given these presuppositions, the remaining notion of *tao* is predictably integrated into the same project of human culture and world making. Far from constituting an elusive path requiring an assiduous willingness to search, the authors perceive *tao*, like the world, as a product of human action:

> An important consideration in understanding Confucius' concept of *tao*—limited as it is to the human world—is that the human being is not only heir to and transmitter of *tao*, but is, in fact, its ultimate creator. Thus we shall argue that the *tao* emerges out of human activity. . . . Ultimately derived from particular efforts at person making, *tao* embraces all aspects of the historical process of organizing and structuring human experience. It is a process of world making unified by the basic coherence of all humans' ongoing achievements in the areas of the various cultural interests.[11]

## II

Written with vigor and zest, *Thinking through Confucius* clearly aims at, and is largely successful in, bringing Confucius closer to the contemporary Western reader. Rescued from confinement in dusty archives, Confucius is transformed from a distant cult figure into a lively interlocutor in present-day philosophical debates. This transformation also has a clear political and ideological significance. Long vilified by Marxists as a spokesman of feudal privilege and elitism, Confucius is tendentially integrated into, or at least approximated to, the dominant contemporary mood of democratic liberalism and its globalizing effects. Hall and Ames's effort of retrieval, however, has potential costs that surface on two levels. On the one hand, with regard to alien texts and cultures, assimilationist strategies always run the risk of being predatory in character and thus of damaging the integrity (or "otherness") of alien lifeworlds. On the other hand, the same strategy may also be counterproductive from the interpreter's perspective. When assimilated with Western existentialism and pragmatism, what additional intellectual contribution can Confucianism make—apart from confirming and underwriting Western presuppositions, especially the premises of a modern (Promethean) worldview? What learning experience can Confucius provide—apart from validating existing beliefs? Thus, the query of the American philosopher—"What is Confucianism good for?"—remains intact. Why should the Western reader bother to consult recondite Asian texts for teachings that are articulated so much more lucidly by Sartre and Mead?

Keeping the philosopher's query in mind, it is desirable to turn to alternative interpretations of Confucius, especially readings that deliberately challenge or unsettle Western "world making" views (without being entirely incommensurable). One such alternative reading, frequently singled out by Hall and Ames for criticism, is that offered by Herbert Fingarette in *Confucius—The Secular as Sacred*. For Hall and Ames, Fingarette's reading is marred by his supposed subjection of *jen* to a higher (ritual) order and his treatment of *tao* as an "externally existing schema." This criticism, however, invites countercritique in turn. Fingarette by no means presents *tao* as an "external" scheme, certainly not as an absolute a priori norm exacting passive obedience. In addition, it is precisely his rejection of "world making" that may provide an antidote to modern Western anthropocentrism or anthropocentric humanism (despite an occasional tendency to slide into non- or antihumanism). Fingarette's study links *jen* or humanity closely with *li* or sacred tradition in a careful balancing act that strongly accentuates (perhaps sometimes over-accentuates) the role of *li*. In his basic approach, Fingarette entirely shares Hall and Ames's contemporary motivations—minus their assimilationist bent. "Increasingly," he writes, "I have become convinced that Confucius can be a teacher to us today," but a real teacher and not merely one who "gives us a slightly exotic perspective on ideas already current." Confucius "tells us things not being said elsewhere," things "needing to be said." In this sense he has "a new lesson to teach." Fingarette's central aim in studying the *Analects* is "to discover what is distinctive in Confucius, to learn what he can teach me," not merely to seek "that somewhat pedantic pleasure we can find in showing that an ancient and alien teacher anticipated some point which is already quite familiar to us."[12]

In his reading of the *Analects*, Fingarette departs from two prominent Western approaches, which treat the text either as offering an "empirical, humanist, this-worldly teaching" or else as paralleling "Platonist-rationalist doctrines." Contrary to the allegations of Hall and Ames, Fingarette is unwilling to inject into the text "a doctrine of 'essences' or 'Platonic Ideas'." His book actually concurs with their basic premise that the central topics of the *Analects* revolve around human behavior and relationships. However, deviating from pragmatist assumptions, Fingarette perceives the more-than-human in the human, the unfamiliar in the familiar, the extraordinary in the ordinary—or, as his title says, the "sacred" in the "secular." This more-than-anthropocentric dimension is uncovered in the Confucian concept of *li*, which Fingarette translates as "holy ritual" or "sacred ceremony." *Li* is not simply convention or tradition, though it also means that, nor is it simply the ordinary lifeworld, though it also means that; rather, it denotes a process of transformation or humanization whereby a merely potentially human life-form is transmuted into something distinctively human and even more-than-human. Moreover, this process is not merely a mode of individualistic or egocentric self-production, but a relational event in which self is continuously and emphatically transgressed in the direction of the more-than or other-than-self. In Fingarette's eloquent and beautiful portrayal, human beings in the *Analects*

> are by no means conceived as being mere standardized units mechanically carrying out prescribed routines in the service of some cosmic or social law. Nor are they self-sufficient, individual souls who happen to consent to a social contract. Men become truly human as their raw impulse is shaped by *li*. And *li* is the fulfillment of human impulse, the civilized expression of it—not a formalistic dehumanization. . . . Explicitly holy rite is thus a luminous point of concentration in the greater and ideally all-inclusive ceremonial harmony of the perfectly humane civilization of the *tao*, or ideal way. Human life in its entirety finally appears as one vast, spontaneous and holy rite: the community of man.[13]

In his discussion of the process of humanization, Fingarette's emphasis is squarely on *li*—without neglecting or omitting *jen*; in his study *li* represents the shaping element and *jen* the self that is being shaped or participates in its shaping. One point repeatedly made is the critique of a "psychologistic" construal of *jen*, which would reduce humanization to a process of internal-spiritual self-cultivation. For Fingarette, the accent has to be placed on human action or behavior, more specifically on inter-human behavior in a community, where *jen* and *li* are seen as two sides of the same coin. As he writes, *li* directs our attention to "the traditional social pattern of conduct" (or sacred ceremony), while *jen* refers to "the person as the one who pursues that pattern of conduct." *Li* points to the normatively shaping dimension of human action; *jen* signals a person's orientation "as expressing his commitment to act as prescribed by *li*." Differently phrased, *jen* designates the willingness of submitting oneself to, or "shaping oneself" in accordance with, *li*—with the result that development of *jen* can occur only insofar as *li* develops or is nurtured. Again, one should note that development does not refer to a purely private mode of self-care, but to an active or interactive form of humanization in relation with others. This aspect concurs well with this statement in the *Analects* (6/28): "If you want to be established yourself, then seek to establish others." Fingarette ultimately returns to the notion of inter-active human life as a rite or sacred ceremony affecting and transforming private self-seeking. Individual selfhood is not expunged in this conception, rather, the individual acquires "ultimate dignity" and even "sacred dignity" by participating in rite or *li*. It is not the individual per se nor the group per se that animates and sustains human dignity; "it is the ceremonial aspect of life that bestows sacredness upon persons, acts, and aspects which have a role in the performance of ceremony."[14]

In many ways, Fingarette's general approach has been ably continued and revised by Tu Wei-Ming, especially in his books *Humanity and Self-Cultivation* and *Confucian Thought: Selfhood as Creative Transformation*. While correcting a tendential overemphasis on *li*, Tu Wei-Ming joins Fingarette in resisting a construal of *jen* in terms of a secularist "world making." In company with his fellow Asianists, Tu's outlook is nonantiquarian and hence also largely inspired by contemporary philosophical concerns in the West; however, his choice of intellectual mentors, which prominently includes Gabriel Marcel, Heidegger, and Martin Buber, is revealing for the nuanced direction of his thought. This direction was sketched in one of his early essays, "The Creative Tension Between *Jen* and *Li*." Significantly, the essay spoke of a "creative tension" rather than a rigid primacy of one concept over the other, although the focus was on *jen*, which somewhat misleadingly was rendered as moral "inwardness" or inwardly moral selfhood. In Tu Wei-Ming's words, *jen* designates a "principle of inwardness" and as such is "not a quality acquired from outside"; by contrast, *li* denotes "an externalization of *jen* in a specific social context." Whereas *li* underscores the fact "that man lives in society," *jen* points to selfhood and personal self-cultivation. Despite this questionable use of inner/outer vocabulary, the essay immediately countered any possible confusion of selfhood with self-centeredness or this-worldly self-creation. Although not tied to a transcendent deity, Confucian thought in Tu's presentation scrambles the immanence/transcendence bifurcation. Confucianism, he writes, "also has a transcendental anchorage," though of a quite "different nature" from Western theism; to this extent, *jen* is "not only a personal virtue but also a metaphysical reality." While *jen* designates morality in a crucial sense, traditional Confucian morality is "not merely confined to the ethical stage" but also conveys "religious significance." Hence, though in an ordinary (Western) context Confucianism may not be a "religion," it is "completely unjustified to deny its religiousness."[15]

The creative balancing act between *jen* and *li* was articulated more carefully in a subsequent essay titled "*Li* as Process of Humanization." Abandoning in large measure the inner/outer dichotomy, the essay accentuated the mutual interpenetration of *jen* and *li*, giving rise to the question: how can *li*, commonly translated as ritual, be adequately understood as integral to "a process of humanization"? As Tu Wei-Ming emphasized, *jen*—though an index of moral selfhood—cannot properly be cultivated or developed outside the context of human relationships, especially the "five basic human relations" thematized in the *Analects*, which are permeated by the standards of *li*. This accent on human "relatedness," in Tu's account, contrasts with Western conceptions of spirituality or religiosity where the latter can only be nurtured in individual isolation, through a plunge either into the "wholly other" or into the abyss of inwardness. While insisting on self-cultivation, Confucianism rejects isolationism. In fact, from a Confucian vantage, Tu writes, sociality is "not only a desirable trait but also a defining characteristic of the highest human attainment." According to central Confucian teachings, humanization occurs not in a vacuum but always in a structured setting, specifically the broader cosmic context of "Heaven, Earth, and the myriad things." Against this background, *li* designates openness to the "other," and humanization a patterned or contextual fostering of *jen* under the auspices of *li*. Tu adds, however, that the interpenetration of *jen* and *li* should not be reduced to a process of individuation, nor to one of external socialization (nor to an internalized "I-me" relation along Meadian lines). Confucian self-cultivation or self-transformation is based on "neither isolated self-control nor collective social sanction"; rather, its sphere is that of a tensional "between": "If we follow this line of thinking, the road to sagehood is a 'narrow ridge' between spiritual individualism and ethical socialism."[16]

Tu Wei-Ming's understanding of humanity and humanization was deepened and refined in several additional essays, assembled together in his volume on *Confucian Thought: Selfhood as Creative Transformation.* The opening chapter clearly delineates the distinctive character of Confucian *jen* in its connection with *li* and its differentiation from Western-style self-creation. The Confucian accent on self-cultivation, Tu notes, may seem to betray a central preoccupation with individual selfhood, inner spirituality, or "one's own private self"; but this impression is misleading. While not neglecting self-concern or self-care, the *Analects* inaugurate a vision of humanity where self is closely enmeshed in "a shared life together with other human beings" and "inseparable from the truth of transcendence." Selfhood appears as a dynamic, open-ended vista opening up not only to society or social conventions but to broader normative and sacred dimensions. Tu at this point pays explicit tribute to Fingarette's portrayal of *li* as a cosmic ritual. These comments lead him to the important observation that, despite its seemingly secular-humanistic bent, Confucianism is

> predicated on a holistic vision of humanity which transcends not only self-centeredness, nepotism, ethnocentrism, nationalism, and culturalism but also anthropocentrism. Indeed, the Confucian vision of "forming one body with Heaven and Earth and the myriad things" is anthropocosmic in the sense that the complete realization of the self, which is tantamount to the full actualization of humanity, entails the unity of humankind with Heaven.

The contrast between this conception and Western "individualism," with its celebration of ego's alienation from society and world, is striking. Yet, as Tu insists, such individualism does not exhaust the full range of *jen* and human self-cultivation. In fact, it is quite possible to accept the Confucian *jen* without being constrained to endorse "Locke's idea of private property, Adam Smith's and Hobbes' idea of private interest, John Stuart Mill's idea of privacy, Kierkegaard's idea of loneliness, or the early Sartre's idea of freedom."[17]

What emerges from Tu Wei-Ming's presentation is a complex notion of *jen* that steers a precarious path between human-centered world making and antihumanist self-effacement. In a series of chapters with such alluring headings as "On Learning to be Human," "The Value of the Human," and "*Jen* as a Living Metaphor" in Confucian thought, this path is carefully explored in a manner that reveals it as a synonym for the Asian *tao* (seen as "way"). Human "relatedness"—though crucial—cannot simply be equated with socialization or adaptation to external rules or conventions; to this extent, Max Weber's characterization of Confucian thought as based on "adjustment to the world" is misleading, because it misconstrues the self-other relation, missing its quality of depth. In Tu's words, Weber's formula ignores the Confucian capacity for both human self-care and "religious transcendence." At the same time, this quality should not be mistaken for an exit route to an inner-human privacy or an other-worldly realm populated by a creator God, or else an abstract set of principles. As previously indicated, Confucian "transcendence" does not point to an extramundane dimension (or radical "exteriority"), but rather to a complex intermingling of elements, particularly the participation of human life in the cosmic rite of "Heaven, Earth, and the myriad things." From this vantage, human self-cultivation necessarily means self-transcendence, and vice versa. Tu Wei-Ming is fond of quoting *The Doctrine of the Mean* or *Chung-yung*, to which he had devoted an earlier study. According to that text, humans can fully develop their own capacities only by also fostering the potential of others, which in turn allows them to assist in fostering "the nature of things." Moreover, in proceeding along this route, humans can assist in "the transforming and nourishing process of Heaven and Earth," which enables them ultimately to form "a trinity with Heaven and Earth." Tu comments perceptively, "Confucian humanism is therefore fundamentally different from anthropocentrism because it professes the unity of man and Heaven rather than the imposition of the human will on nature."[18]

These interpretive insights lead Tu Wei-Ming to some thoughtful comments on the significance of Confucianism in today's world that go a good distance toward answering the American philosopher's query. In large measure, his observations take their bearing from what is often called the "crisis of modernity" (or else the "dialectic of Enlightenment"), discussed by many existentialists under the heading of "alienation" from self and world. In Tu's account, the crisis surfaces in lopsided and erratic conduct. While we "take rights seriously," indeed as our paramount concern, we are reluctant to shoulder obligations; though negligent and even dismissive of cultural traditions, we yet search for artificial means of social cohesion. Thus, as we become "increasingly subjectivistic, individualistic, and narcissistic," we can "neither remember the old nor instruct the young." A major antidote for this malaise is the Confucian emphasis on self-cultivation and humanization, seen not as a passing whim but as the steady practice of "learning to be human." Guided by *li*, self-cultivation here does not mean self-glorification (or a cult of human-centered world making) nor a mere process of social adaptation and conformism. Above all, Confucian-style learning does not involve a one-sided stress on rational knowledge—conducive to (technological) world-mastery—but an equilibrated training of "heart-and-mind" (*hsin*), where cognitive gains must be accompanied by humanization in the sense of ethical self-mastery and self-transformation. Only this transformation is able to rescue humans from self-centered isolation and to embed them again in the great rite of "Heaven, Earth, and the myriad things." Borrowing from Michael Polanyi (and Marcel), Tu speaks in this context of a "fiduciary community," whose participants—without being blandly homogenized—maintain their distinct role through mutual responsiveness and faith-keeping. As he noted in his study on the *Chung-yung*, the Asian *tao* is actually just a synonym for humanization, which in turn is equivalent to cosmic openness in a network of "mutual fidelity."[19]

## III

In Tu Wei-Ming's presentation, Confucian thought appears both distant (or "other") and intensely pertinent to contemporary concerns in the West. He makes no effort to popularize Confucianism by assimilating it blandly to modern Western preferences or prejudgments. On the contrary, Confucian thought in many ways represents a challenge or antidote to these preferences—and precisely in this manner gains its pertinence or relevance for contemporary readers. Against this background, it becomes possible to ponder or perceive how Confucianism may not only have been "good for China" but may also be good for today, offering some valuable lessons. These lessons are not simply exotic doctrines; though historically distant, Confucian discourse is not entirely incommensurable with ours. To some extent, receptivity for its teachings has been prepared by recent intellectual trends. Particularly in the context of Continental philosophy, several prominent strands have called into question basic pillars of modern Western thought, especially the centrality of the *cogito* and hence of anthropocentrism or an anthropocentric humanism. Quite apart from the inflated rhetoric of the "death of man," this centrality has been challenged by a number of major thinkers, including Levinas, Derrida, and Heidegger. In Levinas's writings, the subject is entirely dislodged from its pivotal role as knower and agent and instead exposed to the inroad of otherness, or the "face of the other," especially the face of the "absolutely Other" (*Autrui*). As he observes at one point, his approach—with its stress on interpersonal contact—"does not reduce the other to the same" or self but calls the self "into question," something that cannot happen "within the egoist spontaneity" of selfhood but must be "brought about by the other": "We name this calling into question of my spontaneity by the presence of the Other ethics." Quite appropriately, Levinas's thought has been termed a counterhumanism or a "humanism of the other man," where humanity is not self-propelled or self-created but derives from the encounter with otherness.[20]

The point here is not to endorse the Levinasian position in all its aspects. For a number of reasons, one may be reluctant to accept the Levinasian accent on such notions as "heteronomy," "exteriority," and "asymmetry," and especially on the radical "passivity" of the subject in interpersonal encounters. Still, his approach is valuable if taken as a corrective to modern Western anthropocentrism (anchored in self and world making)—provided interpersonal encounter is transferred from the abstract level of the "Other" to the more concrete level of human relationships (such as the five basic Confucian relationships). A more balanced approach to this set of issues is offered by Heidegger in his famous *Letter on Humanism*. There Heidegger advanced a radical critique of modern egocentrism and anthropocentrism, but without proceeding to delegitimate or disempower human existence in favor of otherness (or passively endured obligation). In his account, "humanism," deriving ultimately from Roman antiquity, has always insisted on ascribing to humans a determinate preeminence or privileged quality, whether this quality was found in human rationality, subjectivity, or personhood. In modern times, this preeminence has been progressively stylized as self-creation and world making. Countering this tradition, the *Letter* found in such ascriptions a diminution of humanity rather than an elevation. Without in any way endorsing the alternatives of counter- or antihumanism, Heidegger preferred to reformulate "humanism" in the direction of existential (or "ek-static") self-transcendence and transformation, reinserting humans in the "chain of being(s)." He wrote, "As the ek-static counterpoint of being, humans are more than rational animals (*animal rationale*) precisely to the degree that they are less compared with their definition in terms of subjectivity. Humanity is not the master of beings, but the shepherd (or guardian) of being."[21]

In his *Letter*, Heidegger did not elaborate on how such a chastized humanism might be cultivated or fostered—beyond some brief references to the notions of "care" and "letting-be" (initially thematized in *Being and Time*). At later points, however, he did offer helpful clues. About a decade after the *Letter*, an essay with the title "*Gelassenheit*" (or "Releasement") indicated how we might nurture a soberly restrained humanness beyond the lure of subjective self-centeredness or external mastery of the world. By letting go of, or being released from, anthropocentric conceit as well as instrumental designs we become ready for a genuine "care" for being and also for an openness to the "mystery" or recessed sacredness of life. Yet, for Heidegger, such openness and releasement are not the result of a sudden whim: "they do not befall us accidentally, but flourish only through persistent and courageous thinking" (and acting). In a somewhat more limited sense, the theme of a cultivation of human being has also been articulated by Michel Foucault in some of his later writings. The theme emerged centrally in *The Care of the Self*, written shortly before his death. In the chapter titled "The Cultivation of the Self," Foucault showed at length (and approvingly) how care for one's humanity was a crucial concern for Greeks and Romans during the early imperial and Hellenistic periods. Yet, self-care here was not simply the antithesis of other-relatedness. Rather, it often happened, and was assumed, that "the interplay of the care of the self and the help of the other blends in preexisting relations, giving them a new coloration and a greater warmth." To this extent, the care of self appears as "an intensification of social relations."[22]

Foucault's study focused on a circumscribed period—late antiquity. Needless to say, self-care has not been the sole province of that period. Under such labels as *paideia, cura sui,* and *Bildung,* humanness and its cultivation have been a persistent concern throughout Western history, although, admittedly, this concern has often been invaded or overshadowed by a narrow anthropocentrism or a self-aggrandizing type of humanism. In the context of Western modernity, no one has expounded the theme of humanity and humanization more eloquently and stirringly than Johann Gottfried Herder. Although critical of the universalizing and blandly homogenizing aspirations of Enlightenment thought, Herder throughout his life persistently extolled and celebrated the topic of humanization and human *Bildung* as a process of self-transcendence and self-transformation—but a transformation that can only happen in concrete and carefully sustained relationships. His *Letters for the Advancement of Humanity* still deserve to be consulted as a primer of ethically responsible (in the sense of genuinely "responsive") conduct. As we read there, humanity (*Humanität*) is the distinctive "emblem of our species"; yet, it is not given to us ready-made, but requires assiduous practice and cultivation. To this extent, *Bildung* is a work or labor that has to be "incessantly continued"; it involves self-transcendence as well as openness to the "divine" so that humanization or *Bildung zur Humanität* appears ultimately as a divine calling.[23] In the Confucian tradition there is a passage by Chang Tsai (1020–1077) often called the "Western Inscription." It is a passage that Tu Wei-Ming loves to quote—and which indeed deserves to be quoted and even memorized:

> Heaven is my father and Earth is my mother, and even such a small creature as I finds an intimate place in their midst. Therefore that which fills the universe I regard as my body and that which directs the universe I consider as my nature. All people are my brothers and sisters, and all things are my companions.[24]

# Notes

1. See Richard J. Bernstein, "Heidegger on Humanism" in his *Philosophical Profiles: Essays in a Pragmatic Mode* (Philadelphia: University of Pennsylvania Press, 1986), pp. 197–220; a version of the essay, under the title "Anti-Antihumanism," had earlier been presented at the annual meeting of the Society for Phenomenology and Existential Philosophy in 1984. Regarding the problematic status of the modern subject see, e.g., Michael E. Zimmerman, *Eclipse of the Self* (Athens, Ohio: Ohio University Press, 1981); Daniel Shanahan, *Toward a Genealogy of Individualism* (Amherst, Mass.: University of Massachusetts Press, 1992); also my *Twilight of Subjectivity* (Amherst, Mass.: University of Massachusetts Press, 1981).

2. David L. Hall and Roger T. Ames, *Thinking through Confucius* (Albany, N.Y.: SUNY Press, 1987), pp. 6–7, 12.

3. Hall and Ames, *Thinking through Confucius*, pp. 12–13, 17–18, 21–23. The term "inseparable complementarity" has been used by Benjamin Schwartz in his contribution to *Confucianism in Action*, ed. David S. Nivison and Arthur F. Wright (Stanford, Calif.: Stanford University Press, 1959), pp. 50–62.

4. Hall and Ames, *Thinking through Confucius*, p. 326. Regarding the importance of the "*interpretandum*" see Hans-Georg Gadamer, *Truth and Method*, 2nd rev. ed., trans. Joel Weinsheimer and Donald G. Marshall (New York: Crossroad, 1989), pp. 266–270.

5. Hall and Ames, *Thinking through Confucius*, pp. 72–74, 80–81. In the authors' view, both existentialism and pragmatism are marred by potential pitfalls that require correction; see Hall and Ames, p. 79: "From the perspective of this work, the fatal disadvantage of existentialism is its individualistic presuppositions, which make of society a derivative, and therefore abstract notion. Pragmatism provides a corrective to the individualism of the existentialist, of course, but in doing so threatens to fall into the equally serious mistake of reducing the concept of person to naturalistic categories that owe altogether too much to the method of the natural sciences." Without endorsing Sartrean existentialism I find

dubious the claim that Sartre neglected the correlation of action and context, of freedom and social situation.

6. *Thinking through Confucius*, pp. 73, 80, 82–84, 100 (italics in the text). The claimed parallelism between Confucianism and existentialist pragmatism does not prevent the authors from registering another caveat: "The turn toward praxis in twentieth-century Western philosophy does seem to make our task somewhat easier, but we must be cautious nonetheless. . . . The reduction of theories to praxis with the consequent construal of ideas in terms of actions, found in existentialism, and to a lesser extent in pragmatism, cannot be wholly satisfactory to the Confucian who does not recognize a breach between the two" (p. 82).

7. *Thinking through Confucius*, pp. 85–86, 89.

8. *Thinking through Confucius*, pp. 92–96.

9. *Thinking through Confucius*, pp. 90, 93–94, 98, 107–110. As on previous occasions, the authors again add a caveat, stating, "One might object that stressing to such a degree the function of *yi* in establishing ritual actions renders incomprehensible Confucius' concern to promote a coherent set of rituals, grounded upon tradition, as a context for human experience" (p. 109). The political motive is forcefully reasserted in one of the concluding notes (p. 345, n. 76), directed against Ts'ai Shang-ssu: "Ts'ai's argument is based on the assumption that Confucius was a spokesman for the feudal powers-that-be, and that he philosophized in service to the rigid continuance of an established political system. Our entire book, step by step, is an argument against collapsing the distinction between the teachings of Confucius and the political order that interpreted it, and against casting Confucius as a conservative advocate of Chou feudalism."

10. *Thinking through Confucius*, pp. 116–121. As they add pointedly, the nexus of love and self-extension "poses an insurmountable problem for those Christian interpreters of Confucius who, given the 'unselfish' implications of *jen*, would equate *jen* with *agape*. For *jen* cannot be *agape*" (p. 120).

11. *Thinking through Confucius*, pp. 200, 205–207, 211, 222, 228, 230. The interpretation of *tao* is contrasted sharply with that of Fingarette, who views *tao* as a "path" with normative implications (pp. 234–237). Despite their strenuous insistence, it seems fair to observe that the authors by no means escape the lure of "transcendentalism." In their emphasis on person making, they merely exchange the creator-God for the creator-Man, and the divine act of *creatio ex nihilo* for an existentialist-pragmatist mode of self-construction.

12. Herbert Fingarette, *Confucius—The Secular as Sacred* (New York: Harper & Row, 1972), pp. vii–viii. See also Hall and Ames, *Thinking through Confucius*, pp. 107–109, 112–113, 236.

13. Fingarette, *Confucius—The Secular as Sacred*, pp. 1–2, 7, 15, 17. In emphasizing the dimension of "humane civilization" and the "community of man" (i.e., human beings), Fingarette presents Confucius not as a backward-looking traditionalist but as a "visionary" anticipating new developments (first of all in China). Confucius was "the creator of a new ideal, not an apologist for an old one"; what Confucius perceived were "the newly *emerging* similarities in social-political practices, the newly *emerging*, widespread sharing of values that had

once been restricted to a small region which included Lu" (p. 60). For this interpretation he invokes the statement in the *Analects* (2/11) that "he who by reanimating the old can gain knowledge of the new is indeed fit to be called a teacher."

14. *Confucius—The Secular as Sacred*, pp. 37, 42–43, 48, 51, 75–76. Fingarette's discussion of the relation between *jen* and *li* is marred by his equation of the two terms with purpose or decision, on the one hand, and actual performance, on the other—which seems again to "psychologize" *jen*. As one should note, his treatment of the "secular as sacred" by no means endorses a bifurcation between immanence and transcendence, this world and other world. "Instead of being a diversion of attention from the human realm to another transcendent realm," he writes, "the overtly holy ceremony is to be seen as the central symbol, both expressive of and participating in the holy as a dimension of all truly human existence" (p. 17).

15. Tu Wei-Ming, "The Creative Tension Between *Jen* and *Li*," in *Humanity and Self-Cultivation: Essays in Confucian Thought* (Berkeley, Calif.: Asian Humanities Press, 1979), pp. 5, 8–12. Regarding his contemporary starting point and orientation compare these comments (p. xxi): "I believe that by employing fresh perspectives on perennial issues, we can dig down through strata of partial and distorted writings on the matter. Only then can we say that we have arrived at an understanding."

16. "*Li* as Process of Humanization," in *Humanity and Self-Cultivation*, pp. 17, 19–22. He adds, seen as a process of humanization, *li* is manifested in four stages or dimensions: cultivating personal life, regulating familial relations, ordering the affairs of the state, and bringing peace to the world; to this extent, "*li* assumes the forms of integrating personality, family, state, and the world" (pp. 27, 29). In several additional essays collected in the same volume, Tu Wei-Ming comments on the meaning of *jen* in the context of later neo-Confucianism. From the perspective of Chu Hsi, he writes, humanity is "both immanent and transcendent," for it reflects both "the character of the mind and the principle of love" (p. 77). With specific regard to humanism, Tu notes that the Confucian and neo-Confucian position "can be labelled as humanist only in a very special sense. The man of humanity . . . must also be able to realize the nature of the 'myriad things' and assist Heaven and Earth in their transforming and nourishing functions. If one cannot transcend one's anthropological structure, let alone egoistic structure, one's self-transformation is still in the initial stage. Unless one can realize the nature of all things to form a trinity with Heaven and Earth, one's self-realization cannot be complete. In this sense, humanity implies a profound care for and deep commitment to the well-being of the natural world—indeed, to the cosmos" (pp. 97, 99).

17. Tu Wei-Ming, *Confucian Thought: Selfhood as Creative Transformation* (Albany, N.Y.: SUNY Press, 1985), pp. 8, 10–12.

18. *Confucian Thought*, pp. 55, 74–75. "In fact," he adds, "the anthropocentric assumption that man is put on earth to pursue knowledge and, as knowledge expands, so does man's dominion over earth is quite different from the Confucian perception of the pursuit of knowledge as an integral part of one's self-cultivation" (p. 75). Compare also Tu Wei-Ming, *Centrality and Commonality: An*

144 Chapter 5

*Essay on Chung-yung*, Monograph No. 3 of the Society for Asian and Comparative Philosophy (Honolulu: University of Hawaii Press, 1976).

19. *Confucian Thought*, pp. 32, 58, 71–73, 82, 137; also *Centrality and Commonality*, p. 9. Compare also Wm. Theodore de Bary, *Neo-Confucian Orthodoxy and the Learning of the Mind-and-Heart* (New York: Columbia University Press, 1981).

20. See Emmanuel Levinas, *Totality and Infinity*, trans. Alphonso Lingis (Pittsburgh, Pa.: Duquesne University Press, n.d.), pp. 39, 43; *Otherwise than Being or Beyond Essence*, trans. Alphonso Lingis (The Hague: Martinus Nijhoff, 1991), pp. 184–185; also Fabio Ciaramelli, "Levinas's Ethical Discourse between Individuation and Universality," in *Re-Reading Levinas*, ed. Robert Bernasconi and Simon Critchley (Bloomington: Indiana University Press, 1991), pp. 92–93.

21. Martin Heidegger, "Letter on Humanism," in *Martin Heidegger: Basic Writings*, ed. David F. Krell (New York: Harper & Row, 1977), p. 221 (translation slightly altered, to correct gendered terminology). Compare also his comment that in its traditional meaning, "humanism is opposed because it does not set the *humanitas* of humans high enough. Of course, the dignity of humans does not consist in their role as the ultimate substance of beings, as their 'subject', a role which would enable them as the master of being to dissolve all being-ness into the all too loudly proclaimed 'objectivity' " (p. 210) of knowledge. For one of Levinas's more extreme formulations compare his statement "The self cannot form itself; it is already formed with absolute passivity. In this sense, it is the victim of persecution that paralyzes any assumption that could awaken in it, so that it would posit itself for itself" (*Otherwise than Being or Beyond Essence*, p. 104).

22. See Heidegger, *Discourse on Thinking, A Translation of Gelassenheit*, trans. John M. Anderson and E. Hans Freund (New York: Harper & Row, 1966), p. 56; and Michel Foucault, *The Care of the Self*, trans. Robert Hurley (New York: Pantheon Books, 1986), p. 53.

23. Johann Gottfried Herder, *Briefe zur Beförderung der Humanität*, in *Sämtliche Werke*, vol. 17, ed. Bernhard Suphan (Hildesheim, Germany: Georg Olms, 1967), p. 138. Among Heidegger's students it was chiefly Gadamer who has called attention again to Herder and his notion of *Bildung*; see Hans-Georg Gadamer, *Truth and Method*, pp. 9–12.

24. See Tu Wei-Ming, *Confucian Thought*, pp. 137, 157.

# 6

# Liberating Remembrance: Thoughts on Ethics, Politics, and Recollection

> . . . the best education, perhaps, is that of preserved, sacred memory.
>
> Dostoevsky, *The Brothers Karamazov*

> The struggle of man against power is the struggle of memory against forgetting.
>
> Kundera, *The Book of Laughter and Forgetting*

"The earliest appearances in our lives of a person who is destined to take our fancy later on assume retrospectively in our eyes a certain value as an indication, a warning, a presage." Thus writes Marcel Proust in *Remembrance of Things Past*; he adds, "It was in this fashion that Swann had often reverted in his mind to the image of Odette encountered in the theatre on that first evening when he had no thought of ever seeing her again." In a subtle and philosophically suggestive way, Proust points to the complex intertwinement in human lives of action and circumstance, purpose and contingency. Without in any way denying the role of human freedom, the passage signals the embeddedness of choice in a welter of happenings that by no means determines deliberate goals but retains the status of an obscure indication or "presage." The lines are suggestive, however, for another reason: for unsettling the notion of a linear temporal sequence in favor of an embroilment of temporalities. Despite its overt title, Proust's novel is not simply backward-looking or nostalgic; far from denoting merely a "lost time" (*temps perdu*), the past for Swann remains a reservoir of sedimentations and hidden trends that actively permeate the present while casting their shadow (or their light) on the future.[1]

The present chapter probes the philosophical implications of Proustian remembrance, particularly in the domains of ethics and cultural politics.

Remembrance or recollection occupies a prominent and indeed preeminent place in philosophical reflection, because it adumbrates the genealogy or oblique beginning of such reflection. The same holds true for ethics or ethical thought. If it is true—as some philosophers claim—that ethics deserves primacy as a "first philosophy," then this status can be warranted only in terms of remembrance, and not by virtue of any "foundational" privilege. Approaching ethics from a Proustian angle brings a new impulse to ethical theory, which today is impaled on the proverbial horns of a dilemma: "descriptivism" and "prescriptivism," inclination and duty. In the eyes of many theorists, sometimes termed "naturalists" or "descriptivists," there is a smooth continuity between empirical inclinations, preferences or institutional settings, and ethical norms; far from being obtuse to moral values, "nature," or factual reality, is said to be pregnant with normative yardsticks. This approach neglects the transformative quality of ethics and the disjuncture commonly prevailing between factual "is" and normative "ought." In sharp opposition to naturalism in its various forms, "prescriptivists" prefer to derive standards from conceptual categories or else from the transcendental "conditions of possibility" of human action; in the Kantian critical framework, moral imperatives encapsulate "noumenally" grounded duties entirely divorced from empirical inclinations or contingent social conditions. While imposing in its moral grandeur, Kantian ethics, however, exchanges one horn of the dilemma for another: in avoiding the "naturalistic fallacy," presciptivism seems to court the danger of a transcendental or "antinaturalistic" fallacy by stripping duty of any impact on concrete behavior and on the actual course of human history.[2]

In steering a course beyond naturalism and prescription, this chapter will draw inspiration from a number of diverse though cognate perspectives, including early critical theory, post-Freudian psychoanalysis, and Heideggerian philosophy. In the context of early critical theory, remembrance or recollection first surfaced as a remembrance of suffering (what Johann Baptist Metz has called a *memoria passionis*).[3] For Walter Benjamin, historical remembering served mainly as an antidote to the constraints of positivist reality and prevailing power structures—an antidote which, by recovering hopes buried in past sufferings, is able to illuminate the present while casting a redemptive light on the future. Directly or indirectly, Benjamin's notion of "redemptive remembering" became an important tributary to the critical theory program of the early Frankfurt School, especially to Adorno's conception of "natural history" or the retrieval of nature in civilization. The link between Adorno's argument and psychoanalytic theory was articulated chiefly by Herbert Marcuse, with an accent on the utopian potential of memory or remembrance. In a different register, the theme of transformative memory-work was

explored by Martin Heidegger in his discussion of recollective or "anamnestic" thinking (*Andenken*), which is attentive to the embeddedness of
reason and action in the "happening" of being and language. Without
asserting any historical or intellectual filiation, the subsequent presentation will follow the sketched sequence of perspectives. Thus, after review-
ing some of Benjamin's writings, section II examines the treatment of
recollection in early critical theory and post-Freudian psychoanalysis. In
a third section, the chapter turns to the role of recollection in Heidegger's
evolving opus, from *Being and Time* to *What Is Called Thinking*. The
conclusion will ponder some of the implications of recollection for contemporary ethics and politics, keeping in mind the possibly redemptive
or liberating potential of remembrance in the context of an emerging
global democracy.

# I

As a theoretical notion or philosophical category, recollection has itself a
distinct history. There is no need here to "recollect" or retrace this complex historical trajectory, as this has been done quite well by a number
of writers.[4] For present purposes, a few comments must suffice. Apart
from serving as a mainstay of empirical (sensualist) psychology, remembrance has occupied a fragile or tenuous place in modern times. From
the vantage of rationalist or idealist philosophy, the past appears as a
prelude to the present, which, in turn, is a mere stepping stone to the
future within the confines of an overarching teleology. Seen in this light,
remembered experience is at best an obscure or corrupted mode of
awareness destined to be superseded by, or "sublated" in, higher and
more transparent forms of reflection.

This view of recollection as an antechamber to knowledge was challenged in our century by a number of philosophical "turns," especially
by the moves to language, historical contingency, and "worldliness" (that
is, a precognitively experienced lifeworld). In the aftermath of these
changes, the past began to emerge as a fabric of deeply sedimented traces
and clues, as a memory-work that permanently resists "sublation" into
cognitive analysis without losing any of its significance as a portent for
the present and the future. One of the first thinkers to adopt this perspective and to explore its implications for a postidealist (or postmetaphysical) view of history was Walter Benjamin. After having participated in
debates on "historicism" during the middle years of the Weimar period,
Benjamin articulated an experiential but nonteleological sense of past
suffering in his study on the origins of German tragic theater or of the
German "mourning play" (*Trauerspiel*). Shortly before his death, Benja-

min dramatically reformulated this outlook in his "Theses on the Philosophy of History," designed as an introduction to his sprawling work on the Paris arcades (*Passagenarbeit*).[5]

The historicism discussion had been triggered by some writings of Ernst Troeltsch, Wilhelm Dilthey, and others. The central issue was whether history could be seen as a positivist record of "actual" events or whether its meaning could be distilled into a transparent teleology or else a set of a priori principles. For Benjamin both approaches were unsatisfactory, since they ignored the crucial role of memory-work. His alternative view of history was outlined in his study on the origin of German Baroque tragedy (*Ursprung des deutschen Trauerspiels*, published in 1928). According to Benjamin, German drama of the Baroque era—deviating sharply from classical canons—allowed history directly to enter the stage and permeate the plot or story line. However, history at this point was not a sequence of glorious deeds, a repository of profound purposes, or a steadily unfolding teleology; instead, it was an arena of non-meaning and non-transparency, where historical occurrences are marked by finitude, radical contingency, and suffering. Seen from this angle, history was close to the domain of nonpurposive nature, the domain of natural mortality, entropy, and physical decay. In Benjamin's words, history in the Baroque tragedy surfaced as a passion play, as a "story of the suffering of the world" (*Leidensgeschichte der Welt*); far from revealing an intelligible purpose, it was occluded by and even synonymous with contingency and mortality. To capture or memorialize this historical non-meaning, Baroque tragedy took recourse to allegory, a literary device uniquely suited to transitoriness and natural finitude. While symbolism—Benjamin notes—tries to transcend decay by revealing a higher, transfigured meaning, allegory presents the troubling image of history as a "congealed prehistorical landscape"; allegory preserves traces of whatever is "untimely, painful, and unfulfilled" in time and thus pinpoints the "peculiar entwinement of nature and history."[6]

As Benjamin elaborated, the Baroque focus on natural contingency and mortality was radically opposed to classical standards of beauty and harmony, especially to the notion of sensual reality as simple "appearance" of the divine. Classical art or aesthetics, he writes, was congenitally unable to perceive the "unfreedom, incompleteness, and brokenness" of sensual nature. Despite certain affinities with the Baroque period, later Romanticism tended to abandon Baroque sobriety, namely, by favoring subjective empathy and spiritual revivalism. By contrast, Benjamin notes, the accent of Baroque tragedy was on "mortification": its goal was not "Romantically to revive consciousness in living [works]," but rather to "settle thought among works of decay." In entering the Baroque stage history bears the legible imprint of finitude and transitoriness; hence, the "allegorical physiognomy of nature-history" is portrayed or represented in the form of ruins. With this preference for fragmentation and decay, allegory occupies a place "beyond beauty"; "allegories are in the realm of thoughts what ruins are in the realm of things," which explains the "Baroque cult" of the latter. Still, this cult or preference was the outgrowth of memory-work, not merely the result of positivist description. More importantly, the Baroque accent on transitoriness and decay was not simply a recipe for pessimism or bleak despair. In Benjamin's account, Baroque theater shifted attention from a redeemed nature, and an intelligible history, to an eschatological promise; while denying an existing harmony or purpose, remembrance of decay uncovered a redemptive spark pointing to the future:

> Since the ruins of large edifices reveal the architect's design more powerfully than do well-preserved small structures, the German Baroque drama has a claim to interpretation. In the spirit of allegory this drama is conceived as a ruin or fragment from the beginning. While other arts are resplendent as on the first day, this art form keeps the image of the beautiful for the last day.[7]

While the role of memory-work was still left somewhat obscure in this historical study, its character was soon more fully delineated in Benjamin's essay on Proust or the "image of Proust" (composed barely a year later). Turning to *Remembrance of Things Past*, Benjamin noted that Proust obviously did not seek to describe a life "as it actually was," but rather a life "as it was remembered by the one who had lived it." But even this statement needed to be amended. For the important thing was not the course of experience but this course as filtered and distilled through remembrance; what concerned Proust was not the past as such but "the weaving of his memory, the Penelope work of recollection." Memory-work was not a deliberate act seeking to expose experience to the searchlight of awareness. Implicit in memory was also a mode of non- or counterintentionality intent on concealing the traces of the past. Instead of speaking of the work of recollection, Benjamin asks,

> should one call it, rather, a Penelope work of forgetting? Is not the involuntary recollection, Proust's *mémoire involuntaire*, much closer to forgetting than what is usually called memory? And is not this work of spontaneous recollection, in which remembrance is the woof and forgetting the warf, a counterpart to Penelope's work rather than its likeness? For here the day unravels what the night has woven.

In contrast with Penelope's labors, nighttime forgetfulness weaves the intricate "tapestry of lived life." As Benjamin adds with some insistence, memory-work for Proust was not backward-looking or nostalgic. While an experienced event may be "finite" by occupying a distinct place in the past, a remembered event is "infinite," since it serves as "a key to everything that happened before it and after it." For Proust himself, remembrance was always saturated with pain and melancholy—but it was also an escape from despair. By submitting to the ordeal of recollection, Benjamin writes, Proust "conquered the hopeless sadness within him" and "from the honeycombs of memory he built a house for the swarm of his thoughts." His relentless pursuit of remembering revealed in an oblique way his "blind, senseless, frenzied quest for happiness." This quest "shone from his eyes; they were not happy, but in them there lay fortune as it lies in gambling or in love."[8]

During the years following this essay, Benjamin began collecting materials for his large-scale study on the Paris arcades, which he conceived as a memorial of the "European capital of the nineteenth century." As a corollary of this study he also wrote his compressed and lapidary "Theses on the Philosophy of History" (completed in early 1940). In these reflections, the role of memory-work looms large—with an accent on the redemptive quality of remembering. One of the opening Theses refers to the theme of happiness as a longing embedded in recollection. This longing, Benjamin notes, has a temporal quality by being closely tied to our existential time frame; this time frame, however, is not a closed clock-time but harbors an emancipatory opening or cleft. Our view of happiness is "indissolubly bound up with the image of redemption." This is particularly true of the remembered past that is the concern of history: "The past carries with it a secret index which points to or adumbrates redemption"; to this extent, every previous generation was endowed with at least a "weak messianic power" to which our present is heir.

As on earlier occasions, historical memory-work is sharply distinguished from positivist description as practiced by historicism. "To articulate the past historically," one Thesis asserts, "does not mean to know it 'as it really was' "; rather, it means "to seize hold of a memory as it flashes up at a moment of danger," a moment of lived need or provocation. Only a historian attentive to this memory-work will have the gift of "fanning the spark of hope in the past." Accentuating a point only implicit in earlier writings, Benjamin's Theses consign redemptive hope not to a futuristic end-time, but make room for an instantaneous eschatology, an irruption of hope in the lived moment. "History," we read, "is the topic of a construction whose site is not homogeneous, empty time, but time filled by the presence of the 'now' " (*Jetztzeit*, the equivalent of the mystical *nunc stans*). This lived moment, or *Jetztzeit*, is the sign or emblem of a "messianic suspension of [ordinary] events"; it is the paradigm of a "messianic time" comprising "the entire history of humankind in an enormous abridgment." From the angle of this "now," the experienced present is seen as "shot through with chips of messianic time"—a view that concurs with the Jewish tradition of recollection (*Eingedenken*), in which every second functions as "the narrow gate through which the Messiah might enter."[9]

# II

Among the founding members of the Frankfurt School, Benjamin's views on history and memory-work most strongly influenced Theodor Adorno. This influence or affinity is not surprising given the prolonged interaction of the two thinkers during the Weimar period, especially in the debates revolving around historicism. Benjamin's outlook was at least in part responsible for Adorno's abandonment of transcendental idealism and his progressive turn during these years toward a nonmetaphysical materialism focused on finitude and natural contingency; in programmatic form, this change was reflected in a paper titled "The Idea of Natural History" (composed in 1932, shortly before his departure from Germany). Faithful to Benjamin's initiative, the paper aimed to steer a course beyond historical teleology, wedded to a transparent purpose, in the direction of "nature" seen as an arena of non-meaning, transitoriness, and fragmentation.

As Adorno commented, paying tribute to the writings of his friend, it was under Benjamin's radical gaze that historical reality was transformed "into a panorama of ruins and fragments, into a golgotha of experience where the key to the nexus of history and nature lies buried." According to "The Idea of Natural History," the key could be uncovered not by a historicist description of "actual" events, nor by their integration into an idealist formula or *telos*, but by a recollection of nature in history, a memory-work seeking to retrieve both the historical transitoriness of nature and the contingent sedimentations of the past in progressive or future-oriented historical projects.[10] On a larger scale, this effort of retrieval was the hallmark of a work jointly undertaken by Max Horkheimer and Adorno during the war years and subsequently published as *Dialectic of Enlightenment* (1947). In dramatic and somber language, the study reexamined the trajectory of modern Western enlightenment, portraying it not as a unidirectional process, but as a fateful collusion of advance and regress; in relentlessly seeking to emancipate human mind from nature, modern history progressively succumbed to instrumental-technological constraints (a corollary of the mastery of nature). To this extent, enlightenment was neither a purposive teleology nor a causal series of events but a manifestation of "natural history." Again, recollection, immune from backward-looking nostalgia, was needed to unravel this intrinsic ambivalence:

> Enlightenment must reflect upon itself, if men are not to be wholly betrayed. What is at issue is not the mere conservation of the past, but the redemption of the hopes of the past. Today, however, the past is preserved only in the form of a destruction of the past.[11]

Although refined and modified in many ways, the accents on natural history and recollection were not put aside in Adorno's later writings. In extremely nuanced fashion, these accents permeate his magisterial *Negative Dialectics* (of 1966), especially the chapters "World Spirit and Natural History" and "Freedom: Toward a Metacritique of Practical Reason." Devoted to a searching review of Hegel's historical teleology, the former chapter offered a trenchant critique of the idealist stress on the advancement of spirit and the concomitant neglect of nature and the countercurrent of historical contingency. In tracing the unfolding of spirit through successive national cultures, Adorno argued, Hegel had tied history's movement to the intentional designs of collective agents, thereby sidestepping or ignoring the broad arena of non-meaning, fragmented meaning, and counterintentionality. Moreover, the celebration of spirit's "march" through history amounted to an endorsement of a long-range project of domination: the mastery of unified reason or spirit over amorphous nature and the contingency of particular events. According to Adorno, the progressive ascendancy of reason to a position of dominance carried a price: its growing entanglement in instrumental calculation and technological fabrication. The postulated trajectory of emancipation was offset by the counterdialectic of steadily tightening disciplines (reflecting the reign of causal-empirical necessity). As an antidote or corrective to Hegelian teleology, Adorno counseled a mode of recollective reflection recovering nature in reason, a memory-work retrieving traces of natural contingency in historical development. From the angle of "critical theory," he observed, the distinction between mind and nature, contingency and purpose cannot simply be erased; yet, a self-critical pursuit of the theory can yield access to their intimate entwinement or nexus—which is the emblem of "natural history." Stepping beyond the confines of idealism, it was the province of recollective reason to "perceive all nature as history and all history as nature."[12]

In a different register and with closer attention to ethical concerns, the issue of recollective thought was further pursued in the chapter on freedom and practical reason. Turning the critical spotlight on Kantian (and post-Kantian) ethics, the chapter underscored the dilemmas besetting strict deontology, especially the antinomial opposition between autonomy and heteronomy, between "noumenal" freedom and "phenomenal" necessity. Lurking behind this opposition was a conflict endemic to modern rationalism and Enlightenment thought: the battle between mind and matter, nature and spirit. As Adorno insisted, the dilemma was not merely of an abstract-metaphysical sort. While designed to emancipate human action from external bonds, deontology rebounded against the status of freedom itself by pitting mind against matter and rational imperatives against "inner nature"—thereby subjugating and thwarting natural inclinations. Moving beyond the confines of Kantian idealism, Adorno's chapter at this point articulated a tensional view of freedom that, without relinquishing rational agency, remained attentive to the limiting constraints of reason and of rational identity structures. Again, recollection played a crucial role in this conception: specifically, recollection of the pre-rational substrate of reason itself. In Adorno's words, what was needed at this point was remembrance of the "untamed impulse" antedating Kant's noumenal self, that is, memory-work recovering an "archaic freedom" not yet governed by the dictates of rational identity. As one should note, "impulse" in this context was not simply a blind force or a synonym for causal necessity, but rather a recollected impulse harboring in its obscure promptings a liberating promise. What was contested or called into question by these promptings was not rational autonomy and responsibility as such but their privileged or dominating status; in revoking this Kantian privilege, the chapter made room for the "diffuseness of nature" and the "multiplicity of non-identity" behind the streamlining effects of enlightened reason. Proposing self-transgression as a further step in human emancipation, *Negative Dialectics* stated:

> Human beings become properly human only where they do not act or posit themselves as (self-identical) persons; the diffuseness of nature which over-reaches such personhood resembles the lineaments of an intelligible creature, of a self delivered from the constraints of the ego. . . . Properly human would be someone who, by means of the strength deriving from identity, would have cast off the encasing of identity.[13]

Although keenly interested in psychology and Freudian thought, Adorno did not explore in detail the link between recollection and psychoanalysis. Among members of the Frankfurt School, the connection was articulated most eloquently by Herbert Marcuse in his *Eros and Civilization* (1955). In Marcuse's treatment, the amorphous freedom or "archaic impulse" invoked by Adorno was located squarely in the Freudian domain of the "unconscious" seen as a welter of drives not yet regulated by the ego and its rational imperatives. From the Freudian angle, civilization and rationalization were so many sources of "discontent" for the human psyche and its striving for happiness and fulfillment. As Marcuse noted, civilized freedom for Freud was a result of accommodation and basically "antagonistic" to happiness; by contrast, the unconscious domain—that "deepest and oldest layer" of psychic life—was inhabited by the "drive for integral gratification," by the striving for a genuinely "free" fulfillment (free from want and repression). It was at this point that recollection showed its psychic importance, for its task was to preserve "the memory of past stages of individual development where integral gratification was obtained." Although reason and its "reality principle" seek to erase the past, psychoanalytic remembrance "explodes" the rational pretenses of the repressed and repressive ego; under the impact of memory-work, the "forbidden images and impulses of childhood begin to tell the truth that reason denies." As Marcuse emphasized (echoing Adorno and Benjamin), memory-work in the psychoanalytic setting was not an outgrowth of nostalgia or a recipe for regression. On the contrary, remembrance was said to serve a "progressive function," with the recollected past yielding critical utopian standards for the present and future:

> The past continues to claim the future: it generates the wish that the paradise be restored on the basis of the achievements of civilization. . . . The liberation of the past does not end in its reconciliation with the present. Against the self-imposed restraint of the discoverer, the orientation to the past tends toward an orientation to the future. The *recherche du temps perdu* becomes the vehicle of future liberation.[14]

Marcuse's reference to Proust was not merely a marginal gloss. Repeatedly, *Eros and Civilization* juxtaposes and correlates Freud and the French novelist. Thus, in discussing the interplay of *"eros"* and *"thanatos,"* of life and death instincts, Marcuse presents recollection as an outgrowth of civilizational discontents and as a counterpoint to forgetfulness and amnesia. More importantly, however, remembrance is portrayed as an antidote to temporal transitoriness, especially to the Nietzschean "resentment" against the passing flight of time. Memory-work is said to shield against such resentment by rescuing experience from the vanishing past. "From the myth of Orpheus to the novel of Proust, happiness and freedom have been linked with the idea of the recapture of time, the *temps retrouvé*." By means of this recapture or restoration, memory retrieves the *"temps perdu"* that was the time of unrepressed *eros* and infantile gratification. Remembered happiness, against this background, is a "thing of the past," but a past that foreshadows and prefigures the present and future. To the extent that civilization progressively demands renunciation of happiness, the *recherche du temps perdu* involves an act of resistance or countercultural rebellion. While unable to fabricate or willfully generate a redeemed social condition, recollection can at least insinuate emancipatory glimpses into prevailing social structures, thereby forestalling both forgetfulness and complacency. In Marcuse's words, "the restoration of remembrance to its rights, as a vehicle of liberation, is one of the noblest tasks of thought."[15]

**III**

In the context of recent Continental thought, the theme of remembrance has not been the sole province of critical theory and psychoanalysis. In novel and philosophically challenging ways, the theme has also been pursued by other intellectual strands or perspectives, including phenomenology, existentialism, and hermeneutics. A central motive animating these strands was a concern with the precognitive underpinnings of reason and subjective identity, that is, with their embroilment in a matrix of experience that can never be transformed or foregrounded into a target of rational analysis. In the confines of phenomenology, an important early impulse was provided by Edmund Husserl in his studies of "internal time consciousness," although in his treatment, time and its various tenses were still seen basically as modalities of consciousness. A more radical turn was performed by Martin Heidegger, whose evolving opus steadily decentered consciousness in favor of a focus on its ontological and temporal moorings.

This decentering move was incipiently manifest in Heidegger's *Being and Time* (1927) and its effort to articulate a "fundamental ontology" via an examination of human existence (or *Dasein*). According to *Being and Time*, the most pressing philosophical issue to be explored and renewed in our era is the question of the "meaning of being," the question how and in which sense anything can be said to be or have being. This question, in turn, was closely linked with the status of time or temporality—the latter viewed not as an accidental property but as a constituent trait of being itself. From the vantage of human existence, the "being question" was accessible in the different temporalities of past, present, and future. Properly construed, the past for Heidegger was not a closed arsenal of historical data, but a sedimented storehouse amenable to experiential retrieval or "repetition" (*Wiederholung*), always pregnant with anticipation and expectancy. Far from being an antiquarian relic, the past was a reservoir of future possibilities or a portent of things to come.[16] The linkage of recollection and the being question became a dominant preoccupation in Heidegger's later writings. In the *Letter on Humanism*, the being question cannot be approached straightforwardly *intentione recta*—which would reify being into a thing or object—but only through a roundabout kind of reflection mindful of the textured horizon that allows thought to proceed in the first place. This type of reflection was termed by Heidegger "recollective" or "commemorative" thinking (*Andenken*). As distinguished from technical reasoning—presented as the hallmark of Western logic and science—recollective thinking does not seek to grasp or master external objects nor exploit available resources; instead, it remains embedded in the matrix that sustains it, in the "element which enables it to be thinking." Such thinking is "recollection of being and nothing else"; it does not claim or seek any palpable "result" or any external "effect."[17]

By the time he wrote the *Letter*, Heidegger had already probed recollection from a number of angles, focusing on prospective remembrance and its insertion in different temporal modes. During the dark years of World War II, Heidegger offered a lecture course in Freiburg on Hölderlin's hymn "Remembrance" (*Andenken*). Heidegger interprets the poet's admonition to "think well" about a recollected experience (a journey to Southern France) as an invitation to recollective or commemorative thinking or remembrance. In turning to a remembered experience, he observes, thinking seems to depart from the present in the direction of the past; yet, curiously, the past returns in a countermovement in the direction of the remembering thought. Still more curiously, the recollected past does not stop in the present or become stationary in its representation:

> If we respect and do not disturb the basic character of remembrance, we discover that, in its return, the recollected past does not make halt in the present in order merely to serve as a substitute for the past through its representation. Rather, the recollected experience leaps beyond the present and confronts us suddenly from the future; in this manner it approaches us from afar, as something still unfulfilled, as an unexplored treasure.

In the context of Hölderlin's hymns, recollective thinking points forward to the encounter and conversation among friends and ultimately to an impending redemptive "bridal feast" (of mortals and immortals).[18]

Recollective retrieval for Heidegger does not simply involve the recovery of transparent meaning or a univocal purpose. Rather, given the latency of being and its withdrawal behind the screen of palpable things or "beings," recollection also means attentiveness to the complex entwinement of presence and absence, of disclosure and concealment (resembling Penelope's work of weaving and unweaving). This theme, together with many related issues, was developed at length in a lecture course that Heidegger offered shortly before his retirement (about a decade after the lecturers on Hölderlin). In the German original the course was titled *Was heisst Denken?*—a phrase that resists easy translation. The title has been translated as *What Is Called Thinking?*, but it may with equal legitimacy be rendered as *What Calls for (or Calls upon) Thinking?* As the opening lecture emphasized, thinking is not merely a cognitive faculty of reasoning that we can exercise or not exercise at will any time. Thinking can only proceed by remaining attentive to what is "to be thought"—which sustains and enables our being and thinking prior to deliberate cognition. Being attentive to this enabling potency, reflection is mindful of what "calls forth" or "calls upon" thinking. This mindfulness or responsiveness to a call is the central emblem of recollection. In Heidegger's words, memory or recollection is "the gathering of thinking. Gathering into or toward what? Toward that which sustains us insofar and inasmuch as we think or recollect it—recollect it precisely because it is what needs to be thought." This kind of gathering or recollecting mode of thinking is largely atrophied in our time under the impact of media and the flood of "interesting" information. Yet, our age is also an extremely needful, troubled, and unsettling time. Many experiences seem to call for and even provoke thinking—but to little avail. According to the lecture, what is most troubling and "thought-provoking" (*bedenklich*) in our troubled time is the fact that "we are not yet thinking" (in a recollective mode).[19]

In probing the status and character of recollection, Heidegger's lecture course returns briefly to Hölderlin's poetry, specifically to a fragment of a hymn titled "Mnemosyne" (or "Remembrance"). As used by Hölderlin, the title invoked Greek mythology, the struggle between Olympians and Titans. In Greek myth, Mnemosyne was a female Titan and, as such, the daughter of heaven and earth; wedded to Zeus, she became in nine nights the mother of the nine Muses. Thus, "drama and music, dance and poetry" issue forth from the womb of Mnemosyne, or remembrance. As Heidegger points out, remembrance or memory does not merely designate the psychological faculty or capacity to retain past events in thought. Instead, remembrance in the image of Mnemosyne thinks or ponders what is or needs to be thought. What needs to be thought, however, is not just some random or arbitrary idea. Remembrance as the mother of the Muses means

> the gathering of thinking into or toward that which everywhere and first of all demands to be thought. As such, remembrance is the gathering of recollection (*Andenken*); in this capacity, it safeguards and shelters that which everywhere and first of all needs to be pondered in the encounter with anything that is or that shows itself in its present or past being. As mother of the Muses, remembrance-Mnemosyne means recollection of what calls for thought; as such, she is the source and fountain of poetry.

The story of Mnemosyne is itself "recollected" for us in the legacy of Greek mythology and its poetic "tale" (*Sage*). Heidegger adds, the mythic tale of the Greeks aimed to "disclose or make manifest" whatever appears in the "epiphany" of its being. To this extent, Greek myth has the character of a calling-forth or an appeal through a tale: "Myth is that which first of all and basically calls upon or appeals to humans by inviting them to think or recollect being in its appearance."[20]

As previously indicated, however, recollection for Heidegger is not simply an act of disclosure revealing a transparent meaning or appearance. Elaborating on the legacy of Greek thinking (as articulated chiefly by the pre-Socratics) Heidegger turns attention to the domain of *"aletheia"* or "unconcealment," the matrix out of which presencing arises or which enables beings of any kind to be present. Presencing or being present, he notes, "arises out of unconcealment; it takes its origin from such an emergence into presence." Yet, in this emergence into presence, the backdrop of unconcealment tends to drop out of sight, to withdraw behind the panoply of manifest appearances. It is part of presencing "to hold back these traits and thus to let come to the fore only that which is present"; even, and in particular, the domain of unconcealment in which this emergence takes place "remains concealed in difference or distinction from unconcealed present beings." The crucial role of difference in thinking comes into view: the difference between absence and presence, concealment and unconcealment, being and beings. For presencing is not possible without the corollary of withdrawal, nor disclosure without the matrix of sheltering reticence; thus, the emergence into presence is always combined and "gathered" together with the "ever-possible absencing into concealment."[21]

## IV

As the preceding discussion has shown, the theme of recollection has been developed in recent Continental thought from diverse angles and with a variety of accents and connotations. Notwithstanding such divergences of emphasis, however, the discussion has also revealed a strand of commonality or shared features. One commonality has to do with the status of recollection itself: far from reflecting simple nostalgia or antiquarian curiosity, recollection is a retrieval of past experiences for the sake of the present and future—with liberating and possibly redemptive implications. Another feature has to do with the "non-foundationalism" of recollection or remembrance. Recollection is not the return to a pristine origin or the recovery of an innate *"logos"* construed as a clear and distinct idea or transparent meaning. Most definitely, remembering is not the deliberate act of a *cogito* or of a rational ego bent on surveying and controlling the psychic field.

In Benjamin's portrayal, remembrance is akin to Penelope's labors with woof and warp, the interpenetration of recovery and forgetting, of nighttime sedimentation and daytime dissection or unraveling. In Adorno's writings, recollection involves a labor of retrieval, a memory-work seeking to recover nature in history and sedimented contingencies in prospective cultural endeavors. In a parallel fashion, remembrance in Heidegger's case points to the differential thought of being/beings and to the intricate entwinement of being and nonbeing, presence and absence, revealment and concealment. In every instance, the remembered experience or the appeal "calling upon" recollective thought is not a foreground amenable to rational mastery, but a background matrix or horizon yielding glimpses or clues only in a roundabout way requiring steadily renewed interpretation.

Although devoid of secure guideposts, recollection's clues are not negligible in the ethical and political domains; its sheltering withdrawal of meaning does not denote randomness or arbitrary whim. In many ways, recollection holds lessons or implications for contemporary ethical debates, especially those revolving around descriptivism and prescriptivism, around (natural) teleology and deontology. Above all, recollection offers an alternative to the conundrums of causality and noumenalism. In terms of post-Freudian psychoanalysis, recollection recuperates the experience of an amorphous symbiosis preceding maturational splits; without prescribing rigid maxims, memory of this experience intimates, at least from afar, the persistence of a latent kinship or affinity behind social and psychic schisms, the possibility of a transformative "selflessness" circumscribing rational self-interest. In terms of normative theory, recollective ethics is neither inferred from empirical conditions nor derived or deduced from principles; in lieu of empirical or logical explanations, behavior is embedded in an ongoing "tale" or story, a tale that, irreducible to simple formulas, stands in contrapuntal relation to prevailing structures and "civilization's discontents," thereby making room for liberating and redemptive hopes.[22]

Among the thinkers discussed in these pages, the ethical implications of recollection were most explicitly developed by Adorno, with emphasis on the "archaic freedom" of recollected motivation. Guideposts for a recollective ethics can also be found, however, in Heidegger's works. In his *Letter on Humanism* Heidegger presents a thinking that attentively recollects differential being as a gateway to ethical sensibility and liberating "care" (antedating theoretical ethics). Commenting on a phrase by Heraclitus—"*ethos anthropo daimon*"—the *Letter* translates *ethos* as the matrix or open horizon of differential being inhabited by humans, suggesting that this matrix provides clues for human conduct through the counseling voice of the heart (or *daimon*). If *ethos* is seen as the backdrop allowing conduct to arise in the first place, Heidegger adds, then a thinking that recollects differential being as the abode of human being-in-the-world is also an "original ethics," although it must not be confused with empirical descriptions or deontological principles.[23]

The political implications of remembrance and recollective ethics have been sketched in recent times by a number of writers, including spokesmen of a humanist Marxism and Christian liberation theology. Proceeding from a broadly Marxist framework modulated by the early Frankfurt School, Christian Lenhardt has articulated the notion of an "anamnestic solidarity," or solidarity of remembrance, seen as an antidote both to unilinear theories of historical progress and to a narrow focus on class struggle. Drawing his inspiration chiefly from Walter Benjamin as well as Horkheimer and Adorno, Lenhardt portrays recollection preeminently as a *memoria passionis* or remembrance of suffering, which, immune to resentment, nurtures a forward-looking, redemptive glance. Past injustices and the sufferings of previous generations, in his account, cannot cancel the prospect of a future human solidarity—but they must also not be forgotten or erased by this future vision. This account is radically opposed to a conception of Marxism as a theory of linear historical progress, in which the future utopia eradicates the past and "total oblivion" appears as the "precondition of bliss." Challenging this construal, Lenhardt asks whether the Marxist theme of liberation is really "the theory and practice of emancipation from remembrance." Taking his cues from Benjamin and early critical theory, he insists on the recollective "sublation" of the past in the present and the future, entailing a vision of solidarity devoid of univocal consensus in which presence and absence, meaning and non-meaning, remain interlaced:

> The evils of prehistory may have been overcome, but they will linger on in the collective *anamnesis* of liberated mankind. They must so linger, or else the achievement of true solidarity is just another form of one-dimensional experience where enjoyment of the Thing and the Other is as unreflective as it is under conditions of late-capitalist affluence.[24]

In his exploration of the role of remembrance, Lenhardt also reviews ancient modes of worship devoted to the recollection of the past, leading him in the end to pose the question of the "relationship of Marxism and religious thought." This relationship has been a prominent concern of European "political theology" during the past several decades. Although occasionally inclined toward a linear progressivism, political theology, like liberation theology, also pays tribute to remembrance; this is particularly true in the case of Johann Baptist Metz. In his *Faith in History and Society*, Metz speaks of the "risky" or "dangerous memory" (*gefährliche Erinnerung*) of Christian freedom in the context of prevailing social-political conditions. This remembrance, he emphasizes, is not merely a backward-looking recollection that "deceptively dispenses from the risks of the future"; on the contrary, it anticipates the future as an emancipatory promise for the oppressed and those without hope. To this extent, Christian *memoria* is a "dangerous and at the same time liberating memory" that challenges and "calls into question the present" in the name of an anticipatory remembrance. As one should note, liberative remembrance for Metz is not the exclusive province of Christians or Christian churches, but extends potentially to humankind at large, thus gaining global significance. In this broader context, Christian faith necessarily comes into contact with, and faces the challenge of, parallel aspirations, especially the Marxist or socialist demand for an "international solidarity with the working class." Christianity cannot distance itself from, or remain neutral in regard to, the struggle for "global solidarity of the underprivileged and needy." Among the pressing problems today is the question how Christianity handles "its own class problem, namely, the gaping contrast between the churches of the North and the South."[25]

Metz's comments on global solidarity expose the gulf between North and South, between First and Third World countries, between development and underdevelopment. Even more than in the Christian West, liberative remembrance has a crucial place in developing societies. As previously discussed (in chapter 3), recollective emancipatory endeavors are present today in other world religions exposed to the pressures of modernization and First World hegemony; preponderantly, remembrance in these settings involves a retrieval of indigenous potentials as an antidote to regressive fundamentalism and Western-style secularism. In the context of Third World countries, recollection is bound to be not only redemptive-invigorating but also painful by keeping alive the memory of dislocation and the agonies of exile and defeat. In the words of the Nepali poet Laxmiprasad Devkota:

> When clouds drift over the earth,
>   over life a sorrow,
> when the tears rain down
>   on parched despairing hearts,
> when lament is everywhere
>   recollecting the heart's pain—
> remember then the full-moon nights
>   in dream cities after the earthquake. . . .

In memory the garden blooms,
winning sap and color; . . .
and in my memory rise from the sleep
the sweet sounds of your voice.[26]

# Notes

1. Marcel Proust, *Swann in Love*, trans. C. K. Scott Moncrieff and Trent Kilmartin (New York: Vintage Books, 1984), pp. 265–266.

2. Regarding descriptivism and prescriptivism see W. D. Hudson, *The Is-Ought Question: A Collection of Papers on the Central Problem in Moral Philosophy* (London: Macmillan, 1969); for an overview of contemporary ethical theory see my "Ordinary Language and Ideal Speech" in *Twilight of Subjectivity: Contributions to a Post-Individualist Theory of Politics* (Amherst, Mass.: University of Massachusetts Press, 1981), pp. 218–254. Regarding the attempt to derive ethics from radical otherness see Emmanuel Levinas, *Ethics and Infinity*, trans. Richard A. Cohen (Pittsburgh, Pa.: Duquesne University Press, 1985); *Otherwise than Being or Beyond Essence*, trans. Alphonso Lingis (The Hague: Nijhoff, 1981). For a critical appraisal of Levinas's approach see Jacques Derrida, "Metaphysics and Violence," in *Writing and Difference*, trans. Alan Bass (Chicago: University of Chicago Press, 1978), pp. 79–153; and Derrida's "At This Very Moment in This Work Here I Am," in *Re-Reading Levinas*, ed. Robert Bernasconi and Simon Critchley (Bloomington: Indiana University Press, 1991), pp. 11–48.

3. Compare Johann Baptist Metz, *Faith in History and Society: Toward a Practical Fundamental Theology*, trans. David Smith (New York: Seabury Press, 1980), p. 195.

4. Metz distinguishes two traditional approaches to remembrance in Western thought, one originating in Platonic metaphysics (*anamnesis*) and the other in Christian eschatology; both were ultimately fused in Hegelian philosophy. In the post-Hegelian era Metz again discusses two main perspectives: hermeneutics from Dilthey to Heidegger and Gadamer; and critical theory from Benjamin to Habermas. See *Faith in History and Society*, pp. 186–194. For historical-philosophical discussions of recollection compare also Janet Coleman, *Ancient and Medieval Memories: Studies in the Reconstruction of the Past* (Cambridge: Cambridge University Press, 1992); David Carr, *Time, Narrative and History* (Bloomington: Indiana University Press, 1986); Richard J. Glinn, *The Present and the Past: A Study of Anamnesis* (Allison Park, Pa.: Pickwick Publ., 1989).

5. Regarding the historicism debates see Susan Buck-Morss, *The Origin of Negative Dialectics: Theodor W. Adorno, Walter Benjamin, and the Frankfurt Institute* (New York: Free Press, 1977), pp. 53–54. On Benjamin's work generally see Richard Wolin, *Walter Benjamin: An Aesthetic of Redemption* (New York: Columbia University Press, 1982); Gary Smith, ed., *On Walter Benjamin: Critical Essays and Recollections* (Cambridge, Mass.: MIT Press, 1991); and Max Pen-

sky, *Melancholy Dialectics: Walter Benjamin and the Play of Mourning* (Amherst, Mass.: University of Massachusetts Press, 1993).

6. Walter Benjamin, *Ursprung des deutschen Trauerspiels,* in *Gesammelte Schriften,* vol. I, bk. 1, ed. Rolf Tiedemann and Hermann Schweppenhäuser (Frankfurt-Main: Suhrkamp, 1974), pp. 343–344.

7. *Ursprung des deutschen Trauerspiels,* pp. 352–355, 357, 409.

8. Benjamin, "The Image of Proust," in *Illuminations,* ed. Hannah Arendt, trans. Harry Zohn (New York: Harcourt, Brace & World, 1968), pp. 204–205.

9. "Über den Begriff der Geschichte," in *Gesammelte Schriften,* vol. I, bk. 2, pp. 693–695, 701, 703–704; for an English translation under the title "Theses on the Philosophy of History" see *Illuminations,* pp. 255–257, 263, 265–266. In the above citations I have altered this translation in light of the original German text.

10. Theodor W. Adorno, "Die Idee der Naturgeschichte," in his *Philosophische Frühschriften (Gesammelte Schriften,* vol. I), ed. Rolf Tiedemann (Frankfurt-Main: Suhrkamp, 1973), pp. 355–364.

11. Max Horkheimer and Theodor W. Adorno, *Dialectic of Enlightenment,* trans. John Cumming (New York: Herder & Herder, 1972), pp. xiii–xv (translation slightly changed).

12. Adorno, *Negative Dialectics,* trans. E. B. Ashton (New York: Seabury Press, 1973), pp. 317–318, 356–359 (translation slightly changed for purposes of clarity). For a fuller discussion of Adorno's chapter see my "Adorno and Natural History" in *Twilight of Subjectivity* (Amherst, Mass.: University of Massachusetts Press, 1981), pp. 211–219.

13. Adorno, *Negative Dialectics,* pp. 212–214, 221–222, 228–229, 256, 277 (translation slightly changed for the sake of clarity). For a fuller discussion of Adorno's chapter see my "Kant and Critical Theory" in *Between Freiburg and Frankfurt: Toward a Critical Ontology* (Amherst, Mass.: University of Massachusetts Press, 1991), pp. 122–127.

14. Herbert Marcuse, *Eros and Civilization: A Philosophical Inquiry into Freud* (New York: Vintage Books, 1962), pp. 17–18. Marcuse in this context linked recollection and memory-work closely with the role of imagination and "phantasy," though without specifying the relation between imagination and cognitive truth.

15. *Eros and Civilization,* pp. 212–213. For additional comments on memory see Marcuse, *One-Dimensional Man: Studies in the Ideology of Advanced Industrial Society* (Boston: Beacon Press, 1964), pp. 98–100. Despite its captivating élan, Marcuse's argument is marred by several flaws that restrict its cogency. One has to do with Marcuse's portrayal of the unconscious as a reservoir of instinctual drives, which conjures up the notion of a biological determinism. Closely connected with this problem is his stress on the revelatory function of recollection, on the capacity of remembrance to disclose the cognitive "truth" of the past. On both of these counts, Jacques Lacan's reformulation of Freudian theory offers important correctives. Lacan presented the unconscious as a "language," a meaning structure governed by its own peculiar grammar or syntax. In performing this "linguistic turn," Lacan's approach forestalled the lure of a biosex-

ual determinism. As in Adorno's case, the preconscious quest for happiness and freedom is not just a natural impulse, but a recollected and imaginatively reconstructed impulse; the past retrieved through psychoanalytic remembrance does not strictly compel, but has a story to tell, recalcitrant to univocal interpretation. On Lacan's notion of the discourse of the unconscious and his treatment of memory-work as repetition/retrieval or "rememoration" see Shoshona Felman, *Jacques Lacan and the Adventure of Insight: Psychoanalysis in Contemporary Culture* (Cambridge, Mass.: Harvard University Press, 1987), p. 123, and Ellie Ragland-Sullivan, *Jacques Lacan and the Philosophy of Psychoanalysis* (Urbana: University of Illinois Press, 1986), pp. 58–67, 100–101. For a more detailed discussion of Lacanian psychoanalysis and its relation to the Frankfurt School compare my "Psychoanalysis and Critical Theory: A Lacanian Perspective," in *Between Freiburg and Frankfurt: Toward a Critical Ontology*, pp. 183–209.

16. Martin Heidegger, *Sein und Zeit*, 11th ed. (Tübingen, Germany: Niemeyer, 1967), pp. 1–5 (par. 1 and 2), 337–339 (par. 68). Heidegger refers explicitly to Kierkegaard, who had articulated the notions of "temporality," existential "moment," and "repetition." See Søren Kierkegaard, *Repetition: An Essay in Experimental Psychology*, trans. W. Lowrie (Princeton, N.J.: Princeton University Press, 1941). Regarding Husserl see his *The Phenomenology of Internal Time Consciousness*, ed. Martin Heidegger, trans. James S. Churchill (Bloomington: Indiana University Press, 1964).

17. Heidegger, *Über den Humanismus* (Frankfurt-Main: Klostermann, 1949), pp. 7, 23, 42; trans. by Frank A. Capuzzi as "Letter on Humanism," in *Martin Heidegger: Basic Writings*, ed. David F. Krell (New York: Harper & Row, 1977), pp. 196, 215, 236.

18. Heidegger, *Hölderlins Hymne "Andenken"* (*Gesamtausgabe*, vol. 52) ed. Curd Ochwadt (Frankfurt-Main: Klostermann, 1982), pp. 54, 69–70, 164–165. The lecture course was presented in 1941–1942. For a fuller discussion of Hölderlin's hymn see my "Homecoming through Otherness" in *The Other Heidegger* (Ithaca, N.Y.: Cornell University Press, 1993), pp. 149–180. The prospective character of recollection had also been thematized in Heidegger's *Kant und das Problem der Metaphysik* (first ed. 1929; 2nd ed. Frankfurt-Main: Klostermann, 1951), p. 211; trans. by James S. Churchill as *Kant and the Problem of Metaphysics* (Bloomington: Indiana University Press, 1962).

19. Heidegger, *Was heisst Denken?* 3rd ed. (Tübingen, Germany: Niemeyer, 1971), pp. 1–3; trans. by J. Glenn Gray as *What Is Called Thinking?* (New York: Harper & Row, 1968), pp. 3–6. (In the above and subsequent citations I have altered the translation for purposes of clarity.) The lecture course was presented in Freiburg in 1951–1952.

20. *Was heisst Denken?*, pp. 6–7; *What Is Called Thinking?*, pp. 10–11.

21. *Was heisst Denken?*, pp. 143–145, 174–175; *What Is Called Thinking?*, pp. 227, 236–238.

22. In one of his recent books, Alasdair MacIntyre distinguishes three "rival versions" of ethics that distantly resemble the alternative positions outlined above, though disguised under the labels of "tradition" (natural teleology), "encyclopedia" (rational deontology), and "genealogy" (Nietzsche and post-Nietz-

scheans); see *Three Rival Versions of Moral Enquiry* (Notre Dame, Ind.: University of Notre Dame Press, 1990).

23. Heidegger, *Über den Humanismus*, p. 41; "Letter on Humanism" in *Martin Heidegger: Basic Writings*, pp. 234–235. From the perspective of political theory, an ethics of care or cultivation has been articulated by William E. Connolly in *Identity/Difference: Democratic Negotiations of Political Paradox* (Ithaca, N.Y.: Cornell University Press, 1991), and *The Ethos of Pluralization* (Minneapolis, Minn.: University of Minnesota Press, 1995). See also Stephen K. White, *Political Theory and Postmodernism* (Cambridge: Cambridge University Press, 1991).

24. Christian Lenhardt, "Anamnestic Solidarity: The Proletariat and Its *Manes*," *Telos* 25 (Fall 1975): 136–138. He adds, "Even in this [future] society there are those who did not make it. Their presence is that of shadows. To pretend that these ancestral shadows have no place in the sun-lit world of solidarity is to be unkind, inhuman" (p. 138).

25. Metz, *Faith in History and Society*, pp. 88–90, 133, 234–236.

26. Laxmiprasad Devkota, "Memory," in *Nepali Visions, Nepali Dreams: The Poetry of Laxmiprasad Devkota*, ed. and trans. David Rubin (New York: Columbia University Press, 1980), p. 100.

## Part II

# Nationalism, Globalism, and Development

# 7

# "Return to the Source": African Identity (After Cabral)

> ... between colonization and civilization there is an infinite distance.
>
> Césaire, *Discourse on Colonialism*

On January 20, 1973, Amilcar Cabral was killed by agents of the Portuguese government. At the time of his assassination, Cabral was Secretary General of the African Party for the Independence of Guinea and the Cape Verde Islands (PAIGC) and as such one of the leading figures in the struggle against European colonialism and imperialism in Africa. Having been educated in Portugal, together with fellow students from other Portuguese colonies like Angola and Mozambique, Cabral was distinguished both by his intense political engagement and his deep theoretical insights garnered not from abstract philosophical doctrines but from the concrete suffering of African peoples at the hands of colonial masters. Faced with the arrogance of colonial elites, Cabral sought to energize indigenous modes of thought and practice—especially among the underclasses of society—as resources in the arsenal of anticolonial resistance. Since his assassination more than two decades have passed, and African countries, including former Portuguese colonies, have all achieved a measure of independence or political autonomy. As a result of this change, the legacy of the independence struggle—Cabral's legacy in particular—seems to have been eclipsed or rendered obsolete. Almost everywhere today, top priority is given to social and economic "development," that is, the integration of non-Western societies into the world economy wedded to market liberalism and industrial progress. In light of this shift, terms like "national liberation" or struggle for self-determination have become suspect and nearly apocryphal; in the eyes of some, they are merely synonyms for regressive or atavistic tendencies that are particularly obnoxious in the African context, given the tradition of "tribal" warfare.

At a closer look, this shift is itself dubious and by no means self-evidently salutary or "progressive." Given the asymmetries of power and wealth prevailing in the global arena, integration into the world economy also conjures up the danger (for "developing" societies) of new forms of economic and cultural tutelage—at a minimum the danger of a "colonization of their life-world" (to use the felicitous phrase of Habermas). In the long run, this colonization is also detrimental to the goal of development itself—the prospect of democracy and democratic self-government. Although no one would want to deny the threat of tribal chauvinism and ethnic "cleansing," the remedy for this peril can hardly be found in a blandly homogenizing and imperialistic globalism. Against this background, the motto for our time cannot simply be *"oublier Cabral"* (forget Cabral). Even less can we endorse or promote globalism through the slogan *"oublier l'Afrique"*—especially the Africa envisaged by Cabral and his associates. A few months before this death Cabral delivered an address on national liberation in which he used the phrase "return to the source." The aim of the present chapter is to commemorate Cabral by means of an extended, tripartite reflection on that phrase. The first section reviews some of Cabral's main arguments, as they were collected posthumously in a booklet titled *Return to the Source*. The second part examines more recent attempts by African philosophers and intellectuals to assess this kind of return and the possibility of distinctly African forms of thinking and acting. By way of conclusion, the third section discusses the meaning and broader implications of the phrase, particularly the prospect of an African identity "after Cabral," where "after" denotes both a temporal distance and an indebtedness, in the sense of the French *selon.*[1]

# I

European colonialism, including its Portuguese variety, always coupled exploitation with a missionary goal: the spreading of a supposedly superior culture to the rest of the world. Even where wholesale conversion proved unfeasible, administrators sought to assimilate at least certain elite sections of society while branding remaining indigenous life-forms as hopelessly backward or obsolete. To this extent, colonialism subscribed to an imperialist version of the "Enlightenment project" by extolling the virtues of Western-style universalism at the expense of local or traditional modes of thought and practice. Given this situation, the struggle against colonial domination had to be waged on many fronts and along many dimensions, including political militancy and cultural resistance. Among leaders of the struggle in Africa, Cabral recognized and perhaps articulated most clearly and poignantly the complexity of the challenge. In a memorial lecture of 1970 commemorating the recent assassination of another African leader, Cabral eloquently underscored the need to link the struggle for "national liberation" with cultural resistance. As he pointed out, colonial domination cannot rely on force alone; in the long run, to ensure the stability of its regime, colonialism can be maintained "only by the permanent, organized repression of the cultural life of the people concerned." This fact did not diminish the need for political pressure and mobilization, but it made clear the "value of culture" as a source of resistance to colonial rule. Such resistance was only a response to European, especially Portuguese, policies that always linked military-political with cultural strategies:

> To take up arms to dominate a people is, above all, to take up arms to destroy, or at least to neutralize, to paralyze, its cultural life. For, with a strong indigenous cultural life, foreign domination cannot be sure of its perpetuation. At any moment, . . . cultural resistance may take on new forms (political, economic, armed) in order fully to contest foreign domination.[2]

Cultural subjugation does not always involve outright repression; sometimes, colonial powers pursued a policy of assimilation seeking to integrate colonized people—or at least significant segments—into the European worldview. Initiated by the French, this "theory of progressive assimilation" was also adopted by Portugal in its African territories. In fact, as Cabral notes, the policy reached its "highest degree of absurdity" when the Portuguese strongman Salazar asserted that "Africa does *not exist*." In the face of such arrogance, cultural resistance became a vital necessity, which, in the case of African colonies, had to take the form at least in part of a reassertion of African identity or a "re-Africanization." For Cabral, such reassertion was not simply a matter of emotional or spiritual self-affirmation. In a quasi-Marxist vein, Cabral always associated cultural features closely with the political and economic (or material) conditions of a society. As his memorial lecture of 1970 pointed out, culture is always in the life of a society "the more or less conscious result of the economic and political activities of that society"; it is "the vigorous manifestation on the ideological or idealist plane of the physical and historical reality of the society that is dominated or to be dominated." Viewed along these lines, historical development or change in a society always has something to do with the prevailing "mode of production" and the evolving "productive forces." Yet, in its historical movement society also productively engenders its cultural life-form, where culture denotes patterned relationships between individuals and groups and between humans and nature or the environment. To this extent, expounding on historical change and development means "also to speak of culture."[3]

Seen in this light, the struggle for national liberation—especially in African territories—necessarily and inescapably signifies an "act of culture," the "organized political expression of the culture" of colonized peoples. Yet, as Cabral makes quite clear, culture is not a uniform phenomenon but is marked by considerable complexity and diversity. For political purposes, it is particularly important in the colonial context to distinguish between popular culture and elite culture, with the latter again showing multiple shadings. As in other societies, Cabral notes, culture in African societies is not blandly homogeneous, since it is not "equally developed" in all sectors of society; these differences in cultural levels and perspectives also affect in a politically crucial way the attitudes of individuals and social groups toward the liberation struggle. On the level of the elite culture, a salient difference exists between members of an "assimilated" or Westernized elite, on the one hand, and traditional local rulers or chieftains, on the other. Whereas members of the first group emulate European lifestyles while shunning or disdaining local customs, members of the second group remain firmly rooted in, and attached to, native traditions—but only for the sake of preserving their own social privileges. As Cabral observes with great political astuteness, colonial powers find it advantageous to support both groups for different reasons. In subjugating a given life-form, colonizers quite deliberately provoke the "cultural alienation" of a part of the population, either by a policy of direct assimilation or by creating a "social gap" between indigenous elites and popular masses. This strategy is particularly attractive to the educated bourgeoisie which, mimicking the colonizer's mentality, "considers itself culturally superior to its own people and ignores or looks down upon their cultural values." However, to promote political stability and a degree of popular loyalty, colonizers also enlist the services of traditional elites by offering them material, educational, and other benefits. In the context of the liberation struggle, both groups—despite their differences—buttress the colonial status quo:

> In the general framework of contesting colonial imperialist domination and in the actual situation to which we refer, among the oppressor's most loyal allies are found some high officials and intellectuals of the liberal professions, assimilated people, and also a significant number of representatives of the ruling class from rural areas. . . . The high official or the assimilated intellectual, characterized by total cultural alienation, identifies himself by

political choice with the traditional or religious leader who has experienced no significant foreign cultural influences. For these two categories of people place above all principles or demands of a cultural nature—and against the aspirations of the people—their own economic and social privileges, their own class interests. That is a truth which the liberation movement cannot afford to ignore without risking betrayal of the economic, political, social and cultural objectives of the struggle.[4]

To the extent that national liberation denotes cultural resistance, the struggle must appeal chiefly to popular culture, rather than the predilection of elites. In Cabral's words, the liberation movement must "embody the mass character, the popular character of the culture—which is not and never could be the privilege of one or of some sectors of society." With regard to the assimilated elite the situation is ambivalent: occasionally, members of that group may join the liberation struggle (though often without abandoning their high-status ambitions). On the basis of their educational background and scientific or technical knowledge, such individuals may even attain leading positions in the movement—but without losing their cultural "biases." In this case, what is needed is a "reconversion of minds," a "re-Africanization" or reconnection with grassroots concerns that can only happen through "daily contact" with the masses in the "communion of sacrifice required by the struggle." Matters are more difficult and recalcitrant in the case of traditional elites. Here too individuals may on occasion decide to join the liberation struggle—but usually only with the goal of recapturing the authority that has been taken away or severely curbed by the colonizers. In this situation, Cabral notes, extreme "vigilance" is indispensable. Preserving the "cultural prejudices" of their class, individuals in this category may wish to use the liberation movement merely as a means to other ends: relying on the "sacrifices of the masses," they may pervert the movement into a simple instrument "to eliminate colonial oppression of their own class and to re-establish in this way their complete political and cultural domination of the people." For Cabral, however, cultural resistance cannot coincide with a regressive traditionalism; above all, re-Africanization cannot simply mean the nostalgic retrieval of a real or imaginary past.[5]

The complexity of cultural resistance is underscored and elaborated in the remainder of the memorial address. Cultural struggle, though vitally important, must be kept free of both complacency and a simplistic reification (that is, the lure of metaphysical "essentialism"). Being the result of prolonged historical accretion, culture is a highly diversified phenomenon exhibiting multiple strands; hence, just as one can detect "the existence of several Africas," so also there are "many African cultures." Moreover, culture is a treasure box reflecting diverse historical sedimen-

tations and containing valuable and not-so-valuable ingredients; to preserve it as a living popular concern, critical scrutiny is called for. In
Cabral's words, it is important not to lose sight of the fact "that no culture is a perfect, finished whole"; as an evolving historical phenomenon,
culture is composed "of essential and secondary elements, of strengths
and weaknesses, of virtues and failings." The same verdict holds for the
culture of European powers—despite its employment for repressive colonial aims. Against this background, anticolonial struggle cannot mean
self-encapsulation or a rigid "us-versus-them" mentality; for some purposes and on some levels, cultural resistance must also make room for
cultural learning. Compiling a list of harmful or counterproductive attitudes and behaviors—harmful to Africa and Africans—Cabral mentions
above all these: "indiscriminate compliments; systematic exaltation of
virtues without condemning faults; blind acceptance of the values of the
culture without considering what presently or potentially regressive elements it contains." What this implies for national liberation is that cultural struggle must be carried on without resentment and in a spirit of
tolerant self-affirmation:

> A people who free themselves from foreign domination will be free cultur-
> ally only if, without complexes and without underestimating the importance
> of positive accretions from the oppressor and other cultures, they return to
> the upward paths of their own culture, which is nourished by the living
> reality of its environment and which negates both harmful influences and
> any kind of subjection to foreign culture.[6]

Nearly three years later, in October 1972 shortly before his death, Cabral delivered another lecture on national liberation and cultural struggle. The theme of "re-Africanization"—with all its complexity and
ambivalence—was rearticulated in terms of a "return to the source" primarily applicable to assimilated intellectuals and professionals who,
while alienated from the native culture, still chafe under the colonial
yoke. As in the previous lecture, Cabral distinguished between popular
culture and elite culture, placing his accent now on the assimilated elite
together with its adjuncts in the diaspora. The struggle for national liberation's main strength and source of mobilization had to be found in the
popular culture or among the common people. This was possible in Africa due to a historical factor: the period of European colonization in
Africa had been too brief to penetrate deeply into the villages and countryside outside a limited number of urban centers. This made it possible
for the common people in most African territories to retain their distinctive popular culture and hence to mobilize an effective cultural resistance
to colonial rule. Indigenous culture hence could act as a bulwark in pre-

serving the "identity" of the people and their "dignity" and self-esteem. No national liberation movement could possibly proceed without relying on this resource. Cabral stated, "Repressed, persecuted, humiliated, betrayed by certain social groups who have compromised with the foreign power, culture took refuge in the villages, in the forests, and in the spirit of the victims of domination."[7]

For popular culture, the issue is not one of re-Africanization, but of a simple, relatively unbroken self-assertion. The situation is different for the assimilated elite, the members of the native bourgeoisie who have become thoroughly Europeanized (or Westernized) and alienated from their native moorings. Cabral's lecture—almost as an aside—makes some intriguing comments on the attractions of assimilation and also on the unintended benefits or side effects of colonization. In a quasi-Marxian vein, Cabral admits that quite apart from its repressive impact European political and economic expansion has also tended to stir up lethargic traditions and promote a growing interpenetration of cultures and peoples. "It is not to defend imperialist domination," he states, "to recognize that it gave new nations to the world, the dimensions of which it reduced, and that it revealed new stages of development in human societies." The main consequence of colonialism was the process of globalization coupled with the search for more and more accurate information about societies around the globe. Against its own repressive aims, colonial rule encouraged a multilateral interaction "not only between different men but also between different societies." To facilitate colonial penetration, knowledge about social conditions around the globe had to be gathered more or less systematically; this gave impulse to new fields of inquiry like sociology, anthropology, ethnography, and world history. This burst of investigation contributed to "a general enrichment of human and social knowledge in spite of the fact that it was one-sided, subjective, and very often unjust." In fact, Cabral adds, "man has never shown as much interest in knowing other men and other societies as during this century of imperialist domination." Assimilated elites in colonized countries in a way participate in this expansion of knowledge and hence contribute to the cross-cultural openness and transformation of their societies.[8]

Yet, these benefits of assimilation have to be weighed against, and in fact are clearly outweighed by, its debilitating subservience to foreign rule. As Cabral points out, assimilated elites occupy a volatile and "marginal" position in colonial society: being wedged precariously between agents of the colonial power and the popular masses, their marginality is not relieved when they enter administrative service or join the diasporic community in the colonizer's country. Although indispensable to colonial rule and frequently "pampered" by the foreign power, such elites ultimately never succeed in "getting past the (political and cultural) barriers" thrown up by the colonial system. Sensing their marginality and nurturing a steadily deepening "frustration complex," members of the indigenous bourgeoisie may decide to join the liberation struggle and the side of popular culture; some of them may even emerge as leaders of the movement. It is in these instances that a certain reconversion of minds is demanded, a "return to the source" or to the concretely situated spirit animating the movement. This return, Cabral notes, is all the more urgent the deeper the alienation of the bourgeoisie and the greater their distance or isolation from the lived experience of the people. Curiously, the most fervent expressions of a desired return often emanate from intellectuals or other elite members most thoroughly infected with alienation and thus far removed from ongoing popular concerns:

> It comes as no surprise that the theories or "movements" such as *Pan-Africanism* or *Negritude* (two pertinent expressions arising mainly from the assumption that all black Africans have a cultural identity) were propounded outside of black Africa. More recently, the Black Americans' claim to an African identity is another proof, possibly a rather desperate one, of the need for a "return to the source."[9]

Reconversion may be an individual predilection or a purely emotional state of mind. However, when the return links up with a broader popular movement, it greatly enriches and energizes the national liberation effort while simultaneously giving to former elites a renewed sense of identity or connectedness. Cabral in this context offers some comments on identity formation that appear broadly relevant beyond the immediate confines of the anticolonial struggle. Features of individual or group identity may be traced either to biological-genetic or to sociological and historical factors; but with respect to cultural resistance and affirmation, the sociological-historical dimension clearly deserves primary attention. Seen as a sociological category, identity is always relational or "dialectical," evident from the fact that "an individual (or a group) is only similar to certain individuals (or groups) if it is also different from other individuals (or groups)." Moreover, social and political identity has a dynamic, historically evolving character that also entails its refraction into multiple strands and sedimentations. "Therefore," Cabral states, "the identity of a being is always a relative quality, even circumstantial, for defining it demands a selection, more or less rigid and strict, of the biological and sociological characteristics of the being in question." His lecture also comments briefly on the issue often raised by Marxists of the economic determinants of social life, the role of the "mode of production" in identity formation. If stress is placed on economic determinants, then identity is bound to be defined as the expression of economic realities, especially of the prevailing class structure. Given the fact that assimilated elites opting for a "return to the source" often do so in defiance of their own class status, Cabral on the whole favors a more "culturalist" approach to the problem:

> If one accepts that culture is a dynamic synthesis of the material and spiritual condition of the society . . . , one can assert that identity is at the individual and collective level and beyond the economic condition, the expression of culture. This is why to attribute, recognize or declare the identity of an individual or group is above all to place that individual or group in the framework of a culture.[10]

# II

For many, both inside and outside of Africa, the days of the liberation struggle are now only a distant memory. As a result, the writings and teachings of Cabral—and those of his associates—seem ready to be consigned to library shelves and historical archives, to be retrieved only for academic exercises. This assessment is far from the mark. Although the overt goal of national independence has for the most part been achieved, the issue of political and cultural liberation is by no means resolved or obsolete. Under radically changed circumstances and in a new global context, the question of Africa (or of the "existence" of Africa) still persists, and with it the problem of African identity and a possible return to the source. As previously indicated, a top priority of non-Western societies today is "development," their rapid integration into the global economy or the liberalized world market. In this situation, some of the key themes or categories highlighted by Cabral resurface, though usually cloaked in new terminology or rhetoric. Seeking rapid economic integration, professional or middle-class segments of these societies often promote full-fledged Westernization or Europeanization, thereby conjuring up the image or example of assimilated elites discussed by Cabral. On the other hand, in wholesale rejection of assimilation, other intellectuals or social groups may choose to revert to a nostalgic, anti-Western traditionalism, thereby copying, at least in part, the attitude of traditional elites seeking to recapture their ancient privileges. In order to sort out the dilemmas of postcolonial Africa, this section turns to some distinguished African thinkers or philosophers who have reflected intensely on the problem of African identity: Valentin Mudimbe (formerly of Zaire), Tsenay Serequeberhan (of Ethiopia), and Marcien Towa (of Cameroon).

Mudimbe is primarily known for his award-winning study of 1988 titled *The Invention of Africa*. More recently he has come forward with another important text, *The Idea of Africa*; however, for present purposes the earlier book seems more instructive. In that work Mudimbe shows himself deeply influenced by recent trends in European philosophy, especially structuralism and poststructuralism. What he absorbed from these trends was the notion of "epistemic grids," the idea that understanding always proceeds within a cognitive framework structuring knowledge in selective ways. Accordingly, he accused earlier Western students of Africa of a practice akin to "Orientalism," that is, of integrating African forms of thought and experience into a preestablished set of European categories and premises. In Mudimbe's terms, this practice could be characterized as a mode of "epistemological ethnocentrism," an inquiry governed by the belief "that scientifically there is nothing to be learned from 'them' unless it is already 'ours' or comes from 'us'." In large measure, this belief animated such academic disciplines as cultural anthropology and ethnography that emerged during the last century as a corollary of colonial expansion. The cultural and political significance of these disciplines was pervasive; their impact was deepened by the rise of an ideological or proselytizing ethnocentrism (paralleling the epistemological variant): the zeal of missionaries and many bureaucrats of spreading Western culture to the "savages." The net effect of both discourses was the same—screening the existence of Africa from view:

> Both types of discourses are fundamentally reductionist. They speak about neither Africa nor Africans, but rather justify the process of inventing and conquering a continent and naming its "primitiveness" or "disorder," as well as the subsequent means of its exploitation and methods for its "regeneration."[11]

One of the merits of Mudimbe's book is its broad historical overview of successive theoretical assessments of Africa originating both inside and outside that continent. As indicated, the dominant mode during the heyday of colonialism was an ethnocentric (or "Orientalizing") inquiry that rigidly classified African cultures as inferior to the paradigmatic model of Western modernity. Largely under the influence of Lévy-Bruhl's work, philosophical anthropology expounded lengthily on the distinction between savagery and civilization and between "primitive" and advanced "rational" states of mind. In a way, this trend was continued in Placide Temples's famous *Bantu Philosophy* (1945), which sought to distill a specifically Bantu ontology or metaphysics—despite a determined effort by Temples to transgress Western categories through "empathy."[12] The period of anticolonial resistance brought a sharp reaction to this legacy of European ethnocentrism.

Intellectually, national liberation was accompanied and undergirded by radical African "self-expression," the effort of African intellectuals to marshal indigenous cultural resources as an antidote to foreign domination. Sometimes styled "ethnophilosophy," this effort included the formulation of ideas like "African personality" and *"négritude"* (by Léopold Senghor and others), and also the attempt to recover precolonial institutions and social structures; a high point of the outlook was Marcel Griaule's *Conversations with Ogotemmeli* (1948), a book extolling native wisdom as expounded by a village elder. Attitudes changed again with the onset of national independence. Following the retreat of colonial powers, African intellectuals again opened themselves more freely to Western or European influences; particularly noteworthy was the rapid influx and assimilation of innovative cognitive or epistemic schemes, like structuralism and poststructuralism (including structuralist Marxism). Attacking ethnophilosophers as regressive, some spokesmen of this trend postulated the need for a "universal" philosophy largely detached from local cultural moorings. As Paulin Hountondji, a leading figure from Benin, stated in 1981, following independence

> it was necessary to begin by *demythifying* the concept of Africanity, reducing it to a status of a phenomenon—the simple phenomenon which *per se* is perfectly neutral, of belonging to Africa—by dissipating the mystical halo of values arbitrarily grafted on this phenomenon by the ideologues of identity. . . . In order to think [objectively] of the richness of African traditions, it was necessary to *weaken* resolutely the concept of Africa, to *rid* it of all its ethical, religious, philosophical, political connotations, etc., with which a long anthropological tradition had overloaded it and [of which] the most visible effect was to close the horizon, to prematurely close history.[13]

On the whole, *The Invention of Africa* reflected the postindependence mood, though without a readiness to abandon indigenous African resources. As stated before, Mudimbe took his bearings chiefly from French structuralism and poststructuralism—a perspective that was bound to render his approach deeply ambivalent. Construed as an epistemology or a social-scientific methodology, structuralism (and its early poststructuralist offshoot) basically provides a cognitive structure of social analysis, which, as a formal method, is invariant across cultures and hence necessarily distances and neutralizes their substantive differences. Mudimbe is vaguely aware of this circumstance when he notes that, despite their resistance against universal rationalism—or "the rule of the Same"—and the "history of its conquests over all regionalisms, specificities, and differences," Lévi-Strauss and Michel Foucault still belong to "the signs of the same power" and thus could be considered "an expression of the 'intelligence' of the Same." On the other hand, by stipulating the determination or fixation of cultural content by a given epistemic grid, structuralism also renders cultural differences in effect incommensurable and mutually unintelligible. Hence, in application to cultural understanding, structuralism exhibits a basic quandary or antimony: treating all cultures as rationally knowable—in fact, as already "known" by virtue of the stipulated method—and simultaneously considering them as substantively unknowable or beyond the pale of universal-rational categories. In its concluding chapter, *The Invention of Africa* speaks of two conflicting theses that divide the "geography" of African knowledge into "two opposed spaces." On the one side, there are "synchronically oriented discourses," operating across time and space, which claim to "unveil the organization" of cultural economies as such; on the other side, "diachronically motivated discourses" seek to uncover the "dialectical discontinuities" and differences of social systems. This contrast points out the antinomy, perhaps the dialectic, between universalism and particularism, which Mudimbe is willing to leave unresolved.[14]

The quandaries of structuralism can be mitigated, if not entirely overcome, by a turn to another prominent perspective in our century: existentialism and existential hermeneutics. As formulated by Heidegger and Gadamer (and in part Ricoeur), this perspective replaces the stark form/content and self/other bifurcation with an emphasis on interactive encounter and a dialogical interrogation in which neither party remains unchanged. In his book *The Hermeneutics of African Philosophy* (1994), Tsenay Serequeberhan vividly illustrates the virtues and social-political implications of this approach. Moving within the limits of concretely "lived finitude," he notes, contemporary hermeneutics explores the present and future possibilities of human existence. In the context of recent philosophy, this direction and "sensibility of thought" has been inaugurated in Heidegger's *Being and Time* and expanded in Gadamer's *Truth and Method*—texts that can be fruitfully mined to probe and elucidate the "concrete historicity of postcolonial Africa." The idea of a "hermeneutics of African philosophy" thus denotes a critically interpretive enterprise and interrogation grounded in the lived experience of postcolonial Africa (seen as a complex background "horizon") and articulated in the medium of reflective "discourse." For Serequeberhan, such an endeavor signifies neither a nostalgic antiquarianism nor a critique divorced from historical moorings, but rather the reflective "appropriation and continuation of African emancipatory hopes and aspirations." This continuation is crucially important in the present postcolonial situation, given the insidious rise of "neocolonial" forms of domination under the aegis of *pax Americana* and Western hegemony in technological, economic, and military fields. In this setting, the proper task of African philosophy is elaborating a "radical hermeneutics" of contemporary African experience, a task that necessarily involves a "politically committed and historically specific critical self-reflection that stems from the negativity of our post-colonial present."[15]

In an effort to profile this radical hermeneutics, Serequeberhan carefully differentiates his outlook from a number of competing perspectives, especially "ethnophilosophy" and pure or "professional" philosophy. While the former seeks to excavate and restore "ethnic African world-views" and practices, the ambition of the second is to assimilate or integrate African thought rapidly into the standards of "universal" philosophy (as established by modern Western rationalism, structuralist Marxism, or Anglo-American analytical philosophy). A leading spokesman of the first alternative was Léopold Senghor of Senegal—though his views were in many ways foreshadowed by Temples's *Bantu Philosophy*. By articulating such notions as *"négritude," "Africanité,"* or "African socialism," Serequeberhan argues, Senghor erected a kind of "essentialist particularism," an outlook that reified or objectified a perennial African identity. For Senghor, the black African or "Negro-African" was basically a creature of "nature" rather than civilization and as such characterized by a unique "docility and lyrical submissiveness to nature"; as a corollary, African thinking was said to be intuitive or instinctive, in contrast to modern Western thought, described as rational, discursive, and utilitarian. Turning to representatives of a Western-style "professional" philosophy, Serequeberhan focuses attention primarily on the orthodox Marxism-Leninism of Kwame Nkrumah of Ghana and subsidiarily on the analytical-structuralist Marxism of Hountondji. In Nkrumah's view, social and cultural conditions in Africa were simply accidental contingencies that could be fully subsumed under such Marxist categories as "scientific socialism" and "historical materialism" (seen as a universal "science of history"). As he observed in writings like "African Socialism Revisited" and "The Myth of the Third World," Senghorian notions of African distinctiveness were entirely spurious, since there was only one reality captured uniformly by modern science (specifically scientific socialism). Enriched by recent analytical trends, Nkrumah's arguments have been endorsed and subtlely continued by Hountondji and other proponents of professional philosophy.[16]

In Serequeberhan's account, invocations of modern universal science by Marxists and others can only have the effect of pushing out of sight the "grounding character of the question of freedom in Africa" and thus of relegating to oblivion the "specific particularity of the African situation." Wedded to the continuing struggle against colonialism and neocolonialism, radical hermeneutics has to steer clear of the two options sketched above, options which, in Cabral's terms, are chiefly attractive to assimilated modernizers, on the one hand, and nostalgic traditionalists, on the other. For Marxists and other proponents of modern scientism, philosophical categories are basically neutral with respect to historical and local circumstances. "Without batting an eye," Serequeberhan comments, "they endorse 'scientific socialism': as if this perspective was devoid of any distinctiveness and cultural-historical specificity. . . . As if, that is, European modernity, properly speaking, spelled the 'true' humanity of the human *as such*." On the other hand, in the wake of Said's *Orientalism*, it is difficult to take seriously Senghor's "*Africanité*," for it is "nothing more than the ontologizing of Eurocentric ideas projected and presented as the African's own self-conception"; in Orientalizing fashion, African identity is elevated to the level of an invariant "Platonic idea." Although opposed on the surface, the two perspectives actually concur in their basic effect: by consigning African culture to the level of premodern or antimodern primitiveness. In Serequeberhan's portrayal, the two contradictory positions implicitly "share a single Eurocentric metaphysics"; both the "abstract universalism" of the modernists and the "particularistic antiquarianism" of their opponents fail to come to grips with the "lived actuality" of postcolonial Africa. Nkrumah's Marxism

metaphysically privileges European modernity by obliterating the specificity and particularity of the African in the name of a *universalistic scientism*. Senghor achieves an analogous result by constructing the being of the African—*Africanité*—out of the Otherness of the Other projected by Europe and internally demarcated by it as the negative exterior of Europe's own positive interiority. Senghor's *essentialist particularism* arrogates to the African a difference which is (in spite of Senghor's "good" intentions) the ground for inferiority and servitude. Nkrumah and Hountondji, on the other hand, "objectively" place the African on the lowest rung of an evolutionary metaphysical ladder, itself constructed out of the generative biases and prejudgments that ground the specificity of European modernity.[17]

In some measure, the project of radical hermeneutics is endorsed by Marcien Towa, one of the leading African thinkers today, though with greater concessions to philosophical universalism. Like Serequeberhan, Towa is opposed both to a rigid traditionalism, as represented by ethnophilosophy, and a radical exit from tradition as proposed by epistemic modernism or scientism. Regarding the former, his critique is more blunt and uncompromising, ascribing to it missionary or theological motives devoid of genuine reflection. He writes, "that which hides itself behind the so-called African philosophy of the ethnophilosophers does not belong properly speaking to philosophy, but rather to theology." Animated by the aim of infusing African tradition with religious (Christian, Muslim, and other) beliefs, ethnophilosophy is "already in possession of its credo," at variance with the "true spirit of research"; in fact, it is "as stiff as the dogmas it propagates." Regarding scientism, Towa's main target is Hountondji's scientific Marxism (or scientific socialism). For Hountondji, he notes, philosophy coincides with scientific epistemology (seen as the "theory of theory"). Since traditionally African thought was not concerned with scientific inquiry, Africa historically is bereft of anything resembling genuine philosophy—an endorsement of the Orientalist claim of the superiority of Western modernism. In Towa's lively language, Hountondji

> is a prisoner of the prejudice that views Africa as primitive and [endowed] with a purely mythical mentality. . . . Such a position amounts to turning our backs on our ancestors without harkening to them, to discouraging research pertinent to traditional thought, and to condemning ourselves to amnesia in that which concerns the principal domain of the thinking of the essential.[18]

The last phrase provides a clue to Towa's own approach to philosophical reflection. In a somewhat "Platonizing" vein, he initially endorses *philosophia perennis*, at least a highly formal conception of philosophy cut loose from distinctive links "with any one particular civilization." Philosophy, he writes, is "the thought of the essential: the methodical and critical examination of that which, in the theoretical or the practical order, has or should have for humanity a supreme importance." Focused on the abstract and "entirely general essence" of reflection, this definition in a way sunders the connection of subject and predicate in the phrase "African philosophy." Yet, almost instantly, Towa tempers this Platonizing formalism by adding an existential or hermeneutical twist. Philosophy, he states, is always elaborated by people who "are not themselves abstractions, but are beings of flesh and bones who belong to a continent, to a particular culture, and to a specific period." Thus, philosophical reflection cannot remain limited to the level of principles that are abstractly universal and hence applicable everywhere and at all times. In order to properly philosophize it is necessary for a thinker "to examine in a critical and methodical manner the essential problems of his milieu and of his period." To this extent, critical reflection will always establish an explicit or implicit relation with a given time or locality. In the same manner, one can also say of a philosophy that it is "African or European"—if one means by that expression that Africans or Europeans have "reflected on their fundamental problems."[19]

## III

Having reviewed some prominent recent reflections by African thinkers, it seems appropriate to return, by way of conclusion, to the question raised at the beginning of this chapter: that of African identity, especially of an African "return to the source" as articulated by Cabral. The latter phrase is at first glance enigmatic if not provocative; its meaning surely cannot be discovered apart from its context and Cabral's philosophical and political position. Today Cabral is being increasingly recognized as a pivotal figure in the development of African thought from colonialism to postcolonialism. As the Tanzanian thinker Wamba-dia-Wamba writes, Cabral is an example of "an authentic African philosopher of today's Africa," someone who "expresses consciously the unconscious historical process of self-organization and struggle of the African masses" against colonialism and for national liberation. The exemplary quality of Cabral resides in his ability to combine theoretical reflection with practical engagement, concrete political struggle with broader philosophical insights. Wamba-dia-Wamba adds, Cabral is "a real hero of the African people" as well as of African intellectuals. Contrary to the philosophers of *négritude* and *Africanité* who subscribe to the Orientalist division of civilization and savagery, Cabral was an "organic intellectual" (in Antonio Gamsci's sense), remaining rooted among the African people whom he guided while simultaneously learning from them.[20]

Among the African philosophers cited before, Cabral figures prominently in Serequeberhan's study. While being indebted to the teachings of Heidegger and Gadamer, his text also pays tribute to leaders of the anticolonial liberation struggle—above all to Aimé Césaire, Frantz Fanon, and Amilcar Cabral. Serequeberhan comments extensively and perceptively on Cabral's phrase "return to the source." The phrase, he notes, has no kinship with an attempted retrieval of a fixed starting point; even less does it denote a nostalgic search for a pristine origin or "golden age." Rather, in Cabral's usage, "source" had the meaning of a resource of resistance, pregnant with untapped possibilities of development and self-discovery. Hence, past and future are curiously and intimately embroiled. As Serequeberhan observes, national liberation is the "overcoming of the colonialist interruption of the historicity of the colonized"; as such, it signals a "reaction to a presently frozen reality in terms of the suppressed possibilities of this reality itself."

The point for Cabral—as also for Césaire and Fanon—was not the abstract affirmation or vindication of a "precolonial culture/history"; instead, what matters in the struggle is the disclosure of "a future out of what has endured against colonialism and out of what European domination itself has established in its historic African odyssey." In the context of the liberation struggle, the notion of a return gained its particular saliency from the fissure or division of society into polarized camps—the colonizers and the colonized, the European masters and the native masses—in which assimilated elites occupied a precarious and tensional status. In the midst of this conflict, the motto of return signaled the overcoming and transformation of the identities of both colonizers and colonized, a process ushering in the release of untapped historical options for previously colonized peoples. In the words of Serequeberhan, for Cabral as well as postcolonial societies, returning does not and cannot mean

> a return to a tradition in its stasis. We are not, therefore, engaged in an antiquarian quest for an already existing authentic past. Rather, we are engaged in the affirmation by the Westernized native of the historicity of the rural indigenous mass. Simultaneously, this is the self-negation by the Westernized native [elite] of its own cultural legitimacy. The obverse of this denial is the positive affirmation of the stunted indigenous culture.[21]

Despite differences of accent and orientation, the teachings of Heidegger and Cabral do not basically conflict regarding the return to the source or to the origin. Since his earliest writings, Heidegger's views of temporality revolved around the peculiar embroilment or contamination of past and future. In *Being and Time*, human existence is portrayed as "historical," but not in the sense of an imprisonment in the past. As the famous section on "historicality" points out, human beings always find themselves "thrown" into a legacy or tradition that they may or may not deliberately shoulder; but in shouldering or retrieving this legacy (in the Kierkegaardian meaning of "repetition"), they do not retreat backward in time but explore untapped potentials for the sake of unfolding future possibilities. In Heidegger's words, "Repetition [*Wiederholung*] may be defined as a resolute mode of shouldering the past whereby human *Dasein* expressly assumes a destiny. But if destiny constitutes the basic historicality of *Dasein*, then history is anchored neither in the past nor in the present and its 'linkage' with the past, but in the genuine happening of existence which derives from *Dasein's* impending *future*."[22] Less than a decade later, Heidegger reflected more extensively on the question of "source" or "origin," with particular reference to the creative source of artworks and especially of poetry. As he observed at the time, such creation is neither the arbitrary-subjective effusion of the creative artist nor is it the mere continuation or transmission of an already settled tradition. Rather, genuine poetic invention involves "the opening up of a dimension into which historical *Dasein* is always already placed or thrown [*geworfen*]." This dimension is for a historical people its sedimented ground, "which carries it along together with everything it latently is or can be." The creative ground of artworks and of poetry, for Heidegger, has the character both of an "origin" (*Ursprung*) and of a "leap" (*Sprung*) beyond every customary or predictable routine. But this unexpected quality of the leap

does not exclude but rather implies that the source or beginning is something that is prepared from farthest back and quite imperceptibly. As a leap,
the genuine beginning is always a leap ahead (*Vorsprung*) whereby everything in the future—though still concealed—is already transgressed. Thus,
the source or beginning always contains latently the ending. But the genuine
beginning has never the character of mere primitiveness.[23]

Nearly another decade later, in the middle of the great war, Heidegger
again pondered the question of "source" and "origin" in his last lecture
course on Hölderlin (held in Freiburg in 1942). The course was devoted
to an interpretation of one of Hölderlin's great hymns titled "Der Ister,"
another name for the Danube. As Heidegger pointed out, Hölderlin's
poetry frequently revolved around and celebrated rivers or streams, because rivers capture the essence of human historical existence—its movement between birth and death, beginning and ending, its "wandering"
(*Wanderschaft*) through life and time. Wandering, one should note, does
not mean an aimless, nomadic errancy but rather a search for a home or
an abode, yet in such a manner that wandering is not merely a means (or
externally related) to an end. In Heidegger's words: "The river *is* the
abode which permeates human life on earth and which determines its
sense of home and belonging." Seen as a corollary of wandering, home
can at best be a form of homecoming; far from being an instant property
or possession, home requires and can be reached (if at all) only through
distant peregrinations. Hölderlin states (in another poem) that human
life is "at home not in the beginning" and needs to "courageously venture
abroad" in the direction of otherness or the alien. In "Der Ister," this
aspect is highlighted by the presence of an alien visitor (Hercules) at the
river's source, and even more pointedly by the observation that in its
upper reaches, the Danube seems to "flow backward" into its source
from afar or from abroad. Bringing together the multiple themes of the
hymn and of his lecture course, Heidegger comments:

> The rule of homecoming means that historical humanity is at the start of its
> history unfamiliar with its proper abode; in fact, it has to become alien
> to itself in order to learn—through an exodus abroad—the path of self-
> discovery or self-appropriation and thus to find its home only on the way
> back, by returning. Likewise, the historical existence of a people must first
> of all encounter otherness [*das Fremde*] in order to discover—via this en-
> counter and struggle—what is the proper mode of returning to its abode.
> For history is nothing else but such a return to the source.[24]

In his address of October 1972, Cabral clearly distinguished the "return to the source" from a mere backward-looking nostalgia or an antiquarian "return to traditions." At the same time, however, the phrase

was not meant to serve as a facile political slogan and least of all as an ideological blueprint or utopian agenda. Attentive to the confluence of temporalities, Cabral defined the "return" not as a willful or "voluntary step" but as an existential response: a "reply to the demand of concrete need, historically determined" by the experience of colonialism and the conflict between colonizers and colonized. A similar stance was taken by Aimé Césaire, the poet-politician, in his actions and his writings. In one of his collection of poems, titled *Return to My Native Land* (*Cahier d'un Retour au Pays Natal*), Césaire penned these lines:

> My Negritude is not a stone, its deafness thrown
> against the clamor of the day,
> My Negritude is not a speck of dead water
> on the dead eye of the earth,
>
> My Negritude is neither tower nor cathedral,
> it thrusts into the red flesh of the soil,
> it thrusts into the warm flesh of the sky. . . .
>
> What I seek for my country are not hearts of dates,
> but hearts of men who beat the virile blood
> to enter the cities of silver
> by the great door of trapezoid.[25]

## Notes

1. The notion of a "colonization of the life-world" can be found in Jürgen Habermas, *The Theory of Communicative Action*, vol. II, *Lifeworld and System*, trans. Thomas McCarthy (Boston: Beacon Press, 1987), pp. 196, 305, 391–396. The phrase "*oublier Cabral*" is freely adapted from Jean Baudrillard, *Oublier Foucault* (Paris: Galilée, 1977).

2. "National Liberation and Culture," in *Return to the Source: Selected Speeches by Amilcar Cabral*, ed. Africa Information Service (New York & London: Monthly Review Press, 1973), pp. 39–40. The lecture, delivered in Syracuse, New York, on February 20, 1970, was dedicated to the memory of Eduardo Mondane, the first president of the Mozambique Liberation Front, who had been killed a year before.

3. *Return to the Source*, pp. 40–42. Occasionally, Cabral lapses into somewhat reductive formulations, for example, when he says that culture is the product of history "just as the flower is the product of a plant" or that "culture has as its material base the level of productive forces and the mode of production" (p. 42).

4. *Return to the Source*, pp. 43–47.

5. *Return to the Source*, pp. 45–47. By allowing for the possibility of diverse orientations within elite structures, Cabral implicitly weakens the (orthodox-Marxist) thesis of the economic determination of cultural relations.

6. *Return to the Source*, pp. 43, 50–51. Cultural self-affirmation, for Cabral, was by no means incompatible with globalization or the emergence of a global community. He noted, it was important to discern "the value of African cultures in the framework of universal civilization" and to compare this value with that of other cultures, "not with a view of deciding its superiority or inferiority" but in order to determine "what contribution African culture has made and can make, and what are the contributions it can or must receive from elsewhere" (p. 52).

7. "Identity and Dignity in the Context of the National Liberation Struggle," in *Return to the Source*, pp. 59–61. The lecture was held on October 15, 1972, at Lincoln University in Pennsylvania, where Cabral received an honorary doctoral degree.

8. *Return to the Source*, pp. 58–59.

9. *Return to the Source*, pp. 61–63.

10. *Return to the Source*, pp. 64–66.

11. V. Y. Mudimbe, *The Invention of Africa: Gnosis, Philosophy, and the Order of Knowledge* (Bloomington: Indiana University Press, 1988), pp. 15, 19–20. Some of Mudimbe's language is reminiscent of Edward W. Said, *Orientalism* (New York: Vintage Books, 1979), especially pp. 1–3. See also Mudimbe, *The Idea of Africa* (Bloomington: Indiana University Press, 1994).

12. Placide F. Temples, *Bantu Philosophy* (1st French ed. 1945; Paris: Présence Africaine, 1959). Mudimbe is fair-minded in assessing this controversial text. "Looking back at the period that saw the publication of *Bantu Philosophy*," he writes, "Temples neatly differentiates himself from anthropologists. . . . While attempting to 'civilize,' Temples found his moment of truth in an encounter with people of whom he thought himself the master. He thus became a student of those he was supposed to teach and sought to comprehend their version of truth. During this encounter, there was a discrete moment of revelation, which radically complicated the convictions of the civilizer." See *The Invention of Africa*, pp. 137, 141.

13. Paulin Hountondji, "Que peut la philosophie?" in *Présence Africaine* 119 (1981): 52. See also Marcel Griaule, *Conversations with Ogotemmeli* (1st French ed. 1948; Oxford: Oxford University Press, 1965); and Mudimbe, *The Invention of Africa*, pp. 36–38, 158–160 (on Hountondji).

14. *The Invention of Africa*, pp. 43, 189, 199. Moving away from a rigidly structuralist method, the study elsewhere strikes a more hopeful note. "I am personally convinced," Mudimbe states, "that the most imaginative works that reveal to us what are now called African systems of thought, . . . can be fundamentally understood through their journey into *Einfühlung*" or empathy (p. 145). This sentiment is backed up by occasional references to Heidegger, Ricoeur, and Gadamer (whose hermeneutics, to be sure, cannot simply be equated with empathy).

15. Tsenay Serequeberhan, *The Hermeneutics of African Philosophy: Horizon*

*and Discourse* (New York and London: Routledge, 1994), pp. 1–2, 6, 15–17. Referring to Heidegger's argument that the core of human existence resides in its "to be" (*zu-sein*), Serequeberhan comments "for us [Africans] to appropriate the 'to be' of our historicalness means to confront European neocolonial subjugation: the politics of economic, cultural, and scientific subordination" (p. 21). Elaborating on the subtitle of his book he adds, "Horizon designates the historico-hermeneutical and politico-cultural milieu within and out of which specific discourses (philosophic, artistic, scientific, etc.) are articulated. . . . Discourse, on the other hand, refers to these articulated concerns interior to the concrete conditions-of-existence made possible by and internal to a specific horizon" (p. 18). Compare in this context Theophilus Okere, *African Philosophy: A Historico-Hermeneutical Investigation of the Conditions of Its Possibility* (Lanham, Md.: University Press of America, 1983).

16. Serequeberhan, *The Hermeneutics of African Philosophy*, pp. 5, 41, 44–45. Regarding ethnophilosophy see especially Léopold Sédar Senghor, *The Foundations of "Africanité" or "Négritude" and "Arabité,"* trans. Mercer Cook (Paris: Présence Africaine, 1971). For Nkrumah's writings see his *Revolutionary Path* (London: Panaf Books, 1980), also his *Class Struggle in Africa* (New York: International Publishers, 1975). See also Paulin J. Hountondji, *African Philosophy: Myth and Reality*, 2nd ed. (Bloomington: Indiana University Press, 1996).

17. Serequeberhan, *The Hermeneutics of African Philosophy*, pp. 5, 7, 33–34, 41–42, 47–48, 52.

18. Marcien Towa, "Conditions for the Affirmation of a Modern African Philosophical Thought," in *African Philosophy: The Essential Readings*, ed. Tsenay Serequeberhan (New York: Paragon House, 1991), pp. 189–192.

19. *African Philosophy*, pp. 193–195. He adds, "What is African are the men of flesh and bones who evoke the problems of supreme importance and to whom these same problems are applicable immediately. . . . Defining philosophy only in terms of epistemology would lead us to exlude from the domain of philosophy works universally recognized as philosophical: works of ethics, ontology, political philosophy, aesthetics, etc. . . . I do not see what we stand to gain from such an amnesia, not even to consider the thought of our ancestors as worthy of being examined and discussed" (p. 195). In light of these comments I cannot agree with D. A. Masolo when he classifies Towa among the group of pure or professional philosophers; see Masolo's *African Philosophy in Search of Identity* (Bloomington: Indiana University Press, 1994), pp. 164–172. For other recent texts on African philosophy see Kwasi Wiredu, *Cultural Universals and Particulars: An African Perspective* (Bloomington: Indiana University Press, 1996); Emmanuel C. Eze, ed., *Postcolonial African Philosophy: A Critical Reader* (Oxford: Blackwell, 1996); Eze, ed., *African Philosophy: An Anthology* (Oxford: Blackwell, 1997).

20. Ernest Wamba-dia-Wamba, "Philosophy in Africa: Challenges of the African Philosopher," in *African Philosophy*, ed. Serequeberhan, p. 237.

21. Serequeberhan, *The Hermeneutics of African Philosophy*, pp. 102–105, 107–108. He adds, "In the process of undoing colonialism the colonized culture as colonized also undoes itself. It destroys the frozen and mummified forms of existence imposed on it. Thus, it should be clear by now that 'the practice of

freedom' is possible only within the context of the 'return to the source' which is the internal structure of African self-emancipation. . . . The 'return' is the liberation of the stunted possibilities of the colonized" (p. 110).

22. Martin Heidegger, *Sein and Zeit*, 11th ed. (Tübingen, Germany: Niemeyer, 1967), par. 74, p. 386 (my translation).

23. Heidegger, "Der Ursprung des Kunstwerkes," in *Holzwege*, 4th ed. (Frankfurt-Main: Klostermann, 1963), pp. 62–63 (my translation).

24. Heidegger, *Hölderlins Hymne "Der Ister,"* ed. Walter Biemel (*Gesamtausgabe*, vol. 53; Frankfurt-Main: Klostermann, 1984), pp. 23, 156, 160–162, 175, 177–178, 182 (my translation). In the above citation Heidegger speaks of a "return to the hearth [*Herd*]," where "hearth" seems to be equivalent to the river's source. Compare also the chapter "Homecoming through Otherness" in my *The Other Heidegger* (Ithaca, N.Y.: Cornell University Press, 1993), pp. 149–180.

25. Aimé Césaire, *Return to My Native Land*, trans. Emile Snyders (Paris: Présence Africaine, 1968), pp. 101, 127. See also Cabral, *Return to the Source*, p. 63.

# 8

# Nationalism in South Asia:
# Some Theoretical Points

In a recent book titled *Thick and Thin: Moral Argument at Home and Abroad*, Michael Walzer comments on our domestic and global situation today, especially on the upsurge of diverse forms of particularism, including ethnic, religious, and national identities, often pejoratively labeled "retribalization." Undaunted by such rhetoric, he states that "the tribes have returned" and that "the drama of their return is greatest where their repression was most severe." In Walzer's account, tribe is a stand-in or synonym for a certain social lifeworld, namely, a "thick moral and political culture" binding people together through a shared language and a dense fabric of meanings and historical experiences. Thickness of this kind is said over time to generate among members a "community of character"—a phrase initially coined by Otto Bauer but recently reinvigorated by Stanley Hauerwas—allowing members to find a measure of "identity, self-respect, and sentimental connections." As Walzer adds, the notion of tribe (in this communitarian sense) has always been fiercely opposed and pilloried by radical modernizers and globalizers wedded to "thin" (or universalized) procedures of conduct. In his view, however, the dilemma pictured by globalizers—"dominance of one tribe or a common detribalization"—does not exhaust our options; the alternative in his book is a continued thickness in the midst of a relentless thinning-out process (associated with globalization):

> Confronted with modernity, all the human tribes are endangered species; their thick cultures are subject to erosion. All of them, whether or not they possess sovereign power, have been significantly affected. We can recognize what might be called a right to resist these effects . . . ; [but] we cannot guarantee the success of the resistance.[1]

191

As even a cursory glance at the literature reveals, the distinction be-tween thickness and thinness has also played a prominent role in discus-sions of nationalism, though usually under different terminological guises. Since Hans Kohn's classical treatise on *The Idea of Nationalism* (1944), it has been customary to distinguish at least two major types of nationhood and nationalism: a liberal and an illiberal kind, where "lib-eral" stands for tolerant, civic-minded, and progressive while "illiberal" refers to a regressive and militant chauvinism. As Kohn observed, liberal (or thin) nationalism arose out of the great revolutions of modernity and in close association with the formation of the nation-state dedicated to the rule of law and equal citizen rights; to this extent, the birth of nation-alism was a "predominantly political occurrence" that was either pre-ceded by the growth of the nation-state or, as in the case of America, coincided with it. By contrast, illiberal (or thick) nationalism was dis-jointed from the institutions of the modern state; in fact, it arose typically "in protest against and in conflict with the existing state pattern," not with the aim of transforming this pattern progressively but in an effort to "redraw political boundaries in conformity with ethnographic de-mands." What renders Kohn's argument pertinent in the present context is the fact that the liberal-illiberal contrast was closely linked in his study with another, geographical dichotomy: that between Western and East-ern or non-Western modes of nationalism. While Western nationalism was closely connected with the "concepts of individual liberty and ratio-nal cosmopolitanism," Eastern or non-Western nationalism—as found, for example, in Germany, Russia, and India—tended toward a "contrary development"; whereas the former was forward-looking and emancipa-tory, the latter was backward-looking, oppressive, and fueled by resent-ment, sometimes against colonial masters. Unable to find a rallying point in "a free and rational order," non-Western nationalism sought refuge in sentimental nostalgia and often in "a mystical integration around the irrational, precivilized folk concept."[2]

Before proceeding further, some definitions and stipulative notions that will guide the chapter's subsequent steps are necessary. It is impor-tant to distinguish between nation or nationhood, on the one hand, and nationalism, on the other. Nation refers to the sedimented lifeworld of a people (or a conglomerate of peoples), nurtured by shared historical experiences that can be, and often are, diverse or conflictual. By contrast, nationalism denotes a political agenda, a deliberate political platform pursued by elites and/or popular movements. Nation is basically a cul-tural phenomenon, a complex background welter of meanings and un-derstandings that always involve interpretation and imagination. Roger Scruton correctly dissociates nation from race or ethnicity and empha-sizes such elements as history, language, and distinctive cultural artifacts.

On the other hand, nationalism belongs to the domain of politics, specifically the domain of *modern* politics and political ideologies. The contrast between liberal and illiberal types does not carry over into the distinction between nation and nationalism; in fact, the latter two relate to each other in multiple and often unpredictable ways. Contrary to Kohn's thesis, "political" (or state-oriented) nationalism is not necessarily liberal, and cultural nationhood or nationality not necessarily illiberal.[3]

This assessment can be backed up by historical evidence. As comparative study shows, "thickly" constituted cultural communities or nations may give rise to "thin" or narrowly circumscribed forms of nationalism (and sometimes to a rejection of nationalism as such). Conversely, "thinly" constituted liberal societies may foster aggressive forms of national expansionism (as evident in Western colonialism). The thickest and most aggressive brand of nationalism arises when cultural nationhood is converted or perverted into a dominant political agenda in an attempt to make background available as a foreground. In the following these points will be illustrated with reference to South Asia, more specifically the Indian subcontinent. After an initial section devoted to a prominent offshoot of Kohn's thesis regarding liberal and illiberal types, attention turns to some leading figures of the national independence movement in India, in particular to Sri Aurobindo, Rabindranath Tagore, Mahatma Gandhi, and Muhammad Iqbal. As historical evidence shows, nationalism on the subcontinent has been by no means uniformly illiberal, especially when the focus is placed on the most prominent leaders of the anticolonial struggle. Moving to the postindependence period, the third section briefly examines more recent discussions of nationalism in India in an effort to show its multidimensional character rooted in the tensional relation between culture and politics. The conclusion comments on implications of these discussions for contemporary regional and global politics.

# I

As articulated in his influential study, Kohn's theory of nationalism was by no means the expression of idiosyncratic preferences, but reflected a broader intellectual design. In its basic approach, the study captured the central lineaments of what has come to be known as the "modern project": the project of the progressive ascent of reason over passion, of (scientific) knowledge over superstition, and of individual freedom over traditional forms of collective bondage. In the privilege accorded to "political" nationalism, Kohn's theory mirrored the modern confidence in rational constitutional engineering, in the benefits of the nation-*state* as an antidote to the ravages of tribalism, primitive communalism, and/or feudal disorganization. As we know, this confidence was not restricted to Western or European nation-building. At least since the time of Hegel, the modern trajectory (or "metanarrative") had disclosed its global significance manifest in the presumed superiority of Western civilization over all other cultures and hence in the Western *"mission civilisatrice"* around the globe. Today, no doubt, all these assumptions and doctrines have been called into question. At least in its overt political form, Western colonialism has suffered shipwreck in our century, although it still persists in covert and more insidious guises. Two world wars and a host of assorted disasters have also cast serious doubt on the modern trust in scientific rationality and technology, a doubt further nurtured by the process of ecological degradation. Even the blessings of the modern nation-state are no longer universally hailed, given the fact that on frequent occasions state apparatuses have tended not to reduce but to aggravate ethnic or religious cleavages.[4]

Although widespread and pervasive, these challenges have not yet fully penetrated discussions about nationalism. In the literature on the topic, Kohn's theory still continues to be recapitulated in a number of variations. A brief review of one of the most subtle and nuanced offshoots of Kohn's approach, namely, John Plamenatz's essay on "Two Types of Nationalism," illustrates this continued influence. Plamenatz follows Kohn in differentiating between liberal (thin) and illiberal (thick) versions of nationalism and also between political and cultural variants—but he does so without immediately stigmatizing the latter. In addition, and as a corollary, he also distinguishes between "Western" and "Eastern" brands of nationalism—a distinction backed up mainly by concrete social-political considerations. Nationalism, especially political nationalism, is basically a modern category growing out of the great revolutionary events of modern times, reflecting a belief in progress or the progressive transformation of social life. In Plamenatz's words, nationalism as a political program is a phenomenon "peculiar to peoples who share a cosmopolitan and secular culture" with a strong orientation to the future; it arises where peoples are aware of cultural change and embrace "some idea of progress which moves them to compare their own achievements and capacities with those of others." Nationalism as a program is commonly undergirded by a cultural sense of nationhood—a sense of historical and cultural distinctness—which in turn is an offshoot of earlier modes of "patriotism" (or communal loyalty). A basic problem here is the relation between culture and politics. For Plamenatz, political nationalism is in the main a reactive strategy; it reflects the desire to preserve or enhance a people's national or cultural identity when that identity is threatened, or the desire to transform or even create it where it is felt to be inadequate or lacking. . . . Thus nationalism is a reaction of peoples who feel culturally at a disadvantage.[5]

With regard to the relation between culture and politics, Plamenatz takes some innovative steps pointing beyond Kohn's modernist paradigm. As he emphasizes, cultural nationalism (or a sense of cultural nationhood) does not necessarily promote an illiberal kind of politics; even a densely woven fabric of cultural distinctness does not inevitably translate into political nationalism and may even reject nationalist agendas as such. A case in point is the outlook of Johann Gottfried Herder—a writer who has often been chided as a reactionary antimodernist. Plamenatz can in no way classify Herder as a "political nationalist," since he clearly did not aspire to the "union of all Germans in one state." Herder's main concern was with cultural distinctness, what makes any people culturally different from other peoples, "what they cherish as peculiarly their own." This emphasis on cultural distinctness was not compatible with a policy of uniformity—as was illustrated in the German case, where some Germans were Protestants and other Catholics, some were governed by the Hohenzollern and others by Habsburg and many lesser princes. In Plamenatz's account, it did not occur to Herder that fostering German culture required German political unification; in fact, he disliked the Prussian state of his day, not because it was superficially multinational but "because he thought it despotic." Consequently, there is "nothing illiberal" about cultural nationhood per se. In Herder's case, in fact, concern for national distinctness went hand in hand with liberalism understood as a generous recognition of difference. Herder put a high value

on both individuality and cultural diversity, and claimed to see a connection between them. . . . Diversity is desirable as much within the nation as between nations if the life of the individual is to be enriched. Herder respected the culture of the illiterate, of peoples and classes held to be uneducated because they lack the skills that bring power and wealth to their possessors. He also sympathized with the Jews in their desire to pursue their communal identity among hostile populations, and with the Slav peoples dominated culturally by the Germans.[6]

Even when cultural nationality is transferred to the political domain, the outcome for Plamenatz is not necessarily illiberal or regressive. In his view—which concurs on that point with Kohn's—political nationalism in the West (or "Western nationalism") was for a long time self-limiting and nonexpansive. Somewhat at variance with his own "reactive" thesis, he ascribes such a moderate or liberal nationalism to Britain and France after the Glorious Revolution and during the age of Enlightenment. It was during this period that "belief in progress was fast catching on in the West," with the British and French being "the preeminently progressive peoples" of that era. Even later, during the nineteenth century when progressive ideas were spreading throughout the rest of Western Europe, nationalism still retained largely its moderate and liberating character. This aspect was manifest in the outlook of Mazzini and Garibaldi in Italy and among the early nationalists in Germany. Mazzini, Plamenatz writes, believed with Herder that "all peoples have their own contribution to make to civilization" and must hence "foster and develop whatever makes them distinctively the people they are"; but they must also "respect in other peoples what they claim for themselves." Things began to deteriorate subsequently as a result of the splitting of the European "concert" into more and less advanced, more and less powerful nations, giving rise among some peoples to an intense feeling of cultural and political inferiority or subordination. This feeling was first triggered in the aftermath of the French Revolution when Napoleon's armies sought to impose both progress and French supremacy on the rest of Europe. During the twentieth century, military and/or economic modes of defeat produced a "stridently illiberal" form of political nationalism, particularly in Germany and Italy and sporadically in other European countries. In Plamenatz's assessment, this illiberal nationalism in the West was "the nationalism of peoples defeated in war or disappointed in victory"; it was "the nationalism of peoples already united politically and humiliated or disregarded in spite of this unity."[7]

So far, the discussion has been restricted to nationalism in the West, chiefly meaning Western Europe. In the remainder of his essay, Plamenatz shifts attention to what he calls "Eastern nationalism," a term applying to nationalist politics among Slavic peoples as well as among peoples in Africa, Asia, and Latin America. The difference between the two types (Western and Eastern) rests on two features: the respective degree of "reactiveness" and of illiberalism. While Western nationalism, even in its reactive modes, proceeded from a broad cultural commonality linking the disadvantaged with the more advanced and successful nation-states, Eastern nationalism derives from a much more thorough rupture or reactivity: namely, the reaction to a Western import fundamentally incongruent with native cultural traditions. Whereas Western nationalism has been mainly liberal and only occasionally illiberal, Eastern nationalism, in Plamenatz's view, has been and continues to be generally illiberal, sometimes virulently illiberal. During their respective periods of nation building, Germans and Italians were already "well equipped culturally" with the standards "they shared with the nations with whom they compared themselves"; above all, they had languages, schools, and professions adapted to "the needs, practical and intellectual, of the consciously progressive civilization to which they belonged." By contrast, the situation of Slavic peoples and of the people in Africa and Asia was radically different. Confronted—often due to colonial intrusion—with Western nationalism and an entire "civilization alien to them," these people had to "re-equip themselves, to transform themselves." Far from being able simply to remedy cultural and political maladjustments, non-Western people had "to make themselves anew, to create national identities for themselves." There was a widespread awareness among these people "that the skills, ideas and customs acquired from their ancestors were inadequate, if they were to raise themselves to the level of the peoples who—by the standards of the civilization into which they were being drawn—were more advanced than they were."[8]

Coupled with this heightened degree of reactivity is a deep sense of urgency and frustration unconducive to a calmly liberal posture. In Plamenatz's account, Eastern nationalism is in the grip of a cultural and political turmoil or confusion unmatched by the moderate differences between Western nations. This confusion results from the need or desire to catch up rapidly with the Western model—and yet simultaneously to reject or resist Western domination. Eastern nationalism, he observes, involves "two rejections, both of them ambivalent": on the one hand, "rejection of the alien intruder and dominator who is nevertheless to be imitated and surpassed by his own standards," and on the other, "rejection of ancestral ways which are seen as obstacles to progress and yet also cherished as marks of identity." Some individuals in non-Western societies may seek to escape from this turmoil through complete assimilation, that is, by joining Westernized elites; but this option is not open to societies as a whole that have to find a path beyond both cultural surrender and a simple return to the past. Caught in this double bind, Plamenatz notes, Eastern nationalism is "both imitative and competitive," seeking to copy the Western model while challenging or resisting it. This predicament is illustrated by the tensional condition of China. "The proud and self-centered Chinese," he writes, "became nationalists only as they came to feel themselves at a disadvantage against the foreigners"; their nationalism grew as they came "to doubt their superiority" and feel the need "to prove to foreigners that they were as good as the foreigners," though they had to prove it by Western or cosmopolitan standards "until recently quite alien to the Chinese." By shouldering this burden of proof, the Chinese in a way admitted that they are "still backward"; but their backwardness was measured "not by their own standards of years ago," but by standards they had adopted from the West.[9]

Embroiled in the turmoil of rejection and appropriation, Eastern nationalism tends on the whole to be illiberal and expansionist (that is, of the "thickly" pasted or chauvinistic variety). To this extent, Plamenatz finds it to be sharply at odds with Herder's legacy, particularly with the latter's stress on cultural distinctness coupled with a distaste for political agendas. Eastern nationalism is "in some ways far removed from the spirit of Herder"; deviating sharply from the Western example, it is "both imitative and hostile to the model it imitates" and hence is "apt to be illiberal." As Plamenatz acknowledges, its illiberal character does not entirely deprive the Eastern version of certain innovative or progressively liberating features given the fact that nationalism or nation building is always an accessory of modernization. In seeking to create modern nation-states, Eastern leaders are bound to unsettle and "transform" traditional societies and thereby provide traditional people with "skills, ideas and values" they did not have before. All these changes, however, do not alter the illiberalism of Eastern regimes; in fact, they are liable to intensify this feature due to the need for harsh discipline in the face of Western superiority. This consideration leads Plamenatz to reassert the disparity between the two types of nationalism: a Western type applicable to people who, though disadvantaged, are "culturally equipped in ways that favor success and excellence" and an Eastern type pertinent to societies that have only recently been "drawn into a civilization hitherto alien to them" and "whose native cultures are not adapted to success and excellence" in terms of Western and increasingly dominant global standards. He concludes, adding a touch of political realism,

> In a world in which the strong and rich people have dominated and exploited the poor and the weak peoples, and in which autonomy is held to be a mark of dignity, of adequacy, of the capacity to live as befits human beings, in such a world this [Eastern] kind of nationalism is the inevitable reaction of the poor and the weak.[10]

## II

The preceding section has dwelled at some length on Plamenatz's essay, mainly because of the subtlety of his arguments and also because of its instructive shortcomings. Attractive and congenial in his approach is his differentiation between cultural nationhood and political nationalism, especially his readiness to appreciate and even vindicate the former in the face of its detractors. Another attractive aspect is his emphasis on reactiveness, particularly on the imported or imposed character of nationalism and nation-state among non-Western peoples and societies largely unprepared for this import. Plamenatz's portrayal of the social and existential turmoil occasioned by this intrusion is gripping and on the mark. His shortcomings emerge in two aspects: his association of non-Western nationalism with illiberalism, and his general conception of the liberal/illiberal criterion. The national liberation struggle on the Indian subcontinent may serve to illustrate the point that non-Western nationalism is not necessarily or tendentially illiberal, even and precisely when it proceeds from a thick fabric of cultural traditions. To this extent, it is much closer to the Herderian legacy than Plamenatz allows. "Illiberal" at this point means aggressive and chauvinistic. In another sense, however, non-Western nationalism may indeed be nonliberal or deviate from the liberal model as identified with the modern nation-*state*. In the light of strongly divergent cultural premises, the struggle for national autonomy in non-Western societies may indeed take the form of an experimental search for alternatives to the secular and bureaucratic state prevalent in the West.

On the Indian subcontinent, modern nationalism as a political idea first arose as a reaction to Western colonialism, especially to the steadily tightening grip of British control. In response to the Western challenge, several reform movements sprang up during the nineteenth century, among them the "Brahmo Samaj" and the "Arya Samaj" movements, which sought to reinvigorate native cultural traditions in diverse ways while adapting them suitably to modern needs. Although not overtly political in a strategic sense, these movements provided many of the impulses and aspirations that subsequently coalesced under the nationalist banner raised formally with the establishment of the Indian National Congress in 1885. Throughout the nineteenth and much of the twentieth century, political nationalism on the subcontinent remained deeply ambivalent, reflecting the profound social and existential turmoil ably depicted by Plamenatz. Among Indian reformers, this turmoil or agony was vividly captured by Swami Vivekananda (1862–1902), the founder of Ramakrishna Missions and ardent disciple of the "guru" of Bengali revival, Ramakrishna Paramahamsa. As Vivekananda wrote in an essay on "Modern India" (1899), the encounter with Western civilization was bound to be greatly unsettling for Indians and other non-Western peoples. Faced with the dazzling achievements of the West, he asked, "is it strange that Indian society should be tossed up and down?" The contrast of cultures could not be more radical: "For the West the goal is: individual autonomy; the language: money-making education; the means: politics. For India the goal is: *mukti* or *moksha* [release]; the language: the Veda; the means: renunciation." Indians on the subcontinent were liable to hear two entirely contradictory messages:

On one side, New India is saying: "If we only adopt Western ideas, Western language, Western food, Western dress and Western manners, we shall be as strong and powerful as the Western nations"; on the other, Old India is saying: "Fools! By imitation, other's ideas never become one's own—nothing, unless earned, is your own. Does the ass in the lion's skin become the lion?" On one side, New India is saying: "What the Western nations do is surely good, otherwise how did they become so great?" On the other side, Old India is saying: "The flashing of lightning is intensely bright, but only for a moment; look out, boys, it is dazzling your eyes. Beware!"[11]

The ambivalence depicted by Vivekananda carried over into the heart of political nationalism organized by the Indian National Congress. For several decades, leadership of the Congress was split into two factions: the so-called "moderates" and "extremists"—with the former relying chiefly on British goodwill and on general liberation from the top down, and the latter seeking to mobilize popular sentiments and frustrations, including resources deriving from native cultural traditions. Yet, even among the "extremists," political nationalism was not always of one type, and certainly not always of the "thickly" chauvinistic sort, although counterexamples are not lacking. A case in point is the lifework of Srí Aurobindo Ghose (1872–1950), as thinker whose outlook evolved from an intense, nearly fanatical nationalism to a soberly reflective cosmopolitanism sharply opposed to nationalist exuberance. Reacting to British policies for partitioning Bengal, as a young man Aurobindo threw himself into oppositional politics as a member of the "extremist" faction. In speeches delivered during the first decade of our century, he extolled nationalism as a religious creed and a divinely inspired mission in a manner that subordinated religion to a mundane political agenda. "What is nationalism?" he asked in one of these speeches, and replied, "Nationalism is not a mere political program" but rather "a religion that has come from God" and "a creed which you shall have to live." If anyone wanted to call himself a nationalist and participate in the struggle for national independence, he or she had to adopt the proper attitude or outlook: proceeding always in a "religious spirit," remembering that nationalists are "the instruments of God." In another speech of the same period, Aurobindo linked nationalism with the *sanatana dharma* (eternal religion) of Hinduism, exclaiming: "The Hindu nation was born with the *sanatana dharma*, with it it moves and lives. . . . The *sanatana dharma*, that is nationalism: this is the message that I bring to you."[12]

Following a deeply mystical experience that happened to him when he was a political prisoner, Aurobindo began to differentiate more soberly between religion and politics. Subsequently, especially after his retreat to the French territory of Pondicherry, he came to bemoan political nationalism, particularly its virulent variety—a change, however, that did not mean a severing of ties with native cultural and religious resources, especially with the *sanatana dharma* of Hinduism. In lieu of the nationalist self-assertion of his youth, Aurobindo embraced the process of mutual learning between cultures and nations, which did not entail self-erasure or self-abnegation. Some three decades after his youthful speeches, in a book on the "foundations of Indian culture," Aurobindo reflected on the encounter between India and Western colonialism, particularly on the possibility of an Indian "renaissance" in the colonial context. It was possible to distinguish between three major phases of the Indian-Western encounter, with the third approximating something like a rebirth. The first was a phase of rapid adaptation or Westernization, triggered in part by a sense of political inferiority and of cultural decline or stagnation. In the eyes of many Indian intellectuals, only a radical transformation could remedy India's ills; impatient with inveterate customs, they fixed their eyes on ideas "borrowed from the West" or centrally inspired by Western models. The second phase witnessed a strong nationalist reaction to Western colonial influence, sometimes involving a "total denial" of what the West offered and an insistence on the "strict letter of the national past." For Aurobindo, this phase was inordinately marked by nostalgia, self-indulgence, and resentment; in his own view, a genuine "renaissance" could happen only when native traditions were mobilized creatively in the service of a vibrant Indian future and in close interaction with other cultures and societies. Just as Europe was willing to learn from others,

> we should be as faithful and as free in our dealings with the Indian spirit and modern influences: correct what went wrong with us; apply our spirituality on broader and freer lines; be if possible not less but more spiritual than our forefathers; admit Western science, reason, progressiveness, the essential modern ideas, but on the basis of our own way of life and assimilated to our spiritual aims and ideals; open ourselves to the throb of life, the pragmatic activity, the great modern endeavor—but not therefore abandon our fundamental view of God and man and nature. . . . India can best develop herself and serve humanity by being herself and following the law of her own nature.[13]

Still later, in the decade before his death, Aurobindo further moderated his native attachments by turning to the idea of a global unity of humankind, promoted by a universal "religion of humanity" predicated on the belief in a "secret spirit" or "divine reality" pervading all cultures and societies. In these cosmopolitan or cross-cultural leanings Aurobindo emulated in many ways Rabindranath Tagore (1861–1941), the great Bengali poet and Nobel laureate. A son of Devendranath Tagore, one of the cofounders of the Brahmo Samaj, Rabindranath was deeply steeped in the *sanatana dharma*, the religious heritage of India; but he never consid-

ered this heritage a uniquely Indian possession nor his country as an is-
land segregated from the world. In his cross-cultural openness the poet
even went so far as to perceive value in British or Western colonialism—an attitude unlikely to gain him many friends at home; but of
course, Western culture for him (as for Aurobindo) was valuable not simply as a foreign import but chiefly as a catalyst triggering an internal or
indigenous resurgence blending native and alien resources. As he noted
in an essay on "Nationalism in India" (penned in the midst of World
War I), it was possible to view as nearly "providential that the West has
come to India"; yet providence must not be confused with imperialistic
designs. In the larger scheme of things, India was "no beggar of West,"
because, like other societies, she had her own contribution to make to
the "history of civilization." What Tagore appreciated most in India's
culture was the differentiated tapestry of her social structure, the rich
profusion of ethnic, religious, and caste diversity recalcitrant to homogenizing ambitions. To be sure, this diversity was tarnished by inequality
and social injustice; however, once cleansed of exploitation and mutual
enmity, India's diversified culture could serve as a model for the larger
global community.[14]

As is evident from his writings, Tagore's sympathies were with a certain form of cultural distinctness or cultural nationhood, which he
treated, however, in a nonexclusive, tolerant, and hence not "illiberal"
way. On the other hand, he was and remained deeply apprehensive of
political nationalism, the program of political unification under the auspices of the modern nation-state. As he asserted at one point, the modern
idea of nationalism was "a great menace"; in fact, it was "the particular
thing which for years has been at the bottom of India's troubles." On this
point, Tagore was in disagreement with Mohandas Gandhi (1869–1948),
with whom he otherwise had a fluctuating friendship. For Gandhi, political nationalism was a necessary tool in the struggle for independence
from British colonial domination; yet his nationalism was also of the
nonexclusive kind and broadly hospitable to ethnic and religious
diversity—a posture that ultimately cost him his life. Moreover, like Tagore, he remained always suspicious of the homogenizing bent of the
modern bureaucratic state, preferring instead a decentralized web of
loosely connected village and local governments. For Gandhi, nationalism was basically a modern Western import that required Indians to respond in kind. Unlike the Bengali poet, he was deeply embroiled in
politics and recognized the importance of political strategies; but in accord with the poet, he was also willing to distinguish between nationalism and cultural nationality or nationhood, which both men saw as a
highly differentiated fabric.

The distinction was already clearly announced in Gandhi's famous early book on *Hind Swaraj* or "Indian Home Rule" (1909). As Gandhi acknowledged there, nationalism as a program tied to the nation-state was brought to the subcontinent by the British; but they did not import or invent the idea of nationality. Culturally, he argued, Indians were "one nation" (*praja*) before the arrival of the British, "nation" denoting a shared history and "mode of life." A shared mode of life, however, does not rule out ethnic and religious differences. A country, Gandhi stated, does not cease to be a nation because "people belonging to different religions" live in it. This is particularly true of the Indian subcontinent, for there we find almost "as many religions as there are individuals." The important thing is that "those who are conscious of the spirit of nationality do not interfere with one another's religion"; otherwise, "they are not fit to be considered a nation." Gandhi continued pointedly, "If the Hindus believe that India should be peopled only by Hindus, they are living in a dreamland."[15]

However, a shared cultural framework for Gandhi was no complete substitute for an active nationalist program—at least so long as India was under colonial control. It was precisely on the issue of political nationalism that Tagore and Gandhi clashed for a period of time, especially during an exchange that occurred in 1921 on the heels of Gandhi's call for a general burning of foreign-made clothing. Targeting this call and more generally Gandhi's policy of noncooperation with British institutions, Tagore charged Gandhian nationalism with harboring a petty spirit of provincialism and xenophobic isolationism. To this charge Gandhi replied:

> I hope I am as great a believer in free air as the great poet. I do not want my house to be walled in on all sides and my windows to be stuffed. I want the cultures of all the lands to be blown about my house as freely as possible. But I refuse to be blown off my feet by any.

The exchange is memorable because of its revealing character; but it is also possible that the two friends talked past each other here. Tagore was legitimately apprehensive of xenophobia, but he was by no means detached from his culture and vernacular language. In his turn, Gandhi was suspicious of a "free-floating" intellectualism or cosmopolitanism that, in being loyal to everything and nothing, was bound to remain politically impotent as well as existentially vacuous; but his own nationalism was limited, open-ended, and responsive to circumstances. This latter aspect was highlighted in another riposte to Tagore, when Gandhi stated, "My patriotism is not exclusive; it is calculated not only not to hurt any other nation but to benefit all in the true sense of the word. India's freedom as conceived by me can never be a menace to the world."[16]

Gandhi's open-ended view of nationalism was shared, with some vari-

ations, by prominent Muslim intellectuals during the anticolonial struggle. The leading spokesman of the Muslim community in the pre-
independence period was Muhammad Iqbal (1873–1938), the Punjabi
poet-philosopher whose prestige nearly rivaled Tagore's. Although educated in England and Germany and influenced by Western philosophy
(especially the teachings of Nietzsche and Bergson), Iqbal's deepest loyalty was to the Islamic tradition in which he was raised; among Islamic
thinkers he was most fondly attached to the Sufi poet Rumi, to whom
he frequently referred in his work. Like Aurobindo and Tagore, Iqbal
appreciated the cultural and religious diversity of the subcontinent—
provided it respected the Muslim heritage; together with Aurobindo, he
did not object to the Indian struggle for national independence (that is,
the agenda of political nationalism)—provided the end result made room
for a certain autonomy of Muslim communities in delimited regions.
Thus, the "unity of the Indian nation" had to be sought not in the "negation" of distinct cultures and religions but in their "mutual harmony and
cooperation." Iqbal added, Indian Muslims were willing to stake their
lives for the "freedom of India" provided a basic principle was accepted:
Indian Muslims would be entitled to the "full and free development" of
their culture and tradition in their own "Indian home-lands"—a principle that was not synonymous with a narrowly exclusive communalism.[17]

    During this period a similar voice was that of Abul Kalam Azad
(1888–1958), a distinguished scholar-politician and a dedicated Muslim-
Indian nationalist. Like Iqbal, Azad was reared in the Islamic tradition;
like the former, he also experienced the influence of European or Western
philosophical teachings, which gave him a "freer" outlook on life (his
adopted pen name "Azad" actually means "free"). In opposition to the
Muslim League policy under the leadership of Mohammed Ali Jinnah,
Azad remained firmly committed to the struggle for an independent, non-
partitioned India; in that spirit he served as president of the Indian National Congress during and immediately after World War II (and later as
minister of education in Delhi). Together with Iqbal, Azad was willing to
support Indian political nationalism—but without relinquishing in any
way his status as a Muslim. As he observed in a presidential speech in
1940, it was the "bounden duty" of Muslims to "march with assured
steps to India's national goal" since the Muslim community was as much
an integral part of "Indian nationality" as any other ethnic or religious
group. For Azad as for Aurobindo, the Indian subcontinent was the fer-
tile crossroads of many peoples and traditions, which accounted for her
rich cultural fabric: "Just as a Hindu can say with pride that he is an
Indian and follows Hinduism, so also we can say with equal pride that
we are Indians and follow Islam." The term "Indian" included not only
Hindus and Muslims, but also Jains, Christians, Parsis, and others. The

task looming for an independent India was to protect and nurture this diversified tapestry, rather than smother it in a uniform bureaucratic mold. It was shared historical experience that had slowly produced this tapestry, which should not now succumb to arbitrary governmental tampering: "Thousand years of our joint life has molded us into a common nationality"; no "fantasy or artificial scheming" should be allowed to destroy or disfigure the sedimentation of history.[18]

## III

Since the departure of the British the political situation in South Asia has changed dramatically—and so has the status and significance of nationalism. With the partitioning of India, the subcontinent was parceled out into a series of formally independent nation-states, often patterned (at least outwardly) on the Western secular model. Despite this incisive transformation, there is at least one aspect of Plamenatz's analysis that remained relatively untouched: the basically "reactive" character of nationalism as a political agenda. While during the colonial period the struggle for national independence was chiefly a response to Western imperialist designs, the postcolonial situation forced South Asian nation-states to react to the international power play, especially to the Cold War. As a result, the leading nation-states of the region were quickly co-opted as pawns in Great Power strategies—notwithstanding India's valiant effort to maintain a policy of "nonalignment."

Given the gravity of domestic and international pressures, South Asian societies have been unable to transcend or exit the agonies of their past; unsurprisingly, nationalism has returned as a major issue of debate and a central theme in what has come to be called "postcolonial discourse."[19] On the topic of nationalism, Indian postcolonial discourse can be differentiated into four major strands or approaches—of which only one is "illiberal" in an exclusivist or chauvinistic way. This illiberal strand—the danger of which should not be minimized—is that of Hindutva and other forms of ethnic and communal fundamentalism. Since the aim here is to show the limitations of the Kohn-Plamenatz analysis, the present section concentrates on the other three "voices" in the discourse, which stand in mutual contestation as well as supplementation. The first voice is that of the modernists or modernizers who extol the progressive virtues of the secular nation-*state*, especially its function as an efficient domestic problem solver and bulwark against foreign threats. The modernists accentuate *political* nationalism, sometimes to the neglect of social and cultural underpinnings. The second voice is that of Marxist or quasi-Marxist oppositional groups who emphasize the role of political economy and often criticize the nation-state as a class-based institution under the control of a managerial or capitalist elite. Yet, opposition to the nation-state here is ambivalent, as Marxists clearly recognize the utility of the state as an instrument of change, especially in the hands of the working class. The last voice is represented by a somewhat amorphous group of intellectuals—often "postmodern" in outlook—who challenge political nationalism and the nation-state as such, shifting the accent to civil society and popular culture, or rather to a welter of multiple and only partially overlapping popular cultures.

The camp of modernizing nationalists is perhaps best represented by the leaders of the two nation-states emerging from the partition of India: Jawaharlal Nehru (1889–1964) and Mohammed Ali Jinnah (1876–1948). The two men were quite different in temperament and ideological leanings; both also played very different roles during the independence struggle—Jinnah spearheading the move toward partition, which Nehru came to accept only reluctantly. Nevertheless, they had much in common. Both went to excellent Western schools and had successful careers as barristers; both were also largely alienated from native traditions and basically aimed at the establishment of a secular, constitutional state patterned on the Western model. In their dedication to secular constitutionalism, their nationalism can be described as progressive and "liberal" and also as "imitative" (in Plamenatz's sense). The same liberalism was also manifest in their commitment to a general, public rule of law applicable to all citizens, irrespective of ethnic, religious, or cultural background. Yet despite these progressive aims, their nationalism was troubled by a deep ambivalence from the beginning. By assisting in the creation of India and Pakistan, Nehru and Jinnah placed their societies into the cauldron of international rivalries, especially the rivalry between their respective states. The two countries soon found themselves in a situation of political, military, and economic confrontation prone to transform liberal nationalism at times into aggressive chauvinism. Moreover, the very idea of a secular state on the subcontinent was in a way paradoxical: partition resulted from suspicion and conflict between Hindus and Muslims and was designed to provide a secure homeland for the respective communities. Against this background, how could India or Pakistan be "liberal" in the sense of being aloof from religious or cultural moorings? How could a secular state forget the heritages that were the sources of its own creation?

The dilemma was bound to surface with particular force in the case of Jinnah, a secularized Muslim who first served as leader of the Muslim League and later as governor-general of the newly emerging Pakistan. Jinnah's devotion to secular constitutionalism was unwavering, but equally beyond doubt was his special concern and solicitude for the Muslim community during the independence struggle. Throughout his life these two commitments were in profound and perhaps irresoluble tension; thus, even when laying the cornerstone of Pakistan, he had to leave open the question of whether the new state was going to be neutral toward any and all religious traditions or toward all religions except Islam. In illustrative fashion, the tension pervaded his speech to the Pakistani Constituent Assembly in 1947. Invoking historical experience, he stated emphatically that "a division had to take place"; given the cultural and religious differences on the subcontinent, "any idea of a united India could never have worked and, in my judgment, it would have led us to terrific disaster." Yet, this remembrance of partition was followed instantly by the endorsement of public impartiality and equal justice in the new state: "We are starting with this fundamental principle that we are all citizens and *equal* citizens of one state." Civic equality was bound to be purchased at a price: namely, the privatization of faith. In Jinnah's words: "You are free to go to your temples, free to go to your mosques or to any other places of worship in this state of Pakistan"; in fact, "you may belong to any religion or caste or creed" because "that has nothing to do with the business of the state." Thus, on the very heels of affirming religious difference (and its political effects), Jinnah extolled the Western model of the neutral state:

> Now, I think we should keep that in front of us as our ideal and you will find that in course of time Hindus would cease to be Hindus and Muslims would cease to be Muslims—not in the religious sense, because that is the personal faith of each individual, but in the political sense as citizens of the state.[20]

Jinnah's vision of constitutional government was fully shared by Nehru, although the latter's outlook included a strong dose of socialist planning absent from the former's agenda. The point on which Jinnah and Nehru strongly concurred was the commitment to a modern nation-*state* modeled mostly along Western lines. This commitment included the postulate of secularization, the privatization of religious faith, a need that was particularly strong in the emerging India given the sheer size of the Hindu majority that was liable to dwarf all other creeds. Like Jinnah, Nehru saw the antidote to communal or religious conflicts in the process of careful constitutional engineering that could find helpful guidance in Western models of nation building and liberal democracy. In his speech to the Indian Constituent Assembly in 1946, Nehru appealed to the lessons of modern constitutional history, in particular to the Philadelphia Convention that drafted the American constitution and the successive constituent assemblies that laid the groundwork for the French republic.

Throughout his long political career Nehru remained solidly wedded to progress, which signified for him a steady advance in industrialization and democratization under the auspices of a centralized nation-state. As he noted in a speech delivered shortly before his death, India's future had to be sought in the achievement of "full democracy," a goal that implies the "full realization by people of their political and economic demands." The linking of political and economic objectives imposed on India the burden of a "tremendous experiment . . . of maintaining our democratic structure and at the same time of planning for as rapid a progress, industrial and scientific, as is feasible for us." The experiment could only be successful by utilizing centralized institutions as well as "modern methods of science, technology, and the like," for there is "no other way of doing it."[21]

Nation-building Nehru- (or Jinnah-) style has not gone unopposed in the post-independence period. The Marxist-inspired strand of postcolonial discourse questions the nation-state not only as a Western import but also as a tool in the hands of managerial and capitalist elites. For adepts of this position, especially members of the "Subaltern Studies" group during its early phase, the transition from colonialism to national independence had been altogether too smooth and continuous, involving at best an internal readjustment among sections of the bourgeois establishment; seen from the grassroots level, the change was experienced largely as a "passive revolution," with little or no effect on the lot of the toiling masses. Despite their strenuous objections, however, members of this school also share important accents with the Nehruvian project. In alignment with the nation-building ethos, their outlook has tended to be basically modernist and secularist in character; wedded to rapid social change, it implies a certain aloofness from, if not rejection of, popular culture, especially native religious traditions. Among more orthodox Marxist intellectuals, commitment to social change also entails acceptance of economic planning under centralized state control.

Partha Chatterjee, a social scientist teaching in Calcutta, is a prominent spokesman of this oppositional strand. Among Chatterjee's numerous writings the most pertinent for present purposes is his study on *Nationalist Thought and the Colonial World: A Derivative Discourse* (1986), which has been hailed as "required reading" for anyone interested in the "politics of nationalism." As the subtitle of the book indicates, nationalism for Chatterjee is an imported or borrowed ideology; in effect, it involves the transfer of power from colonial rulers to the leaders of the nation-*state*, which means a simple shift from negation to affirmation.[22] Drawing mainly on the teachings of Antonio Gramsci and Louis Althusser, Chatterjee proceeds to delineate the successive stages nationalist thought in India passed through from the heyday of colonialism to national independence. The first stage marked the initial encounter between Indian self-awareness and Western modernity as displayed in colonial rule. Embarrassed by the success of foreign intervention, nationalists at this point were willing to accept Western superiority in the fields of science, technology, and material progress, while simultaneously asserting Eastern superiority in the "spiritual" domain. In the eyes of early nationalists, genuine progress in India had to involve a fusion of Western materialism and Eastern spirituality—a formula destined to appeal only to a small intellectual elite. The second stage aimed at the mobilization of popular masses, especially peasants, for the nationalist cause, though excluding them from political and economic emancipation. The goal was to lay the groundwork for "expanded capitalist production" while operating behind the screen of a vaguely populist or anticapitalist ideology (a cover-up that for Chatterjee was performed by Gandhi). The final stage occurred with the achievement of independence. At this point, anticolonial nationalist thought transformed itself into a "discourse of order" wedded to the "rational organization of power" articulated with supreme eloquence by Nehru.[23]

Critique of the nation-state as embodiment of political nationalism has not been restricted to Subaltern writers. The complaint of the third strand mentioned above is lodged not only against the bourgeois elite monopolizing state institutions, but also against the intrinsic character of the *state* itself: its tendency to usurp the functions of society and to smother the dynamism of popular culture, especially the profuse welter of popular ethnic and religious cultures sedimented in India over the centuries. Nationalism, in its linkage with the nation-state, becomes the target of a radically "deconstructive" scrutiny aimed more broadly at Western modernity with its emphasis on relentless rationalization and bureaucratization. No one has articulated this position more eloquently and persistently than Ashis Nandy, cofounder and senior member of the Centre for the Study of Developing Societies in Delhi. As Nandy argued in his Third World manifesto or "credo" penned in 1987, recourse to indigenous cultures was an urgent need in the face of the relentless Westernization and uniformization of the world. "Culturalism" was not synonymous with cultural nostalgia or a regressive traditionalism, but rather contained a liberating potential: the aim of enabling common people to participate in shaping their future on *their* own terms and in *their* vernacular languages. Given the hegemonic status of Western modernity, resistance to domination—in Nandy's view—has to challenge critically a whole panoply of modernist concepts, such as development, science, technology, and nation-state, which have become in the Third World "not only new 'reasons of state' but mystifications for new forms of violence and injustice."[24]

More recently, Nandy has more critically addressed the issue of nationalism and nation-state. Titled *The Illegitimacy of Nationalism*, one of his newer books (1994) invokes the legacies of Gandhi and Tagore, particularly Tagore's antistatist and antinationalist outlook (hence the subtitle of the book: *Rabindranath Tagore and the Politics of Self*). As Nandy notes, nationalism and nation-state have been critiqued in India from two angles: modernist and culturalist. From the vantage of modernists or progressivists, the nation-state was at best a halfway house on the road to rational enlightenment and full emancipation that would ultimately usher in a "One World" scenario "free of all ethnic and territorial loyalties." On the other hand, Gandhi and Tagore—"dissenters among dissenters"—viewed the nation-state as a corollary of Westernization, a byproduct of the "deculturation brought about by British colonialism in India." Their alternative scenario was a "distinctive civilizational concept" of the world, one "embedded in the tolerance encoded in various traditional ways of life in a highly diverse, plural society." In the end, their dissent was "doomed": the achievement of independence eclipsed their critique of nationalism and their refusal to embrace the nation-state "as the organizing principle of the Indian civilization." Yet today, with the dilemmas of the nation-state in full view, their legacies acquire new significance. As Nandy writes, both Gandhi and Tagore accepted the need for a national ideology for limited strategic purposes as a means of cultural survival; but both also recognized that, for the same reason,

India would either have to make a break with the post-medieval Western concept of nationalism or give the concept a new content. As a result, for Tagore, nationalism itself became gradually illegitimate; for Gandhi, nationalism began to include a critique of nationalism. For both, over time, the Indian freedom movement ceased to be an expression of only nationalist consolidation; it came to acquire a new stature as a symbol of the universal struggle for political justice and cultural dignity.[25]

## IV

By way of conclusion, some general theoretical comments seem in order. Nationalism has been and continues to be a highly contested and controversial topic—properly so given the great diversity of its manifestations. While clearly deplorable in its virulent or chauvinistic version, its general assessment requires careful attention to both historical circumstance and semantic meaning. Following Plamenatz, the present chapter distinguished between nation or nationality in the sense of a historically sedimented lifeworld and political nationalism as a program oriented toward nation-state building. Our discussion also concurred with him in dissociating the former from any necessary connection with illiberalism (as stipulated by Kohn). We departed from Plamenatz by extending the latter point to Eastern or non-Western forms of nationalism and nationhood. Invoking some of the leading figures of the anticolonial struggle on the subcontinent, we showed that chauvinist illiberalism is not a necessary feature of Indian nationalism in both its political and cultural modalities; as particularly the example of Tagore illustrates, cultural rootedness can even serve as an antidote or source of resistance to political nationalism (in a manner reminiscent of Herder).

These observations lead us back to Walzer's distinction between "thick" and "thin" forms of social life. Our historical example tends to confirm his thesis that thick social attachments are not necessarily a bar to broader, global horizons. What renders thick loyalties objectionable, from a liberal vantage, is the potential erection of walls or the closing of windows to the world, a closure inimical to cross-cultural learning. But on this point, "thinness" holds no advantage. As championed by liberal proceduralists or "neutralists," cultural thinness often means a cosmopolitanism detached from all local or cultural moorings, defeating learning. Moreover, as has often been noted, thinness may conceal cultural hegemony (of the West). In order for transformative learning to occur, agents have to proceed from a distinct position or background and then open themselves to the challenges of the other—which is impossible in the case of permanent or free-floating spectators. This point was well grasped by Gandhi when, in his exchange with Tagore, he welcomed the winds of all cultures to blow freely around his house, but refused "to be blown off my feet by any."

Gandhi's comments were particularly salient in the context of colonial domination; but they have lost none of their significance today. As our review of Indian postcolonial discourse indicates, the respective virtues of cultural loyalty and thin (or secular) impartiality are still hotly debated in our time. Again, assessment of this debate has to move beyond rigid thin-versus-thick or liberal-versus-illiberal alternatives. All the protagonists in our sketch of postcolonial discourse—excepting Hindutva and other forms of fundamentalism—bring important considerations to bear on the nationalism issue and cannot readily be dismissed. Secular nationalists in the Nehruvian mold accentuate features of the modern nation-*state* which it would be foolish to brush aside summarily: features like constitutionalism, an impartial rule of law, and equal liberties or citizen rights. Although first developed in the West, these aspects today (in some form) are requisites of nonrepressive or democratic regimes around the globe. To be sure, procedures alone are insufficient to ensure popular rule. Marxists and Subalternists have been quick to point to the limits of "formal" democracy: its inability to affect or restructure existing social and economic disparities, especially the unequal access to modes of production. In the context of present-day economic "liberalization" policies, these disparities are likely to be deepened rather than ameliorated. Still, in seeking to promote rapid social change, Marxists have traditionally tended to rely on the very mechanism of centralized bureaucracy that they have customarily denounced in the case of liberal nation builders. In an effort to exit from this dilemma, the third strand in postcolonial discourse takes recourse to indigenous cultural traditions and beliefs—while refraining from unduly homogenizing these legacies. In this manner, culturalists hope to initiate a grassroots approach to democratization and social change that avoids blind imitation both of the Western nation-state model and the model of central economic planning imported by Marxism.

There is no ready-made formula to adjudicate this postcolonial debate. To a considerable degree, the dispute among the protagonists hinges on the relation between culture and politics (and also culture and economics). For secular nation builders, politics, meaning state control exercised through central public institutions and a properly organized legal and judicial system, has primacy over, and in effect shapes, culture. While native traditions may not be completely ignored, they tend to be treated mainly as obstacles or barriers on the road to modernization. Under modified auspices, a similar priority scheme marks the second camp. For Marxists (and many Subalternists), politics—now in the form of political economy and centralized planning—takes absolute precedence over cultural traditions, which tend to be sidestepped or devalued as mere remnants of a feudal and superstitious past. In opposition to both nation builders and central planners, culturalists assert the primacy of the life-world or culture, a diversified fabric of local customs and religious beliefs, over state-centered politics. The chief objection of this third camp is to the pretense of public expertise manifest in the program of "social engineering" from the top down, which is felt to be in violation of the deeper aspirations of popular self-determination and democratic self-rule (or *swaraj*).

What resurfaces at this point is the antagonism alluded to at the beginning: the tension between lifeworld and politics, between cultural background and politically managed foreground. This tension is by its nature irresoluble; in fact, any attempt to blend or collapse the two sides is bound to do serious harm to both culture and politics. Cultural lifeworld is always in excess of political management, especially by the modern nation-state; to this extent, culture is not an external but a constitutive limit of politics. What nation builders and central planners have to remember is that public policies—especially nationalist policies—are always partial and selective, and hence contestable, formulations of the "common good." To this extent, political agendas are always "imagined constructions," not in the sense that public life is up for grabs and at the disposal of expert social engineers, but in the sense that policies are imaginative interpretive exercises that can never exhaust available possibilities and need to be self-limiting. In turn, culturalists must remember that, especially in modern times, culture cannot be a replacement of, or substitute for, politics; recourse to indigenous traditions cannot offer a dispensation from political thought and action. What culturalism can and should provide is a reminder of the inevitably partial and selective character of political agendas and of the rich reservoir of alternative resources or sources of inspiration. In emphasizing the aspect of selectivity, culturalism can also generate important incentives toward a rethinking of central categories of modern politics, including nationalism and the nation-state. Our contemporary global situation is in urgent need of such rethinking, that is, of the imaginative reconceptualization and experimental testing of new political institutions and practices suitable to democratic self-rule in different contexts. On this point Chatterjee correctly states that the root of postcolonial malaise lies "not in our inability to think out new forms of the modern community but in our surrender to the old forms of the modern state."[26]

Rethinking of the modern state is also bound to involve a rethinking of community, especially the national community: the latter cannot or should not become an overarching political agenda by collapsing the culture-politics tension. In this respect, recent political developments on the subcontinent have brought to the fore certain nationalist tendencies that friends of Indian culture cannot readily welcome or endorse. Harking back to the "extremist" days of the independence struggle, some groups or movements have sought to reforge a fusion of religion and politics—precisely the kind of blending that Aurobindo initially endorsed but was able to overcome in a lifetime of serious reflection and dedicated service. It cannot and should not be left to secular modernists alone to denounce this kind of relapse; it is precisely the task of culturalists and religiously sensitive people to attack this political abuse of religion. In this critique they can find ample support from leading anticolonial figures, especially Gandhi, Tagore, and Iqbal. What Gandhi called *ramarajya* was not a motto for Hindu revivalism, but the expression of a hope or promise of interethnic and cross-cultural peace and justice. The same might be said of the Muslim notion of *umma* or *dar al-Islam*, the pledge of general brotherhood/sisterhood. In Western (Christian) terms, when believers speak of the "coming kingdom" they mean a promised and hoped for, not a politically engineered condition—hoped for in the midst of mundane politics.

In Iqbal's *Mysteries of Selflessness* we find these lines:

> Now brotherhood has been so cut to shreds
> that in the stead of community
> the country has been given pride of place
> in men's allegiance and constructive work.
> The country is the darling of their hearts,
> and wide humanity is whittled down
> into dismembered tribes. . . .
> Vanished is humankind; there but abide
> the disunited nations. Politics
> dethroned religion.

And in Tagore's *Gitanjali* we read:

> Where mind is without fear and the head held high;
> where knowledge is free; and where the world
> has not been ruptured into fragments by domestic walls;
> where words come out from the depth of truth;
> where tireless striving stretches forward to perfection;
> where clear reason has not lost its way
>      into the dreary desert sand of habit;
> where mind is led and lifted upward
>      into ever-widening thought and action—
> into that heaven of freedom, my Father, let my country awake.[27]

# Notes

1. Michael Walzer, *Thick and Thin: Moral Argument at Home and Abroad* (Notre Dame, Ind.: University of Notre Dame Press, 1994), pp. 63, 69, 72. Compare also Tom Bottomore and Patrick Goode, eds., *Austro-Marxism* (Oxford: Clarendon Press, 1978), pt. 3 (regarding Otto Bauer); and Stanley Hauerwas, *A Community of Character: Towards a Constructive Christian Social Ethic* (Notre Dame, Ind.: University of Notre Dame Press, 1981).

2. Hans Kohn, *The Idea of Nationalism: A Study in Its Origins and Background* (New York: Macmillan, 1944), pp. 329–331, 351. Kohn's dichotomy was anticipated nearly a century earlier by Lord Acton in his distinction between "political" and "ethnological" types of nationality; see his "Nationality" (1862), in *The Theory of Freedom and Other Essays* (Freeport, N.Y.: The Free Press, 1967), pp. 277–298. I am grateful to Ivelin Sardamov for alerting me to this essay. Compare also Carlton J. H. Hayes, *The Historical Evolution of Modern Nationalism* (New York: Smith, 1931).

3. Here I fully agree with Walzer when he writes, "What has been called 'the

national question' does not have a single correct answer, as if there were only one way of 'being' a nation, one version of national history, one model of relationships among nations. History reveals many ways, versions, and models." See *Thick and Thin*, p. 70. I also agree with Walzer's comments on the notion of "imagined communities" (made prominent by Benedict Anderson) when he notes that, in the absence of a plausible alternative, the phrase is largely redundant (p. 68). See also Roger Scruton, "In Defense of the Nation," in *The Philosopher on Dover Beach*, Scruton (Manchester: Carcanet, 1990), pp. 299–337; and Benedict Anderson, *Imagined Communities: Reflections on the Origin and Spread of Nationalism*, rev. ed. (London: Verso, 1992). For some recent studies challenging Kohn's claims see, e.g., Yael Tamir, *Liberal Nationalism* (Princeton, N.J.: Princeton University Press, 1993); Julia Kristeva, *Nations without Nationalism*, trans. Leon R. Roudiez (New York: Columbia University Press, 1993).

4. Compare in this context Basil Davidson, *The Black Man's Burden: Africa and the Curse of the Nation-state* (New York: Times Books, 1992). As one may note, Kohn is known not only for his book on nationalism, but also for a number of texts that clearly reflect a Eurocentric or "Orientalist" outlook. Compare Kohn, *Die Europäisierung des Orients* (Berlin: Schocken, 1934), and *A History of Nationalism in the East* (New York: Harcourt, Brace & Co., 1929).

5. John Plamenatz, "Two Types of Nationalism," in *Nationalism: The Nature and Evolution of an Idea*, ed. Eugene Kamenka (New York: St. Martin's Press, 1967), pp. 23–24, 27. He adds, "Nationalism is confined to peoples who, despite their rivalries and the cultural differences between them, already belong to, or are being drawn into, a family of nations which all aspire to make progress in roughly the same directions" (p. 27).

6. Plamenatz, "Two Types of Nationalism," pp. 2, 27–28. For Kohn's ambivalent treatment of Herder see *The Idea of Nationalism*, pp. 331, 427–451. In his defense of cultural diversity, Herder went so far as to praise the nonliterate simplicity of the Haitians of his time—a praise that elicited a strongly modernist response from Immanuel Kant.

7. Plamenatz, "Two Types of Nationalism," pp. 25–26, 28–29. One may, of course, question the benignly liberal character of French and British nationalism during the eighteenth and nineteenth centuries, given the close linkage of liberal progress and colonial expansion.

8. Plamenatz, "Two Types of Nationalism," pp. 29–30.

9. Plamenatz, "Two Types of Nationalism," pp. 33–34.

10. Plamenatz, "Two Types of Nationalism," pp. 33–36.

11. Swami Vivekananda, "Modern India," in *Sources of Indian Tradition*, 2nd ed., ed. Stephen Hay (New York: Columbia University Press, 1988), vol. 2, p. 80.

12. Hay, *Sources of Indian Tradition*, vol. 2, pp. 152, 154. A similar "extremist" view of nationalism was upheld without wavering by Bal Gangadhar Tilak and Vinayak Savarkar, the chief founder of the doctrine of "Hindutva."

13. Sri Aurobindo Ghose, "The Renaissance in India," in *Sri Aurobindo Birth Centenary Library*, vol. 14 (Pondicherry: Sri Aurobindo Ashram Trust, 1972), pp. 411–412, 431–432.

14. Rabindranath Tagore, "Nationalism in India," in *Nationalism*, 2nd ed. (London: Macmillan, 1950), pp. 130–131, 147–148.

15. Mohandas Karamchand Gandhi, *Hind Swaraj*, in *The Moral and Political Writings of Mahatma Gandhi*, vol. 1, ed. Raghavan Iyer (Oxford: Clarendon Press, 1986), pp. 220–223.

16. Gandhi, *The Collected Works of Mahatma Gandhi* (New Delhi: Government of India Publications, 1958–1984), vol. 20, p. 159, vol. 23, p. 340. The exchange is quoted from Dennis Dalton, *Mahatma Gandhi: Nonviolent Power in Action* (New York: Columbia University Press, 1993), p. 75. In assessing the exchange, Dalton observes that Tagore "had the courage to denounce Gandhi's doctrines when they lapsed into dogma or *duragraha*. Yet both Tagore's theory and practice fell short of a method of political and social change. Enveloped in a system of imperialism and social injustice, he remained a powerful critic with no potential for exercising real political power. If his hold on *swaraj* was firm, his grasp of *satyagraha* was weak" (p. 76).

17. Muhammad Iqbal, "Presidential Address of 1930" (before the All-India Muslim League in Allahabad), in *Sources of Indian Tradition*, vol. 2, Hay ed., pp. 219–220. He explained, "The principle that each group is entitled to free development on its own lines is not inspired by any feeling of narrow communalism. There are communalisms and communalisms. A community which is inspired by feelings of ill-will toward other communities is low and ignoble. I entertain the highest respect for the customs, laws, religions, and social institutions of other communities. Nay, it is my duty according to the teaching of the Qur'an, even to defend their places of worship, if need be. Yet I love the communal group which is the source of my life and behavior and which has formed me what I am by giving me its religion, its literature, its thought, its culture and thereby recreating its whole past as a living factor in my present consciousness" (p. 220). Susequently Iqbal modified his outlook somewhat along more separatist lines.

18. Abul Kalam Azad, "Presidential Speech," in *Sources of Indian Tradition*, vol. 2, pp. 239–241. Compare also Ian Henderson Douglas, *Abul Kalam Azad: An Intellectual and Religious Biography* (Delhi: Oxford University Press, 1993).

19. On "postcolonial discourse" and its diverse facets see, e.g., Bill Ashcroft, Gareth Griffiths, and Helen Tiffin, eds., *The Postcolonial Studies Reader* (London: Routledge, 1995); Patrick Williams and Laura Chrisman, eds., *Colonial Discourse and Postcolonial Theory: A Reader* (New York: Columbia University Press, 1994); Francis Barker, Peter Hulme, and Margaret Iversen, eds., *Colonial Discourse, Postcolonial Theory* (Manchester: Manchester University Press, 1994); and Gayatri Chakravorty Spivak, *The Postcolonial Critic* (London: Routledge, 1991).

20. Jamil-ud-din Ahmad, ed., *Speeches and Writings of Mr. Jinnah*, vol. 2 (Lahore: Ashraf, 1942), pp. 402–404; quoted here from Hay, *Sources of Indian Tradition*, vol. 2, pp. 386–387. Compare also Saad R. Khairi, *Jinnah Reinterpreted: The Journey from Nationalism to Muslim Statehood* (Karachi: Oxford University Press, 1995). Jinnah's notion of a privatization of Islamic faith was completely at odds with Iqbal's view, expressed in an address in 1930, that Islam

could never be simply a "private affair" and that, consequently, the "construction of a polity on [secular] national lines" was "unthinkable for a Muslim." See Hay, ed., *Sources of Indian Tradition*, vol. 2, pp. 219–220. The subsequent history of Pakistan has been entirely overshadowed by the tension between Islam and constitutional democracy. For an instructive discussion of the tension see the report issued by Muhammad Munir, the Chief Justice of Pakistan, following religious riots in 1953, in Hay, *Sources of Indian Tradition*, vol. 2, pp. 394–399.

21. Jawaharlal Nehru, *Independence and After* (New Delhi: Government of India, 1949), pp. 346–348, and *Speeches, 1949–1964*, vol. 5 (New Delhi: Government of India, 1954–1964), pp. 42–43, 65–66; quoted from Hay, *Sources of Indian Tradition*, vol. 2, pp. 323–324, 351–352.

22. Partha Chatterjee, *Nationalist Thought and the Colonial World: A Derivative Discourse*, 2nd impr. (Minneapolis: University of Minnesota Press, 1993), p. 42. Chatterjee starts his book with a discussion of Plamenatz's "two types" of nationalism. He prefers, however, to speak of "three types" (p. 20): European "linguistic nationalism"; "Creole nationalism" in the Americas; and "official nationalism" (mainly in Russia). The phrase regarding "required reading" is taken from Gayatri Spivak's endorsement of the book.

23. Chatterjee, *Nationalist Thought and the Colonial World*, pp. 50–51, 161. Chatterjee writes, with Nehru "nationalism has arrived. It has now constituted itself into a state ideology; it has appropriated the life of the nation into the life of the state. It is rational and progressive, a particular manifestation of the universal march of Reason; it has accepted the global realities of power" (p. 161). More recently, Chatterjee has begun to analyze nationalism in a more differentiated way, attentive to post-Marxist and poststructuralist developments; see *The Nation and Its Fragments: Colonial and Postcolonial Histories* (Princeton, N.J.: Princeton University Press, 1993).

24. Ashis Nandy, "Cultural Frames of Social Transformation: A Credo," *Alternatives* 12 (1987): 113–117. The essay also appeared in Bhikhu Parekh and Thomas Pantham, eds., *Political Discourse: Explorations in Indian and Western Political Thought* (New Delhi: Sage Publ., 1987), pp. 238–248. For a fuller discussion of the essay see my "Modernization and Postmodernization: Whither India?" in *Beyond Orientalism: Essays on Cross-Cultural Encounter* (Albany, N.Y.: SUNY Press, 1996), pp. 149–174.

25. Nandy, *The Illegitimacy of Nationalism: Rabindranath Tagore and the Politics of Self* (Delhi: Oxford University Press, 1994), pp. x–xi, 1–3. Nandy uses the term "patriotism" (p. 81) instead of nationalism to characterize Tagore's outlook. For the recent retrieval of this older notion see, e.g., Alasdair MacIntyre, "Is Patriotism a Virtue?" in Ronald Beiner, ed., *Theorizing Citizenship* (Albany, N.Y.: SUNY Press, 1995), pp. 209–228; and Mary Dietz, "Patriotism," in *Political Innovation and Conceptual Change*, ed. Terence Ball, Russell Hanson, and James Farr (Cambridge: Cambridge University Press, 1989), pp. 297–325.

26. Chatterjee, *The Nation and Its Fragments*, p. 11.

27. Quoted from Hay, *Sources of Indian Tradition*, pp. 211, 280.

# 9

# Global Development?
# Alternative Voices from Delhi

> The idea of alternatives . . . signifies a major dissatisfaction with
> both the existing state of *affairs* and the existing state of *analytics*.
>
> Kothari, *Rethinking Development*

Into its farthest corners, the entire world today is in the grip of "development"—the meaning or direction of which, however, remains obscure.
The two world wars of our century were fought to make the world "safe
for democracy," but the sense of that phrase was ambivalent. According
to some observers, there were several plausible and viable interpretations
of the phrase: Western liberal democracy, socialist "people's democracy,"
and indigenous democracies in "developing" societies. The Cold War
soon consolidated these options under the aegis of three competing international power blocs, thereby effectively splitting the globe into three
antagonistic "worlds": the liberal-capitalist West, the Soviet East, and
the so-called "nonaligned" nations (comprising most of the Third World
countries).[1] All these demarcations have recently been thrown into disarray if not entirely erased. The end of the Cold War has also meant the
end of many previously cherished possibilities. Emerging from the cauldron of competing "worlds," our time is increasingly under the spell of
"one world" formulas backed up by the hegemonic status of Western
societies and worldviews. Although seemingly conducive to global peace,
such formulas are bound to cause alarm among friends of democracy. In
the words of the dean of contemporary European philosophy, Hans-
Georg Gadamer: "The hegemony and unchallengeable power of any one
single nation—as we now have with just *one* superpower—is dangerous
for humanity. It would go against human freedom."[2]

Gadamer's indictment is directed not so much against liberal Western democracy, as against its elevation to a uniform and universal standard imposed on all other societies with or without their consent (and thus possibly without popular democratic support). In both philosophical and political terms, Gadamer's comments challenge a univocal and one-dimensional conception of a "world" without alternatives and diversity, one whose meaning is no longer open to questioning. Neatly streamlined and hegemonically managed, such a world, he correctly perceives, would also be without hope, without vision or excess, without (ontological) difference. Despite the intensive efforts of one world protagonists, the nightmare of uniformity feared by Gadamer has not yet become fully entrenched on a global scale. Both in the West and the non-West, there are voices of dissent diverging from the hegemonic mainstream, sometimes muted or confused, sometimes sharply articulated. The present chapter illustrates this critical temper by drawing attention to a prominent locus of intellectual and political ferment on the Indian subcontinent: the Centre for the Study of Developing Societies in Delhi. Established in 1963 by Rajni Kothari and some of his associates, the Centre has emerged during the past four decades as one of the most stimulating and clear-sighted institutions of academic and political nonconformism in South Asia, and in the "developing" world at large.

The focus here is purposely restricted and not meant in any way to disparage or silence other expressions of dissent. India is a richly diversified social fabric with a variety of oppositional strands. One of the more prestigious oppositional perspectives is linked with the so-called "Subaltern Studies" project, initiated by Ranajit Guha and his associates, a project that has already resulted in a string of publications offering critical new views on colonialism and postcolonialism.[3] Despite the undeniable merit of these endeavors, the project is bypassed here for several reasons. First of all, Subaltern Studies have been widely acclaimed and thus are relatively familiar to scholars and intellectuals in the West. Second, and more importantly, as inaugurated by Guha and his associates, the project was in many ways still closely wedded to traditional premises of Marxist political economy, which today have become questionable. Even within the confines of the Delhi Centre, this chapter's presentation will necessarily have to be selective. Akin in many ways to the Frankfurt School of Social Research, the Centre from the beginning has been a collective enterprise of scholars from many disciplines, including the humanities, social sciences, and psychology. Over the years, the studies sponsored by the Centre have been both empirical and theoretical in character and have dealt with a broad spectrum of issues ranging from the ethnic and social-psychological components of change to problems of rural development and ethno-agriculture to the role of science and technology in the modern world.[4] For present purposes, two leading spokesmen of the Centre are singled out: Rajni Kothari, its founder and longtime director, and Ashis Nandy, one of its senior members (and also recent director). Following a review of some of their main works, the concluding section assesses their contributions in light of our contemporary global context.

# I

More than ever before, critical intellectuals today cannot be neutral spectators; according to an old adage, reflection without practical commitment is empty, commitment without reflection is blind. Among members of the Delhi Centre—and perhaps among Indian intellectuals at large—no one exemplifies this adage better than Rajni Kothari. Trained both in India and the West, Kothari has distinguished himself as an accomplished scholar, institution builder, and political activist on all levels (local, national, and international) of politics. The Delhi Centre was designed both to facilitate broadly interdisciplinary research and to reduce—and if possible to overcome—the theory-praxis hiatus afflicting modern higher education.

While some of Kothari's early publications, like *Politics in India* (1970), showed him strongly indebted to Western social scientific paradigms (especially functionalism), he soon freed himself from such subservience in favor of more innovative and experimental modes of inquiry. In 1974 he was instrumental in launching the quarterly *Alternatives*, a journal that soon emerged as a leading forum for the discussion of issues relating to social change and global transformation. Roughly at the same time, he became actively involved in the Janata Party, a leftist movement that was raising basic questions about the direction of the Indian government under Congress leadership. During the period of the Emergency imposed by Indira Gandhi (in 1975), Kothari surfaced as a vocal spokesman of the anti-Emergency campaign and one of the chief leaders of the civil liberties movement in India. Both his scholarly and political talents coalesced in 1980 when, together with other Centre colleagues, he inaugurated "*Lokayan*" (meaning "dialogue among people"), designed as an arena for the meeting of scholars, policymakers, and activists concerned with local or rural grassroots initiatives. His moment of greatest visibility came in 1989 when, following the defeat of Rajiv Gandhi, he joined the Janata Dal-led National Front government as a member of the national Planning Commission.[5]

As a scholar and critical intellectual, Kothari has produced an impressive corpus of writings that so far has not gained the recognition it deserves in the West. Pervading these writings, broadly speaking, is a radical democratic humanism that does not fit neatly into any ideological blueprint or partisan program. This outlook is announced in the subtitles of many of his publications, especially those published in rapid succession during the past decade. 1988 saw the publication of two important volumes, titled respectively *State against Democracy: In Search of Humane Governance* and *Transformation and Survival: In Search of a Humane World Order.* These texts were followed a year later by three additional books: *Rethinking Development: In Search of Humane Alternatives* and *Politics and the People: In Search of a Humane India* (the latter comprising two volumes). Although linked together by common thematic concerns, the books are differentiated by their distinctive accent or focus.

*State against Democracy* was written mainly in protest against the policies of Indira and Rajiv Gandhi, whose regimes were denounced for their attempt to marshal state power against the democratic aspirations of the people. In large measure, the book was meant as a challenge to the relentless process of centralization that, during the postindependence period, was steadily molding India into a uniform "nation-state" along Western lines. Buttressed by the resources of modern technology and corporate business, this nation-state—in Kothari's view—was erecting or deepening a structure of stratification or inequality that the struggle against colonialism had meant to erase. The situation was further aggravated by the progressive militarization of the state promoted in the name of "national security" interests. These and related factors conspired to produce a social-political crisis that, according to Kothari, was changing, or rather perverting, the character of the state: namely, from "being an instrument of liberation of the masses to being a source of so much oppression for them."[6]

The critique of state-sponsored accumulation of power was carried into the global arena in *Transformation and Survival*. Paralleling the bifurcation of domestic society into a propertied elite and impoverished, marginalized masses, the operation of the international state system promoted and, in fact, steadily reinforced a global structure of asymmetry between North and South, "developed" and "developing" societies, and center and periphery. As on the national level, this global asymmetry was compounded by the concentration of technological, economic, and military resources in the hands of hegemonic (developed) states. In combination, these forces posed a threat to the natural environment, international peace, and ultimately the survival of humankind itself. As an antidote to those perceived dangers, the two volumes of 1988 formulated an alternative vision of human existence and social-political life that was not beholden to any of the reigning ideologies of the time. In fact, as Kothari insisted, it was necessary to move beyond both the liberal-capitalist and the classical Marxist paradigms, since both were "offshoots of the same philosophic pedigree of the Enlightenment and nine-teenth-century (mechanistic) humanism" with their unlimited faith in progress abetted by technological mastery over nature.

In lieu of this "modernist" pedigree, the books invoked the legacy of Gandhi, who, in writings like *Hind Swaraj* as well as in his political ac-tions, had challenged Western imperialism while at the same time pro-moting democratic mobilization at the grassroots level; in his entire lifework, Gandhi had thus honored "the moral imperative of treating people as a source in the recovery of a humane order." In addition to Gandhian teachings, the texts also drew inspiration from left-leaning modes of political radicalism wedded to the promotion of human free-dom and social justice. "Freedom" meant not only an act of withdrawal or negative abstinence but a capacity for social well-being and public participation. To this extent, human rights—a central concern for Ko-thari—denoted not so much private entitlements or privileges as basic constituents of a good social order. As we read in *State against Democ-racy,* "Human rights movements, ecology movements, women's move-ments, the peace movement are all about restoring the first principles of the 'good' and 'good life' in the conduct of human affairs."[7]

For present purposes, it must suffice to highlight some particularly in-structive passages or sections in Kothari's *Rethinking Development* (1989) and the more recent *Growing Amnesia* (1993). The opening chap-ter of the former provides important clues to his alternative vision. Enti-tled "Alternatives in Development: A Conceptual Framework," the chapter immediately zeroes in on the basic problem besetting "develop-ment" debates: the confusion regarding its meaning and direction. Both in mainstream literature and mainline policy planning, development has tended to be identified with unfettered economic and industrial expan-sion propelled by advances in modern science and technology. In Ko-thari's view, this outlook has not only engendered a deadly arms race and a wasteful, consumption-driven civilization, but also a pernicious class structure on both the national and the global levels pitting the "de-veloped" North against the "underdeveloped" South and Westernized elites in the South against large marginalized masses of people. As a re-sult, democracy is under seige both at home and in the world at large. For Kothari, the trouble with the dominant "economistic" model is not only that it is difficult to implement due to various roadblocks, but that it is inherently flawed and mistaken. For too long, he notes, development has been fueled by a faulty vision, namely, by the idea of a "uniform end product to be achieved by all societies," a goal characterized by "a state of urban, industrial affluence, managed by experts at the top running secular affairs through a 'rational' bureaucracy, and backed by a capital-intensive technology." The increasingly evident costs exacted by this model, especially in terms of human suffering, give impetus to an alternative vision, or alternative visions, of development. The notion of alternatives implies

> two considerations: that the world is becoming too uniform, too standardized, too dominated by a single conception of life and its meaning, with little scope for other available cultural and historical propensities and potentialities; and that such domination of a single conception has led to political and cultural domination by a single region of the world over all the others.[8]

In proceeding to outline details of his own alternative vision, Kothari cautions against some pitfalls or simplistic shortcuts: especially reactionary antimodernism and rampant cultural relativism (following the "anything goes" maxim). Faced with domestic and international inequities, he writes, the temptation is great to launch into a virulent attack on the West or the "Western model" or else to retreat into the shell of cultural narcissism or self-enclosure. What these shortcuts neglect is the inextricable entwinement of North and South, that is, the fact that different modes of social life and development inevitably condition each other in our age. Although there may be radically different options and even different "worlds," these are still embedded in, and held together by, our global (or globalizing) context. According to Kothari, the philosophical principle that must guide us in such a setting should "steer clear of both imperialist claims to universality and the normless striving for relativity." Concretely, this involves a double gesture or affirmation that endorses both "the principle of *autonomy* of each entity (human as well as social) to seek out its own path to self-realization" *and* "the principle of *integration* of all such entities in a common framework of interrelationships based on agreed values."

In terms of specific policies or development strategies, his chapter offers a list of recommendations, among which several major points stand out. One set of proposals has to do with the fostering of alternative lifestyles, in opposition to the high consumption patterns present among elites. Borrowing from Gandhi, Kothari advocates an "ethic of consumption" that discourages ostentatious living in favor of a frugal limitation of wants. Closely linked with this policy is the establishment of normative guidelines regarding "minima and maxima" of income and wealth. Another set of proposals deals with the "organization of space," the promotion of a more equitable balance between urban and rural spaces, town and countryside, and agriculture and industry; Gandhian-style decentralization serves as a key to curbing the unchecked growth of metropolitan centers. In a sense, decentralization also animates Kothari's educational policy, dedicated to a "basic cultural attack" on illiteracy (with special attention given to villages and the education of women). All these items are rounded out by the demand for broad-scale popular participation in economic production and public life. Kothari states, "I am firmly convinced that it is only on the basis of a clear acceptance of a decentralized and highly participatory democratic structure that social justice can be realized."[9]

The contours of his alternative vision are further sharpened in a subsequent chapter titled "Alternative Development and the Issue of Environment." In examining the crisis features of our time, the chapter draws attention to recessed philosophical premises undergirding these dilemmas: specifically, the post-Cartesian bifurcation of mind and matter and, as a corollary, the ascendancy of human mastery over nature by means of science and technology. Buried in the myriad problems of our age, Kothari notes, lies a "dominant philosophical doctrine" that, although originating in Europe, is now encircling the globe: the "doctrine of modernity" according to which "the end of life is narrowly defined as to be within the grasp of all—progress based on economic prosperity." Fueled by Enlightenment teachings, this doctrine presents social progress entirely as a matter of social engineering, superseding old-style beliefs. All that human beings and societies have to do in this model is to "discard tradition and superstition and become rational and 'modern'." A crucial backbone of this model is modern "science-based technology" or rather science in the service of technology. Subservient to technical needs, science (and knowledge in general) becomes a mere instrument of power, "an instrument of domination over the sinister and unpredictable forces of nature" that later spills over into domination over "social forces and institutions" and, ultimately, over "relations between societies and between cultures and races." Echoing insights articulated earlier by Horkheimer and Adorno (regarding the "dialectic of Enlightenment"), the chapter queries:

> Isn't the theory of progress, as developed in the West, based on an anthropocentric view of nature and a positivist conception of knowledge and science, which are responsible for a model of development spelling domination and exploitation? And if these be the essence of Occidental culture and its contribution to human thought and values, shouldn't we discard large parts of it, and look for alternative modes of thought and values embedded in some other cultures? . . . It is essential to come to grips with this particular worldview, of which science and technology are but means, that stands for steamrolling almost the entire world into uniformity, reducing its rich diversity to a predictable and predetermined state.[10]

Given the deleterious effects of this worldview of modernity, as shown in its domestic and global repercussions, the search for alternatives has to be attentive to ideas or perspectives originating outside or at the periphery of the modern West, especially perspectives indigenous to developing societies. In forthright language—bound to be shocking to radical modernists—Kothari refers approvingly to the cultural, including religious, traditions of non-Western countries. "The religions and civilizations of India, of the Islamic world, of the complex web of humanist thought that has informed China, and of Buddhism," he writes, "provide major streams of thought that could substantially contribute to the present search for alternatives" (although this possibility is presently only latent or embryonic). Possible contributions of these cultures extend to the domain of knowledge and science by offering an alternative to technological mastery. The major cultural regions of the non-Western world have important traditions of science and human learning, but what is common to them is a view of science as basically "a search for truth" or "a means of self-realization and self-control," not "a means of bringing anything, least of all nature, under domination."

As in the previous chapter, the turn to alternative cultural traditions is hedged in again by important caveats having to do with the lure of purely negative or reactionary sentiments. As Kothari emphasizes, modernity is not something that can simply be "wished away" or ignored; to a significant degree, modernity is "not just Western or Occidental" but is "part of us all," just as "the West itself is part of us all." What needs to happen in our world is not a mutual encapsulation but a reciprocal openness and engagement, an effort to relate the "presently dominant tradition" (of Western modernity) to "other civilizational traditions and meaning systems" and thus to evolve a "process of critical interaction" or dialogue between them. To promote such interaction, what must be avoided above all is "intellectual brainwashing" on all sides, especially that which preaches that there is only one "uniform and homogeneous end product for all societies": an "all-encompassing modernity." Such reciprocal learning must be coupled with the critique of prevailing domestic and global inequities, a shift from elitism to a popular and ecologically sensitive perspective. Such a perspective

> must promote a view of human welfare that does not assume some linear progression on some uniform pattern but, instead, allows for autonomy and self-reliance in a variety of local contexts so that everyone participates with a first-hand knowledge of actual conditions.[11]

*Growing Amnesia* is separated from the developmental study by an interval of four years. That interval was marked by momentous historical events on a global scale: chiefly, the dismantling of the Soviet Empire and, as a result, the termination of the Cold War resulting in the waning of a viable "nonalignment" policy (as sponsored by India and other Third World countries). Although widely hailed in the West as the dawn of a new "world order"—and even as the goal or "end of history"—the emerging global situation raises serious qualms and critical reservations for Kothari. In his view, the turn of events signaled basically the triumph of capitalist market economics and corporate free enterprise, processes that augur ill for the cause of social justice and participatory or grass-roots democracy. Given the concentration of power and wealth in developed countries (and multinational conglomerates), the existing gulf between North and South, center and periphery was prone to be further deepened, while the fate of underprivileged masses around the world was bound to be abandoned to apathy or else consigned to "growing amnesia." As *Growing Amnesia's* opening chapter observes, economic liberalism by itself is unlikely to be a harbinger of democracy. In fact, the priority granted to the market principles of "liberalization" and "privatization" puts an entirely new slant on the notion of development: "Among other things, the whole rationale of development as a reduction of poverty and the promotion of equity goes. The whole focus shifts to deregulation, mainly for foreign investors and multinationals." Thus, the slogan of "liberalization" should not be confused with emancipation or popular liberation. Sanctioned by global-hegemonic and multinational forces, implementation of the slogan "can and probably will destabilize the democratic polity, put the masses under severe strain, turn against labor and further marginalize the poor."[12]

Although he bemoans the sway of liberalization, Kothari is far removed from endorsing a communist-style planned economy under the auspices of a centralized state. As he is well aware, the Indian state—once an engine in the struggle for independence—has itself become an instrument of oppression by being captive to privileged elites. We know, he writes, that the state and its various agencies "have increasingly become repressive and cruel vis-à-vis the poor and the radical movements that support the poor." Yet, for Kothari, available options should not be restricted to the competing dystopias of an unchecked market and a centralized state bureaucracy. Above all, in developing societies, a viable agenda cannot consist of the simple cancellation of the latter in favor of the former. Given the powerful sway of globalization, such a cancellation in effect becomes the surrender of national or local self-rule to hegemonic economic forces—which, in turn, is a synonym for a form of neocolonialism. Addressing himself to the post–Cold War leadership in India, he states bluntly:

They have quite blindly gone in for an erosion of the role of the state, for an acceptance of the market as the key mediator in the development process,

and for globalization. In doing so, they have walked into a trap laid by
global hegemonic interests, not just a debt trap but also a trap for recoloniz-
ing large parts of the world.[13]

In order to avoid this trap, a move beyond both a centralized bureaucracy (the backbone of the traditional nation-state) and a mindless globalization (governed by hegemonic market forces) is needed. Kothari
at formulates a Third World vision designed to fill the vacuum created
by the "world without alternatives" (emerging in the wake of socialism
and nonalignment): the modern state is retained but sharply recast in a
popular-democratic direction as the arena of democratic participation
and self-rule. With this redefinition, the state ceases to be the monopoly
of traditional elites; it also ceases to be the preserve of an upwardly mobile middle class increasingly alienated from the broader community. The
latter is particularly important in the Indian context. As Kothari notes,
while previously a mainstay of Gandhian ideas and of the movement
toward a "humane and progressive" India, the Indian middle class has
progressively adapted itself to the global bourgeoisie, in the process abandoning their social conscience in favor of a "vulgar consumerism" and
the relentless pursuit of private wealth and pleasure. Against the backdrop of these developments, Kothari assigns the state the role of "preserving spaces for the underprivileged" as well as "protecting peoples
and cultures from globalizing trends." Partially shielded by the state,
peoples and cultures emerge as sources of resistance to global hegemony—notwithstanding the danger of degenerating into xenophobic forms
of populism or communalism. For Kothari, the basic issue is how to
counterbalance the implacable sway of globalism and thus to salvage the
mediating role of cultures in the crucible "between tradition and modernity" and hence "between external and indigenous structures and values." Only a properly democratic politics can accomplish this goal when
democracy means

> not just electoral politics but a politics based on critical interventions that
> will once again give a sense of hope and confidence to the poor and margin-
> alized sections of society, generate a process of empowerment, a new re-
> alignment of forces and, out of it all, a new agenda for the state.[14]

From this angle democratic politics requires a serious effort of decentralization, both in the public administrative and the economic spheres.
In this context, Kothari again pays tribute to the legacy of Gandhi—
without subscribing in every detail to Gandhian programs or policies
such as the program of village autonomy. The important point is that
social and economic life must be built from the ground up rather than

from the top down in a managerial or technocratic style. Contrary to the centralized strategies still favored by traditional Marxists, *Growing Amnesia* starts from the ordinary lifeworld of concrete experience, guided by the commitment to take "people seriously," by "respecting their thinking and wisdom" and by fostering institutions and technologies that "respond to their needs." Only by following this maxim is it possible to counteract managerial elitism and establish an economic system that, in Gandhi's words, "not only produces for the mass of the people but in which the mass of the people are also the producers." The turn to the ordinary lifeworld also entails a certain respect for popular or indigenous beliefs, including religious and cultural traditions. As Kothari notes, some of the most intense conflicts and resentments arise from threats to "the cultural and social identity of a people." Although traditions and customary beliefs are certainly not immune from change or critique, Kothari strongly counsels a transformative approach that proceeds from within, and with the resources of, a given cultural context, precisely as an antidote to chauvinism or aggressive xenophobia:

> If minority (or, for that matter, the majority) groups in this country are to be weaned away from the influence of fundamentalism, they must be made to feel socially and economically secure. Their culture and religion must be protected from external violence and from unnecessary moralizing. It must be recognized that social transformation can only legitimately come from within a society or community. . . . External threats to the identity of such communities only strengthen the traditionalists and fundamentalists within them, and marginalize the progressive forces.[15]

## II

Kothari's insider perspective—his view of the world "from the bottom up"—is also emphatically shared by Ashis Nandy, his senior associate at the Delhi Centre. Like Kothari, Nandy has long been a spokesman of democratic politics and democratic transformative change—but change that is popularly or locally legitimated rather than imposed by hegemonic (colonial or neocolonial) forces or self-appointed middle-class elites. If there is a difference between the two thinkers, it is one of emphasis and disciplinary focus: whereas Kothari centerstages issues endemic to political economy and sociology, Nandy—a trained psychologist and psychoanalyst—is more concerned with the psychic (or psychocultural) wellsprings of popular resistance as well as with the inner traumas of colonial oppression. One of his early publications, *At the Edge of Psychology* (1980), perceptively traced the intersections and crosscurrents linking politics, culture, and psychology, especially as experienced in non-Western societies. His next book, *The Intimate Enemy* (1983), probed these intersections more concretely by focusing on the psychic effects of colonial domination, primarily on the introjection or internalization of the colonizer's worldview, which, among the colonized, lead to a "loss of self" and an ensuing struggle for self-recovery. In psychotherapeutic fashion, Nandy sought to unearth submerged or suppressed layers of an "uncolonized mind" that might be mobilized as possible sources of resistance and self-transformation.[16]

In a relatively clear and concise manner, Nandy's alternative vision is articulated in *Traditions, Tyranny and Utopias* (1987), especially in the chapter titled "Towards a Third World Utopia." The chapter immediately takes its stand at the grassroots level by viewing the world "from the bottom up." As Nandy emphasizes, the notion of the "Third World" is not a timeless, metaphysical idea; rather, it is a political and economic category "born of poverty, exploitation, indignity and self-contempt." Given this stark historical background, the formulation of an alternative future for non-Western societies must start from the experience of "man-made suffering"—not for the sake of inducing self-pity or self-hatred, but in order to permit a therapeutic "working through" of the traumas of oppression. Nandy's approach is guided by the belief that the only way the Third World can transcend colonialism—as well as the "sloganeering of its well-wishers"—is by "becoming a collective representation of the victims of man-made suffering everywhere in the world" and then by "owning up" to the forces of oppression and "coping with them as inner vectors."

As helpmates in this process of coping and working through Nandy invokes healing powers latent or buried in indigenous traditions, especially powers like those mobilized in the Gandhian struggle for independence. A prominent resource is the relative distance of non-Western cultures from modern (Cartesian) dualisms or dichotomies, those of subject and object, humans and nature, and colonizers and colonized. Nandy construes Gandhian notions of nonviolence and noncooperation as therapeutic exit routes from domination. For Gandhi, he states, the aim of the oppressed was not "to become a first-class citizen in the world of oppression instead of a second- or third-class one," but rather "to build an alternative world where he can hope to win back his humanity." In this manner Gandhi sought "to free the British as much as the Indians from the clutches of imperialism." Nandy sees here a parallel with forms of (nonorthodox) Marxism as well as Christian liberation theology, and he quotes a statement by Gustavo Gutierrez: "one loves the oppressors by liberating them from their inhuman condition as oppressors, by liberating them from themselves."[17]

The publication of *Traditions, Tyranny and Utopias* coincided roughly with the appearance of one of Nandy's most widely discussed essays, "Cultural Frames for Social Transformation: A Credo." The essay took as its point of departure the anticolonial struggle in Africa, especially from Amilcar Cabral's stress on popular or indigenous culture as a counterpoint to external oppression. In Nandy's view, Cabral's stance could be extended to other colonial or postcolonial societies; basically, it implies a turn to the lived world of people at the grassroots (and thus a perspective "from the bottom up"). The emphasis on culture and cultural traditions signals a defiance of the modern (Western) idea of intellectual and scientific "expertise" uncontaminated by popular customs or beliefs; it gives voice to societies and peoples "which have been the victims of history and are now trying to rediscover their own visions of a desirable society." In our postcolonial world, the issue of cultural resistance and self-assertion is by no means obsolete; on the contrary, it is gaining added significance due to the relentless momentum of globalization or global standardization under Western auspices. Thus, the stress on "cultural frames for social transformation" constitutes in our time "a plea for a minimum cultural plurality in an increasingly uniformized world."[18]

An important objective of Nandy's essay is to sort out the spectrum of possible (ideal-typical) responses on the part of non-Western societies to the inroads of colonialism and globalization. One such response is that of modernizing elites, especially urban middle-class professionals, entrepreneurs, and intellectuals. Having received much of their education and training in the West, these elites are essentially committed to Western-style modernization—"the values of European Enlightenment"—although they may be willing to fit selected fragments of native traditions into their modernist scheme. In contrast to this mode of "critical modernism," radical traditionalists are intent upon repulsing and ostracizing all Western influences and encapsulating themselves in native traditions, in effect, ossifying or "museumizing" the latter. Nandy's own sympathies are with neither of these options. He pleads for a different path, termed "critical traditionalism," which seeks to marshal the resources provided by cultural traditions or inherited "cultural frames" for purposes of social and political transformation. The chief exemplar of this approach in the Indian context was Gandhi. Gandhi's *Hind Swaraj* launched a "savage" critique of Western civilization and Western modernity (which Gandhi at one point did not hesitate to call "satanic"), but this critique did not in any way inhibit him from denouncing traditional abuses like the caste system and untouchability. In fact, Nandy writes, Gandhi's inweighing against untouchability was only "the other side of his struggle against modern imperialism"; "neither of the two struggles could be conceived without the other." Unlike radical traditionalists,

Gandhi did not want to defend tradititions; he lived with them. Nor did he, like Nehru, want to museumize cultures within a modern frame. Gandhi's frame was traditional, but he was willing to criticize some traditions violently. He was even willing to include in his frame elements of modernity as critical vectors. He found no dissonance between his rejection of modern technology and his advocacy of the bicycle, the lathe and the sewing machine. Gandhi defied the modern world by opting for an alternative frame.[19]

Elaborating further on the path of critical traditionalism, Nandy emphasizes the difference between this path and a backward-looking historicism that retrieves the past for merely academic purposes. A recollection of the role of cultural traditions in the lived experience of peoples is needed; this, in turn, requires attention to the internal fissures in traditions, especially the fissures between oppressors and oppressed. In Nandy's words, critical traditionality invokes the memory of traditions in their embroilment with (overt or covert) modes of oppression; to be valid or legitimate, recollection of traditions has to foster also "an awareness of the nature of evil," of the persistence of "man-made *dukkha* or suffering" from the past into the present. Conversely, to be pertinent and intelligible, a theory or account of oppression has to be cast "in native terms or categories," that is, "in terms and categories used by the victims of our times." The latter postulate militates against certain modernist theories of oppression, including orthodox Marxism, which, couched in the idiom of post-Enlightenment rationalism, are disdainful of vernacular languages and experiences. Resorting to popular culture privileges the voice of the victims. In emphatic terms, Nandy insists on

> the primacy that should be given to the political consciousness of those who have been forced to develop categories to understand their own suffering and who reject the pseudo-indigenity of modern theories of oppression using—merely using—native idioms to conscientize, brainwash, educate, indoctrinate the oppressed or to museumize their cultures. The resistance to modern oppression has to involve, in our part of the world, some resistance to modernity.

These arguments lead Nandy ultimately to articulate a "general skepticism" toward some key premises of Western modernity. His doubts boil down to a general distrust of the ideas sponsored by "the winners of the world and their allies," prompting him to turn from mainline doctrines to "the faiths and ideas of the powerless and marginalized. That way lie freedom, compassion and justice."[20]

Nandy's *The Illegitimacy of Nationalism* (1994) is a critical indictment of one of the key features of Western modernity: the centralized nation-state and, as a corollary, the idea of "nationalism" as the driving engine of that state. Nandy follows Partha Chatterjee in perceiving the nation-state in India as a basically British import foisted on a more or less amorphous Indian society and civilization. Yet, whereas for Chatterjee—and for many "Subaltern" as well as progressivist writers—the nation-state was merely a halfway house or obstacle on the road toward a more global vision (either that of a global free market or a classless world society), Nandy invokes indigenous cultural resources as critical buffers against the homogenizing effects of both nationalism and (Western-style) cosmopolitanism. In pursuing this path, he expresses his strong indebtedness to Rabindranath Tagore who differed from many leaders of the independence struggle in his ambivalent and quasi-dialectical attitude toward nationalism and the nation-state. Although initially willing to marshal nationalist sentiments in the struggle against colonialism, Tagore's more seasoned work came to suspect nationalism as an accomplice of neo-imperialist modernization schemes. In Nandy's portrayal, many leaders of the independence movement saw nationalism as a "premodern concept" that functioned merely as a "pathological by-product of global capitalism." Once India and humanity at large had overcome the seductive charms of this "vestigial medievalism," nationalism and the nation-state were expected to "wither away" in favor of an "enlightened, secular universalism" greeted as harbinger of a "future One World." In opposition to this outlook, Tagore and a small band of dissenters regarded nationalism as an outgrowth of the Western system of nation-states, but also and more importantly as an ally in the steadily accelerating process of globalization and global standardization. Shunning cultural relativism, the alternative vision of these dissenters was a global civilizational perspective rooted in "the tolerance encoded in various traditional ways of life in a highly diverse, plural society."[21]

Nandy includes Gandhi in the band of dissenters in the independence movement as well as Tagore—notwithstanding some pronounced differences of emphasis and orientation between the two. The main difference had to do with the type of cultural resources each mobilized in the anticolonial struggle. Tagore was primarily attracted to India's "high culture" as represented by its classical traditions; Gandhi turned chiefly to the popular or folk traditions (both in India and the West) for support. What linked the two, in Nandy's account, was their assessment of nationalism. Both recognized "the need for a 'national' ideology of India as a means of cultural survival"; yet both also recognized that, for the same reason, India "would either have to make a break with the post-medieval Western concept of nationalism or give the concept a new content." As a result, nationalism became gradually illegitimate for Tagore, while for Gandhi it had to involve an internal self-critique coupled with a critique of the nation-state. For both, the latter critique did not entail the endorsement of a bland globalism, but the need to strengthen cultural and popular sources of resistance to imperial or neo-imperial designs. For both also, such an accent was completely at odds with ethnic chauvinism or exclusivism, especially the notion of a "single-ethnic Hindu *rashtra*"; instead, whatever meaning India might have could only be the work of continuous interpretation and renegotiation, a process yielding fragile unity only "through acknowledgment of differences."[22]

## III

The presentation in these pages has offered glimpses, or highlighted major accents, of the Delhi Centre for the Study of Developing Societies by focusing on the work of Kothari and Nandy. As indicated before, the focus in this regard is highly selective, given the multifaceted character of the Centre's activities. As an institution devoted to research on social policy issues, the Centre counts among its associates—in addition to Kothari and Nandy—numerous practioners whose leanings are more empirical or social-scientific in character, or else straddle empirical, theoretical, and practical domains; on several occassions, collaborative projects have also been undertaken by associates from diverse disciplines. In all these respects, the Centre bears a resemblance to the Frankfurt Institute of Social Research established by Horkheimer, Adorno, and several others during the later years of the Weimar Republic. Curiously, the parallel between the two institutions breaks down when applied to the present period. While initially committed to the critical analysis of capitalist developments in the West—and hence also to an investigation of the dark underside of modernity (or the "dialect of Enlightenment")—the Frankfurt School has emerged in recent decades as a chief protagonist of Western modernity and of the global process of modernization and secularization. To this extent, the Delhi Centre recaptures strands of the earlier Frankfurt program that have been cast aside or sidelined by recent representatives of the latter school.

Not being a neutral onlooker of global affairs, I find myself harboring a strong sympathy for the overall pattern, though perhaps not all the details, of the Centre's perspective. Above all, the Centre's accent on popular culture and folk traditions strikes me as preferable to a narrow political-economy approach that has tended to characterize "Subaltern Studies" (at least during their formative years). From the vantage of developing societies, political economy—especially when couched in a traditional Marxist idiom—is likely to be experienced as a Western import, as part and parcel of the arsenal of conceptual frameworks (including the nation-state) bequeathed to subaltern peoples by colonial or neocolonial policies. Moreover, in its orthodox Marxist mode, political-economic analysis is prone to compress social life into a polar opposition of classes in a fashion that ignores the complex welter of differentiated interactions and antagonisms prevalent in non- or partially industrialized societies. This problem as been duly noted by Edward Said, in his foreword to one of the Subaltern volumes. If Subaltern history, he writes, follows this polarizing strategy and construes itself as simple antithesis, it runs the risk of "just being a mirror opposite" of official historiography, thus becoming "as exclusivist, as limited, provincial and discriminatory" as the "master discourses" of colonialism and capitalist elitism.[23] Finally and most importantly, in its bent toward secularist universalism, Marxist analysis rides roughshod over and thus homogenizes local experiences and traditions by subjecting them to a global design. Futurist in orientation, such analysis strips oppressed people of their cultural memories just when they are most needed as points of resistance.

Although in many ways partial to the Centre, I am not unaware of certain quandaries besetting its perspective. One of the more troubling and recalcitrant problems has to do with the role of politics, particularly the role of the state. On this point, the writings of Kothari and Nandy reveal a notable ambivalence and also a certain difference of emphasis. Both are opposed to the homogenizing threat of centralized power; yet Kothari seems unwilling to jettison the modern state entirely—at least in the absence of other mediating and policy-setting agencies. While moving away from an earlier progressivism (supporting the Indian welfare state), his recent work grants the state at least a limited function—as long as it provides a protective shield for popular resistance to global or multinational pressures. As he writes in *Growing Amnesia*, there is a need not to allow the complete erosion of the state's "legitimacy"—for experience shows that, lacking alternatives "the poor and the marginalized have nowhere to turn other than to the state."

For Kothari, salvaging a properly chastized, transformed or "humanized" state also means salvaging a "democratic space" or public forum for the redress of grievances. On this point, Nandy's position appears more adamant. In an essay titled "Culture, State, and the Rediscovery of Indian Politics," Nandy distinguishes between two basic approaches to politics: a "culture-oriented" and a statist or "nation-state-oriented" approach. In the latter, culture serves merely as a tool for the promotion of state power; in the former the state is a handmaiden of culture (or for the "enrichment of culture"). Nandy finds it imperative to abandon the primacy-of-state theory—adopted by India from the West—in favor of an outlook privileging culture or civilization. A basic premise of that outlook is the belief "that a civilization must use the state as an instrument and not become an instrument of the state."[24]

Nandy's position raises difficult questions regarding the relation between culture and politics (some of which were alluded to in the previous chapter). A central query might be, How can culture "use the state as an instrument" or provide an agenda for state policy? Also, can culture be a "frame" (a cultural frame) for social transformation? I am fully in accord with Nandy's critique of the modern nation-state as a totalizing project and, more generally, of a narrowly "state-oriented" approach to politics intent upon merely "using" or abusing cultural traditions. His critique can be extended to a recently fashionable thesis according to which culture is nothing but a political product or artifact, hence something that can be willfully constructed and "deconstructed" by political elites or agents—a thesis reflecting an excessive sway of subjectivism and social engineering. On the other hand, culture cannot be completely immunized from politics or policy concerns, as might be suggested by the notion of a "culture-oriented" or "primacy-of-culture" approach. To treat culture as such a non- or prepolitical domain that only subsequently utilizes state policy endorses, or leans in the direction of, cultural "essentialism" or "foundationalism" (terms that today have a pejorative ring). As it seems to me, culture always requires interpretation (which, in a sense, is a political act); but it is also always in excess of any given interpretation, with the result that interpretations remain contestable. Culture or the cultural lifeworld is a background that can never be fully "foregrounded," although politics tends to court such a foregrounding attempt. These considerations point up the complex entwinement of lifeworld and policy, of culture and agency, where both are mutually implicated, thereby constraining and modulating each other.[25]

The privileging of culture raises additional questions, when it implies a privileging of native or indigenous cultural resources over alien (mainly Western) cultural and political-economic influences. As has often been pointed out (especially by Western intellectuals), such favoritism conjures up the danger of cultural exclusivism or self-segregation, coupled perhaps with the utopian imagery of the "*bon sauvage.*" Despite occasional overtures in this direction, Nandy's as well as Kothari's writings are on the whole remarkably free of this temptation. As both have persistently emphasized, the voices of the marginalized and dispossessed in Third World countries can only be heard or come into their own when placed in the broader public forum of the emerging world community— provided they are not drowned out by standardizing hegemonic refrains. In *Traditions, Tyranny and Utopias* Nandy states that the issue is not choosing between Westernization and a static "reactive Indianness," but finding a path for cross-cultural encounter in the context of Western global hegemony. Such encounter, he writes, inevitably succumbs to the hierarchy of power "unless the dialogue creates a shared space for each participant's distinctive, unstated theory of the other cultures." Cross-cultural dialogue inevitably spills over at this point into intracultural dialogue, the "dialogue within each participating culture among its different levels or parts." This insight is corroborated by Kothari in his comments on the internal complexity and multivocity of Indian cultural life. A passage from *Growing Amnesia* ably reflects his alternative vision for India—and possibly for the rest of the world:

> One of the continuing cultural traits of the Indian civilization has all along been in terms of its high tolerance of ambiguity. Only the modern hi-tech elite wants to regulate things, "resolve" contradictions along some rationalist calculus. . . . The age of these modernists . . . is fast coming to a close, here and elsewhere in the world. This does not mean any return to some pristine past as if such a "past" were ever there for us to "revive." This is then the ambience of a new awakening, a redefinition of Indian identity, one that is at once so uncertain about what lies in store and so pregnant with possibilities.[26]

## Notes

1. Compare, e.g., Irving Louis Horowitz, *Three Worlds of Development: The Theory and Practice of International Stratification* (New York: Oxford University Press, 1966). Regarding different models of democracy see C. B. Macpherson, *The Real World of Democracy* (Oxford: Clarendon Press, 1966); also his *The Life and Times of Liberal Democracy* (Oxford: Oxford University Press, 1977).

2. See Thomas Pantham, "Some Dimensions of the Universality of Philosophical Hermeneutics: A Conversation with Hans-Georg Gadamer," *Journal of Indian Council of Philosophical Research* 9 (1992): 132.

3. For a good introduction to the Subaltern project see Ranajit Guha and Gayatri Chakravorty Spivak, eds., *Selected Subaltern Studies*, with a foreword by Edward W. Said (New York: Oxford University Press, 1988). The first volume of *Subaltern Studies* was published in Delhi in 1982; since then, at least eight additional volumes have appeared.

4. A brief introduction to the perspective and work of the Centre is provided by Rajni Kothari in "Towards an Alternative Process of Knowledge," in his *Rethinking Development: In Search of Humane Alternatives* (New York: New Horizons Press, 1989), pp. 23–43. (The book was first published in India by Ajanta Publications, Delhi.) The Centre issues periodic *Research Reports*, among which the most detailed and comprehensive was the report published in 1988 on the occasion of the Cenre's Silver Jubilee.

5. *Lokayan* in the meantime has become an autonomous institution with its own statutes; six times a year it publishes a journal known as *Lokayan Bulletin* (in English and Hindu).

6. Rajni Kothari, *State against Democracy: In Search of Humane Gover-*

*nance* (Delhi: Ajanta, 1988), p. 60. As one should note, Kothari did not entirely condemn the modern state. In a progressive democratic vein, he endorsed the state provided it served as an "instrument" of democratization. The state was to be in the service of democracy and the people (not the other way around).

7. See Kothari, *State against Democracy*, pp. 2–3, 151; also his *Transformation and Survival: In Search of a Humane World Order* (Delhi: Ajanta, 1988), pp. 6, 170–171. In the latter text, Kothari states his vision in these terms: "My preferred world is one in which the individual enjoys *autonomy* for his self-realization and creativity—what is generally known as freedom. This is my principal value. . . . The primary condition of freedom is sheer survival, a protection against violence—local, national and international violence, as well as conditions tending towards either annihilation of the properties of life or towards a deadening uniformity of all forms of behavior and social structure" (p. 173).

8. Kothari, *Rethinking Development*, pp. 3–5. The chapter was first presented as a paper at a Pugwash Conference on Science and World Affairs held in Madras in 1976.

9. *Rethinking Development*, pp. 7–21.

10. *Rethinking Development*, pp. 48–49, 51. The chapter was first presented as a paper at a conference on alternative development strategies held in Bangkok in 1979. Compare in this context also Max Horkheimer and Theodor W. Adorno, *Dialectic of Enlightenment*, trans. John Cumming (New York: Herder & Herder, 1972).

11. *Rethinking Development*, pp. 50, 52, 54–55. Regarding ecology compare also the chapter "On Eco-Imperialism" (a critique of Garrett Hardin), pp. 107–117. The book contains an important chapter on "Ethnicity," pp. 191–224, where ethnicity is not merely castigated (as a possible ally of xenophobic communalism), but also affirmed and celebrated as a possible source of human empowerment and an emblem of cultural diversity (against the encroachments of globalizing uniformity).

12. Kothari, *Growing Amnesia: An Essay on Poverty and the Human Consciousness* (New Delhi: Viking, 1993), pp. 8–9. The book was published in England under the title *Poverty: Human Consciousness and the Amnesia of Development* (London: Zed Books, 1993). I quote from the Indian edition. Kothari adds, "Quite apart from the decline in the role of the state in preserving spaces for the underprivileged and protecting peoples and cultures from globalizing trends, there is the danger of the whole normative framework of democracy being undermined. The assumption that the liberalization of the economy would lead to a more liberal policy and generate more liberties for individuals and groups is thoroughly unfounded" (p. 26).

13. *Growing Amnesia*, pp. 17, 28.

14. *Growing Amnesia*, pp. 22–23, 26, 28–29, 31.

15. *Growing Amnesia*, pp. 123, 134, 149, 151. He adds, "Basically, without the deeper cultural base, it is not possible to achieve human well-being. Even if it is temporarily brought about through some administrative or technological means . . . it will soon disappear" (p. 90).

16. See Ashis Nandy, *At the Edge of Psychology: Essays in Politics and Cul-*

*ture* (Delhi: Oxford University Press, 1980); *The Intimate Enemy: Loss and Recovery of Self under Colonialism* (Delhi: Oxford University Press, 1983). Nandy has also been a prolific writer on the politics and culture of science. One of his early texts in this field was *Alternative Sciences: Creativity and Authenticity in Two Indian Scientists* (Delhi: Oxford University Press, 1980).

17. Nandy, *Traditions, Tyranny and Utopias: Essays in the Politics of Awareness* (Delhi: Oxford University Press, 1987), pp. 21, 31–35. The importance of Gandhi's legacy for the future of developing societies is spelled out with eloquence and subtlety in the book's concluding chapter, titled "From Outside the Imperium: Gandhi's Cultural Critique of the West," pp. 127–162. As one should note, in exploring therapeutic alternatives, Nandy did not postulate a latent Indian "essence" untouched by external intrusion. It is not easy, he writes, "to live with an alien culture's estimate of oneself, to integrate it within one's selfhood and to live that self-induced inner tension. It is even more difficult to live with the inner dialogue within one's own culture which is triggered off by the dialogue with other cultures because, then, the carefully built defenses against disturbing dialogues . . . begin to crumble" (p. 17). See also Gustavo Gutierrez, *A Theology of Liberation* (Maryknoll, N.Y.: Orbis Books, 1973), p. 276.

18. Nandy, "Cultural Frames for Social Transformation: A Credo," *Alternatives* 12 (1987): 113–114.

19. "Cultural Frames for Social Transformation," pp. 114–116.

20. "Cultural Frames for Social Transformation," pp. 117, 123. Nandy's distrust of some key categories of Western modernity is evident in a subsequent volume edited by him, *Science, Hegemony and Violence: A Requiem for Modernity* (Delhi: Oxford University Press, 1988).

21. Nandy, *The Illegitimacy of Nationalism: Rabindranath Tagore and the Politics of Self* (Delhi: Oxford University Press, 1994), pp. x–xi. Compare also Partha Chatterjee, *Nationalist Thought and the Colonial World: A Derivative Discourse* (Tokyo: Zed Books, 1986; second impr.: Minneapolis: University of Minnesota Press, 1993).

22. Nandy, *The Illegitimacy of Nationalism*, pp. 1–2, 6, 87.

23. Edward W. Said, foreword to *Selected Subaltern Studies*, ed. Ranajit Guha and Gayatri Chakravorty Spivak (New York: Oxford University Press, 1988), p. viii. Since the publication of the first volume in 1982, the Marxist and Gramscian moorings of Subaltern Studies have been transformed by a series of other influences, including structuralism and poststructuralism as well as British political sociology. To this extent, Said is entirely correct in noting that "none of the Subaltern Scholars is anything less than a critical student of Karl Marx" and that today "the influence of structuralist and poststructuralist thinkers like Derrida, Foucault, Roland Barthes and Louis Althusser is evident, along with the influence of British and American thinkers, like E. P. Thompson, Eric Hobsbawm, and others" (p. x).

24. See Kothari, *Growing Amnesia*, p. 95 ("Role of the State"); Nandy, "Culture, State, and the Rediscovery of Indian Politics," in *Interculture* 21, no. 2, issue 99 (1988): 2–3, 8.

25. On the relation of culture and politics see, e.g., Margaret Archer, *Culture*

*and Agency: The Place of Culture in Social Theory* (Cambridge: Cambridge University Press, 1988); Gayatri Chakravorty Spivak, *In Other Worlds: Essays in Cultural Politics* (New York: Methuen, 1987); and Marshall Sahlins, *Culture and Practical Reason* (Chicago: University of Chicago Press, 1976).

26. Nandy, *Traditions, Tyranny and Utopias*, pp. 16–17; Kothari, *Growing Amnesia*, p. 179. Compare also Nandy's comment in "Culture, State, and the Rediscovery of Indian Politics": "Unlike the modernists and Hindu revivalists, those viewing Indian politics from outside the framework of the nation-state system believe it possible for a state to represent a confederation of cultures, including a multiplicity of religions and languages. To each of these cultures, other cultures are an internal opposition rather than an external enemy" (p. 11).

# 10

# Culture and Global Development

> . . . the general characteristic of *Bildung*: keeping oneself open to what is other.
>
> Gadamer, *Truth and Method*

Development is the global watchword today. Commonly the topic is discussed from the angle of economists and social scientists, a not inappropriate but very restricted approach. The comments I want to offer in the present chapter are of a reflective or theoretical kind, nurtured by my background in philosophy and social-political theory. The question raised here is, on the surface, quite simple: What is "development"? or What do we mean by "development," especially global development? The response I propose (in somewhat condensed and schematic form) is that the question cannot be adequately addressed without a consideration of "culture."

1. The notion that development presupposes a consideration of culture is likely to be challenged or rejected by economists and many empirical social scientists. For mainstream economists, development tends to consist in the growth of the gross national product (GNP), particularly in the expansion of industrial productivity coupled with the acceleration of capital accumulation and steadily higher levels of consumption. For economists trained in orthodox Marxist doctrine, development involves a change in the mode of production, a shift from feudal landlords and entrepreneurs to industrial labor, with culture relegated to a superstructural status. On the other hand, empirical social scientists tend to classify development under the rubrics of division of labor and growing structural complexity, with an accent on the transition from agriculture to industry, from village to urban centers—changes that permit empirical analysis and resort to quantitative-statistical measurement.

Approached from these angles, development and culture are only marginally correlated. To be sure, economists are often willing to recognize that the efficiency of specific production techniques and marketing strategies depends in good measure on the prevailing cultural context. Accordingly, economic planners and company managers are often exhorted to learn something about foreign cultures where they wish to do business or introduce economic changes. The purpose of this exhortation is of a purely utilitarian sort, however; learning about a foreign culture is encouraged not for the sake of that culture, but in order to maximize corporate efficiency and to increase the chances of economic gain in the face of prevailing cultural constraints. Empirical social scientists, on their part, are often ready to acknowledge culture as one of the ingredients or variables in a growingly complex social structure, as one of the "subsystems" of society (alongside the economy and the polity) contributing to the maintenance and evolution of societal goals over time.[1] Again, the significance of culture is reduced to a subordinate and utilitarian role: as one variable among many others, culture is invoked to enhance the possibility of empirical social prediction and control.

2. The assertion of a close link between development and culture—the dependence of development on a consideration of culture—means to go beyond such marginal concessions. The question What is development?, or What do we mean by development?, cannot be answered in strictly economic or social-scientific terms. Even the notions of "economic development" or "social development" exceed in principle the disciplinary confines of economics and social science. To assess the meaning of these notions requires a reflective judgment (about higher/lower, better/worse) that transgresses the competence of these disciplines. In the absence of such judgment, the pronouncements of economics and social science on development are bound to have the character of dogmas. For on what grounds and with what justification can one say that development equals growth of the GNP or the enhancement of societal complexity? What are the criteria of judgment that allow us to say that some societies—richer, technologically advanced societies—are "more developed" than others? Economists and social scientists may at this point invoke their expertise. But acceptance of this expertise again requires criteria that lie outside their professional disciplines.

Talk of development thus requires evaluative criteria—that is, resort to theoretical or philosophical reflection. Clearly, philosophical reflection is not confined to any one of the established scientific disciplines. If one wishes to locate it at all academically, philosophy belongs to the so-called "humanities," the field of the "human" or "cultural sciences." To this extent, one may say that philosophy has its home in culture. Given that development questions presuppose reflective judgment, their adequate treatment can consequently be shown to depend on a consideration of culture. To be sure, reflective judgment is not the exclusive province of professional philosophers; it is an everyday occurrence and as such the task and privilege of every human being. In its everyday mode, reflection does not occur in a vacuum but is always inserted in a cultural and linguistic context (without being imprisoned by the latter). Like philosophy, everyday thinking involves a reflection—sometimes critical—*of and on* culture. By "culture" I mean here not merely a set of artifacts but rather a way of life, a manner of thinking and acting shared by a group of people over time.[2] Captured in reflective judgment, culture provides an overall framework through which we understand the world; it offers a frame of reference that gives sense or meaning to individual terms or concepts like the concept of development.

3. The linkage of development and culture, however, is still more intimate than has so far been suggested. What today is termed development was in earlier times often, if not usually, discussed under the heading of culture; in fact, the slogan of development has today usurped the place previously occupied by culture. The latter term at this point signifies no longer simply a general frame of reference but an experiential process: a process of human cultivation, educational growth, or "formation." During the classical period of German thought and literature, this process was captured by the term *Bildung* (which is commonly rendered in English as "formation" or "culture"). In his magisterial work *Truth and Method*, Hans-Georg Gadamer has evoked this tradition in stirring and lucid language. He writes, "The concept of self-formation or cultivation [*Bildung*] which became supremely important at the time, was perhaps the greatest idea of the 18th century—and it is this concept which became the natural element or soil of the humanities during the 19th century (even if they were no longer able to provide an epistemological justification)."[3]

Crucial for the rise to prominence of *Bildung*, in Gadamer's account, was the work of Herder, particularly the latter's notion of "human cultivation" (*Bildung zum Menschen*) and of a "rising up to humanity through culture" (*Emporbildung zur Humanität*)—phrases that preserved and transformed Enlightenment ideals of education. Herder's lead was continued by German classical philosophy, especially by Hegel whose *Phenomenology of Spirit* was nothing but a detailed account of the process and successive stages of human self-formation (*Bildung*). Gadamer also reminds his readers of the linkage of *Bildung* (formation/culture) and *Bild* (image/icon)—*Bild* referring to the divine image implanted in the human heart (recollecting the biblical story of the creation of humans "in the image of God"). This linkage, Gadamer notes, had not yet been forgotten in that period: "The cult of *Bildung* in the 19th century preserved the profounder dimension of the word, and our notion of *Bildung* is determined by it. . . . The rise of the term *Bildung* evokes the ancient mystical tradition according to which humans carry in their soul the image of God after whom they are fashioned and which they must cultivate in themselves."[4]

4. The notion of educational formation or *Bildung* is not limited to the German classical period, nor to Western culture in general. Virtually all the cultures of the globe have stories or mythical-religious narratives that recount a formative process of humankind—stories that sometimes date back several millennia. In the West, such a story is part and parcel of the basic religious patrimony. Gadamer refers to "medieval mysticism," but the story has a broader foundational character. Drawing on older Hebrew teachings, Christianity depicts the development or formative process of humankind as a "salvation history": a story that starts from a condition of initial bliss, proceeds to a period of corruption, loss, and separation, and finally points to the promise of recovery, healing, or redemption. The basic pattern of this story persisted well beyond the time of medieval speculation and mysticism. In the wake of the Enlightenment and at the height of German classical thought, Hegel portrayed historical development as a movement from initial immediacy to a stage of alienation, loss, and dispersion to the final epiphany of "absolute spirit"— thus transforming salvation history in the mode of a self-formation of reason (*Bildung zur Vernunft*). Although dubious as an account of actual or secular history, Hegel's "metanarrative" preserved the earlier nucleus of a deeper formative experience.[5]

5. In different guises, parallel stories can be found in most world civilizations. A case in point are the great epic narratives of India, the *Ramayana* and the *Mahabharata*. In both narratives the heroes are divine-human beings, that is, human beings that carry preeminently within themselves the image of God. In both stories, this image is subjected to severe tests: the heroes have to undergo prolonged agonies of separation, loss, and exile before they can return to their true home and fulfill their divine destiny. In the *Ramayana*, the leading hero is an *avatar* of Vishnu, while his wife Sita is an offspring (a "furrow") of the earth goddess. Due to the cabal and deceit of his stepmother, Rama is deprived of his kingdom and together with his wife is forced into exile. While they are dwelling in a forest far from home, Sita is abducted by the demon-king Ravana and carried off into the distant land of Lanka. Only after a protracted search and after enlisting the help of the monkey king is Rama able to face and defeat the demons, recapture his wife, and bring her back to his native Ayodhya, where, after further trials, the two finally find peace and heavenly transfiguration.

In the *Mahabharata*, the heroes—named Pandavas—are sons of human mothers and gods, thus likewise carrying within themselves a divine imprint. As a result of the trickery and deceit of their cousins (the Kauravas), the heroes are expelled from their kingdom and compelled to live in a far-off forest region. It is there, in suffering the agonies of exile, that the Pandavas slowly begin to discover their sense of purpose or mission. After having assembled an army, they finally face their cousins and other relatives on a large battle field—the field of "rightness" or *dharma*. Having vanquished their foes, the Pandavas establish in their homeland a rule of peace, harmony, and general well-being—whereupon they retreat into the Himalayas, thus completing their process of divine-human formation (*Bildung*).[6]

Similar stories of formation can also be found in the Chinese tradition, though with different accents. In Confucianism everything—including the peace of the family and of the political regime—depends on the proper formation of humans in the spirit of nobility, that is, on the cultivation of the qualities of the *chün-tzu*. Foremost among these qualities are the virtues of humaneness or fellow-feeling (*jen*) and of the propriety of behavior (*li*) in accordance with given contexts. As one may note, K'ung-fu-tzu—the teacher of these noble virtues—was himself the victim of political intrigues and cabals and was forced to live in exile for many years before he was allowed to return to resume his pedagogical mission.[7]

The notion of formation or self-formation also plays a prominent role in Asian Taoism and Buddhism, though in a form transgressing traditional morality. In Buddhism, the basic task is to overcome the lure of selfishness or self-centeredness and thus to reach the level of *sunyata*, or emptiness, where the world can be experienced in its "suchness" (*tathata*) beyond the bifurcations of knower and known, of being and nonbeing. Ascent to this level is far from easy and requires a strenuous process of self-formation, a kind of pilgrim's progress along the "eightfold path" in accordance with the *shilas* handed down by Sakyamuni. Taoism likewise counsels self-abandonment or abandonment of self-centeredness for the sake of a higher recovery, mainly for the sake of living in accord with the "way" of things and with cosmic harmony as expressed in the correlation of *yin* and *yang*. Like K'ung-fu-tzu, Lao-tzu was also forced by political intrigues to leave his post at the court and to travel far afield to the borders of China (the Western mountain pass). Regarding self-formation, Lao-tzu states, "A sound man by not advancing himself / Stays the further ahead of himself. / By not confining himself to himself/Sustains himself outside himself: / By never being an end in himself / He endlessly becomes himself."[8]

6. Let me return to the issue of development in our present global setting. How much of these older stories of formation, culture (*Bildung*), and self-development still lives on in contemporary conceptions of social development? One has to admit not very much, although this verdict

probably needs to be qualified somewhat in the interest of fairness. Development theory presents itself today in two major forms or versions:
an empirical or social-scientific variant and a philosophically more ambi-
tious or sophisticated model. In large measure, the empirical version presents development as an evolutionary process patterned after the process
of biological survival and growth. In the field of economics, the model
was outlined in succinct fashion in Rostow's trendsetting *Stages of Economic Growth* that emphasized the progressive expansion of industrial
productivity and the potential for capital accumulation.[9] In the domain
of social and political science, writers on development have tended to rely
heavily on the founders of modern sociological analysis—from Auguste
Comte to Herbert Spencer and Max Weber—with their stress on the progressive differentiation of social structures and functions coupled with
the steady rationalization or secularization of worldviews.

In line with neo-Darwinian teachings on natural selection, human societies in this model are portrayed as quasi-organic structures seeking to
increase their survival chances through the enhancement of internal complexity and external-environmental adaptability. Following in the footsteps of Spencer and Emile Durkheim, proponents of the model view
social evolution as a process of differentiation manifest in the division of
labor and growing "subsystem" autonomy, requiring ever renewed efforts of system integration to ensure effective environmental control. On
the cultural level, Comte and strands of Marxism have furnished the formula of the steady rationalization of worldviews, the progressive ascendancy of science and technology over traditional beliefs.[10] If at all, the
notion of culture as self-formation (*Bildung*) surfaces only dimly or
furtively in the empiricist model; scant traces of it can be found in the
postulated evolutionary transition from "status" to "contract," from *Gemeinschaft* to *Gesellschaft*, from tradition to modernity—but the meaning of these formulas tends to be left obscure.

7. Much of this obscurity is removed in the second model, which offers
a philosophically grounded view of modernization and development inspired mainly by Enlightenment teachings. According to this view, development signifies the progressive emancipation of humankind from modes
of political and religious tutelage characterizing past ages; in the Kantian
formulation, Enlightenment is the resolute awakening of humankind
from a condition of self-induced immaturity. In large measure, the model
has inspired revolutionary transformations in the modern age, from the
French Revolution to recent "velvet revolutions" in Eastern Europe. In
terms of political theory, the model furnishes the central ingredients of
modern Western liberalism with its focus on the enhancement of individual rights and freedoms. Viewed under liberal auspices, development or
modernization basically involves an exodus from past constraints, a

movement from dogmatically held beliefs to rational knowledge, from collective social structures to individual autonomy, and from geographically circumscribed accidents of birth to more universal or cosmopolitan aspirations. In our century, this outlook was articulated in stirring language by the founder of phenomenology, Edmund Husserl, in his portrayal of historical teleology as the progressive unfolding of rational reflection and moral autonomy throughout the world.[11]

Although elevating and inspiring in many ways, the discussed philosophical model is not without drawbacks, especially from a cultural perspective. The model in essence heralds an exodus from tradition—basically from historically grown culture. With its focus on individual autonomy, moreover, liberal Enlightenment thought has difficulty in reconciling individual rights with the notion of culture as a way of life shared by a larger group or community of people. In addition, individualism is coupled with a rationalizing bent. Despite its cosmopolitan aims, the model's celebration of "universal" human rationality is couched unmistakably in the idiom of modern Western philosophy—a fact that is liable to arouse suspicion among non-Western societies wedded to different modes of reasoning or thinking. The situation is aggravated by the linkage of rationality and modern science. To this extent, the liberal model is an accomplice (or provides insufficient antidotes) to the ongoing process of global rationalization, the standardization and homogenization of the world under the auspices of Western science and technology—a process which, again, is bound to evoke resentment and opposition among non-Western cultures while simultaneously shortchanging the process of cultural self-formation.

8. Against the backdrop of prevailing development theory (in both its empirical and universalist-philosophical versions), the importance of a consideration of culture clearly emerges. For present purposes, I want to highlight this importance under three headings.

a) Culture is important for providing a frame of reference through which development of any kind can be discussed and formulated. Culture is a framework of meanings and assumptions presupposed by economics and empirical social science; this framework is provided by philosophical reflection that has its home in the human or cultural sciences, which, in turn, are embedded in a broader cultural context.

b) Culture is important as an antidote to the ongoing process of global standardization and Westernization, a source of resistance for non-Western societies in the grip of Western hegemony. Culture here has connotations of "counterculture." The need for resistance against global standardization and homogenization has recently been articulated, especially by spokesmen of poststructuralism or postmodernism (from Michel Foucault to Jean-François Lyotard). In the context of development strategies, countercultural resistance is stressed by many non-Western writers, from Frantz Fanon to Ashis Nandy. In his Third World manifesto or "credo," Nandy has underscored the significance of indigenous cultural traditions as a counterpoise to the steamrolling effect of Westernization and global uniformization; resort to such traditions constitutes a bulwark to "the modern idea of expertise," that is, to the technocratic rule of scientists, bankers, and development experts. Invoking directly Foucaultian teachings, Tariq Banuri likewise emphasizes the importance of indigenous cultures as vehicles of non-Western societies "to retain control over their own actions and their own environments."[12]

c) Countercultural resistance might lead (or is sometimes accused of leading) to parochialism or communal self-enclosure. For this reason it is important to remember a third dimension: the notion of culture as cultivation, self-formation, and self-transformation (*Bildung*). By retaining the memory of traditional legacies, societies—both in the North and the South—preserve the memory of older stories of human development, where development is a learning process proceeding through loss and self-abandonment, or rather a process leading to self-discovery through loss and abandonment. Culture in this sense is crucial both for salvaging the human (or humanistic) meaning of development and for providing a bulwark against cultural isolation or self-enclosure.

9. Culture as cultivation (*Bildung*) has always had on interpersonal (that is, not self-centered) and dialogical character. This aspect has been eloquently articulated by Charles Taylor in his recent essay on "multiculturalism." As Taylor points out, stories of cultivation or self-formation in pre-modern times were always embedded in shared ways of life which were interpersonal or transpersonal by definition; given the fragility of shared life-forms in modernity, the link of interpersonal mutuality has to be deliberately cultivated today through dialogue, giving rise to a complex "politics of recognition." Hence: "The genesis of the human mind" (self-formation or *Bildung*) is "not monological, not something each person accomplishes on his or her own, but dialogical. . . . We define our identity always in dialogue with, sometimes in struggle against, the things our significant others want to see in us." What is distinctive of the modern age is not the need for mutuality or recognition as such but "the conditions in which the attempt to be recognized can fail. That is why the need is now acknowledged for the first time."[13] This transpersonal and dialogical character of culture is likewise underscored in the work of Gadamer, Mikhail Bakhtin, and Raimundo Panikkar. What Panikkar calls a "dialogical philosophy" is not the imposition of one point of view or the adoption of a superior standpoint but "the forging of a common

universe of discourse in the very encounter" among people (a process that does not necessarily yield consensus or a complete fusion of horizons).[14]

10. In light of the preceding discussion, what are the concrete implications of culture for a politics of development on both the regional and global levels? Here are a few things I do *not* mean to suggest. I do not mean to propose a mere substitution of cultural for social and economic development, and certainly nothing like a ban or moratorium on the latter. Least of all am I proposing a governmentally or state-sponsored culture policy (or *Bildungspolitik*) that would transform culture into an instrumental-political agenda. What I *do* endorse is culture as a source of ferment, of contestation, and also as a resource for countering the "iron cage" portrayed by Max Weber: the relentless process of standardization, homogenization, and global bureaucratization.

Although not immune from political intrusion, cultivation of this resource is not (or not in the first instance) the province of the state or state officials. In the context of modern society, cultural and religious legacies are preferably nurtured in the family and civil society, "civil society" being that dimension of social life beyond the confines of narrowly economic market relations, including schools, churches, universities, and the welter of voluntary associations marking a complex modern lifeworld. Cultivation cannot and should not be the mere perpetuation of elite culture and class privilege nor the imposition of standards of conduct from the top down. In line with Taylor's stress on mutual recognition and dialogue, cultivation must embrace popular culture and remain an open-ended, nondogmatic learning process where *Bildung* is neither willfully imposed nor willfully rejected. Such a learning process is akin to what A. C. Graham has called the "disputation of the Tao," and it resonates with these lines from the *Tao Te Ching*:

> A sound man's heart is not shut within itself
> But is open to other people's hearts:
> I find good people good,
> And I find bad people good
> If I am good enough.[15]

## Notes

1. The treatment of culture as one of the subsystems of society was particularly prominent in structural functionalism, as articulated chiefly by Talcott Parsons. See especially Parsons, *The Structure of Social Action* (New York: McGraw-Hill, 1937); *The Social System* (Glencoe, Ill.: Free Press, 1951); *Politics and Social Structure* (New York: Free Press, 1969). Parsonian theory has exerted

a strong influence on political development literature; compare, e.g., Lucian W. Pye and Sidney Verba, eds., *Political Culture and Political Development* (Princeton, N.J.: Princeton University Press, 1965).

2. In large measure I follow here the view of culture articulated by Clifford Geertz in *The Interpretation of Cultures: Selected Essays* (New York: Basic Books, 1973): "The concept of culture I espouse . . . is essentially a semiotic one. Believing, with Max Weber, that man is an animal suspended in webs of significance he himself has spun, I take culture to be those webs, and the analysis of it to be therefore not an experiential science in search of law but an interpretive one in search of meaning" (p. 5). Compare also James Clifford and George Marcus, eds., *Writing Culture: The Poetics and Politics of Ethnography* (Cambridge, Mass.: Harvard University Press, 1986).

3. Hans-Georg Gadamer, *Truth and Method*, 2nd rev. ed., trans. Joel Weinsheimer and Donald G. Marshall (New York: Crossroad, 1989), p. 9.

4. Gadamer, *Truth and Method*, p. 10. Compare also Johann Gottfried Herder, *Auch eine Philosophie der Geschichte zur Bildung der Menschheit*, with a postscript by Hans-Georg Gadamer (Frankfurt-Main: Suhrkamp, 1967); Georg W. F. Hegel, *Phenomenology of Mind*, trans. J. B. Ballie (New York: Harper & Row, 1967).

5. Compare Hegel, *Lectures on the Philosophy of History*, trans. J. Libtree (New York: Dover, 1956). For the notion of "metanarratives" and their critique, see Jean-François Lyotard, *The Postmodern Condition: A Report on Knowledge*, trans. Geoff Bennington and Brian Massumi (Minneapolis: University of Minnesota Press, 1984), pp. xxiii–xxv.

6. For perceptive comments on the two epics in terms of a human-divine formation process (*itinerarium mentis in Deum*) see J. L. Mehta, "My Years at the Center for the Study of World Religions: Some Reflections" (especially the section "Considerations on the Ramayana") and "The Discourse of Violence in the Mahabharata," in *Philosophy and Religion: Essays in Interpretation*, Mehta (New Delhi: Manoharlal, 1990), pp. 65–82, 254–271.

7. Compare in this context my "Tradition, Modernity and Confucianism," *Human Studies* 16 (1993): 203–211; also Tu Wei-ming, Milan Hejtmanek, and Alan Wachman, eds., *The Confucian World Observed: A Contemporary Discussion of Confucian Humanism in East Asia* (Honolulu: East-West Center, 1992).

8. Lao-Tzu, *The Way of Life*, trans. Witter Bynner (New York: Perigee Books, 1972), p. 35 (Chapter 7).

9. W. W. Rostow, *The Stages of Economic Growth* (Cambridge, Mass.: Harvard University Press, 1960); Robert T. Holt and John E. Turner, *The Political Basis of Economic Development* (Princeton, N.J.: Van Nostrand, 1966).

10. Compare, e.g., Gabriel A. Almond and G. Bingham Powell, *Comparative Politics: A Developmental Approach* (Boston: Little, Brown, 1966); Lucian W. Pye, *Aspects of Political Development* (Boston: Little, Brown, 1966); A. F. K. Organski, *The Stages of Political Development* (New York: Knopf, 1965).

11. See Edmund Husserl, *The Crisis of European Sciences and Transcendental Phenomenology*, trans. David Carr (Evanston, Ill.: Northwestern University Press, 1970); compare also Jürgen Habermas, *Communication and the Evolution of Society*, trans. Thomas McCarthy (Boston: Beacon Press, 1969).

12. See Ashis Nandy, "Cultural Frames for Social Transformation: A Credo," in *Political Discourse: Explorations in Indian and Western Political Thought*, ed. Bhikhu Parekh and Thomas Pantham (New Delhi: Sage, 1987), pp. 238–248; Tariq Banuri, "Modernization and Its Discontents: A Cultural Perspective on the Theories of Development," in *Dominating Knowledge: Development, Culture, and Resistance*, ed. Frédérique Apffel Marglin and Stephen A. Marglin (Oxford: Clarendon Press, 1990), pp. 73–99.

13. See Charles Taylor, "The Politics of Recognition," in *Multiculturalism and "The Politics of Recognition,"* ed. Amy Gutmann (Princeton, N.J.: Princeton University Press, 1992), pp. 32–35. My only reservation vis-à-vis Taylor is that "recognition" for me is not so much cognitive as ethical-ontological in character, implying a shift from Hegelian dialectics to Heideggerian "letting-be." To this extent I concur with Krzysztof Ziarek when he writes that Heideggerian *Mitsein* (being-with) implies a mutual openness, which "does not amount to a disclosure of the content of the other that would simply result in the eventual cognition, thematization, and thus absorption of the other." Hence, Heidegger's thought culminates "not in a dialectics of (re)cognition but precisely in proximity to their respective, noncognizable, otherness." See his *Inflected Language: Towards a Hermeneutics of Nearness* (Albany, N.Y.: SUNY Press, 1994), p. 57.

14. Raimundo Panikkar, "What Is Comparative Philosophy Comparing?" in *Interpreting Across Boundaries: New Essays in Comparative Philosophy*, ed. Gerald J. Larson and Eliot Deutsch (Princeton, N.J.: Princeton University Press, 1988), p. 132. See also Tzvetan Todorov, *Mikhail Bakhtin: The Dialogical Principle*, trans. Wlad Godzich (Minneapolis: University of Minnesota Press, 1984).

15. Lao-tzu, *The Way of Life*, p. 76 (Chapter 49). Compare also William Theodore deBary, *East Asian Civilization: A Dialogue in Five Stages* (Cambridge, Mass.: Harvard University Press, 1988); and A. C. Graham, *Disputers of the Tao: Philosophical Argument in Ancient China* (LaSalle, Ill: Open Court, 1989).

# 11

# "Rights" Versus "Rites":
# Justice and Global Democracy

Whose justice? Which rationality?

Alasdair MacIntyre

Ours is a time of perplexing crosscurrents. As we approach the end of the second millennium, we seem to enter the stage of a new *pax Romana* on an unprecedented scale: a world order or world civilization, basically of Western design, encircling the globe with a network of universal/ uniform ideas and practices. Among these ideas, easily the most prominent and influential is that of liberal democracy, a regime founded on popular self-determination and equal citizenship rights. Thus, the near-providential advance of liberal democracy, apprehended dimly by de Tocqueville over a century ago, seems to have reached in our time its destined goal and global fulfillment—an event celebrated by some observers as the completion and "end of history."[1] Yet, behind the din of global celebration we cannot fail to perceive discordant sounds or disruptive noises emanating chiefly from the upsurge of ethnic, national, and religious rivalries. The reasons for this upsurge are multiple, not simply a backward obstinacy. Even when transmitted through noncoercive means, the blessings of the new *pax Romana* (or *pax Americana*) are bound to reach non-Western societies (and unassimilated groups in the West) as the offshoots of imperial hegemony—and thus are prone to be resented and resisted precisely in the name of popular self-determination. On a more philosophical plane, global hegemonic rules—likes all rules—cannot possibly encompass or absorb the full range of otherness and historical contingency, an insight that inevitably disrupts or unsettles the sway of liberal cosmopolitanism.[2]

Our global scenario may induce despair, or at least stark disillusionment. In contrast to the champions of historical fulfillment, some observers perceive our time as the completion of *realpolitik*, manifest in the relentless clash between center and periphery, global domination and local particular resistance; in lieu of the triumph of universal rule, world order signals only global oppression or—in Max Weber's phrase—the advent of a "polar night of icy darkness." Although capturing elements of our situation, this outlook seems too bleak. Despite its hegemonic bent, *pax Americana* also buttresses the dissemination of universal democratic principles, especially equal rights and liberties, around the world. To this extent, liberal democracy, raised to the level of global order, is not entirely divorced from considerations of public justice and equity, and thus not simply equivalent to *realpolitik*. To be sure, care must be taken not to ignore the limits of these ethical concerns, that is, the complicity of liberal rule in the process of global standardization at the expense of local and cultural differences. Hence public justice today requires a highly nuanced treatment, perhaps something like a double gesture of affirmation and denial. Such a move was at least latently present in traditional conceptions. According to well-known classical formulas, justice means to "give to each his or her due" or to "treat equal things equally and unequal things unequally." Buried in these formulas are complex questions of a judgmental sort: What precisely is everyone's "due"? and What are the relevant respects in which things are either equal or unequal? For clearly, equality and inequality presuppose an act of comparison or, in Aristotle's phrase, an "intuitive grasp of the similarity in dissimilars" (and of dissimilarity in similars).[3]

In modern Western philosophy, this comparison has been weighted almost entirely in favor of equality or the principle of equal rights, resulting in inequality, or dissimilarity, being marginalized if not obliterated. Equality of rights or "equal liberty" is assumed to be a natural fact (operative in a presocial "state of nature"), while inequality or difference is attributed to social convention. With regard to public justice, this means that the presumption is in favor of the equal treatment of all individuals alike, while unequal treatment requires justification in the light of circumstances. The proverbial "blindness" of justice has come to be viewed entirely in this light: the rule of justice (or "rule of law") is postulated to apply "blindly" or equally to all individuals, irrespective of their color, creed, race, or gender. Undoubtedly, blindness of this kind is an enormous advance over the arbitrary or willfully prejudicial modes of treatment found in autocratic regimes; to this extent, "due process"—a process due to everyone—is surely an unrelinquishable part of modern democratic life. Yet, approbation here cannot entirely escape critical scrutiny or the double gesture of dialectical inquiry, giving rise to questions like these: Is the vaunted blindness of justice perhaps itself unjust?

Construed in terms of radical indifference or neutrality, is the rule of law, with its accent on universal sameness of treatment, perhaps itself oppressive or repressive in suppressing or shunting aside important differences or distinctions that matter deeply to people in concrete situations? At this point, law as universal rule seems to hover precariously at the border of justice and injustice by not giving people their "due" (not respecting the "dissimilarity in similars").

What is at stake at this juncture is not only the notion of justice as law but also, and more importantly, the question of the status and meaning of democracy, especially liberal democracy. This chapter cannot discuss—let alone resolve—all the facets of these complex issues. Its more modest ambition is to bring into view the basic tension or ambivalence intrinsic to justice: its inevitable sliding or prevarication between neutral indifference and solicitous attention to difference. The approach will be in part phenomenological and in part dialectical (in Adorno's sense of "negative dialectics"); it starts with commonsense assumptions regarding justice and explores their tensional implications for ethical theory. The first section probes commonsense beliefs undergirding modern Western conceptions of rule-governance, using as a reference point chiefly Jürgen Habermas's portrayal of the fabric of "moral consciousness." This portrayal leads Habermas to vindicate the prevalent (liberal) priorities of proceduralism over substantive ethics, of universal rule over conceptions of the "common good," and generally (using summary labels) of "justice" over "solidarity." The second section turns to other commonsense assumptions that, though usually sidestepped by liberal-individualist theories, have an equal prima facie appeal: they centerstage the role of particular traditions and cultural frameworks, thus affirming, or at least suggesting, the primacy of difference over sameness, of concrete context over rule-governance. Raised to the level of theoretical reflection, these beliefs support recent Western formulations of a "differential" justice, attentive to group or community rights as well as the ethical relevance of gender and ethnicity. The concluding section extends the dispute over justice to the international scene, the arena of global (or globalizing) democracy. Here the basic question concerns the relation between Western-style equal rights and community bonds and between secular rationality and cultural-religious attachments. In light of the contest between global power and local resistance, the issue is ultimately "whose justice and which rationality" shall prevail.

# I

Theories of justice sometimes start from abstract theoretical premises from which logical inferences are then drawn. Although fashionable among some professional philosophers, such theories seem to begin their construction with the roof. More plausible, and also sanctioned by a venerable Socratic tradition, are efforts that build from the ground up, namely, by exploring the commonsense opinions of ordinary, nonacademic people, in order to extract the "kernel of truth" or theoretical yield of such opinions. Some prominent philosophical initiatives in recent times have essentially followed this inductive-experiential approach. In *A Theory of Justice*, John Rawls took his point of departure from commonsense opinions widely held in Western liberal democracies, views that tend to accentuate the value of individual liberty and self-realization in a context of equal opportunities. Sifted through a theoretically imposed screen (called "veil of ignorance") bracketing all nonrelevant differences or particularities, these opinions were then shown to yield a general conception of justice centered around the primary principle of equal liberty (of individuals).[4] In a somewhat modified form, a similar approach has also been adopted by Jürgen Habermas in his elaboration of a communicative or "discourse ethics," which guides this section because of its instructive insights. As Habermas observed in an important text meant to lay the groundwork for his discursive framework, access to the moral domain can only be found from the vantage of ordinary experience and concrete lifeworld interactions; to this extent, ethical theory inevitably relies on a "phenomenology of morals": "As long as moral philosophy takes it as its task to clarify the everyday intuitions into which we are socialized, it must take its bearings (at least virtually) from the attitude of those participating in the communicative practice of everyday life."[5]

In delineating this grassroots approach to ethics, Habermas invoked the testimony of Peter Strawson who, in a number of writings, had articulated something like a "linguistic phenomenology of ethical consciousness." In Strawson's account, ethical theorizing had to be anchored in concrete moral sentiments or experiences like the indignation or resentment arising from personal insults, with secondary attention being given to the articulation of such feelings in ordinary language or speech. Moral sentiments were embedded in concrete lifeworld interactions and hence genuinely experienced only by participants, not by mere onlookers of such interactions; in terms of linguistic (or speech-act) theory, ethics happens in an illocutionary or performative, rather than merely denotative, mode. In Habermas's reading of these arguments, moral sentiments arise in everyday practices that are "accessible to us only in a performative attitude." This insertion in everyday practices lends moral feelings "a certain ineluctability": we cannot "revoke at will our engagement in a lifeworld to which we belong," for instance, by absconding into a spectator's perspective. This insight has to guide or inform ethical theorizing intent on distilling the core of moral experiences. Thus, naturalistic or empiricist approaches that look at morals merely from the outside, the vantage of a detached observer, cannot possibly have an enlightening or "clarifying effect" in this domain. Habermas shares Strawson's conclusion that

> the personal reactions of an offended party—for instance, resentments—are possible only in the performative attitude of a participant in interactions. By contrast, the objectifying attitude of a detached observer cancels the communicative roles of I and thou (first and second persons) and thus neutralizes the realm of moral phenomena as such. The third-person attitude causes this realm of phenomena to vanish.[6]

So far, Habermas's argument has remained close to the phenomenal domain of experience and thus seems largely unobjectionable. In further pursuing his theoretical objectives, however, his text makes a number of subtle moves that in light of the preceding appear somewhat startling. One has to do with the proclivity to individualize moral experience, to examine ethical questions chiefly from the "first person" perspective of individual agents. Thus, taking instruction from Kantian teachings, Habermas formulates the root question of ethics as the quandary of conscience: "What shall I do?" or "What ought I to do?" Although legitimate in certain respects, this question immediately distances the individual agent from the ordinary life context from which we began, "our engagement in a lifeworld to which we belong"; for all practical purposes, this life context now appears unreliable or unhelpful and perhaps radically defective in a moral or ethical sense. This distance or alienation is reinforced in the text by a second, more crucial move: the ascent to the level of "discourse" or discursive argumentation where agents encounter each other as rational *cogitos* pressing against each other contested normative claims; temporarily suspending ordinary interactions, discourse functions here as a quasi-transcendental platform predicated on idealized conditions of speech (guaranteeing the equal liberty of participants). With this ascent, the ban pronounced earlier against the detached onlooker seems to be nearly revoked. In Habermas's account, moral experiences point to broader "normative expectations" beyond the level of ego-alter interactions, to the realization that in committing a moral offense, the perpetrator has "also violated something impersonal or at least transpersonal, namely a generalized expectation that both parties hold." To this extent, feelings of guilt or obligation "transcend the particular sphere of what concerns individuals in specific situations":

> Emotional responses directed at individual persons in specific situations would be devoid of moral character were they not connected with an *imper-*

*sonal* kind of indignation over some breach of a generalized norm or behavioral expectation. It is only their claim to *general* validity that lends to an interest, a volition, or a norm the dignity of moral authority.[7]

The accent on discourse or discursive validation is clearly the most distinctive and innovative feature of Habermas's theoretical approach. For present purposes, the most noteworthy aspect of this approach is its centerstaging of the liberty and equality of participants, accomplished through the medium of idealized speech (rather than a Rawlsian "veil of ignorance"). In a theory of justice, this centering is a vindication of the moral weighting noted earlier in the case of Rawls: the assignment of priority to universal rules over particular contexts, to "equal liberty" over "difference" (where difference might arise from local contingencies or cultural-religious traditions). This weighting is clearly evident in Habermas's formulation of the "principle of universalization," a "bridging principle" allowing moral consensus, and also of the more specific "principle of discourse ethics" construed as the avenue for the argumentative validation of moral claims. The first principle is simply a modified continuation of the Kantian categorical imperative, according to which only those norms that express a "general will" or can be suitably elevated to the status of "universal laws" can be accepted as valid. Universalization requires that "*all* affected persons can accept the consequences [of a norm] as well as the side effects that its *general* observance is likely to have for the satisfaction of the interests of *every* affected individual." For the sake of its procedural implementation, this principle of universalization is further coupled with the second principle (of discourse ethics), which stipulates that "only those norms can claim to be valid that meet (or could meet) with the approval of all potentially affected individuals in their capacity as *participants in a practical discourse*."[8]

As can be gathered from these comments, justice in Habermas's account is basically equivalent to universal rule-governance—with rules being sanctioned through general (free and equal) argumentation; as in most liberal theories, justice is assumed to be blind to differences of status, race, creed, or gender (as well as differences of intellect or moral striving). This procedural blindness or indifference is further accentuated and argumentatively fleshed out in the concluding part of Habermas's text. As he points out, discourse ethics is basically procedural and formal in that it revolves only around a method of argumentation or a means for validating contested norms; it provides "no substantive ethical guidelines" and no framework of "justified norms." Although not entirely devoid of content, discursive practices depend on contingent content being "brought into them" or being "fed into them from outside." The distinction between form and content also carries over into the division between procedural rule-governance and conceptions of the "common good," or of the "good life," which may pervade "the entirety of a particular life-form or of a particular life history." Ethical formalism or proceduralism is said to be "incisive in a literal sense": for the universalization principle "acts like a knife that makes razor-sharp cuts" between evaluative assessments of life-forms and strictly normative statements, "between goodness and justice." This division deeply affects the status of cultural traditions and beliefs as well as the concrete meaning patterns of individual lives enmeshed in distinct cultural lifeworlds. In Habermas's words, these patterns and beliefs are so inextricably intertwined with the whole fabric of particular life-forms that "they cannot by themselves claim normative validity in the strict sense"; they can at best function as "*candidates* for an embodiment in norms that are designed to express a general interest" or general will.[9]

Habermas at this point considers the complex and tensional relation between substantive goodness (of life-forms) and procedural justice—generally concluding in favor of the primacy of the latter over the former. Individuals living in societies cannot entirely distance or extricate themselves from their cultural lifeworld or from the personal life history that has shaped their identity; yet, they can extricate themselves, he insists, from contested norms or normative clusters set off from the larger social fabric and thus adopt "a hypothetical attitude toward them" by placing themselves on the quasi-transcendental level of discourses. Habermas also reviews certain hermeneutical qualms concerning procedural justice arising from the indisputable need to interpret procedural rules and their application in given circumstances. Discourse ethics, he acknowledges, cannot "resolve problems regarding its own application"; rather, rule application requires a "practical prudence" or judgment that seems to be already "presupposed" by the rationality of discursive argumentation. Despite this acknowledgment, however, Habermas is adamant in asserting the ultimate priority of rule-governance over interpretive judgment. Hermeneutical insights cannot "undercut the claim of discourse ethics to transcend all local conventions or traditions"; in fact, no participant in argumentation can escape this claim "as long as he takes seriously the meaning of normative validity in a performative attitude." To illustrate this superior or "transcending" force, Habermas turns to the history of human rights in modern constitutional regimes, which is said not to vary contingently but to follow a "straight line" or teleology. Rules always take precedence over their application, which, in a given case, may "distort the meaning" of normative principles. Thus, while rules are universal (and presumably univocal), "we can operate in a more or less biased way in the domain of prudent application."[10]

Behind the tension between substantive goodness and justice—

Habermas argues further—there ultimately looms the deeper gulf between history or historical contingency and reason or the "transcending
claims and interests" of rationality. Using Hegelian terminology, the tension might also be rendered as the conflictual relation between "morality" and "ethical life" (*Sittlichkeit*), where morality retains a distinct
Kantian flavor. Interpreting Hegel somewhat freely, perhaps misleadingly, Habermas views ethical life simply as a synonym for ordinary life
practices and everyday beliefs that are "distanced" and called into question on the level of discourses. The ordinary lifeworld, he asserts, is an
arena where "taken-for-granted cultural beliefs of a moral, cognitive or
expressive sort are closely interwoven with each other"; in this sense, it
functions as a "sphere of ethical life (*Sittlichkeit*)." In this sphere, questions of justice arise only "within the horizon of questions concerning
the good life, where the latter are *always already settled*." Seen in their
everyday context, questions of the good life are not "theoretical axioms
incorporating an abstract 'ought' "; rather, they "shape the identities of
groups and individuals in such a manner that they form an intrinsic part
of the respective culture or personality." Discourse ethics, by contrast,
operates on an entirely different level. From the vantage of participants
in discourses "the relevance of lifeworld contexts pales" completely; the
experiences of ordinary life are seen from "an artificial, retrospective
angle." Under auspices of procedural justice, the lifeworld nexus is un-
hinged: "Under the stern moralizing gaze of the participant in discourses,
this nexus has lost its taken-for-granted quality"; hence, "the normative
potency of reality has vanished." Due to this moralizing gaze, the entire
"traditional storehouse of norms" has disintegrated and split into those
norms that can be "justified in terms of principles" and those that "operate only *de facto*":

> Thus the development of the moral viewpoint goes hand in hand with a
> differentiation in the practical realm between *moral* and *evaluative* ques-
> tions. Moral questions can in principle be decided rationally, that is, in
> terms of *justice* or the generalizability of interests. Evaluative questions, by
> contrast, present themselves at the most general level as issues of the *good
> life* (or of self-realization); they are accessible to rational discussion only
> *within* the unproblematic horizon of concrete historical life forms or the
> conduct of an individual life.[11]

Habermas does not entirely ignore the need somehow to correlate
goodness and justice, or lived experiences and procedural rationality.
However, he finds the solution not in a genuine mediation or mutuality,
but in the adaptation and transformation of everyday practices, in their
progressive "rationalization" in the direction of a greater conformity

with discursive rules. Universalist modes of morality, he writes, have somehow to compensate or "make up" for the loss of concrete ethical substance, if they wish to retain their practical efficacy. To this extent, universalist moralities are dependent on life-forms that are "sufficiently 'rationalized' to permit the prudent application of universal moral insights" and that thus move close to universalist principles. The weighting of priorities and presumptions surfaces again—now with clearly political implications that sanction the hegemony of universal rule-governance. The same weighting also emerges in another essay, dating roughly from the same period, in which Habermas juxtaposed and ranked the respective roles of "justice and solidarity." In its ordinary (or premoral) sense, solidarity for Habermas signifies the concrete context of everyday life, the shared "engagement in a lifeworld to which we belong." Solidarity hence is equivalent to conventional practices that need to be sifted through the filter of discursive argumentation and universal procedural rules. Once this happens, in tandem with a rationalization of lifeworld beliefs, a transformation occurs: solidarity—now construed as a "post-conventional" category—becomes a corollary of justice by safeguarding the integrity of the context of moral discourses. In his words, justice concerns the "equal freedom of unique and self-determining individuals," while solidarity protects the "welfare of consociates who are linked in an intersubjectively shared life-form—and also the maintenance of the integrity of that life-form itself."[12]

## II

Moral proceduralism, as outlined above, is by no means the unique preserve of Habermasian discourse theory, though his formulation is distinguished by its verve and trenchant internal consistency. As indicated before, modern liberal democracy is to a large extent pervaded by a procedural conception of justice (with or without Kantian overtones) privileging universal rule anchored in equal rights for all citizens. Despite its broad influence—and its salutary effect as an antidote to autocracy—this conception is not as incontestible or solidly grounded, however, as its proponents claim. With respect to discourse ethics, its limitations have been pointed out repeatedly not only by overt opponents, but by writers otherwise quite sympathetic to Habermas's perspective. Their criticisms have brought to light certain deficits of proceduralism—especially in the areas of rule application and hermeneutical exegesis—that are more serious than Habermas has been willing to admit. Thus, relying in part on Wittgensteinian teachings, Herbert Schnädelbach has drawn attention to the nexus of rule and rule application and the impossibility of exhaustively capturing application in rules (which would involve an infinite regress of rule formulation). Proceeding from a slightly different angle, Albrecht Wellmer has shown the close interlacing of form and content, of procedural justice and qualitative "goodness"—a linkage illustrated by the fact that, to be meaningful, discursive exchanges already presuppose a sense of what "counts as" a good argument and thus a shared framework of understanding (or pre-understanding).[13] Pressing this point further, one might question Habermas's "distancing" of normativity from lifeworld practices (or of "ought" from "is"). If this distancing is radically performed—if lived experience is radically stripped of "normative potency"—then justice is literally stranded, suspended "lifelessly" in the void of abstract speculation.

Apart from theoretical quandaries, there are also political considerations affecting the role of proceduralism, having to do with our contemporary global situation. In light of the asymmetry of center and periphery, of hegemonic power and nonhegemonic societies or groups, universal rule-governance can also mean the subjection of cultural particularities to hegemonic imperatives. In this situation, even the dissemination of equal human rights can entail a kind of disempowerment by disaggregating shared life-forms, and thus denuding them as reservoirs of resistance. An example is the Spanish *conquista*. Propagating Western (Christian) standards, Spanish missionaries typically treated natives as individuals destined for personal salvation, thereby disrupting traditional cultural meaning patterns. Examples of this kind, illustrating "divide and conquer" policies, could readily be multiplied. What emerges is a closer correlation, perhaps contamination, of justice and solidarity than Habermas allows—a correlation buttressed by moral experience or the "phenomenology" of moral sentiments. Our sense of justice is violated not only when equal cases are treated unequally or prejudiciously, but also when relevant differences (of cultures or persons) are ignored or repressed in favor of universal sameness. The plight of North American Indians and of aboriginal populations elsewhere can serve as a reminder of the deleterious and subjugating effects of individualizing and homogenizing rule-governance.[14]

In recent times, sensitivity to such problems has greatly increased, even in the confines of Western liberal democracy. As a result, procedural blindness is no longer uniformly treated as the only yardstick of justice and/or ethical life. Attention to the relevance of difference (or non-sameness) can be found in recent philosophical initiatives, both in North America and in Europe. In North America, the most eloquent treatment of the theme has been offered by Charles Taylor, without any deprecation of equal rights. Elaborating on the Hegelian notion of mutual "recognition," Taylor has distilled two diverse meanings or implications of this term. On the one hand, he notes, recognition means "equal" recognition, that is, acceptance of a symmetrical relation. To this extent, the term endorses "a politics of universalism, emphasizing the equal dignity of all citizens," with an attendant commitment to the "equalization of rights and entitlements." Equality militates against hierarchical social gradations and any kind of prejudicial discrimination; in this sense, sameness of treatment (of citizens) has become a cornerstone of modern liberal democracies everywhere. On the other hand, a second meaning of recognition gives rise to and supports a "politics of difference" nurturing and preserving precisely the distinctiveness or non-sameness of cultures or groups. Taylor notes a peculiar paradox operative in the latter meaning, because recognition of difference is usually postulated as a general or universal rule. To this extent, we are asked to give general acknowledgment to something that is "peculiar to each," thus in a way universalizing the particular. For Taylor, the two meanings are not just juxtaposed, but interpenetrate (and sometimes collide). In terms of equal citizenship,

> what is established is meant to be universally the same, an identical basket of rights and immunities; with the politics of difference [by contrast], what we are asked to recognize is the unique identity of this individual or group, their distinctness from everyone else. The idea is that it is precisely this distinctness that has been ignored, glossed over, assimilated to a dominant or majority identity. . . . Where the politics of universal dignity fought for forms of non-discrimination that were "blind" to the ways in which citizens differ, the politics of difference often redefines non-discrimination as requiring that we make these distinctions the basis of differential treatment.[15]

In Taylor's presentation, the two strands or meanings of recognition are linked with prestigious philosophical or metaphysical traditions. In the case of equal citizenship, the underlying idea is basically that all humans are "equally worthy of respect" due to a "universal human potential" that all humans share. The chief inspiration comes from Enlightenment philosophy, especially the writings of Kant and Rousseau (although the latter's impact is circumscribed by his demand for public unity). It was Kant who centerstaged the notion of equal respect or dignity as something owed to humans as "rational agents" capable of directing their lives "through principles." The accent on difference or differential treatment, on the other hand, can be traced back to Herder (and, in part, to Hegel), with the chief credit going to Herder's stress on distinct particularity functioning on two levels: "the individual person among other persons" and "the culture-bearing people among other peoples." In modern democracies, the two strands or legacies inevitably come into contact, leading to pragmatic sorts of accommodation. Yet, on a theoretical level, and often also in practice, the two orientations clash and are difficult to reconcile. The principle of equal liberty requires "that we treat people in a difference-blind fashion," while the other strand counsels us "to recognize and even foster particularity." This contrast fuels charges and countercharges. "The reproach the first makes to the second," Taylor observes, "is just that it violates the principles of nondiscrimination. The reproach the second makes to the first is that it negates identity by forcing people into a homogeneous mold that is untrue to them." The latter complaint is aggravated by the asymmetry or power differential between hegemonic and nonhegemonic cultures that presses minority life-forms into an alien mold. This, in turn, leads to the frequently voiced charge "that 'blind' liberalisms are themselves the reflection of particular cultures."[16]

Taylor's essay does not leave matters in this state of conflict or mutual recrimination. Faithful to the Platonic-Hegelian heritage of dialectical-dialogical reasoning—and also to the more recent work of Mikhail Bakhtin—Taylor explores the possibilities of a genuine reconciliation that without abandoning equal rights would be properly responsive to the claims of otherness or human difference. He distinguishes between two types of liberalism or liberal politics, of which only the second is found to be sufficiently nuanced or "differentiated." The first type is a narrowly procedural liberalism that emphatically privileges justice (as universal rule) over goodness and allows equal individual rights always to "trump" other considerations of ethical life. In Taylor's account, this type is associated today with the names of John Rawls, Ronald Dworkin, and Bruce Ackerman, although Taylor might well have included strands in Habermas's argument. In its distilled form, this approach sees liberal society as devoid of any "particular substantive view about the ends of life," while being united only around "a strong procedural commitment to treat people with equal respect." This approach's strong scheme of priorities has "become more and more widespread in the Anglo-American world" and derivatively in the rest of the Western world (as a hegemonic scheme). Taylor's own sympathies go toward another, more supple type of liberal democracy, which tempers equal rule-governance with a greater Herderian (and Hegelian) appreciation of diversity and thus makes room for a stronger recognition of distinct life-forms. "A society with strong collective goals can be liberal, on this view," he asserts, "provided it is also capable of respecting diversity, especially when dealing with those who do not share its common goals; and provided it can offer adequate safeguards for fundamental rights." As illustrated by issues raised in French-speaking Quebec, such an approach might be willing "to weigh the importance of certain forms of uniform treatment against the importance of cultural survival, and opt sometimes in favor of the latter." In view of the increasingly multicultural character of many societies, the "rigidities" of procedural liberalism might turn out to be "impractical in tomorrow's world."[17]

In recent Western philosophy, attention to otherness or difference is nurtured not only by Herderian or Hegelian sources, but also by perspectives loosely gathered under the label of poststructuralism or postmodernism. Although frequently accused of moral indifference, and even of harboring nihilism, these perspectives have generated their own ethical arguments, which, though not entirely incompatible with earlier (Hegelian) teachings, are distinguished by their stress on "nonessentialism," on the difference of everything from itself. This stress entails an openness to the distinctness of fellow beings, to their "alterity" above and beyond rule-governance (or in Heideggerian terms, to the excess of "being" over concepts). Among contemporary postmodern thinkers, crucial initiatives in this domain have been formulated by Jacques Derrida. In an important essay titled "Force of Law," Derrida not only delineated a theoretical view of justice, but one that in effect equates justice with deconstruction. Deviating from procedural terminology (and perhaps from commonsense usage), Derrida opposes "law" (*droit*) as universal rule to "justice" seen as the disturbance or disruption of rules by the power of "unruly" particularities or contingencies. The term "law" (*droit*) denotes basically equivalence or rule-governance conceived as a conceptually determinate and calculable principle. The term "justice," in its strong or primary sense, by contrast, refers to the domain of the unruly, incalculable, or "undecidable." In large measure, the essay revolves around the correlation and conflict between these terms, around the

> difficult and unstable distinction between justice and *droit*, between justice (infinite, incalculable, rebellious to rule and foreign to symmetry, heterogeneous and heterotropic), and the exercise of justice as law or right, legitimacy or legality, stabilizable and statutory, calculable, a system of regulated and coded prescriptions.

Invoking a notion with which his work has been prominently affiliated, he adds that it is precisely in the aporias of the ruled and the unruly, in the interstices between law and justice, that "deconstruction find its privileged site—or rather its privileged instability."[18]

The accent on justice as excess or radical heterogeneity does not entail a simple dismissal of rule-governance or of the principle of equal rights. As Derrida emphatically states, the fact "that justice exceeds law and calculation, that the unrepresentable exceeds the determinable cannot and should not serve as an alibi for staying out of juridico-political battles, within an institution or a state or between institutions or states and others." The relation between law and justice is not one of thesis and antithesis or of affirmation and (logical) negation. Everything would be quite simple, he notes, if the relation were a "true distinction, an opposition whose functioning was logically regulated and permitted mastery." But law (*droit*) "claims to exercise itself in the name of justice," while justice is "required to establish itself in the name of a law that must be 'enforced'." This ambivalence is clearly evident in the context of judicial interpretation where the court must "decide" or render a judgment about a particular case not foreseen by established rules. For a decision to be "just and responsible" in this situation, Derrida writes, it must be "both regulated and without regulation": it must "conserve the law and also destroy it or suspend it enough to reinvent it in each case." Since each case is different, each judgment is new and requires "an absolutely unique interpretation which no existing, coded rule can or ought to guarantee absolutely." On the other hand, if a decision were automatic, bypassing the "ordeal" of judgment, it would be only a "programmable application" or deduction: "it might be legal; it would not be just." These observations lead Derrida to comment on the "infinite idea of justice." This idea is infinite

> because it is irreducible, irreducible because owed to the other, owed to the other before any contract, because it has come, the other's coming as the singularity that is always other. This "idea of justice" seems to be irreducible in its affirmative character, in its demand of gift without exchange, without circulation, without recognition or gratitude, without economic circularity, without calculation and without rules, without reason and without rationality. . . . And deconstruction is mad about this kind of justice. Mad about this desire for justice.[19]

In various modulations and combinations, arguments reminiscent of Taylor and/or Derrida have also infiltrated contemporary political and feminist theorizing. In the field of political theory, reference should briefly be made to the innovative study by Iris Marion Young entitled *Justice and the Politics of Difference*. Young critiques prevalent procedural conceptions as being wedded too closely to abstract standards of universality (or universalization) that tend to reduce equal liberty to equivalence and substitutability. This defect is manifest, in her view, in Rawls's model, especially in his bracketing of significant differences on the level of moral reflection (under the "veil of ignorance"). Although favoring some aspects of discourse ethics (especially the accent on public deliberation), Young also takes issue with Habermas's work, which she accuses of harboring a rationalist bias manifest in his privileging of general rights or interests over particular situations, and of reason over affectivity. Generally speaking, adepts of procedural justice claim to occupy a higher, de-contextualized standpoint for the sake of fairness or "impartiality," a claim Young takes to task for its neglect of the "heterogeneity" of life-forms and personal life histories and also for its tendency to homogenize individuals (at the expense of both social and personal differences). Drawing on a number of postmodern writers including Derrida and Adorno, she articulates a normative conception of the "politics of difference" where the latter steers a course between the pitfalls of radical exclusivism (or essentialism) and harmonious convergence. This approach also involves a reformulation of the notion of "pluralism," which has long served as a staple in liberal political theorizing. In Young's account, the politics of difference underscores the genuine diversity of life-forms against a mere juxtaposition of aggregate interests:

> The vision of liberation as the transcendence of group differences seeks to abolish the public and political significance of group difference, while retaining and promoting both individual and group diversity in private, or nonpolitical, social contexts. . . . Radical democratic pluralism [by contrast] acknowledges and affirms the public and political significance of social group differences as a means of ensuring the participation and inclusion of everyone in social and political institutions.[20]

In the domain of feminist theory, the "politics of difference" has in recent years animated lively discussions that commonly (like Young's work) seek to bypass both essentialism and gender sameness. For present purposes, a brief glance at some of Luce Irigaray's writings must suffice. In Irigaray's view, prevalent Western conceptions of ethics and justice blend out or bracket gender differences while celebrating universal rule in the sense of procedural neutrality and impartiality; this celebration is part of traditional "patriarchy" with its entrenched male dominance masquerading under the veil of gender blindness. Drawing on Derridean teachings and also, in part, on Lacanian terminology, Irigaray equates universal rule with the "calculability" of law (*droit*) and the "symbolic" structure of logical discourse (in opposition to the dimensions of the "imaginary" and the "real"). Being abstract and deductively linked, calculable rules inevitably have an exclusionary effect: screening out and repressing concrete particularities, including above all the particularity of gender. Referring to the comprehensive system of rule-governance, as sanctioned by patriarchy, and its effect on women, she notes that the latter's "exclusion is internal to an order from which nothing escapes: the order of [man's] discourse." Given the concreteness of gender differentiation, the effect of the patriarchal order points up an issue that is prominent in postmodern thought: the excess of being over categorical concepts or, in Lacanian terms, of the "real" over the "symbolic." This excess deeply pervades gender relations, in a manner that is bound to unsettle "equal liberty" or the simple postulate of the equalization of calculable rights. For Irigaray, genders are not substitutable; "one sex is not entirely consumable by the other. There is always a *remainder.*" The accent on gender difference by no means implies an endorsement of "essentialism" or of invariant (biological or cultural) essences that would freeze both genders again in logical-symbolic categories. What it does encourage, however, in a very emphatic way, is attention to the political and ethical significance of gender difference; for, flexibly cultivated, such difference might act "as a brake upon and a storehouse of resistance against a formalization that threatens life."[21]

## III

Having outlined prominent Western conceptions of justice, as well as their tensional or conflictual relation, this final section turns to the implications of these concepts for global politics, especially for the prospects of global democracy. Our global scene is overshadowed today by a political asymmetry or conflict between the hegemonic center and the nonhegemonic periphery, an asymmetry that can be translated into the contrast between "universal" Western rule-governance and non-Western societies, cultures or traditions not yet fully submerged in this orbit. This contrast also raises profound issues of justice: To which extent is the justice of (Western) rule-governance itself just? What are appropriate, fair, or "just" modes of response and resistance to this rule? The questions "whose justice, which rationality?" surface again and with full vigor. Seen from this vantage, our global world requires a large-scale "politics of recognition" as delineated by Taylor. Such a politics is bound to involve worldwide struggle and antagonism; hopefully it can advance beyond a harsh "clash of civilizations"—to borrow Samuel Huntington's phrase—in the direction of a mutual learning process among cultures. The obstacles to such learning are formidable on all sides. If one follows Hegel's portrayal of the "struggle for recognition," as manifest in the master-slave relationship, then the chances for learning (and a learning that liberates) may be brighter on the side of peripheral or developing societies than on the side of the West in its role as hegemonic master. The conceit of superiority, the complacent assumption of holding the key to justice and ethical truth, obstructs (or may obstruct) learning on the part of Western culture. Against this posture, the idea of an "imparative" philosophy, as formulated by Raimundo Panikkar, in which commonalties are sought rather than presupposed, is inspiring. "Imparative" is the very opposite of the "imperative" belonging to the model that treats the West as "imperator" in a globally orchestrated *pax Americana*.[22]

What renders learning difficult, of course, are not only philosophical presumptions but real-life political and economic constellations, especially the noted asymmetry between center and periphery. Given the vast reach of Western media and market principles, the very encounter between West and non-West no longer takes place on any "impartial" ground, but under the auspices of Western civilization. This fact is illustrated by the undisputed status of English as the worldwide *lingua franca*. Westerners, especially Americans, are notoriously loathe to acquire fluency in other languages, on the assumption or conviction that everything relevant is or can be made accessible in English, which implies that everything is universally translatable without loss. The problems arising from language barriers—and especially from the monolingual bias of most Americans—are ably pinpointed by Iris Young in her discussion of bilingual education. As she shows, the Bilingual Education Act of 1978 has largely remained a paper declaration. Half a decade later, three-fourths of Hispanic children in America still received no special bilingual instruction of any kind, while in Texas an even larger number of school districts were out of compliance with the legal mandate. In 1986 a referendum was passed in California declaring English the official language of that state. The issue is not the requirement of a reasonable proficiency in English, but rather "whether linguistic minorities are recognized as full participants in their specificity, with social support for the maintenance of their language and culture."[23]

In seeking to promote "universal" standards, including the principle of universal rights, Western culture paradoxically tends to foster monolingual conformity that is at variance with rights (or rightness). Precisely under democratic auspices, non-Western societies and people must be able to speak or "write back"—and they must be able to do so in their native tongue, which invariably is part of a cultural fabric or tradition. Hence it cannot be entirely correct to restrict the notion of rights to equal individual claims, as adepts of universal procedural justice are wont to do; in some contexts and under certain circumstances, claimants must also be entitled to speak on behalf of communal bonds, such as a shared language and distinctive conceptions articulated in that language. In his essay on multiculturalism, Taylor refers to the francophone community in Quebec, arguing cogently that the "survival and flourishing" of French language and culture in Quebec cannot be entirely a matter of individual choice (given the fact that there cannot be a completely individualized or "private" language game). This flourishing is also mandated by the Canadian Charter of Rights and Freedoms that proclaims as one of its objectives "the preservation and enhancement of the multicultural heritage of Canadians." Taylor also briefly alludes to the status of native Americans and aboriginal peoples in general—an issue more fully developed by Iris Young. In Young's account—which no one can seriously dispute—American Indians (whether on or off the reservation) suffer "the most serious marginalization and deprivation of any social group"; by every conceivable measure they are "the poorest Americans." At the same time, however, at least on an abstract legal level, Indians are not completely individualized but recognized as communities; in fact, they are "the only group granted formally special status and rights" by the American government. Thus, in a manner confounding proceduralist axioms, the justice of recognizing collective group's needs and rights has a "clear precedence" in American law. This precedent in the meantime has been extended to the global level, in the form of international charters of the rights of endangered communities (charters that match earlier declarations of the equal rights of individuals or citizens).[24]

To be sure, the notion of collective or cultural rights—like the principle of rights in general—must not be construed in a parochial or narrowly exclusivist fashion. In our steadily globalizing context, the "politics of recognition" necessarily has to be a two-way street, involving a process of mutual learning. On the part of non-Western societies or cultures, such learning is complicated by the legacy of colonialism with its tarnishing effects on Western liberal-democratic ideas. Faced with the realities of global hegemony, non-Western cultures have to engage in a complex double gesture, to affirm or defend cultural traditions and identities while simultaneously opening the latter up to critical scrutiny and revision (perhaps even of a radical kind). This double move has been at the heart of the more inspiring national liberation movements in our century that struggled valiantly against colonialism without retreating into a safely secluded or nostalgic counteridentity. Gandhi's entire lifework can be understood along these lines. A similar outlook has pervaded liberation struggles in Africa—at least as seen from the angle of Amilcar Cabral and Frantz Fanon. As presented in Fanon's *Black Skin, White Masks*, Africans had to liberate themselves first of all from "Negrophobia" or an internalized self-hatred induced by the colonizers; this effort led naturally to the endorsement and counteraffirmation of blackness or "*négritude*" that is not simply a negation, but a term that must constantly renegotiate its meaning in a domain beyond fixed racial markers.[25]

As indicated before, justice in the sense of universal rule is today contested, or at least supplemented, in the West by alternative conceptions stressing individual and cultural differentiation. There is no simple "rule" to settle this contestation or tension. In Aristotelian language, the tension requires cultivation of prudential judgment (*phronesis*), which in turn demands attentiveness to the complex fabric of social and cultural lifeworlds in the global arena. Both the cultivation and the exercise of such judgment are bound to be difficult and fraught with political hazards. In political terms, the issues are how to recognize difference without sanctioning discrimination and individual or group privilege, and how to promote universalism without becoming a pawn in hegemonic power plays.

Prudential judgment is meant to adjudicate between justice as procedural norm and justice as goodness or the "good life," between the principle of universally equal rights and the ethical demands of particular relationships and situated life contexts, in a sense negotiating the difference between Western and non-Western modes of ethical sensitivity. Fortunately, the tension cuts across the East-West divide. On both sides of the ledger, the tensional character of ethics and justice has long been acknowledged, at least on a recessed speculative level. Aristotle's views on justice were recalled at the beginning of this chapter. Equally suggestive, however, is the example of Confucianism. In traditional Confucian thought, a distinction has commonly been made between *fa*, meaning law, rule, or legality, and *li*, denoting appropriateness or rightness of conduct (or conduct in conformity with proper "rites") in a given circumstance. When linked with the assumption of a universal humaneness (*jen*), *fa* could be interpreted as anticipating a general rule of law guaranteeing universal "rights" in contrast to contextually sanctioned "rites" (which were a special concern of Confucian ethics).[26]

Broadly parallel views can be found in other major civilizations. In the confines of Islam, rule-governance finds a loose equivalent in the *sharia*, law equally governing all Muslims. Yet, this rule has always been tempered by the manifest need of interpretation, with different legal schools offering diverse interpretive schemes, and more thoroughly challenged by Sufism's emphasis on contingent and incalculable modes of experience. In the case of Hinduism, a distinction has traditionally been made between *samanya dharma* (general rule) and *visesa dharma* (a differentiated moral conduct)—with the two terms seen not so much as polar opposites, but as closely interpenetrating perspectives. The closest interlacing of rule and nonrule can probably be found in the Asian notion of *tao*, usually rendered as "way" or way of life. Referring to the Western infatuation with universal calculable rules, D. T. Suzuki has pointed to the complicity of such rules with homogenizing forms of domination and control that are at variance with the Buddhist attention to nonessential distinctiveness or "suchness" (*tathata*). The task facing most non-Western cultures, in our age of globalization, is preserving this attention to distinctness without lapsing into parochialism, to democratize their life-forms without becoming a mere appendage of Western rule-governance. In Rajni Kothari's words:

The philosophical perspective that should guide us . . . should steer clear of both imperialist claims to universality and the normless striving for relativity: it should affirm both the principle of *autonomy* of each entity (human as well as social) to seek out its own path to self-realization, and the principle of *integration* of all such entities in a framework of interrelationship based on agreed values.[27]

# Notes

1. See especially Francis Fukuyama, *The End of History and the Last Man* (New York: Free Press, 1992); and for a recent critique Jacques Derrida, *Specters of Marx*, trans. Peggy Kamuf (New York: Routledge, 1994), pp. 56–68.

2. On the upsurge of particularisms see, e.g., Crawford Young, ed., *The Rising Tide of Cultural Pluralism: The Nation-State at Bay?* (Madison, Wisc.: University of Wisconsin Press, 1993); Mark Juergensmeyer, *The New Cold War? Religious Nationalism Confronts the Secular State* (Berkeley: University of California Press, 1993). In the above I do not mean to deny that certain rivalries are the result of "backward obstinacy" and hatefulness (witness the atrocities committed in Bosnia and in Rwanda).

3. Aristotle, *Poetics* 1459a 3–8. For Weber's phrase see his "Politics as a Vocation," in H. H. Gerth and C. Wright Mills, eds., *From Max Weber: Essays in Sociology* (New York: Oxford University Press, 1958), p. 128.

4. See John Rawls, *A Theory of Justice* (Cambridge, Mass.: Harvard University Press, 1970), pp. 3–22, 46–53, 60–65, 136–142. The study also clearly illustrates the weighting of presumptions mentioned before: Rawls explicitly grants primacy to the "principle of equal liberty" over the "difference principle." More recently, Rawls has reformulated his approach among more pragmatic lines, without modifying this priority scheme. See Rawls, *Political Liberalism* (New York: Columbia University Press, 1993).

5. Jürgen Habermas, "Discourse Ethics: Notes on a Program of Philosophical Justification," in his *Moral Consciousness and Communicative Action*, trans. Christian Lenhardt and Shierry Weber Nicholson (Cambridge, Mass.: MIT Press, 1990), p. 48. (In the above and subsequent citations I have slightly altered the translation for purposes of clarity.)

6. Habermas, "Discourse Ethics," pp. 45–48. Habermas refers mainly to Strawson's arguments in *Freedom and Resentment, and Other Essays* (London: Methuen, 1974).

7. Habermas, "Discourse Ethics," pp. 45, 48–49.

8. "Discourse Ethics," pp. 63, 65–66. Habermas distinguishes between "theoretical discourses" concerned with the validation of empirical or logical "truth" claims and "practical discourses" concerned with the validation of normative claims.

9. "Discourse Ethics," pp. 103–104.

10. "Discourse Ethics," pp. 104–105.

11. "Discourse Ethics," pp. 106–108. For a broader discussion of the relation

between morality and ethical life (largely from a Habermasian prespective) see Wolfgang Kuhlmann, ed., *Moralität und Sittlichkeit: Das Problem Hegels und die Diskursethik* (Frankfurt: Suhrkamp, 1986). I have discussed this relation—and Habermas's vulnerability to Hegelian rejoinders—in my "Kant and Critical Theory," in *Between Freiburg and Frankfurt: Toward a Critical Ontology* (Amherst, Mass.: University of Massachusetts Press, 1991), pp. 105–131.

12. See Habermas, "Discourse Ethics," p. 109; also his "Justice and Solidarity: On Kohlberg's Stage Six," in *The Moral Domain: Essays in the Ongoing Discussion between Philosophy and the Social Sciences*, ed. Thomas E. Wren (Cambridge, Mass.: MIT Press, 1989), p. 118. Some of these points are developed in greater detail in Habermas, *Between Facts and Norms: Contributions to a Discourse Theory of Law and Democracy*, trans. William Rehg (Cambridge, Mass.: MIT Press, 1996). Compare in this context also Micha Brumlik and Hauke Brunkhorst, eds., *Gemeinschaft und Gerechtigkeit* (Frankfurt: Fischer, 1993); William Rehg, *Insight and Solidarity: The Discourse Ethics of Jürgen Habermas* (Berkeley: University of California Press, 1997).

13. See Herbert Schnädelbach, "Remarks about Rationality and Language," and Albrecht Wellmer, "Practical Philosophy and the Theory of Society: On the Problem of the Normative Foundations of a Critical Social Science," in *The Communicative Ethics Controversy*, ed. Seyla Benhabib and Fred Dallmayr (Cambridge, Mass.: MIT Press, 1990), pp. 270–292, 293–329. See also Wellmer, *Ethik und Dialog* (Frankfurt: Suhrkamp, 1986), and *The Persistence of Modernity: Essays on Aesthetics, Ethics and Postmodernism* (Cambridge, Mass.: MIT Press, 1991). Compare on the same issues Georgia Warnke, *Justice and Interpretation* (Cambridge, Mass.: MIT Press, 1993). Partly in response to these and similar critiques, Habermas has modified his position somewhat, acknowledging the limitations of an abstract universalism. See his *Justification and Application: Remarks on Discourse Ethics*, trans. Ciaran P. Cronin (Cambridge, Mass.: MIT Press, 1995), especially p. 15. Doubts persist, however, when one reads in quick succession that morality's "exercise of abstraction explodes the culture-specific lifeworld horizon" and that nevertheless "the connection to the pretheoretical knowledge of everyday life remains intact" (pp. 24–25).

14. To mention just a few episodes: In 1868, a federal commission on Indian affairs recommended that "their barbarous dialect should be blotted out and the English language be substituted," reasoning that "through sameness of language is produced sameness of sentiment and thought," such that "in the process of time, the differences producing trouble would have been gradually obliterated." Another government official is recorded as saying a decade earlier that "the great cause of civilization, . . . in the natural course of things, must exterminate Indians." Quoted from *Washington Post*, 14 March 1993 and a bulletin of the American Indian Relief Council of August 1994. Regarding the Spanish *conquista* compare especially Tzvetan Todorov, *The Conquest of America: The Question of the Other*, trans. Richard Howard (New York: Harper & Row, 1984).

15. Charles Taylor, "The Politics of Recognition," in *Multiculturalism: Examining the Politics of Recognition*, ed. Amy Gutmann (Princeton, N.J.: Princeton University Press, 1994), pp. 37–39.

16. Taylor, "The Politics of Recognition," pp. 31, 41–44, 51. Taylor is at least in partial agreement with this charge. Pointing to the Salman Rushdie affair and the general linkage of politics and religion in Islamic societies, he states that "liberalism is not a possible meeting ground for all cultures, but is the political expression of one range of cultures, and quite incompatible with other ranges" (p. 62).

17. "The Politics of Recognition," pp. 52–54, 56, 59–61. Apart from Rawls's *A Theory of Justice,* Taylor refers chiefly to Ronald Dworkin, *Taking Rights Seriously* (Cambridge, Mass.: Harvard University Press, 1977), and Bruce Ackerman, *Social Justice in the Liberal State* (New Haven, Conn.: Yale University Press, 1980). The volume on multiculturalism also contains an essay by Habermas designed at least in part as a response to Taylor. In his essay, Habermas seems willing to move some steps in the direction of Taylor's second type of liberalism—but without renouncing his basic priority scheme favoring universal rule-governance. With specific reference to the Canadian situation, Habermas asserts somewhat blandly that "when properly understood the theory of rights is by no means blind to cultural differences" and that, in fact, that theory is blind "neither to unequal social conditions nor to cultural differences." These statements, however, do not in any way abrogate the trump card held by equal individual rights, for liberal democracy demands "first and foremost, the right to equal individual freedom of choice and action, which in turn presupposes comprehensive legal protection of individuals." Hence, recognition of cultural distinctiveness "does not require an alternative model that would correct the individualistic design of the system of rights through other normative perspectives. All that is required is the consistent actualization of the system of rights." See "Struggles for Recognition in the Democratic Constitutional State," in *Multiculturalism,* trans. Shierry Weber Nicholson, pp. 112–113, 122.

18. Jacques Derrida, "Force of Law: The 'Mythical Foundation of Authority'," in *Deconstruction and the Possibility of Justice,* ed. Drucilla Cornell, Michel Rosenfeld, and David G. Carlson (New York: Routledge, 1992), pp. 21–22. As Derrida notes, there are similarities as well as differences between his approach and that of Levinas—where the differences are also of a terminological sort (with Levinas approximating "justice" closer to rule-governance and ethics to the genuine excess of alterity). Compare Emmanuel Levinas, *Totality and Infinity,* trans. Alphonso Lingis (Pittsburgh, Pa.: Duquesne University Press, n.d.), especially pp. 82–101.

19. Derrida, "Force of Law," pp. 22–25, 28. With regard to the status of human rights, Derrida adds without circumlocution, "Nothing seems to me less outdated than the classical emancipatory ideal. We cannot attempt to disqualify it today, whether crudely or with sophistication, at least not without treating it too lightly and forming the worst complicities" (p. 28). While generally attracted to Derrida's account, I am somewhat troubled by his categorial juxtaposition of law and justice, rule and nonrule, reason and nonreason—and especially by his later association (in a second part devoted to an exegesis of Walter Benjamin) of justice with force or violence. On these points see my "Justice and Violence: A Response to Jacques Derrida," *Cardozo Law Review* 13 (1991): 1237–1243;

also my "Hermeneutics and the Rule of Law," in *Deconstruction and the Possibility of Justice*, pp. 283–304. In another context, I have discussed Heidegger's reflections on justice; see "Heidegger on Ethics and Justice," in *The Other Heidegger* (Ithaca, N.Y.: Cornell University Press, 1993), pp. 106–131.

20. Iris Marion Young, *Justice and the Politics of Difference* (Princeton, N.J.: Princeton University Press, 1990), pp. 7, 100–107, 118, 166–168. Although emphasizing the public importance of difference, Young also seems willing to accept (p. 36) the priority of justice over the good life. In the domain of political theory, mention should also be made of William E. Connolly, *Identity/Difference* (Ithaca, NY: Cornell University Press, 1991), especially the chapter on "Liberalism and Difference," pp. 64–94; Michael Walzer, *The Spheres of Justice* (New York: Basic Books, 1983); and Hannah Pitkin, *Wittgenstein and Justice* (Berkeley: University of California Press, 1972).

21. See Luce Irigaray, *Sexes and Genealogies*, trans. Gillian C. Gill (New York: Columbia University Press, 1993), p. 171; also her *This Sex Which Is not One*, trans. Catherine Porter (Ithaca, N.Y.: Cornell University Press, 1985), p. 88; and *An Ethics of Sexual Difference*, trans. Carolyn Burke and Gillian C. Gill (Ithaca, N.Y.: Cornell University Press, 1993), p. 14. Compare also Drucilla Cornell, *Beyond Accommodation: Ethical Feminism, Deconstruction, and the Law* (New York: Routledge, 1991); and Deborah L. Rhode, *Justice and Gender* (Cambridge, Mass.: Harvard University Press, 1989).

22. See Raimundo Panikkar, "What is Comparative Philosophy Comparing?" in *Interpreting Across Boundaries*, ed. Gerald J. Larson and Eliot Deutsch, (Princeton, N.J.: Princeton University Press, 1988), pp. 116–136, especially pp. 127–128; also Samuel P. Huntington, "The Clash of Civilizations?" in *Foreign Affairs* 72 (1993), pp. 22–49.

23. Young, *Justice and the Politics of Difference*, pp. 178–181.

24. Prominent among such charter declarations are the African Charter on Human and Peoples' Rights, adopted in Nairobi in June 1981, and the Declaration of Principles of Indigenous Rights, adopted at the World Conference of Indigenous Peoples in Panama in September 1984. For these and other documents, and their discussion, see James Crawford, ed., *The Rights of Peoples* (Oxford: Clarendon Press, 1992), especially pp. 179–212. Compare also Taylor, "The Politics of Recognition," pp. 52, 58; Young, *Justice and the Politics of Difference*, pp. 181–183; and William F. Felice, *Taking Suffering Seriously: The Importance of Collective Human Rights* (Albany, N.Y.: SUNY Press, 1996).

25. See Frantz Fanon, *Black Skin, White Masks*, trans. Charles Lam Markman (New York: Grove Weidenfeld, 1967), pp. 14, 134–135, 160. Regarding Gandhi see, e.g., Bhikhu Parekh, *Gandhi's Political Philosophy* (Notre Dame, Ind.: University of Notre Dame Press, 1989); also my "Gandhi as Mediator Between East and West," in *Margins of Political Discourse*, Dallmayr (Albany, N.Y.: SUNY Press, 1989), pp. 22–38.

26. The main title of this chapter is a variation on the phrasing used by Roger T. Ames in his "Rites as Rights: The Confucian Alternative," in *Human Rights and the World's Religions*, ed. Leroy S. Rouner (Notre Dame, Ind.: University of Notre Dame Press, 1988), pp. 199–216.

27. See Rajni Kothari, *Rethinking Development: In Search of Humane Alternatives* (New York: New Horizons Press, 1989), p. 9. Compare also K. J. Shah, "Of Artha and Arthasastra," in *Comparative Political Philosophy*, ed. Anthony J. Parel and Ronald C. Keith (New Delhi: Sage Publ., 1992), pp. 141–162; Daisetz T. Suzuki, *An Introduction to Zen Buddhism* (New York: Grove Press, 1964); and Christopher Ives, *Zen Awakening and Society* (Honolulu: University of Hawaii Press, 1992), especially pp. 114–144 (ch. 6: "Zen Formulation of the Social Good").

## 12

# An "Inoperative" Global Community? Reflections on Nancy

> Those who would take over the earth
> And shape it to their will
> Never, I notice, succeed.
>
> *Tao Te Ching*

Perspective matters. Seen from a sufficient distance—perhaps that of an orbiting spaceship—our earth appears as a smoothly rounded globe devoid of rugged edges or fissures. On closer inspection, however, this smoothness quickly gives way to a spectacle of stunning diversity: mountains and plains, forests and deserts, oceans and dry land. Similarly, viewed from the altitude of speculative metaphysics, humankind seems to exhibit a pleasant homogeneity, anchored perhaps in a common "human nature"; again, however, this pleasantness is disrupted by the stark experiences of conflict and turmoil in human history. Recently, in an essay that aroused considerable controversy, Samuel Huntington exposed a new phase of political conflict now occurring on a global scale: an emerging "clash of civilizations." The essay was provocative for a number of reasons, particularly because of its timing, following the Cold War. Just when the dismantling of the Iron Curtain had engendered visions of a harmonious global "world order," Huntington shattered public euphoria by pointing to profound ruptures. According to Huntington, political battle lines have shifted over the centuries. While the beginning of modernity (after the Peace of Westphalia) witnessed rivalry among princely states, the French Revolution inaugurated a new phase of intensified struggle between nations or nation-states. Following the Russian Revolution, this phase in turn gave way to a contest between ideologies—chiefly between liberal democracy and communism—that fueled the Cold War.

With the demise of this era, now dawning is a new and unprecedented pattern of conflict: one no longer propelled chiefly by ideological or economic, but by cultural or "civilizational," motives. Although nation-states will remain powerful actors in world affairs, it is the "clash of civilizations" that will dominate global politics; "The fault lines between civilizations will be the battle lines of the future."[1]

The vision of conflict projected by Huntington was perhaps over-drawn, and certainly remains questionable in many details. Nevertheless, several features deserve close attention. Huntington deliberately removed the Eurocentric (or Western-centered) blinders from the study of world politics. Up to the close of the Cold War, he notes, international politics was overshadowed by struggles among Western states, nations, and ideologies; to this extent, international conflicts were chiefly conflicts "within Western civilization" or, in a sense, "Western civil wars." In the present era, by contrast, international politics for the first time moves out of its "Western phase," and its central focus becomes the "interaction between the West and non-Western civilizations and among non-Western civilizations." While in previous periods non-Western peoples and governments were reduced to the status of "objects of history" (mainly by being targets of Western colonialism), they now enter the world arena and join the West as "movers and shapers of history." Coupled with this feature is another transgression of the traditional paradigm of international politics: namely, the change from the primacy of states (or other public organizations) as chief actors in the world arena to that of cultures seen as comprehensive meaning patterns animating the lives of ordinary people (and not only ruling elites) in a given context. Attentive in part to the post-Wittgensteinian turn to language (or to language games as life-forms), Huntington defines civilization as "the highest cultural grouping of people and the broadest level of cultural identity people have"; its fabric is constituted both by "common objective elements, such as language, history, religion, customs, institutions," and by "the subjective self-identification of people." He realizes that civilizations of this kind are not compact or historically invariant entities; in fact, they often blend, overlap, or are transformed. Nevertheless, despite elements of flux, civilizations are "meaningful entities" in the global arena, and "while the lines between them are seldom sharp, they are real."[2]

In focusing on cultural meaning patterns, Huntington shifts the accent from competing elite structures—the traditional "anarchy" of states—to the domain of concrete human experience in ordinary lifeworlds; in useful terminology coined by Hedley Bull, emphasis is placed on the emerging "world society" as distinguished from the familiar international "society of states."[3] To be sure, the turn to world society—or what is sometimes called our "global village"—cannot be credited to Huntington alone; the same shift was articulated by other writers before him, some-times in more cogent and circumspect language. Yet, the issue here is not one of originality. Whatever its drawbacks, Huntington's essay stands out both because of its dramatic flair and because of the prestigious status of its author in the profession of international studies. Behind his argu-ment, however, lurks a question that so far has not received much atten-tion in the literature: the concrete character of the impending world society or global family of peoples.

To the extent that parallels can be drawn between global and domestic politics, several prominent alternatives come into view. Is global society going to be an assortment of autonomous individuals and social group-ings, after the fashion of Toennies's model of *"Gesellschaft"*? Or will it be a more tightly knit community—a *"Gemeinschaft"*—held together by shared beliefs and practices? In Western political theory, this contrast has recently been debated at great length under the labels of "liberalism" (or liberal universalism) versus "communitarianism"—perhaps to the point of exhaustion.[4] The present chapter concentrates on a different possibil-ity or conception of social life, one in which "difference" plays a crucial role: the "inoperative community" as formulated by Jean-Luc Nancy. The first section presents Nancy's basic line of argument in an effort to profile it against competing, more customary views. Next, inferences for the study of world politics, invoking some prominent recent initiatives in this field, are drawn. The final section points to some normative implica-tions of an "inoperative" or nonmanagerial model for cross-cultural en-counter on a global plane.

# I

Jean-Luc Nancy's *La communauté désoeuvrée* was first published in 1986, in an intellectual climate saturated with the teachings of Heideg-ger, Derrida, Foucault, and Georges Bataille (among others). Subtle in its argumentation, Nancy's work gathered in itself, but also innovatively rethought, all the major themes animating recent Continental philoso-phy: the end of traditional metaphysics, the decentering of subjectivity (or the *cogito*), the turn to language as a reservoir always in excess of particular speech acts, and, above all, the conception of human existence as an "ekstatic" mode of being (or, in Heidegger's terms, as a *Dasein* in the grip of self-transcendence). Politically, the context surrounding its publication was marked by monumental changes on a global scale: the progressive disintegration of "official" (or Stalinist) communism, the im-pending demise of the Cold War, and the worldwide upsurge of a self-confident neoliberalism intent upon submerging public life in market economics and in considerations of private self-interest. Against this background, Nancy's book acquired its distinctive, and even boldly provocative, contours—contours manifest already in its title (which resists easy translation). While acknowledging the bankruptcy of official communism (and all forms of regimented communitarianism), Nancy was not ready to endorse a militantly refurbished individualism that would only restore a defunct metaphysical "subject." Taking cues from both Heidegger and "poststructuralist" writers, Nancy reasserted the primacy of "the political" over economics (and technology), the preeminence of a public space seen as an arena of democratic interactions. To this extent, *La communauté désoeuvrée* reaffirmed a notion of "community," but a community without substance, communion, or communism—an unmanageable, "unworking," or "inoperative" community beyond instrumental control.[5]

The backdrop of global transformations is closely and eloquently addressed in the opening chapter of Nancy's book. Referring to the cancerous decay infesting the Soviet empire and its satellites, the chapter ponders the implications of this decay for political theory in general and for the concept of community in particular. The "gravest and most painful" experience of our era, he notes, is "the testimony of the dissolution, the dislocation, or the conflagration of community," inextricably linked with the demise of communism. In Nancy's portrayal, communism was not simply, or in its intent, a synonym for corruption; rather, the term signaled the desire to rediscover a sense of community "at once beyond social divisions and beyond subordination to technological dominion"— and hence also "beyond such wasting away of liberty, of speech, or of simple happiness as comes about whenever these are subjugated to the exclusive order of privatization." Despite some redeeming virtues, however, communism as a political regime was from the beginning afflicted by a fundamental, even metaphysical flaw: its bent on reducing everything to production, management, and effective control. Quite apart from despotic or corrupt leanings of its leaders, "it was the very basis of the communist ideal that ended up appearing most problematic": "human beings defined as producers" and, most importantly, as "the producers of their own essence in the form of their labor or their work." Under the aegis of production and operational control, public community was itself conceived as a constructed or operational goal, a goal effected by humans producing "their own essence as their work, and furthermore producing precisely this essence *as community*." This accent on management sidestepped or ignored the aspect of excess or "ekstatic" self-transgression—which accounts in large measure for the "totalitarian" or confiningly "immanentist" character of communism:

It is precisely the immanence of man to man, or it is *man*, taken absolutely, considered as the immanent being par excellence, that constitutes the stumbling block to a thinking of community. . . . Economic ties, technological operations, and political fusion (into a *body* or under a *leader*) represent or rather present, expose, and realize this essence [of community] in themselves. Thus, essence is set to work in them; through them, it becomes its own work. This is what we have called "totalitarianism," but it might be better named "immanentism."[6]

The flaw intrinsic to communism is equally shared by other, less radical forms of "communitarian" politics, including unorthodox, left-Hegelian modes of Marxism—all of which have been wedded to the goal of a totalizing and manageable community; like their Soviet counterpart, these forms too "have by now run their course." Neoliberal individualism, the most timeworn staple of modern Western politics, has stepped into the void left by communism/communitarianism almost everywhere. Nancy is scathing in denouncing this individualist creed. "Some," he writes, "see in its invention and in the culture, if not the cult built around the individual, Europe's incontrovertible merit of having shown the world the sole path to emancipation from tyranny" as well as "the norm by which to measure all our collective or communitarian undertakings." For Nancy, however, the individual is merely the "residue" or leftover of the dissolved community; in its atomistic "indivisibility," it shows itself as the "abstract result of a decomposition." More importantly, like the totalizing community, the individual reveals an "immanentist" streak: this time the immanentism of the self-contained and "absolutely detached" subject "taken as origin and as certainty." What cannot be derived or extrapolated from atomistic individualism is any notion of a social world, any sense of a "*clinamen*," of a declination or declension of individuals with or toward each other. This inability has been the traditional defect of modern individualist theories, and it persists in more recent existentialist and neoliberal guises. As Nancy pointedly observes: "Neither 'personalism' nor Sartre ever managed to do anything more than coat the most classical individual-subject with a moral or sociological paste"; although talking profusely about the subject's situatedness, "they never *inclined* it, outside itself, over that edge that opens up its being-in-common."[7]

Like every form of immanentism, self-contained individualism is not only stifling but also paradoxical and ultimately self-defeating: to know oneself as a distinct individual already presupposes one's differentiation from others. "To be absolutely alone, it is not enough that I be so," Nancy comments; "I must also be alone being alone—which of course is contradictory." Thus, the very logic of absolute self-containment violates and undermines this containment, by implicating it in a relation that it refuses and that "tears it open from within and from without." Hence, the absolute separateness of individuals is ruptured in favor of a relationship (which itself cannot be absolutized): this relation is "nothing other than what undoes in its very principle—and at its closure or its limit—the autarchy of absolute immanence." In a philosophically pathbreaking way, such a nonabsolute and nondialectical relation was prefigured in Heidegger's notion of "being-in-the-world" and also in his delineation of *Dasein's* "ekstatic" transgression toward "being" and toward others. As Nancy perceptively notes, being for Heidegger was neither a thing, nor a concept, nor a totalizing essence, but rather the very emblem of a differential relation rupturing every kind of self-enclosure. Properly understood, he asserts, "being 'itself' comes to be defined as relational, as nonabsoluteness, and, if you will (in any case this is what I am trying to argue) *as community.*" Community in Nancy's sense is far removed from any compact or totalitarian type of communism/communitarinism; instead, its relational character is predicated on the very rupture or ekstatic transgression of compactness. Ecstasy defines the "impossibility of absolute immanence" and consequently the "impossibility either of an individuality in the strict sense of that term, or of a pure collective totality." The challenge presented by this outlook is the difficult task of seeing community and ecstasy as inseparably bound together in a manner that disrupts community's "operational" management. In a shorthand formula, community might be described as "the being-ecstatic of being itself."[8]

In Nancy's portrayal, community is not simply an empirical reality or presence, but rather an advent, a calling, or something lying in wait. Above all, it is not the emblem of a primitive past or a golden age to be retrieved (as imagined by communitarian visionaries). Nancy is stern in castigating longings for a lost innocence. One of the most prominent modern spokesmen of such longings was Rousseau who, perhaps more intensely than others, experienced modern society as resulting from "the loss or degradation of a communitarian (and communicative) intimacy." Actually, however, retrospective dreams have been part of Western self-awareness or historical consciousness from the beginning: "At every moment in its history, the Occident has given itself over to the nostalgia for a more archaic community that has disappeared, and to deploring a loss of familiarity, fraternity and conviviality." Irrespective of the concrete character of the dream or the precise imagery employed—the natural family, the Athenian city, early Christianity, communes, or brotherhoods—always

> it is a matter of a lost age in which community was woven of tight, harmonious, and infrangible bonds and in which above all it played back to itself,

through its institutions, its rituals, and its symbols, the representation, indeed the living offering, of its own immanent unity, intimacy, and autonomy. Distinct from society (which is a simple association and division of forces and needs) . . . community is not only intimate communication between its members, but also its organic communion with its existence.

Nancy corrects Toennies's evolutionary sequence of community and society as well as related developmental schemes. "No *Gesellschaft* has come along to help the State, industry, and capital dissolve a prior *Gemeinschaft*." What accounts, or may account, for developmental schemes of this kind is the (strategic) desire of present generations to impose their own longings on the past, which remains recalcitrant; to this extent, modern communitarianism may well be "nothing than a belated invention." In Nancy's contrary opinion, community—far from being "what society has crushed or lost"—is "*what happens to us . . . in the wake* of society."[9]

The "happening" invoked is not akin to an external fate or inexorable destiny; instead it presupposes a proper human responsiveness or responsibility: above all the readiness to "rethink" the meaning of community, to remain alert to its "insistent and possibly still *unheard* demand." Rethinking involves moving out into uncharted terrain by setting aside the familiar formulas of communism/communitarianism and individualism. Of particular urgency is the replacement of self-contained individuality by the notion of "singularity" or singular human beings. For Nancy, singularity stands in contrast with the structure of individuality: it never occurs "at the level of atoms, those identifiable if not identical identities"; rather, it is "linked to ecstasy" and as such takes place "at the level of the *clinamen*, which is unidentifiable." Singular beings are finite beings who, in their finitude, are exposed to mortality as well as the transgressive incursion of otherness (and of being in every form). "What the thematic of individuation lacked," he notes, "as it passed from a certain Romanticism to Schopenhauer and to Nietzsche, was a consideration of singularity, to which it nevertheless came quite close." Whereas individuation proceeds by detaching closed-off entities from a formless ground, singularity "does not proceed from anything" because it is not "a work resulting from an operation" (which might be called "singularization"). In their finitude, singular beings do not emerge against the background of a prior chaos, the foil of an original unity, or a process of "becoming" and willful construction. Rather, singular beings always emerge together from the beginning; their finitude "co-appears or compears (*comparaît*)" in a shared space or world:

A singular being *appears*, as finitude itself: at the end (or at the beginning) with the contact of the skin (or the heart) of another singular being, at the confines of the *same* singularity that is, as such, always *other*, always shared, always exposed. . . . Community means, consequently, that there is no singular being without a singular being, and that there is, therefore, what might be called, in a rather inappropriate idiom, an originary or ontological "sociality" that in its principle extends far beyond the simple theme of man as a social being (the *zoon politikon* is secondary to this community).[10]

What is involved in this originary sociality is neither fusion nor exclusion, but a kind of "communication" that is vastly different from a mere exchange of information or messages. In opposition to technical information theories (and also theories of communicative interaction), Nancy locates communication on a more primary level: the "sharing and compearance (*com-parution*) of finitude"; on that level there is a dislocation and interpellation that "reveal themselves to be constitutive of being-in-common—precisely inasmuch as being-in-common is not a common being." Nancy returns at this point to the theme of an "inoperative" or nonoperational community, seeking to clarify further that notion. As a mode of "compearance" or a shared space, he observes, community properly understood is not constituted or constructed, nor does it arise from an act of "intersubjective" bonding (contractual or otherwise); "It does not set itself up, it does not establish itself, it does not emerge among already given subjects." Rather, reflecting a mutuality or mutual transgression without fusion, community signals the place of "the *between* as such," a dash or incision: "you *and* I (between us)—a formula in which the *and* does not imply juxtaposition, but exposition" or exposure. Recasting the famous Cartesian adage regarding the *cogito*, Nancy substitutes the phrase "*ego sum expositus*," meaning "I am first of all exposed to the other, and exposed to the exposure of the other"—signaling the contours of a mutuality "about which Descartes seems to know so little, or nothing at all." Located in the interstices of mutual exposure, in the between-space of coappearance, community is not producible or "workable," but rather marked by a basic lack or absence of a substance or stable identity that could be fixated once and for all. What characterizes community is finitude or, more precisely, the "infinite lack of infinite identity (if we can risk such a formulation)." Hence community is formed by "the retreat or the subtraction of something," and "this something, which would be the fulfilled infinite identity of community, is what I call its 'work' " (or its "*oeuvre*," hence *communauté désoeuvrée*).[11]

From this inoperative vantage, a new vista is opened up onto political life, or at least onto a public space in which politics and political struggles can occur. Nancy takes up a distinction, which has become current in recent Continental thought, between "politics" and "the political," where the former designates partisan strategies and concrete institutional devices, and the latter the arena or *mise en scène* presupposed by these strategies. He suggests that the term "the political" may serve to denote "not the organization of society but the disposition of community as such"; as long as public life is not entirely dissolved into the "sociotechnical element of forces and needs," the term can stand as a synonym for "the sharing of community." Pushing the issue further by invoking the difference between "working" and "unworking" (or nonmanagement), he states:

> "Political" would mean a community ordering itself to the unworking of its communication, or destined to this unworking: a community consciously undergoing the experience of its sharing. To attain such a signification of the "political" does not depend, or in any case not simply, on what is called a "political will." It implies being already engaged in the community, that is to say, undergoing, in whatever manner, the experience of community as communication.

The accent on sharing or a shared space need not, and in fact should not, imply a neglect of concrete political struggles. Nancy is keenly aware of prevailing power differentials and hegemonic asymmetries on both the domestic and global levels. Although the political cannot be reduced to power (or an instrumental "will to power"), one cannot escape the sphere of power relations, for we never stop "being caught up in it, being implicated in its demands." To remedy oppressive or exploitative power differentials, counterenergies must be mobilized and, in a sense, be put to "work." Yet, caution must be taken in the pursuit of strategic aims or counteraims, lest they become "totalizing" and oppressive in turn. Hence, strategic struggles must remain mindful of a recessed inoperative domain, of a shared public space that allots to politics its sense and measure.[12]

## II

Having retraced the main steps of Nancy's argument, we return now to the global context thematized at the beginning, and especially to the "clash of civilizations" evoked by Huntington. In light of Nancy's notion of an inoperative community, both the virtues and the defects of Huntington's essay come more clearly into view. As indicated before, the chief virtue of the essay resides in the shift from international anarchy (of states) to the level of cultural beliefs and practices, from governmental elite structures to the lived world of ordinary people. This shift is closely linked with the attention paid to religious customs and traditions, heralding an incipient departure from homogenizing modes of secularism (as well as social-scientific canons of value neutralism). Unfortunately, these initiatives are marred by a number of drawbacks or defects. Huntington basically views civilizations or cultures as power constellations, which, after the demise of the Cold War, now confront each other in the global arena. To this extent, the traditional model of international politics is modified but not radically transformed: the "clash of civilizations" simply takes the place of the clash of superpowers and the customary conflict between nation-states. Although acknowledging a certain flux or "fuzziness" of cultural identities, Huntington nonetheless affirms the relatively compact status of cultures as "meaningful entities"—a claim that predictably (and quite properly) has exposed him to charges of reification or a reifying "essentialism" bypassing internal fissures as well as cross-cultural overlaps. In the terminology employed by Nancy, cultures or civilizations are presented as self-enclosed "individuals" or totalizing entities—at the expense of their flexible "singularity" as well as their "compearing" relationships. A close corollary of this individualizing treatment is the reduction of Western civilization to one power constellation (or cultural actor) among others; even where its special role in global politics is recognized, this recognition takes the form of a dichtomizing opposition (under the label "the West versus the Rest").[13]

In Huntington's portrayal, civilizations are bound to collide in our age—along "cultural fault lines"—for a host of interrelated reasons, among which the following seem to be most crucial (and indicative of his individualizing bent). First of all, differences between cultures are located on a basic experiential level nourished by history, language, literature, and religion; to this extent, they are "far more fundamental than differences among political ideologies and political regimes." Secondly, our world is becoming a "smaller place," with interactions between cultures steadily increasing—which, in turn, leads to intensified "civilization consciousness" or awareness of cultural identity. Next, the weakening of ideological attachments in the wake of the Cold War prompts traditional cultures and religions to move in "to fill this gap." Finally, cultural characteristics and differences, in Huntington's view, are "less mutable" and hence "less easily compromised and resolved" than political and economic rifts along nation-state or class lines—a fact amply illustrated by the upsurge of ethnic and religious conflicts around the globe. While these and related factors sharpen and deepen intercultural cleavages in our time, the same reasons also foster a rallying movement within a given civilizational sphere, a strengthening of intracultural cohesion. Huntington claims that "civilization commonality"—what others have called the "kin-country syndrome"—is today in the process of "replacing political ideology and traditional balance of power considerations as the principal basis for cooperation and coalitions." Occasionally, especially in response to Western ascent or supremacy, this rallying process may extend across narrowly civilizational lines, as is evident in the emerging "Confucian-Islamic connection." All these developments clearly spell trouble for our global future:

> History has not ended. The world is not one. Civilizations unite and divide humankind. . . . What ultimately counts for people is not political ideology or economic interest. Faith and family, blood and belief, are what people identify with and what they will fight and die for.[14]

The cleavage of civilizations also affects Western culture in its relations with the outside world. Huntington is by no means unaware of the distinctive, hegemonic status of Western culture, accounting for the close entwinement of modernization and Westernization. In discussing the reasons of contemporary conflicts, he refers explicitly to the "dual role" of the West: its simultaneous roles as hegemonic or master culture and as foil or target of worldwide reactions, strivings, and frustrations. This duality, however, quickly shades over again into harsh contrast or totalizing mutual exclusion. Borrowing a phrase from Kishore Mahbubani, Huntington's essay pits the West as a global power constellation "versus the rest" of the world. On the one hand, the West today is at the top of the global pyramid; at the same time, however, and perhaps as a result, a "return to the roots phenomenon" is occurring among non-Western civilizations. Thus, Western culture "at the peak of its power"—in fact, at "an extraordinary peak of power in relation to other civilizations"— today confronts "non-Wests" that increasingly have "the desire, the will and the resources to shape the world in non-Western ways." In unusually blunt language, Huntington's argument pierces the rhetorical veil seeking to cloak Western hegemony in the guise of "one-world" or "world order" formulas. The very phrase "the world community," he writes, has become "the euphemistic collective noun" employed to give "global legitimacy to actions reflecting the interests of the United States and other Western powers." Behind the screen of international agencies global political and security issues are "effectively settled by a directorate of the United States, Britain and France," while world economic issues are jointly managed by the United States, Germany, and Japan. Thus, the West is in effect "using" international institutions and other resources to "run the world in ways that will maintain Western predominance, protect Western interests, and promote Western political and economic values." While much depends here on perspective, and while complaints against global mastery arise mainly from non-Western societies, there is at least "a significant element of truth in their view."[15]

Huntington's bluntness extends from power politics to global cultural

aspirations, above all the vision of "cosmopolis" or a universal civilization of humankind. Such a vision is often promoted by champions of
Western culture—including middle-class intellectuals and professionals
in non-Western countries—who view cosmopolis simply as a globalized
extension of Western standards and ways of life. Such a globalizing process is indeed happening in our time; Huntington readily grants that "at a
superficial level" much of Western culture has infiltrated and permeated
the rest of the world. Yet, appearances here are deceptive; for "at a more
basic level," Western standards and concepts are seen to "differ fundamentally" from those found in other civilizations. The contrast affects
and jeopardizes the idea of cosmopolis itself. "The very notion that there
could be a 'universal civilization' is a Western idea" that collides head-
on with "the particularism of most Asian societies" and their emphasis
on "what distinguishes one people from another." The contrast perco-
lates down to the level of basic political beliefs and practices inhabited
by such key tenets of Western culture as individualism, liberalism, human
rights, democracy, and the separation of church and state. Finding "little
resonance" on foreign soil, Western attempts to propagate or impose
these beliefs tend to conjure up charges of blatant interference and even
of "human rights imperialism." The reasons for these charges are not
hard to detect, given the long history of Western expansionism. Seeing
that modern democratic government originated in the West, Huntington
notes, its emergence in non-Western societies has typically been "the
product of Western colonialism or imposition." Such imposition has not
come to an end with the dismantling of colonial empires, auguring ill for
the prospects of globalism. On the whole, Huntington's global analysis
remains tied to the West/rest bifurcation. As such, it allows only for an
"operative" or managerial type of world community, leaving little or no
room for another alternative.[16]

In order to profile more clearly the limitations of Huntington's approach, juxtapose his argument with that of another renowned expert in
international politics: Immanuel Wallerstein, the most prominent spokesman of so-called "world-system" theory. In opposition to the prevalent
model of international anarchy (among states), Wallerstein for some time
has focused attention on the emergence of a "world-system" or a global
civil society cutting across nation-state boundaries; in a body of work
stretching over the past several decades, he and his associates have delineated the features of a capitalist "world-economy" as the driving force
behind social and political developments on a global scale. Despite this
breakthrough to the societal level, however, it is fair to say that the focus
of world-system analysis in the past has been on economic factors, primarily on the structural determinants of capitalist markets and on economic "center-periphery" relations.[17] More recently, however, the range

of concerns has been dramatically expanded beyond the confines of traditional political economy; this change is particularly evident in Wallerstein's pathbreaking study on *Geopolitics and Geoculture*, where global cultural inquiries are placed on an equal footing with geopolitical (or rather geoeconomic) considerations. Like Huntington's essay—but a few years earlier—Wallerstein's study alerted readers to the looming "clash of civilizations," more specifically to the importance of culture(s) as the "intellectual battleground" in the contemporary "world-system." As in Huntington's case, this cultural confrontation was presented as the latest stage in a long historical sequence of global constellations leading from "multiple mini-systems" over "world-empires" to the modern capitalist "world-economy." Innovative and challenging in Wallerstein's approach, however, is his move beyond individualizing or "essentializing" modes of conceptualization in the direction of a mere nuanced and quasi-dialectical account. Viewed from this angle, cultures are fluid, open-ended meaning patterns, while the syndrome "West versus the Rest" appears as a complex differential entwinement.[18]

One of the central topics of Wallerstein's study is precisely the latter syndrome: more specifically, the relation between indigenous (chiefly non-Western) cultures, on the one hand, and the prevalent global order or world economy, on the other. The relation is often portrayed as the opposition between universalism and particularism, between global civilization (in the singular) and local civilizations (in the plural), with the evaluative accent squarely resting on the first of the paired terms. Stated in this categorical fashion, the distinction is a bald metaphysical shibboleth that Wallerstein is at pains to dislodge and overcome. One reason for its deceptive character is the long-standing collusion of universalism with concrete power constellations—as is evident in France's *"mission civilisatrice"* historically used as a prop of colonialism. Recalling the legacy of the Enlightenment and the French Revolution, Wallerstein pointedly reiterates the linkage between French revolutionary ideas and Napoleon's armies flooding the rest of Europe in a burst of military conquest. On the one hand, these armies were greeted by many Europeans as the carrier of a universal and emancipatory message of liberal "civilization"; but, on the other hand, these same Europeans "soon reacted as local 'nationalists' against French 'imperialism.' " To be sure, the lure of this message goes deeper and antedates Napoleon. According to Wallerstein, universalism is "dear to the Western heart," finding its roots both in monotheistic religion and in the modern "Baconian-Newtonian paradigm" with its attachment to universal laws of behavior. During the nineteenth century, the lure received powerful new support and impetus from the doctrine of "progress" and from evolutionary theories of social development. According to one such theory, human life on earth has always exhibited a "linear tendency toward one world." While originally the globe may have contained a large number of disparate groups, the movement of history has been such that these groups have progressively merged, so that "bit by bit, with the aid of science and technology, we are arriving at one world," a unified cosmopolis. In another account—the "stage theory" of human development—differences between cultures are structural in kind, but they all form part of a patterned sequence. Since all groups are destined to move through parallel pages (though at a different pace), again "we end up with a single human society and therefore necessarily with a world culture."[19]

In terms of political programs or ideologies, universalism has been the backbone of modern liberalism and its global repercussions: specifically the process of modernization in its close embroilment with Westernization. In Wallerstein's words, the "liberal dream"—seen as product of the "self-conscious ideological *Weltanschauung*" of the modern world-economy—has been "that universalism will triumph over racism and sexism." This dream or program, in turn, has been translated into "two strategic operational imperatives": "the spread of 'science' in the economy, and the spread of 'assimilation' in the political arena." Seen as outgrowth of a specific socioeconomic design, these imperatives could easily be criticized or debunked as ideological by oppositional (say Marxist) movements that hold that "the ruling ideas are the ideas of the ruling class." Yet, as Wallerstein shows, oppositional or "antisystemic" movements long remained attached to the very same liberal vision, in a way that colored their proposed remedies. Faced with existing inequalities or social constraints, they demanded the removal of these barriers through reliance on more rather than less "science" and through an ever more thoroughgoing "assimilation" of all groups within the prevailing social system:

> In the political arena, the fundamental problem was interpreted to be exclusion. . . . The unpropertied were excluded. Include them! The minorities were excluded. Include them! The women were excluded. Include them! Equals all. The dominant strata had more than others. Even things out! But if we are evening out dominant and dominated, then why not minorities and majorities, women and men! Evening out meant in practice assimilating the weaker to the model of the strong. . . . This search for science and assimilation, what I have called the fulfillment of the liberal dream, was located deep in the consciousness and in the practical action of the world's antisystemic movements, from their emergence in the mid-nineteenth century until at least the Second World War.[20]

In the meantime, the situation has changed in a way that renders political struggles more complex and multidimensional—and also less uniformly manageable. During recent decades, Wallerstein notes, several oppositional movements have begun to express doubts about "the utility, the reasonableness of 'science' and 'assimilation' as social objectives." Thus, ecological, or "green," movements have raised questions about the damaging and sometimes counterproductive "productivism" inherent in the nineteenth-century linkage of science and progress. At the same time, feminist groups and ethnic minorities have "poured scorn" upon the demand for assimilation, insisting instead on a greater respect for otherness and difference. Yet, the issue is not simply a reversal of priorities, an option for particularism over universalism, for (plural) cultures over (world) civilization. No matter how attractive or tempting, the strategy is bound to fail and even to backfire, by ceding the "cultural high ground" to the defenders of world order or the prevailing world economy. By equating their opponents with a backword-looking parochialism, these defenders can readily present themselves as the "high priests" of world culture. For Wallerstein, the crucial move today is the attempt to extricate oneself from traditional dichotomies and priority schemes, instead of remaining "enveloped" in the paired ideologies of universalism and parochialism. In any event, his study strongly counsels against a lapse into a "mindless cultural pluralism" that would simply substitute the atomism of (incommensurable) cultures for the traditional anarchy of states. He writes, "I am skeptical we can find our way via a search for a purified world culture." But "I am also skeptical that holding on to national or to ethnic or to any other form of particularistic culture can be anything more than a crutch"—at least as long as particularism denotes self-enclosure.[21]

These considerations bring into view the need for a differential strategy beyond global synthesis and its denial, a kind of double gesture proceeding cautiously in the interstices of affirmation and negation. To avoid totalizing enclosure, universalism or world culture can neither be wholly embraced nor wholly rejected. Although, in its linkage with the dominant world economy, universalism can readily be shown to be "hypocritical," this is only part of the story. In the face of prevailing hegemonic structures and power inequalities, the idea of universalism continues to matter as a refuge and a corrective. While it may serve, on the one hand, as a mere palliative or "deception," it also functions, on the other, as "a political counterweight which the weak can use and do use against the strong." The problem, Wallerstein notes, is not purely ideological but structural in a global sense. If universalism were merely a cloak or a smokescreen for oppressive designs, "we would not be discussing it today." As things stand, however, universalism is "a 'gift' of the powerful to the weak" that confronts the latter with "a double bind: to refuse the gift is to lose; to accept the gift is to lose." The only plausible reaction of the weak (including minorities and Third World cultures) is "neither to refuse nor to accept, or both to refuse and to accept"—that is, to pursue a seemingly zigzag course that preserves cultural and group difference or distinctiveness while allowing it to grow and mature in a broader global context:

> The way to combat the falling away from liberty and equality would be to create and recreate particularistic cultural entities—arts, sciences, identities; always new, often claiming to be old—that would be social (not individual), that would be particularisms whose object (avowed or not) would be the restoration of the universal reality of liberty and equality.[22]

## III

Though exceptional in its clarity and conceptual rigor, Wallerstein's approach is today not entirely unique in the study of international or world politics. His nuanced, quasi-dialectical mode of analysis is seconded, and sometimes further radicalized, by a number of practitioners exploring more fully the hermeneutical premises of cross-cultural relations and the political underpinnings of cultural identity formation; inspired in part by recent poststructuralist literature, these writers tend to centerstage the porousness of cultural boundaries as well as the nonantithetical "difference" of universalism and localism.[23] Rather than pursuing this line of inquiry, this section returns to the central theme of this work: the character of our "global village" or of the emerging global community—the last term taken in the complex (and noncommunitarian) sense articulated by Nancy. What are the implications—above all, the political and moral implications—of an "inoperative community" in the midst of our "clashing civilizations"? Clearly, Nancy's work offers more than a descriptive account. Apart from its ontological resonances (deriving in part from Heidegger), his conception also carries a profound normative significance resulting chiefly from his pronounced "antitotalizing" or antisystemic stance. Politics and "the political" cannot be neatly divorced. The absence of communitarian substance does not mean a lack of bonding, just as the accent on "inoperation" does not entail a lapse into indifference or apathetic inaction. The disruption or "interruption" of total structures carries with it a political and moral momentum:

> The passion of and for "community" propagates itself, unworked, appealing, demanding to pass beyond every limit and every fulfillment enclosed in the form of an individual. It is thus not an absence, but a movement, it is unworking in its singular "activity," it is the propagation, even the conta-

gion, or again the communication of community itself that propagates itself or communicates its contagion *by its very interruption*.[24]

Being non- or antimanagerial in outlook, Nancy's argument cannot align itself with the defense of prevailing hegemonic power structures, even while recognizing their "operative" existence. To this extent, his perspective collides with the major thrust of Huntington's essay. As a strategic policy analyst, Huntington views the struggle among civilizations chiefly with an eye to its impact on the foreign policy objectives of the United States (and the West). Regarding policy recommendations, his essay is as blunt as his assessment of global power constellations. In the short run, he argues, it is "clearly in the interest of the West" to "promote greater cooperation and unity within its own civilization" and to "incorporate into the West societies in Eastern Europe and Latin America" whose cultures display features of kinship. Most crucial, however, is the effort

> to limit the expansion of the military strength of Confucian and Islamic states; to moderate the reduction of Western military capabilities and maintain military superiority in East and Southwest Asia; to exploit differences and conflicts among Confucian and Islamic states; to support in other civilizations groups sympathetic to Western values and interests; [and] to strengthen international institutions that reflect and legitimate Western interests and values.

In the long run, the predictable advances of non-Western societies in both economic and military fields dictate a policy of overall containment (not too dissimilar from the earlier containment of communism), for the West obviously needs to maintain "the economic and military power necessary to protect its interests in relation to those civilizations." To be sure, Huntington's view of civilizational encounters is not entirely conflictual. The future may also require the West "to develop a more profound understanding of the basic religious and philosophical assumptions underlying other civilizations and the ways in which people in these civilizations see their interests." Yet, understanding seems to serve mainly a strategic goal here: containing or subduing other cultures more effectively (as Tzvetan Todorov has shown with regard to the European "conquest of America").[25]

As in the case of global diagnosis, Wallerstein's work again offers an instructive contrast or corrective. Despite his focus on the (macro) level of "world-system" or world economy, his normative or policy preferences clearly have an antisystemic edge. Precisely in view of the consolidation of economic and military hegemony, *Geopolitics and Geoculture* accentuates the role of "cultural resistance" and antisystemic movements throughout the world, thus replicating on the cultural level the "preferential option for the poor" (postulated by liberation theology). As he observes, one of the most "striking" features of global politics today is the persistence and intensification of resistance movements ready to challenge hegemonic prerogatives (as part of the differential nexus of "civilization/ civilizations"). Yet—and here a crucial distinction comes to the fore—Wallerstein does not confine these challenges to the level of power struggles, especially struggles for global management and control. "We have had planned social change ad nauseam," he writes, "from Jeremy Bentham to the Bolsheviks; and the results have been less than happy." Planned social change has mainly yielded increased "rationalization" both in Weber's sense and in Freud's sense, with the outcome pointing to a worst-case scenario: "the Iron Cage *and* self-deception." Wallerstein's reflections on the future of world politics in many ways resonate with Nancy's non- or countermanagerial vista:

> we should deconstruct [systems] without the erection of structures to deconstruct, which turn out to be structures to continue the old in the guise of the new. Perhaps we should have movements that mobilize and experiment but not movements that seek to operate within the power structures of a world-system they are trying to undo. Perhaps we should tiptoe into an uncertain future, trying merely to remember in which direction we are going.

In moving along this path, traditional cultures and civilizations have an important role to play in helping to maintain both global and cross-cultural difference.[26]

In helping to maintain difference, cultural movements also carry a broader political significance: they prevent the monopolization of "the political" (seen as a global public space or arena). This monopolization is clearly one of Nancy's central concerns. In the face of the prevailing economic, military, and technological concentration of power, the chances of political democracy on a global scale are placed in jeopardy. Although progressive in some sense, the one-sided liberalization of markets is not by itself a substitute for political self-determination: " 'democracy' more and more frequently serves only to assure a play of economic and technical forces that no politics today subjects to any end other than that of its own expansion." A good part of humanity is "paying the price for this." The notion of an "inoperative community" is meant to serve as a bulwark against both a totalizing globalism (dominated by hegemonic powers) and the surrender of politics to the relentless self-interest of atomistic agents (be they states, corporations, or private individuals):

> If we do not face up to such questions, the political will soon desert us completely, if it has not already done so. It will abandon us to political and

technological economies, if it has not already done so. . . . Being-in-common will nonetheless never cease to resist, but its resistance will belong decidedly to another world entirely. Our world, as far as politics is concerned, will be a desert, and we will wither away without a tomb—which is to say, without community, deprived of our finite existence.[27]

# Notes

1. Samuel P. Huntington, "The Clash of Civilizations?" *Foreign Affairs* 72 (Summer 1993): 22–23.

2. "The Clash of Civilizations?", pp. 23–24. The essay mentions "seven or eight" major, historically grown civilizations: "These include Western, Confucian, Japanese, Islamic, Hindu, Slavic-Orthodox, Latin American and possibly African civilization" (p. 25). The Western type is further divided into "European and North American" variants, and Islam into "Arab, Turkic and Malay" subdivisions.

3. See Hedley Bull, "Human Rights and World Politics," in *Moral Claims in World Affairs*, Ralph Pettman (New York: St. Martin's Press, 1979), pp. 79–91; also Hedley Bull and Adam Watson, eds., *The Expansion of International Society* (Oxford: Clarendon Press, 1984).

4. See, e.g., Shlomo Avineri and Avner de-Shalit, eds., *Communitarianism and Individualism* (New York: Oxford University Press, 1992); David Rasmussen, ed., *Universalism vs. Communitarianism* (Cambridge, Mass.: MIT Press, 1990).

5. Jean-Luc Nancy, *La communauté désoeuvrée* (Paris: Bourgeois, 1986). For the English translation see Nancy, *The Inoperative Community*, ed. Peter Connor, trans. Peter Connor et al. (Minneapolis: University of Minnesota Press, 1991). The difficulty of translating "*désoeuvrée*" is discussed there on p. 156, note 1. The completion of Nancy's study coincided roughly with the publication of Maurice Blanchot's *La communauté inavouable* (Paris: Minuit, 1983), which has been translated by Pierre Joris as *The Unavowable Community* (Barrytown, N.Y.: Station Hill Press, 1988).

6. Nancy, *The Inoperative Community*, pp. 1–3. A similar analysis is offered by Claude Lefort in *Democracy and Political Theory*, trans. David Macey (Minneapolis: University of Minnesota Press, 1988). Compare also Hannah Arendt, *The Origins of Totalitarianism* (New York: Harcourt, Brace & World, 1951).

7. Nancy, *The Inoperative Community*, pp. 3–4.

8. *The Inoperative Community*, pp. 4–6. Over long stretches the chapter proceeds in the form of a critical commentary on the work of Georges Bataille— whose outlook is shown precisely to be split between the poles of ecstasy and community. Bataille "remained suspended, so to speak, between the two poles of ecstasy and community" (pp. 20–21). While the pole of ecstasy was "linked to the fascist orgy," the pole of community was "bound up with the idea of communism." The outcome of this conflict was "community refusing itself ecstasy, ecstasy withdrawing from community." In the end, Bataille was able only to oppose

"a *subjective* sovereignty of lovers and of the artist," and also the exception of "darting 'heterogeneous' flashes," to the " 'homogeneous' order of society, with which they do not communicate."

9. *The Inoperative Community*, pp. 9–11. In Nancy's own retrospective view, past societies exhibited a fabric that was much too complex and diverse to be captured by the term *Gemeinschaft*. "It would undoubtedly be more accurate to say," he writes, "that *Gesellschaft*—'society,' the dissociating association of forces, needs, and signs—has taken the place of something for which we have no name or concept, something that issued at once from a much more extensive communication than that of a mere social bond (a communication with the gods, the cosmos, animals, the dead, the unknown) *and* from much more piercing and dispersed segmentation of this same bond, often involving much harsher effects . . . than what we expect from a communitarian minimum in the social bond. *Society* was not built on the ruins of a *community*" (p. 11).

10. *The Inoperative Community*, pp. 6–7, 22, 27–28.

11. *The Inoperative Community*, pp. xxxviii–xxxix, 29–31.

12. *The Inoperative Community*, pp. xxxvii, 40–41. I have invoked the distinction between "politics" and "the political" in my "Rethinking the Political: Some Heideggerian Contributions" and "Post-Metaphysical Politics: Heidegger and Democracy?" in *The Other Heidegger* (Ithaca, N.Y.: Cornell University Press, 1993), pp. 50–51, 87–88. The phrase *"mise en scène"* is borrowed from Lefort, *Democracy and Political Theory*, pp. 10–11.

13. The charge of a fixating essentialism was advanced chiefly by Fouad Ajami in his response to Huntington titled "The Summoning," *Foreign Affairs* 72 (September/October 1993): 2–9. Unfortunately his and related rejoinders are marred by drawbacks of their own, namely, either a return to the anarchy of states or else the flip side of essentialism: the endorsement of assimilationism or a "melting pot" ideology of globalism (under Western auspices). In his subsequent reply, Huntington correctly labeled these two options respectively as a "pseudo-alternative" (the statist paradigm) and an "unreal alternative" (the one-world paradigm). See "Response: If not Civilizations, What?" *Foreign Affairs* 72 (November/December 1993): 191.

14. See Huntington, "The Clash of Civilizations?" pp. 25–27, 35, 45; "Response: If Not Civilizations, What?", p. 194. The last passage contains a veiled (critical) reference to Francis Fukuyama, *The End of History and the Last Man* (New York: Free Press, 1992).

15. Huntington, "The Clash of Civilizations?" pp. 26, 39–40. Compare also Kishore Mahbubani, "The West and the Rest," *The National Interest* 28 (Summer 1992): 3–13; and his "The Dangers of Decadence: What the Rest Can Teach the West," *Foreign Affairs* 72 (September/October 1993): 10–14.

16. Huntington, "The Clash of Civilizations?" pp. 40–41. Despite his accent on radical cleavage, Huntington delineates three possible responses of non-Western civilizations to Western power and values: a strategy of isolation from the West; a "band-wagon" strategy of rapid Westernization; and finally a critical middle path attempting "to 'balance' the West by developing economic and military power and cooperating with other non-Western societies against the West,

while preserving indigenous values and institutions, in short, to modernize but not to Westernize" (p. 41).

17. While cultural aspects were not entirely ignored, they were strongly subordinated to economic analysis (along quasi-Marxist lines). As Wallerstein and Terence Hopkins noted in 1982, there is a "broadly 'cultural' aspect which needs to be mentioned" alongside the specifically economic and political dimensions (dealing respectively with division of labor and formation of states). But "little is systematically known about it as an integral aspect of world-historical development"; hence "we do not focus" on it because "so much preliminary conceptual work needs to be done first." See "Patterns of Development of the Modern World-System," in *World-System Analysis: Theory and Methodology*, Terence K. Hopkins and Immanuel Wallerstein (Beverly Hills, Calif.: Sage Publications, 1982), p. 43.

18. See Wallerstein, *Geopolitics and Geoculture: Essays on the Changing World-System* (Cambridge: Cambridge University Press, 1991). One of the chapters (pp. 158–183) is titled "Culture as the Ideological Battleground of the Modern World-System," but the running banner line reads "Culture as the Intellectual Battleground." For the historical evolution of world politics see the chapter on "The Modern World-System as a Civilization," especially pp. 222–223.

19. *Geopolitics and Geoculture*, pp. 186–187, 217, 233.

20. *Geopolitics and Geoculture*, pp. 181–182.

21. *Geopolitics and Geoculture*, pp. 182, 198, 235. In Wallerstein's view, universalism today is challenged not only by antisystemic movements but "from *within* science, and on scientific grounds." For while classical dynamics was predicated on the calculation of "linear trajectories" that were said to be "lawful, determined and reversible," contemporary science has discovered "intrinsic randomness and intrinsic irreversibility" as the "basis of physical order" (p. 233).

22. *Geopolitics and Geoculture*, pp. 171, 199, 217.

23. Compare, e.g., James Der Derian and Michael J. Shapiro, eds., *International/Intertextual Relations: Postmodern Readings of World Politics* (Lexington, Ky.: Lexington Books, 1989); also the chapter on "Global Political Discourse" in William E. Connolly, *Identify/Difference: Democratic Negotiations of Political Paradox* (Ithaca, N.Y.: Cornell University Press, 1991), pp. 36–63.

24. Nancy, *The Inoperative Community*, p. 60.

25. Huntington, "The Clash of Civilizations?" pp. 48–49. See also Tzvetan Todorov, *The Conquest of America: The Question of the Other* (New York: Harper, 1984), especially pp. 247–248.

26. Wallerstein, *Geopolitics and Geoculture*, pp. 199, 229–230, 234. Wallerstein adds, non-Western cultures or civilizations are "indeed the foci of important antisystemic movements. We may deconstruct more rapidly in their wake than without them. Indeed, can we deconstruct without them? I doubt it" (p. 230).

27. Nancy, *The Inoperative Community*, pp. xxxvii, xli.

# Index

# About the Author

Fred Dallmayr is Packey J. Dee Professor of Political Theory at the University of Notre Dame. He holds a Doctor of Law degree from the University of Munich (1955) and a Ph.D. in political science from Duke University (1960). He has been a visiting professor at Hamburg University in Germany and at the New School for Social Research in New York, and a Fellow at Nuffield College in Oxford. He has been teaching at Notre Dame since 1978. During fall of 1991 he was in India on a Fulbright research grant. Among his publications are: *Beyond Dogma and Despair* (1981); *Twilight of Subjectivity* (1981); *Language and Politics: Why Does Language Matter to Political Philosophy?* (1984); *Polis and Praxis: Exercises in Contemporary Political Theory* (1984); *Critical Encounters: Between Philosophy and Politics* (1987); *Margins of Political Discourse* (1989); *Between Freiburg and Frankfurt: Toward a Critical Ontology* (1991, American edition); *Life-World, Modernity and Critique* (1991, British edition); *G.W.F. Hegel: Modernity and Politics* (1993); *The Other Heidegger* (1993); *Beyond Orientalism: Essays on Cross-Cultural Encounter* (1996); and numerous journal articles.